Financialisation and the Financial and Economic Crises

NEW DIRECTIONS IN MODERN ECONOMICS

Series Editor: Malcolm C. Sawyer, *Professor of Economics, University of Leeds, UK*

New Directions in Modern Economics presents a challenge to orthodox economic thinking. It focuses on new ideas emanating from radical traditions including post-Keynesian, Kaleckian, neo-Ricardian and Marxian. The books in the series do not adhere rigidly to any single school of thought but attempt to present a positive alternative to the conventional wisdom.

For a full list of Edward Elgar published titles, including the titles in this series, visit our website at www.e-elgar.com.

Financialisation and the Financial and Economic Crises

Country Studies

Edited by

Eckhard Hein

The Institute for International Political Economy (IPE), Berlin School of Economics and Law, Germany

Daniel Detzer

The Institute for International Political Economy (IPE), Berlin School of Economics and Law, Germany

Nina Dodig

The Institute for International Political Economy (IPE), Berlin School of Economics and Law, Germany

NEW DIRECTIONS IN MODERN ECONOMICS

Edward Elgar
PUBLISHING

Cheltenham, UK • Northampton, MA, USA

Published by
Edward Elgar Publishing Limited
The Lypiatts
15 Lansdown Road
Cheltenham
Glos GL50 2JA
UK

Edward Elgar Publishing, Inc.
William Pratt House
9 Dewey Court
Northampton
Massachusetts 01060
USA

Paperback edition 2017

A catalogue record for this book
is available from the British Library

Library of Congress Control Number: 2016931736

This book is available electronically in the **Elgar**online
Economics subject collection
DOI 10.4337/9781785362385

ISBN 978 1 78536 237 8 (cased)
ISBN 978 1 78536 238 5 (eBook)
ISBN 978 1 78811 682 4 (paperback)

Typeset by Servis Filmsetting Ltd, Stockport, Cheshire
Printed and bound by CPI Group (UK) Ltd, Croydon, CR0 4YY

Contents

v

Contributors

Serdal Bahçe got his BSc degree from the Department of Computer Engineering at Middle East Technical University in 1994. He completed the master's program and his PhD at the Department of Economics in the same university in 1998 and 2003, respectively. He worked as a research assistant in the same department between 1997 and 2003. In 2006, he began to work in the Department of Public Finance at Ankara University. He has been studying income distribution, public finance and history of economic thought.

Ricardo Barradas is a PhD candidate in Economics at ISCTE – University Institute of Lisbon. He is a teaching assistant at the Higher School of Communication and Media Studies and Higher School of Accounting and Administration of Lisbon (Polytechnic Institute of Lisbon) and a research assistant at Dinâmia'CET – IUL. His main research interests are in the fields of financial markets, financial systems, monetary policy and other related areas. He has worked for four years in the Portuguese banking system as a financial markets analyst.

Carlos A. Carrasco is a CONACYT Postdoctoral Research Fellow at the School of Economics, National Polytechnic Institute (SEPI-ESE-IPN, Mexico) and a member of the National System of Researchers of Mexico (SNI-I). Previously, he was a FESSUD Research Fellow at the Department of Applied Economics V of the University of the Basque Country (UPV/EHU) where he obtained a PhD degree in Economic Integration. His current and past research fields include macroeconomic stabilisation in Latin America, inflation targeting implementation and functioning, global and European imbalances, and European integration. He has lectured in macroeconomics, macroeconomic policy, fiscal policy and introductory econometrics.

Hasan Cömert is an Assistant Professor of Economics at the Department of Economics at Middle East Technical University (METU), Turkey. Cömert received his PhD from the University of Massachusetts at Amherst in 2011. His research interests include central banking, financial markets, financial flows and developing countries and the Turkish economy. Among others, he is the author of *Central Banks and Financial Markets: The Declining Power of*

US Monetary Policy (published by Edward Elgar in 2013) and he has edited another forthcoming book (with Rex McKenzie) called *The Global South after the Crisis*, which will be published by Edward Elgar. Cömert has contributed to different work packages of the FESSUD project as a researcher.

Gérard Cornilleau is a macroeconomist and a specialist in neo-Keynesian models and he was involved in the building of three important models of the French economy: The REGINA model that simulated the French economy disaggregated in five big regions; the MOGLI model, one of the first generation of dynamic macro models, and the Trimestrial model of OFCE, used for short and medium term economic forecasts. From 1974 to 1987 he was a researcher at the Group of Applied Macroeconomic Analysis (GAMA) of the University of Paris-X. From 1988 to 1998 he was Scientific Advisor and Deputy Director of the econometrics department of the OFCE. From 1999 to 2002 he was Deputy Director of Syntheses, Economic Studies and Evaluation at the Directorate of Studies, Research, Evaluation and Statistics (DREES) of the Ministry of Employment and Solidarity and, since July 2002, Deputy Director of the Department of Studies of the OFCE. He is now a scientific advisor at OFCE.

Jérôme Creel is Director of the Research Department at Observatoire Français dés Conjonctures Economiques (OFCE/Sciences Po, Paris) and Associate Professor of Economics at ESCP Europe. He holds a PhD from University Paris-Dauphine in Economics. His recent works have dealt with economic policies in the Euro area, notably with regards to reforms of the Stability and Growth Pact, published in *Journal of Economic Dynamics and Control*, and the relationships between financial stability, monetary policy and economic performance, published in *Economic Modelling* and *Journal of Financial Stability*. Jérôme Creel participates in the iAGS reports, in the EU funded projects FESSUD and RASTANEWS, and in the OFCE team working as Expert for the European Parliament Economic and Monetary Affairs Committee for the Monetary Dialogue with the European Central Bank.

Daniel Detzer obtained a BA in Economics and a MA in International Economics. He works as FESSUD Research Fellow at the Department of Business and Economics of the Berlin School of Economics and Law. His current and past research fields include banking and financial systems, financial crises, financial regulation, macroeconomics and European imbalances. He also has four years of practical experience in finance, having worked for German and French banking institutions.

Nina Dodig has degrees in Economics of Tourism from the University of Perugia and in International Economics from the Berlin School of

Economics and Law. She is a lecturer in macroeconomics and in European economic policies at the Berlin School of Economics and Law. Her main research interests are in the field of finance and financial systems, financial crises, European economic policies and post-Keynesian macroeconomics.

Nilgün Erdem received her PhD from the University of Ankara in Economics. In 1999–2000 she studied as a visiting researcher at the Department of Economics at the University of Notre Dame (USA). Her current research is on financial crises, labour markets, development and international political economy.

Trevor Evans has degrees in Political Science from the University of Kent at Canterbury and in Economics from the University of London. He worked for many years at the Centre for Economic and Social Research in Managua, Nicaragua, and was Professor of Monetary Theory, Monetary Policy and International Monetary Relations at the Berlin School of Economics and Law from 2006 until 2015.

Jesús Ferreiro is Associate Professor of Economics at the University of the Basque Country UPV/EHU, in Bilbao, Spain, and an Associate Member of the Centre for Economic and Public Policy, University of Cambridge, and an Associate Member of the NIFIP, University of Porto. His research interests are in the areas of macroeconomic policy, labour markets and international economy. He has published a number of articles on those topics in edited books and in refereed journals such as *American Journal of Economics and Sociology*, *Applied Economics*, *Economic and Industrial Democracy*, *European Planning Studies*, *International Labour Review*, *International Review of Applied Economics*, *Journal of Economic Issues*, *Journal of Economic Policy Reform*, *Journal of Post Keynesian Economics*, *Panoeconomicus* and *Transnational Corporations*, among others.

Giampaolo Gabbi is Professor of Financial Investments and Risk Management at the University of Siena, Italy, and he is Director of the Banking and Insurance Department of SDA Bocconi School of Management. He holds a PhD in Banking and Corporate Management from Bocconi University. He has been a lecturer at City University, London (2009–2013). He has published many books and articles in refereed journals, including *Journal of International Financial Markets, Institutions & Money*, *Nature Scientific Report*, *Managerial Finance*, *PlosOne*, *The European Journal of Finance*, and the *Journal of Economic Dynamics and Control*.

Catalina Gálvez is Associate Professor of Economics at the University of the Basque Country, in Bilbao, Spain. Her research interests are in the areas of urban and regional developments, macroeconomic policy and labour markets. She has published a number of articles on those topics in edited books and in refereed journals such as *Tourism Economics*, *Panoeconomicus*, and *Corporations*, among others.

Carmen Gomez is Associate Professor of Economics at the University of the Basque Country, in Bilbao, Spain. Her research interests are in the areas of macroeconomic policy, labour market and international economy. She has published a number of articles on those topics in edited books and in refereed journals such as *American Journal of Economics and Sociology*, *Economic and Industrial Democracy*, *Journal of Economic Issues*, *Journal of Post Keynesian Economics*, *Panoeconomicus*, and *Transnational Corporations*, among others.

Ana González is Associate Professor of Economics at the University of the Basque Country, in Bilbao, Spain. Her research interests are in the areas of macroeconomic policy, labour markets and urban and regional development. She has published a number of articles on those topics in edited books and in refereed journals such as *Tourism Economics*, and *Panoeconomicus*, among others.

Eckhard Hein is Professor of Economics at the Berlin School of Economics and Law, Co-Director of the Institute for International Political Economy Berlin (IPE), member of the coordination committee of the Research Network Macroeconomics and Macroeconomic Policies (FMM), and managing co-editor of the *European Journal of Economics and Economic Policies: Intervention*. His research focuses on money, financial systems, distribution and growth, European economic policies and post-Keynesian macroeconomics. His latest books are *The Macroeconomics of Finance-dominated Capitalism – and its Crisis* (Edward Elgar 2012) and *Distribution and Growth after Keynes: A Post-Keynesian Guide* (Edward Elgar 2014). He is the coordinator of Work Package 3 'Causes and Consequences of the Financial Crisis' of the FESSUD project.

Egert Juuse is a PhD student and Junior Research Fellow at Ragnar Nurkse School of Innovation and Governance (the Chair of Innovation Policy and Technology Governance), Tallinn University of Technology, Estonia. His main research areas are financing of economic development, financial and innovation policies in catching-up economies, especially in Central and Eastern Europe. He has been involved in several national research projects, e.g. Public Administration and Development in Small States; Innovation Policies and Uneven Development. Currently, he is involved in the 7th EU Framework Programme FESSUD: Financialization, Economy, Society and Sustainable Development (2011–2016).

Elif Karaçimen is Assistant Professor of Economics in the Department of Economics at Recep Tayyip Erdogan University, Turkey. Her research interests include the political economy of banking and credit, financialisation in emerging capitalist economies and household debt. She has published articles in *Cambridge Journal of Economics* and *Review of Radical Political Economy*. She obtained her BS in economics from the Middle East Technical University, and her PhD in economics from SOAS London.

Ahmet Haşim Köse is Professor in the Department of Economics, Faculty of Political Sciences, at Ankara University. His research interests are political economy and development economics. He has published books and articles on the political economy of Turkey, labour markets and income distribution. He has co-authored a book with Fikret Şenses and Erinç Yeldan, *Neoliberal Globalization as New Imperialism: Case Studies on Reconstruction of the Periphery* (Nova Publisher 2007).

Sérgio Lagoa is Assistant Professor at Instituto Universitário de Lisboa (ISCTE-IUL) and a researcher at DINÂMIA'CET-IUL. His research interests and publications are in macroeconomics, monetary economics and labour economics. He has recent publications in *Open Economies Review*, *Research in Economics*, *Economic and Industrial Democracy*, and *Economics and Labour Relations Review*.

Emanuel Leão holds a PhD in Economics from the University of York. He is Assistant Professor at ISCTE-University Institute of Lisbon and a researcher at DINÂMIA'CET-IUL. His research interests are in the areas of banking, financial markets, public finance and monetary policy. His main published articles have appeared in the *Journal of Economics* and *Economic Modelling*.

John Lepper, BA, MSc, PhD, is Adjunct Professor at the Alfred Deakin Research Institute of Deakin University. He was a member of the Government Economic Service in the UK advising predominantly on telecommunications and broadcasting matters. He worked on secondment as Senior Adviser at the National Lottery Commission and Research Fellow at the Institute of Advanced Studies at Lancaster University. He was previously Interim Head of Performance and Analysis and Economic Advisor in the Department for Culture, Media and Sport principally on gambling economics. His previous experience includes economic policy advice to the Deputy Prime Minister of New Zealand where he worked on the Gambling Act 2003. He has also been a director of a private economics consultancy, a senior economic adviser in the finance industry in both London and New Zealand and a teacher of economics at a number of universities in the UK, New Zealand and China.

Özgür Orhangazi is Associate Professor of Economics at Kadir Has University in Istanbul. He is the author of *Financialization and the US Economy* (2008) and numerous articles and book chapters on financialisation, financial crises, and alternative economic policies. He holds a PhD from the University of Massachusetts Amherst (2006) and previously taught economics at Roosevelt University in Chicago (2006–2011).

Gökçer Özgür is an Associate Professor at Hacettepe University, Ankara, Turkey. He obtained his PhD in Economics at University of Utah in 2006. His research interests are in money and macroeconomic theory.

Ricardo Paes Mamede is Assistant Professor of Political Economy at ISCTE – University Institute of Lisbon and a researcher at Dinâmia'CET-IUL since 1999. Between 2008 and 2014 he also coordinated the Research and Evaluation Department at the NSRF Observatory, the government agency responsible for monitoring the use of EU structural funds in Portugal during the period 2007–2013. In 2007 and 2008 he was Head of Unit of Economic Analysis at the Research Bureau of the Portuguese Ministry of the Economy and Innovation. He has a PhD in Economics from Bocconi University (Italy) and a Master in Economics and Management of Science and Technology from ISEG/University of Lisbon. His research interests are in the fields of innovation and industry dynamics, structural change, European integration, and public policies. In 2014 he co-edited (with Aurora Teixeira and Ester Silva) the book *Structural Change, Competitiveness and Industrial Policy: Painful Lessons from the European Periphery* (Routledge).

Mimoza Shabani obtained her PhD from SOAS, University of London, in December 2014. She is currently Lecturer in Financial Economics at the University of East London in the Department of Finance, Economics and Risk.

Alexis Stenfors is Senior Lecturer in Economics and Finance at Portsmouth Business School. He holds a Civilekonom degree and an MSc from the Stockholm School of Economics, a CEMS-Master from the Community of European Management Schools and a PhD in Economics from SOAS, University of London. Having previously worked 15 years in the foreign exchange and interest rate derivatives markets at various global banks, his research mainly focuses on issues relating to financial markets and political economy. His recent research has been published in journals such as the *Journal of International Financial Markets, Institutions & Money* and the *Review of Political Economy*. Alexis has also been working on behalf of the University of Leeds within the project 'Financialisation, Economy, Society, and Sustainable Development' (FESSUD).

Elisa Ticci is a FESSUD research fellow at the Department of Economics and Statistics of the University of Siena. She holds a PhD in Development Economics from the University of Florence. Between 2007 and 2011, she worked for the European University Institute, UNICEF and The World Bank. She has published in *Development Policy Review, Ecological Economics, Environment and Development Economics, Journal of Economic Dynamics and Control* and *PLoS ONE.*

Jan Toporowski is Professor of Economics and Finance at the School of Oriental and African Studies, University of London, and Visiting Professor of Economics at the University of Bergamo, and International University College, Turin.

Lefteris Tserkezis studied Economics at the University of Athens, where he also completed his Master degree in Economic Theory. He is a PhD candidate in the Faculty of Economic Sciences in the University of Athens. He has worked as a research associate in institutions of economic research in Greece. He is currently employed in the General Accounting Office of the State in the Greek Ministry of Finance.

Judith Tyson is a research fellow at the ODI, specialising in international private finance and financial sector development in Asia and sub-Saharan Africa. Her papers include commissions for the UK's Department of International Development, the United Nations Economic Commission for Africa, UN-Wider, the European Commission and the Initiative for Policy Dialogue at Columbia University, and Women's World Banking. Her work has been widely featured in the media, including the BBC, CNBC, CNN, the *Financial Times,* the *Guardian* and the *Wall Street Journal.* She holds a doctorate in Economics from SOAS, University of London.

Yanis Varoufakis studied Mathematical Economics at the University of Essex. He received his Master degree in Mathematical Statistics from the University of Birmingham and his PhD in Economics from the University of Essex. He has taught at the University of East Anglia, the University of Glasgow and the University of Sydney. He is Professor of Economic Theory at the Faculty of Economic Sciences at the University of Athens and Visiting Professor at the Lyndon B. Johnson School of Public Affairs at the University of Texas at Austin. He is the author of numerous articles in refereed journals, books and chapters in edited volumes. His main research interests include political economy, game theory, experimental social sciences and industrial relations.

Pietro Vozzella is Research Fellow at the Department of Management and Law of the University of Siena on the project 'Financialisation, Economy,

Society and Sustainable Development' (FESSUD), and obtained the post-graduate School of Banking Management Diploma from the University of Siena. His current and past research fields include banking and financial systems, financial regulation and access to bank credit and SME financing. He has also worked for two years in an Italian banking institution within the credit risk management unit. He has published in *European Journal of Finance, Intereconomics: Review of European Economic Policy* and *PLoS ONE.*

Galip L. Yalman, a graduate of the Middle East Technical University, Department of Political Science and Public Administration, is Associate Professor of Political Science in the same department, and Chairperson for the European Studies Graduate Programme at the Middle East Technical University. He received his MSc in International Relations from the University of Southampton and his PhD in Development Studies from the University of Manchester, UK. His research interests extend from state theory to international and comparative political economy. He is currently the President of the Turkish Social Sciences Association.

Preface and acknowledgements

The chapters of this book are parts of the results of the project Financialisation, Economy, Society and Sustainable Development (FESSUD) (2011–2016), which has received funding from the European Union Seventh Framework Programme (FP7/2007–2013) under grant agreement No. 266800.

The current book is based on the theoretical and historical analyses of financialisation and the financial and economic crises provided in our previous book emanating from the FESSUD project, too (Hein, Detzer, and Dodig (eds), *The Demise of Finance-dominated Capitalism: Explaining the Financial and Economic Crises*, Edward Elgar 2015). The present volume contains a selection of 11 (out of 15) shortened and revised country studies on financialisation and the financial and economic crises carried out in the FESSUD project. Furthermore, we have included an introductory chapter covering the theoretical framework and a cluster analysis for the 15 economies examined in the FESSUD project, as well as a final chapter focusing on the European Union and its member countries.

Outlines and provisional versions of the countries were presented at the annual FESSUD conferences in Amsterdam in October 2013 and in Warsaw in October 2014. Draft versions of the first and the final chapters of the book were discussed at a FESSUD workshop in Berlin in May 2015. We are most grateful to the presenters and our authors for the fruitful collaborations and to the participants in the conferences and the workshop for their very helpful comments. Furthermore, we are heavily indebted to Roel van Geijn, Jim Masterson and Enisa Serhati, who have assisted us in the editing process. And finally, we would like to thank the staff of Edward Elgar for the reliable support throughout this project, as usual.

Eckhard Hein, Daniel Detzer and Nina Dodig
Berlin, October 2015

1. Financialisation and the financial and economic crises: theoretical framework and empirical analysis for 15 countries

Nina Dodig, Eckhard Hein and Daniel Detzer

1.1 INTRODUCTION

This chapter provides an overview of the effects of financialisation on the macro-economy and of the financial and economic crises for 15 countries. As is well known, the succession of crises started in 2007 as a financial crisis, then became the Great Recession in 2008/09, which was followed by the euro crisis starting in 2010. The focus here will be on the first two crises, and the euro crisis will only be considered to the extent that the policy reactions towards the crisis extended the duration and intensity of the crisis in certain countries in our set. What is of particular importance and interest are the long-run developments of finance-dominated capitalism and the inherent inconsistencies and contradictions of this period of modern capitalism, which have led to the crises.

In this chapter we will draw on the material supplied by 15 extensive country studies;[1] shortened versions of most of them can be found in the following chapters of this book. However, in this chapter we will also provide some additional data analysis required by our approach. In Section 1.2, the theoretical and general empirical framework for the country studies and this synthesis will be briefly outlined. Section 1.3 will then deal with the long-run development before the financial and economic crises, and we will provide a typology of regimes and cluster the 15 countries accordingly into debt-led private demand boom, export-led mercantilist and domestic demand-led economies. The focus in our analysis, based on a coherent dataset for all the countries, will be on the trade cycle before the financial and economic crises. Section 1.4 will then concentrate on the crises in each of these clusters, considering transmission mechanisms and the main obstacles to recovery, if there have been any. Section 1.5 will summarise and conclude.

1.2   THEORETICAL AND GENERAL CONCEPTUAL FRAMEWORK

From a macroeconomic perspective, the development of finance-dominated capitalism or financialisation can be characterised by the following elements, as reviewed and elaborated in Hein (2012, 2014, Chapter 10), Hein and Dodig (2015), and Hein and van Treeck (2010), for example, and briefly summarised in Hein, Dodig and Budyldina (2015):

1. With regard to distribution, financialisation has been conducive to a rising gross profit share, including retained profits, dividends and interest payments, and thus a falling labour income share, on the one hand, and to increasing inequality of wages and top management salaries and thus of personal or household incomes, on the other hand. Hein (2015) has recently reviewed the evidence for a set of developed capitalist economies since the early 1980s and finds ample empirical support for falling labour income shares and increasing inequality in the personal/household distribution of market incomes with only a few exceptions, increasing inequality in the personal/household distribution of disposable income in most of the countries, an increase in the income share of the very top incomes particularly in the US and the UK, but also in several other countries for which data is available, with rising top management salaries as one of the major driving forces. Reviewing the empirical literature on the determinants of functional income distribution against the background of the Kaleckian theory of income distribution, it is argued that features of finance-dominated capitalism have contributed to the falling labour income share since the early 1980s through three main channels: the falling bargaining power of trade unions, rising profit claims imposed in particular by increasingly powerful rentiers, and a change in the sectoral composition of the economy in favour of the financial corporate sector at the expense of the non-financial corporate sector or the public sector with higher labour income shares.

2. Regarding investment in capital stock, financialisation has meant increasing shareholder power vis-à-vis firms and workers, the demand for an increasing rate of return on equity held by rentiers, and an alignment of management with shareholder interests through short-run performance related pay schemes, such as bonuses, stock option programmes, and so on. On the one hand, this has imposed short-termism on management and has caused a decrease in management's animal spirits with respect to real investment in capital stock and long-run

growth of the firm and increasing preference for financial investment, generating high profits in the short run. On the other hand, it has drained internal means of finance available for real investment purposes from non-financial corporations, through increasing dividend payments and share buybacks in order to boost stock prices and thus shareholder value. These 'preference' and 'internal means of finance' channels should each have partially negative effects on firms' real investment in capital stock. Econometric evidence for these two channels has been supplied by Stockhammer (2004), van Treeck (2008), Orhangazi (2008), and Onaran et al. (2011), confirming a depressing effect of increasing shareholder value orientation on investment in capital stock, in particular for the US but also for other countries, like the UK and France.

3. Regarding consumption, financialisation has generated an increasing potential for wealth-based and debt-financed consumption, thus creating the potential to compensate for the depressing demand effects of financialisation, which were imposed on the economy via re-distribution and the depressing impact of shareholder value orientation on real investment. Stock market and housing price booms have each increased notional wealth against which households were willing to borrow. Changing financial norms, new financial instruments (credit card debt, home equity lending), deterioration of creditworthiness standards, triggered by securitisation of mortgage debt and 'originate and distribute' strategies of commercial banks, made credit increasingly available to low income, low wealth households, in particular. This potentially allowed consumption to rise faster than median income and thus to stabilise aggregate demand. But it also generated increasing debt-income ratios of private households. Several studies have shown that financial and housing wealth is a significant determinant of consumption, particularly in the US, but also in countries like the UK, France, Italy, Japan and Canada (Boone and Girouard 2002; Ludvigson and Steindel 1999; Mehra 2001; Onaran et al. 2011). Furthermore, Barba and Pivetti (2009), Cynamon and Fazzari (2008, 2013), Guttmann and Plihon (2010), van Treeck and Sturn (2012) and van Treeck (2014) have presented extensive case studies on wealth-based and debt-financed consumption, with a focus on the US.

4. The liberalisation of international capital markets and capital accounts has allowed for rising current account imbalances at the global, but also at the regional, levels, in particular within the Euro area, as has been analysed by several authors, including Hein (2012, Chapter 6, 2014, Chapter 10), Hein and Dodig (2015), Hein and Mundt (2012), Horn

et al. (2009), Stockhammer (2010, 2012, 2015), UNCTAD (2009) and van Treeck and Sturn (2012). Simultaneously, it also created the problems of foreign indebtedness, speculative capital movements, exchange rate volatilities and related currency crises (Herr 2012).

Under the conditions of the dominance of finance, income re-distribution at the expense of labour and low income households, and weak investment in the capital stock, different demand and growth regimes may emerge, as has been analysed by the authors mentioned in the previous paragraph, using different terminologies. Considering the growth contributions of the main demand aggregates (private consumption, public consumption, investment, net exports) and the sectoral financial balances of the main macroeconomic sectors (private household sector, financial and non-financial corporate sector, government sector, external sector), we shall in this contribution distinguish three broad types of regimes, with two sub-types for the third regime: (a) a debt-led private demand boom regime, (b) an export-led mercantilist regime and (c) a domestic demand-led regime.

The debt-led private demand boom regime is characterised by negative financial balances of the private household sector, in some countries accelerated by corporate deficits and thus deficits of the private domestic sector as a whole, positive financial balances of the external sector, and hence, current account deficits, high growth contributions of private domestic demand, and negative growth contributions of the balance of goods and services. The extreme form of the debt-led private demand boom regime is the debt-led consumption boom regime, in which the private household sector is running deficits and private consumption demand is the main contributor to GDP growth (Hein 2012, Chapter 6). However, the broader concept of a debt-led private demand boom regime also includes deficit financed expenditures by the non-corporate and the corporate business sectors for private investment purposes. This broader category also takes into account that in the national accounts the private household sector contains non-corporate business, and thus, depending on the institutional structure of the respective economy, private household deficits to a certain extent may in fact be business deficits.

The export-led mercantilist regime is characterised by positive financial balances of the domestic sectors as a whole, and hence negative financial balances of the external sector, and thus, current account surpluses. The growth contributions of domestic demand are rather small or even negative in certain years, and growth is mainly driven by positive contributions of the balance of goods and services and hence rising net exports. Hein and Mundt (2012) have also considered a weakly export-led type, which is characterised by positive financial balances of the domestic sectors as a whole, negative financial balances of the external sector, and hence current account surpluses, positive growth contributions of domestic demand, but negative growth contributions of external demand, and hence falling export surpluses.

The domestic demand-led type is characterised by positive financial balances of the private household sector as well as the external sector, and hence, current account deficits. Here it is usually the government and, to a certain degree, the corporate sector, running deficits. We have positive growth contributions of domestic demand without a clear dominance of private consumption, and negative growth contributions of the balance of goods and services. In this type of regime we will distinguish between low-growth mature economies driven by domestic demand, and high-growth catching-up domestic demand-led economies.

1.3   DEVELOPMENTS IN THE YEARS LEADING UP TO THE CRISES

Considering the typologies outlined in the previous section, we now take a look at the sectoral financial balances of the main macroeconomic sectors and also at the growth contributions of the demand aggregates for each of the countries under consideration. Doing so, we can identify which type of long-run development prevailed in these countries during the trade cycle[2] before the crises. We find that a debt-led private demand boom regime was experienced by the USA, the UK, Spain, Estonia, Greece, and South Africa. Conversely, an export-led mercantilist type can be found in Germany, Japan, and Sweden. Given their contrasting characteristics and their positions at the 'extremes' in our classification, the countries belonging to these two groups are easier to identify and to allocate. The remaining countries under consideration, however, need to be examined more closely, as they do not clearly belong to either of the two groups. These are, namely, France, Hungary, Italy, Poland, Portugal, and Turkey. They all exhibit indicators of a domestic demand-led type of development, as will be seen below. However, within the group there is much less coherence in terms of their respective stage of development and other characteristics of their economies. We will therefore take a closer look at these countries. In what follows, we will first discuss the debt-led private demand boom group; secondly, we do the same for the export-led mercantilist group. Then we will focus on the countries belonging to the domestic demand-led group, looking at their similarities but also at their differences.

Developments before the Crises in the Debt-led Private Demand Boom Countries

Countries of the debt-led private demand boom type are those that, on average over the trade cycle before the crises (our period of consideration), saw negative financial balances of the private household sector, but also of the corporate sector in some countries, as well as the public sector. This was associated with high private consumption and high domestic demand growth contributions, and relatively high GDP growth rates, compared to the export-led mercantilist economies in particular. These countries – especially the USA given its size and economic importance – were the drivers of world demand, displaying significant negative growth contributions of their net exports to the rest of the world and considerable current account deficits.

As can be seen in Table 1.1, all six countries of this group (the USA, the UK, Spain, Estonia, Greece and South Africa) had negative financial balances of the private household sector, or, as in South Africa, of the private sector as a whole. In the cases of the USA, the UK, and Greece, it was only in the household sector, rather than in the corporate sector, where financial balances were negative. We can therefore say that these countries experienced a debt-led consumption boom. Spain and Estonia, meanwhile, show even stronger negative financial balances of their corporate sectors,

Table 1.1   Sectoral financial balances as a share of nominal GDP, in per cent, average values for the trade cycle, for the USA, the UK, Spain, Estonia, Greece and South Africa

	USA	UK	Spain	Estonia	Greece	South Africa*
	2001–2008	2002–2008	2002–2008	1999–2008	2002–2008	2000–2008
External sector	4.7	2.2	6.3	9.6	10.4	3.2
Public sector	−4.4	−3.4	0.0	−0.3	−5.3	−0.5
Corporate sector	0.4	1.5	−4.2	−4.4	3.9	−2.8*
Private household sector	−0.5	−0.3	−2.1	−4.9	−9.1	

Note: *Financial balance of the private sector (corporate and private household sectors).

Source: European Commission (2015), authors' calculations, Hein and Mundt (2012) for South Africa.

which would normally not be of concern – as we would expect the corporate sector to be in deficit and the private household sector to be in surplus in a healthy economy.[3] However, in these two countries this was not the case. Accelerating investment in real estate and construction led to housing bubbles and thus increasing fragilities. South Africa also experienced strong increases in house prices, with the credit expansion being supported by substantial capital inflows. Moreover, in all countries it is also visible that the public sector was in deficit; Spain is the interesting exception with a balanced government budget on average. Finally, as expected, all six countries show relatively high positive financial balances of the external sector, meaning they suffered from substantial current account deficits.

In the debt-led private demand boom type countries we expect private consumption to be the main driver of GDP growth. This is exactly what we see in these six countries when looking at the respective growth contributions in Table 1.2. Negative growth contributions of the balance of goods and services are also observed for each country. Overall, such a debt-led private demand boom type of development allowed these countries to achieve relatively high growth rates in the cycle of the early 2000s – something that would not have been possible had the private sector not compensated for the slowly growing or stagnating demand out of mass incomes by accumulating debt.

From the 1980s the USA, the UK, Spain, Greece and South Africa all saw changes in functional as well as in personal income distribution at the

Table 1.2   Real GDP growth, in per cent, and growth contributions, in percentage points, average values for the trade cycle, for the USA, the UK, Spain, Estonia, Greece and South Africa

	USA	UK	Spain	Estonia	Greece	South Africa
	2001–2008	2002–2008	2002–2008	1999–2008	2002–2008	2000–2008
Real GDP growth	2.1	2.5	3.1	5.8	3.5	4.2
Contribution to the increase of GDP of:						
Private consumption	1.7	1.7	1.6	3.8	2.6	3.0
Public consumption	0.3	0.5	0.9	0.5	0.7	0.9
Investment	0.2	0.4	1.1	2.8	1.1	1.6
Balance of goods and services	−0.1	−0.1	−0.7	−1.5	−0.8	−1.2

Source: European Commission (2015), World Bank (2015) for South Africa, authors' calculations.

expense of the wage share and of lower household incomes, respectively.[4] In the USA, a significant weakening in the position of labour and a marked strengthening in the position of financial capital was initially brought about by the response of the rentier class and of the government to the period of high inflation in the 1970s. The labour market and social policies of the Reagan government as well as a wave of corporate take-overs, downsizing and outsourcing led to a decline in trade union power and in their bargaining position. The wage share in the US shows a moderate downward trend, falling from an average of 65.5 per cent in the 1980s to 64 per cent in the cycle leading up to the crisis (Evans 2015). According to Duménil and Lévy (2011), the USA national income figures actually mask a more serious decline in the share of income for all but the highest paid 5 per cent of employees since the 1980s. They estimate that, for the corporate sector, if the top 5 per cent is excluded, the share of wages for the remaining 95 per cent fell from 62.2 per cent of income in 1980 to 51.5 per cent in 2009. These developments help explain why private households had to resort to accumulating debt to sustain their relative living standards. Following a short recession after the bursting of the 'dot com' bubble in 2001, the Federal Reserve (Fed) reduced interest rates sharply and thereby contributed to creating the conditions for a further phase of expansion from 2002 to 2007. This expansion was characterised by a wave of mergers and takeovers and a major boom in house prices, enabling, in particular, wealth-based consumption. This framework has then, up until the crisis, allowed to compensate for the dampening effects that rising income inequality had on the ability to consume out of income, but it also triggered increasing debt-income ratios of private households and thus increasing financial fragility. This scenario, as we will see, is not much different for other countries of this group as well.

In the UK, income inequality, and in particular asset inequality, had been rising since the 1980s, due to significant weakening of traditional labour unions during the Thatcher governments and the development of 'flexible labour markets' under successive government legislation which removed protection for employees. In the UK, the adjusted wage share (in per cent of GDP at current market prices) declined from nearly 70 per cent of national income in 1975 to a low of 55 per cent in 1996, thereafter stabilising at around 59 per cent (European Commission 2015).[5] Regarding asset inequality, Lepper et al. (2015) report that in 2010 the Gini coefficient for asset wealth was as high as 0.61. The top decile of households was 4.3 times wealthier than the bottom 50 per cent of households combined, and in 2010 nearly a quarter of households had negative financial wealth. It was the UK's position as an international financial intermediary that made finance available to more people than ever before, in particular through a residential housing market whose inflation was fed by credit inflows and growing shortages of affordable housing (Lepper et al. 2015).

In Spain, the rise in unemployment rates in the late 1970s and early 1980s and the wage moderation policies implemented at that time brought about a major decline in the adjusted wage share (as a percentage of GDP at current market prices) until the late 1980s. After a temporary recovery, the adjusted wage share entered a period of sustained decline from 1995 onwards decreasing from 60 per cent to about 53 per cent of GDP (European Commission 2015). In the trade cycle preceding the crises, a housing bubble developed in Spain and the corporate sector's financial balance deteriorated from −2 to around −7.5 per cent of GDP at its peak in 2007. Similarly the financial balance of private households worsened significantly, from −0.44 per cent of GDP in 2002 peaking at −3.7 per cent of GDP in 2007 (European Commission 2015). The greater availability of external financial resources also allowed for an increase in external imbalances, both in terms of current account deficits and external debt (Ferreiro et al. 2014).

In Greece, income distribution worsened starting in the early 1990s. This was due mostly to the weakening of the Greek labour movement, as well as to the proliferation of part-time and precarious employment (Varoufakis and Tserkezis 2014). The adjusted wage share fell from around 58 per cent of GDP (at current market prices) in 1983 to around 48 per cent in 1996, but it rose again between 2000 and 2010 (European Commission 2015). With the entrance of Greece into the European Monetary Union (EMU), its current account deteriorated markedly. This was accompanied by large net-capital inflows needed to finance the sustained deficit. The financial inflows were mainly in the form of private and public debt, all of which made Greece, more than other Euro area countries, extremely fragile, with a high fiscal deficit and a record current account deficit compared to other EMU countries.

The case of Estonia is rather specific because the country went through a transition process in the 1990s, driven by foreign direct investment (FDI), and featuring a high presence of foreign banks, which were the main source of household borrowing. During the transition process income inequality was generally high, but this should be seen in the context of socio-economic turbulences and the wave of privatisations of the time. The wage share, which had been decreasing throughout the 1990s, remained relatively stable in the 2000s (Juuse and Kattel 2014). The high(er) growth in the trade cycle before the crises was largely based on consumption and investment demand, alongside a developing housing bubble, and was accompanied by high current account deficits.

South Africa experienced a brief growth spurt from the mid-2000s until the global financial crisis, driven by household consumption and capital investments associated with large infrastructure projects. While current account deficits were moderate in the 1990s, they increased rapidly during the 2000s. The wage share was declining in the same period up until 2007 (Newman 2014). In general, income inequality in South Africa was quite high and was rooted primarily in high unemployment associated with de-industrialisation, whereas wage inequality had its roots in corporate restructuring, namely downsizing and outsourcing and in increasingly precarious employment standards. Growth in consumption was particularly relevant in the period from 2000 to 2007. Credit expansion in general, including credit to private households on a large scale, was correlated with capital inflows. The largest part of credits to private households consisted of mortgage loans, and the country saw strong increases in house prices in the 2000s.

Developments before the Crises in the Export-led Mercantilist Countries

For the export-led mercantilist we would expect rather opposite developments relative to those described for the debt-led private demand boom countries. The countries of this group – namely Germany, Japan, and Sweden – did not see rising indebtedness of the private sector in the face of slowly growing or stagnating mass incomes. Quite the contrary as we can see from Table 1.3: In all three cases relatively high surpluses in the financial balances of the private household sector can be observed in the trade cycle before the crises. In fact, the domestic sector as a whole exhibits positive financial balances. These are consequently accompanied by strongly negative financial balances of the external sector, meaning high current account surpluses for these countries. In Germany and Japan we also observe negative financial balances of the public sector.

Table 1.3   Sectoral financial balances as a share of nominal GDP, in per cent, average values for the trade cycle, for Germany, Japan and Sweden

	Germany	Japan	Sweden
	2003–2008	1998–2008	2001–2008
External sector	−4.9	−3.0	−6.9
Public sector	−2.0	−5.6	1.0
Corporate sector	1.2	5.5	3.2
Private household sector	5.7	2.8	2.4

Source: European Commission (2015), authors' calculations.

Table 1.4   *Real GDP growth, in per cent, and growth contributions,*
in percentage points, average values for the trade cycle, for
Germany, Japan and Sweden

	Germany	Japan	Sweden
	2003–2008	1998–2008	2001–2008
Real GDP growth	1.5	0.8	2.6
Contribution to the increase of GDP of:			
Private consumption	0.3	0.4	1.0
Public consumption	0.2	0.3	0.2
Investment	0.4	−0.3	0.9
Balance of goods and services	0.6	0.4	0.5

Source: European Commission (2015), authors' calculations.

In terms of growth contributions, the contribution of private consumption is relatively small (Table 1.4), with Sweden being somewhat of an exception here for reasons which will be outlined below. The balance of goods and services, on the other hand, features prominently and is, in the case of Germany in particular, the most important growth contributor. Overall, the growth rates are lower in comparison to those of the debt-led private demand boom countries.

Both Germany and Japan indeed have a long tradition of net export surpluses, however over the last decades several developments have strengthened their reliance on export-led growth. Again, as with the previous group, one of these reasons can be found in changing income distribution. In the case of Germany, the private household sector has traditionally been a net saver. However, in the early 2000s labour market and social policy reforms under the Schröder government led to extreme nominal wage moderation and a redistribution of income at the expense of wage earners and low income households, and this led to private household surpluses increasing even more (Detzer and Hein 2014). In the last trade cycle before the crises, the adjusted wage share (as a percentage of GDP at current market prices) decreased from 58 per cent to around 54 per cent (European Commission 2015). Low domestic demand meant low imports. This coupled with the improved price competitiveness of Germany vis-à-vis its EMU trading partners, and in particular, with a flourishing world demand for German export goods contributed to rising net exports.

Japan, on the other hand, has had a current account surplus since 1981. But in the 2000s up until the outbreak of the crisis its current account registered a substantial increase in surpluses. This occurred alongside a decline in the wage share: the adjusted wage share (as a percentage of GDP at current market prices) fell from around 77 per cent in the mid-1970s to 59 per cent in 2007, with the most significant decreases occurring in the early 2000s (in the 1990s the wage share remained relatively stable) (European Commission 2015). Regarding personal income distribution, despite the relatively stable Gini coefficient for disposable income, the top 0.1 income share has been increasing consistently since 1992 and in particular during the 2000s (Shabani and Toporowski 2015).

Sweden, as mentioned above, differs somewhat from the previous two countries, primarily because it experienced a house price boom with high wealth and high debt increases. Financial balances of the private households remained nonetheless positive, and for these reasons Sweden demonstrates some elements of a domestic demand-led development – which helps explain its better growth performance relative to Germany and Japan. Regarding income distribution in Sweden, the adjusted wage share, expressed as a percentage of GDP at current market prices, remained relatively stable since the mid-1990s, but there was a significant deterioration in personal income distribution. Top income shares (including capital gains) increased strongly from the mid to late 1980s onwards, while the Gini coefficient for disposable income increased from 0.21 to 0.26 between 1995 and 2006. Overall, Sweden belongs to the countries with the highest increases in inequality (Stenfors 2014).

Developments before the Crises in the Domestic Demand-led Countries

Generally, the domestic demand-led economies are characterised by positive financial balances of the private household and external sectors, and hence, current account deficits, but with negative financial balances of the governments, being the main counterpart to the external sector surpluses. GDP growth is driven by positive growth contributions of domestic demand without a dominance of deficit-financed private consumption. Growth contributions of the balance of goods and services are negative.

Here, we broadly distinguish between the catching-up domestic demand-led economies, on the one hand, and the mature domestic demand-led economies, on the other hand. The former consists of dynamic, high(er) growth countries, which are characterised by a strong presence of financial inflows into their economies. We identify Turkey, Poland, and Hungary, as part of such a group. The latter sub-group, consisting of more mature economies with relatively lower growth rates, features France, Italy and Portugal. It ought to be noted at this point that within this typology there is much less coherence among countries, relative to the debt-led private demand boom type or the export-led mercantilist type. As we go further, we will try to acknowledge these differences, yet it remains our primary aim to stress the commonalities.

Catching-up domestic demand-led countries

The group of catching-up domestic demand-led countries is characterised by significant foreign financial inflows. This also increases vulnerability and makes these countries more susceptible to balance of payment crises. However, these countries, unlike our mature domestic demand-led group, also have their own currencies.

This is broadly what we see when taking a look at Tables 1.5 and 1.6

Table 1.5   Sectoral financial balances as a share of nominal GDP, in per cent, average values for the trade cycle, for Turkey, Poland and Hungary

	Turkey	Poland	Hungary
	2001–2008	2002–2008	2003–2008
External sector	3.3	3.7	7.4
Public sector	−6.5	−4.5	−6.6
Corporate sector	3.2*	0.1	−2.0
Private household sector		0.7	1.2

Note: * Financial balance of the private sector (corporate and private household sectors).

Source: European Commission (2015), authors' calculations.

Table 1.6   Real GDP growth, in per cent, and growth contributions, in percentage points, average values for the trade cycle, for Turkey, Poland and Hungary

	Turkey	Poland	Hungary
	2001–2008	2002–2008	2003–2008
Real GDP growth	4.5	4.4	3.0
Contribution to the increase of GDP of:			
Private consumption	3.3	2.6	1.3
Public consumption	0.4	0.7	0.3
Investment	1.1	1.4	0.7
Balance of goods and services	−0.3	−0.5	0.8

Source: European Commission (2015), authors' calculations.

for Turkey, Poland, and Hungary: All three countries had high current account deficits in the cycle before the crises, as can be seen from the positive financial balances of the external sector, and all three countries also registered substantial public sector deficits. In Poland and Hungary the balances of the private household sector were positive as well and therefore, their growth was not private household debt led. We cannot say this with certainty for Turkey where the available data is only for the private sector as a whole. The yearly data for Turkey shows that the trade cycle average is driven by very high surpluses of the private sector following the 2001 crisis, while from 2005 until 2008 the private sector was in substantial deficit (European Commission 2015). Taking this into consideration, Turkey could also be described as a debt-led private demand boom country for the immediate pre-crisis years. However, given that we have thus far focused on average values over the full pre-crisis trade cycle, we will consider Turkey as part of the domestic demand-led group.

In terms of real GDP growth we see very high growth rates, also relative to those in the debt-led private demand boom group. The main growth contributor was in all cases private consumption, but we can observe also a relatively high growth contribution of investment and of public consumption and, except for Hungary, a negative growth contribution of the balance of goods and services.

Both Turkey and Hungary were very dependent on foreign financial inflows, especially from the early 2000s until the crisis. Neither of these countries has a leading currency like the euro or dollar, which made it much harder for them to borrow in their own currency. Domestic sectors, in particular public sectors in these countries, therefore accumulated foreign debt, which gave rise to a particular sort of vulnerability and a possible balance of payment crisis. There is a risk of sudden stops of capital inflows, and even significant capital outflows, which may lead to the inability to pay for essential imports and/or service debt denominated in foreign currency. Financial inflows dominated the developments of the Turkish economy, particularly after 2002. Large capital inflows brought about an appreciation of the domestic currency and led to increasing imports while restricting export growth. At the same time, large capital inflows meant an expansion of domestic credit, increased asset prices and lower interest rates. In this context, we can say that Turkey, which indeed experienced long-lasting exchange rate appreciation periods, increasing borrowing from the rest of the world and increasing current account deficits, was showing some features of the debt-led private demand boom type, despite positive financial balances of the private sector. It remains an open question how the situation would have progressed had the global financial crisis not erupted. A development that cannot be excluded is that Turkey would have transformed from a domestic demand-led country to a debt-led private demand boom one. In fact, private consumption, which was a key driver of growth from 2001, relied heavily on consumer credit. The ratio of consumer credit and credit card debt to consumption of households increased from 3 per cent in 2002 to 31 per cent in 2013 (Bahçe et al. 2015). Alongside this development, the housing sector was showing signs of a real estate boom, with housing loans increasing from 1 per cent of total loans in 2002 to about 4 per cent in 2008 (Bahçe et al. 2015). All this was accompanied by a strong decrease in the adjusted wage share (as percentage of GDP at current market prices) from 52 per cent to below 33 per cent between 1999 and 2008 (European Commission 2015), and overall a relatively low wage growth, especially in the export goods sector resulting in increasing competitiveness. The nonetheless rising current account deficits are ultimately due to the fact that Turkey exports low-value added products, whereas it is heavily reliant on importing large amounts of energy, as well as intermediary and capital goods.

The main forces driving growth in Hungary during the short and intensive growth period between 1996 and 2006 were household consumption and residential investment, accompanied by massive inflows of foreign direct investment (Badics and Szikszai 2015). In the last trade cycle before the crises, the adjusted wage share (as percentage of GDP at current market prices) fell from about 53 per cent to around 51 per cent. In this period, consumption increased faster than median income. Both the corporate and the public sectors were in deficit, and were hence counterparts to the surpluses of the foreign sector, as well as small surpluses of the household sector. Hungary's current account deficit was substantial, at times reaching up to 10 per cent of GDP (Badics and Szikszai 2015). These deficits were associated with rising foreign debt, mainly through the banking sector and the corporate sector. However, since households' financial savings stayed positive for most of the period and the contribution of the foreign sector to growth was positive after 2004, the long-run development pattern does not fit the debt-led private demand boom type but rather that of the domestic demand-led economies.

Poland went through a transition process in the 1990s. The economic transformation was based on neo-liberal premises – the so-called 'shock therapy' – aimed at reducing inflation, liberalising the markets, and completing a far-reaching privatisation of the economy (Dymarski 2015). In the face of rapidly growing labour productivity, the adjusted wage share (calculated at current market prices) declined from 62 to 54 per cent of GDP, between 1992 and 2002. In the last trade cycle before the crises, the adjusted wage share fell even further to 48 per cent of GDP in 2008 (European Commission 2015). However, in the years preceding the crisis, Poland experienced fast and accelerating growth, with an increase in GDP of 39 per cent, relative to the year 2000, and with growth being driven mainly by private demand.

Mature domestic demand-led countries

France, Italy and Portugal are in our view best described as mature domestic demand-led economies during the trade cycle before the crises. Relative to the former sub-group, these countries are characterised by somewhat lower growth rates, and of course they also have the euro as their common currency. Taking a look at the financial balances of the main sectors (Table 1.7), we can see that all three countries had high public sector deficits and surpluses in the private household sector. All three also had current account deficits, although they differed substantially in size. France exhibited a rather small current account deficit, whereas that of Portugal was very large. Overall, France outperformed the other two countries of the group in several aspects. In terms of real GDP growth (Table 1.8) France fared better than the others, with healthy growth

Table 1.7   Sectoral financial balances as a share of nominal GDP, in per cent, average values for the trade cycle, for France, Italy and Portugal

	France	Italy	Portugal
	2003–2008	2003–2008	2003–2008
External sector	0.4	1.2	8.5
Public sector	−3.1	−3.2	−4.7
Corporate sector	−0.2	−0.7	−5.5
Private household sector	2.9	2.6	1.7

Source: European Commission (2015), authors' calculations.

Table 1.8   Real GDP growth, in per cent, and growth contributions, in percentage points, average values for the trade cycle, for France, Italy and Portugal

	France	Italy	Portugal
	2003–2008	2003–2008	2003–2008
Real GDP growth	1.7	0.9	1.0
Contribution to the increase of GDP of:			
Private consumption	1.0	0.5	1.0
Public consumption	0.4	0.1	0.3
Investment	0.7	0.2	−0.2
Balance of goods and services	−0.4	0.0	−0.2

Source: European Commission (2015), authors' calculations.

contributions of private consumption and investment, whereas in the other two countries the growth contribution of investment was very low (Italy) or even negative (Portugal).

France possibly demonstrated one of the healthiest developments among the countries we consider here before the recent crises. After having experienced a drastic fall in the labour income share in the course of the 1980s, functional income distribution remained roughly constant up to the Great Recession. Personal income distribution also remained more stable than in other countries, in particular through government redistribution (Cornilleau and Creel 2014). In this context, and alongside a stable average propensity to save since the early 1990s, consumption has been growing in line with income, i.e. income-financed consumption dominated the scene. No housing boom and no debt-financed consumption bubble could be observed. The foreign trade balance, which had improved from the mid-1980s until the late 1990s, showed a downward trend, with negative values in the 2000s. French competitiveness suffered particularly from the overly restrictive wage policies of its main trading partner, Germany.

Italy has presented characteristics of a domestic demand-led economy since the 1980s, with private consumption rather than investment being the main driver of growth, and with saving rates of private households remaining roughly constant even in the years leading up to the crises. The adjusted wage share in net national income was falling from the early 1980s until the early 2000s, but has been rising again since then. Personal income distribution saw a tendency towards rising inequality in the 1990s, but has shown declining inequality in the 2000s (Gabbi et al. 2014). The Italian current account worsened from the mid-1990s until the crisis, becoming negative in the early 2000s, mainly driven by falling net exports. These deficits led to a deterioration of the Italian international investment position, making it a net debtor in the mid-2000s. Slight, but constant losses of price competitiveness were witnessed in the 2000s.

Throughout the 1990s, and in the context of waves of privatisation and financial sector liberalisation, the Portuguese economy boomed but this was associated with increasing indebtedness of the domestic private sectors. From the mid-1980s until the late 1990s, in fact, the average saving rate of private households dropped dramatically. High indebtedness levels of private households inherited from previous periods prevented the development of asset price or stock market bubbles in the years leading up to the crises (Lagoa et al. 2014). Overall, the 2000s were characterised by a stable labour income share and relatively stable (only slightly increasing) bank credits to households as a share of GDP. Nevertheless, the current account balance deteriorated in this period, due to, on the one hand, a deterioration of the balance of net primary incomes (high foreign indebtedness and a decline in remittances and EU transfers) and, on the other hand, the negative balance of goods or services due to the loss of price competitiveness. The main counterparts of the external sector surpluses were the public and corporate sector deficits.

1.4   THE EFFECTS OF THE CRISES – CONTAGION, TRANSMISSION AND ECONOMIC POLICY RESPONSES

In this section we deal with the contagion and transmission mechanisms of the financial and economic crises, whereby we distinguish between:

1.   contagion effects of the crisis in the international financial markets;
2.   problems related to financial flows (balance of payment channel);
3.   uncertainty and expectations channel of transmission;
4.   transmission of the economic crisis into the respective economy via international goods markets, i.e. exports and imports;
5.   the role of economic policies in dampening or accelerating the financial and economic crises.

The first two of the aforementioned channels are the financial contagion and transmission channels of the crisis, where the former should be more important for lender countries, and the latter should be applicable rather to debtor countries which are vulnerable to sudden stops of capital inflows. The third channel refers to the adverse effects of an increase in uncertainty, be it for investors leading to negative consequences for the financial sector, or for the general public, resulting in a contraction of private spending. The fourth channel focuses on contagion through exports and imports. And, finally, we will consider the responses of fiscal and monetary policies in dealing with the crises. Here we will distinguish between the developments in those countries with monetary policy autonomy and those without autonomy.

The aim of this section is to see how the crises affected different countries and country groups. Again we will present the data on sectoral financial balances and growth contributions of the demand aggregates, focusing on the period since 2009. It should be noted that the trade cycle after the Great Recession is not yet complete, however the average values might give us an approximate idea of what has occurred since the crisis and, in particular, whether any shifts in the type of development can be observed among countries.

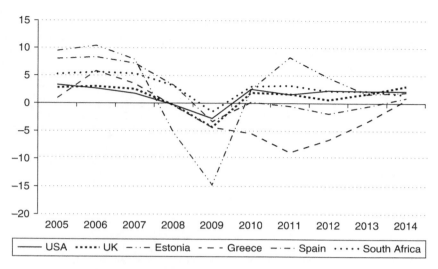

Source: European Commission (2015), authors' calculations.

Figure 1.1   *Real GDP growth in the USA, the UK, Spain, Estonia, Greece*
                and South Africa, 2005–2014, in per cent

The Crises in the Debt-led Private Demand Boom Countries

Figure 1.1 shows the real GDP growth in the USA, the UK, Spain, Estonia, Greece, and South Africa. The financial crisis that broke out in the USA in 2007 hit all of these countries, but whereas the USA and the UK began a slow recovery process from 2009 onwards, Greece was in a recession up until 2014. Spain experienced a double-dip recession due to the euro crisis while Estonia, which was especially negatively affected by the financial crisis, experienced a strong return to growth until 2011, but has had a much weaker performance since. South Africa appears to have managed to contain the effects of the global financial crisis. After experiencing a short-lived recession in 2009 it returned to positive, although weak, growth. In general, as of 2014 all of the countries in this group exhibit sluggish recoveries and none has returned to their pre-crisis growth rates.

In Tables 1.9 and 1.10, we again show the sectoral financial balances and growth contributions, respectively, for each of the six countries in the period 2009–2014. The most obvious development is related to the financial balance of the respective public sectors, all of which have registered enormous deficits (with the exception of Estonia where the average government deficit is rather small). Moreover, in each country the financial

Table 1.9 Sectoral financial balances as a share of nominal GDP, in per cent, average values, for the USA, the UK, Spain, Estonia, Greece and South Africa

	USA	UK	Spain	Estonia	Greece	South Africa*
	2009–2014	2009–2014	2009–2014	2009–2014	2009–2014	2009–2013
External sector	2.7	3.1	1.2	−2.9	5.5	3.4
Public sector	−9.1	−7.9	−8.7	−0.9	−9.8	−4.3
Corporate sector	3.3	2.8	4.2	2.1	12.4	0.9
Private household sector	4.0	1.9	3.3	1.6	−8.3	

Note: *For South Africa the private sector financial balance (corporate and private household sectors) was calculated as the residual from the other two balances.

Source: European Commission (2015), IMF (2015) for South Africa, authors' calculations.

Table 1.10 Real GDP growth, in per cent, and growth contributions, in percentage points, average values for the trade cycle, for the USA, the UK, Spain, Estonia, Greece and South Africa

	USA	UK	Spain	Estonia	Greece	South Africa
	2009–2014	2009–2014	2009–2014	2009–2014	2009–2014	2009–2013
Real GDP growth	1.3	0.8	−1.0	0.7	−4.7	1.8
Contribution to the increase of GDP of:						
Private consumption	1.0	0.3	−0.8	−0.2	−3.4	1.6
Public consumption	0.0	0.2	0.0	0.2	−0.9	0.6
Investment	0.1	0.1	−1.7	−0.2	−2.5	0.3
Balance of goods and services	0.1	0.1	1.5	0.9	2.3	−0.7

Source: European Commission (2015), World Bank (2015) for South Africa, authors' calculations.

balances of the private sector went from deficit to (substantial) surplus, due to deleveraging by both households and corporations, and due to the exhaustion of deficit financing possibilities. In terms of the current account, the USA, the UK and South Africa continued to have current account deficits. Whereas in the case of the USA these are somewhat smaller than in the pre-crisis period, in the UK and in South Africa they have actually increased. The remaining three countries, however, have seen considerable improvements of their external balances. Estonia successfully turned into a current account surplus country, while Spain and Greece have substantially reduced their current account deficits on average over the period. In terms of growth contributions, the most notable changes can be seen in the cases of Spain, Estonia, and Greece, all of which have registered negative growth contributions of private consumption and investment but exhibit strongly positive contributions of the balance of goods and services. However, neither in Spain nor in Greece has this been able to offset depressed domestic demand, which resulted in negative real GDP growth rates on average over this period. The USA, the UK and South Africa, on the other hand, have continued to be led primarily by private consumption, albeit with weaker overall growth than before the crises.

In the following we analyse in more detail which channels of contagion and transmission of the crisis were present in each of these countries, in an attempt to also explain their differing developments over the past five years.

The USA is the country of origin of the financial crisis, and from here the crisis spread worldwide, in the first place through the financial contagion channel. Furthermore, the international trade channel to other countries became important in the course of the deep recession in 2008/09, which had a negative impact particularly on Europe. By 2012, the USA's economic output recovered to the pre-crisis level, not least due to wide government rescue measures for the financial sector and stimulus packages for the non-financial business sector, as well as immediate and prolonged supportive action by the Fed (Evans 2015).

The UK was affected immediately and strongly by the crisis in the USA, due to its strong linkages to global financial markets, resulting in a series of massive government-backed recapitalisation of banks as well as an immediate response from the Bank of England, which enacted a substantial package of measures to prevent the breakdown of the financial system (Lepper et al. 2015). Thus, in the UK, the government stimulus was mainly to save the City of London. After a brief introduction of austerity measures in 2012, this policy was relaxed and the UK has been slowly recovering since.

In South Africa the crisis was relatively mild. The financial sector had little exposure to US toxic assets and no bailouts were needed. The South African economy was affected by the crisis via two channels. South African exports are primarily in metals and minerals, which makes its economic growth particularly susceptible to external market conditions and world commodity prices. With the onset of the crisis, exports declined substantially in 2009, associated with a collapse in commodity prices. The second channel of contagion was the collapse of capital inflows in 2009. This led the financial sector to scale back credit, which hit manufacturing, retail and wholesale sectors. In this situation, the government decided not to scale down large infrastructure projects and was thus able to stabilise demand. Another reaction to the crisis consisted in further liberalisation of the capital account. Once the capital inflows returned, the financial sector rapidly resumed with extending credit, which allowed consumption to recover and aided wholesale and retail sectors (Newman 2014). South Africa, therefore, experienced a rather quick recovery both in exports and in capital inflows.

The cases of Spain, Estonia and Greece are specific, as these three are EMU countries (Estonia only since 2011) and were thus affected by the euro crisis and the government responses since 2010. In Spain, which had become highly dependent on external funding in the years preceding the crisis, the collapse of international financial and inter-banking markets led to massive deleveraging both by financial and non-financial private agents and thus resulted in a sharp abrupt decline in private demand (Ferreiro et al. 2014). With the Greek crisis in 2010, Spanish risk premiums on government bonds reached record levels. In Spain the banking crisis went hand in hand with a sovereign debt crisis that obliged the Spanish government to request financial assistance from the European Stability Mechanism (ESM) in 2012. Since then, the main obstacle to Spanish recovery has been the nature and effect of austerity policies that Spain had to implement.

In Estonia, two channels of transmission of the crisis were relevant. These were, on the one hand, the liquidity and funding channel, because of a high presence of foreign banks, which reduced lending even faster than Estonian domestic banks after the outbreak of the crisis in 2008. This led to a drop in asset prices and high uncertainty, weakening investment and consumption. On the other hand, Estonia was affected by the external trade channel, to which it was especially vulnerable due to its high openness. This aggravated the situation further since Estonia was indebted in foreign currency and depends on foreign exchange income to pay for debt services and imports (Juuse and Kattel 2014). Overall, the crises hit Estonia hard, due to the absence of both fiscal stimulus and of monetary policy interventions tackling the banking crisis, because the country at the time had a currency board. However, quick recovery occurred soon there-after, largely thanks to net exports. However, since then Estonia has seen only meagre growth.

The international financial crisis of 2008 was transmitted to the Greek economy through three main channels. The first operated through the domestic banking system, which was adversely affected by the credit crunch and the almost total collapse of interbank financing, although it was not particularly exposed to toxic financial assets. The second operated through the inability of financing the public fiscal deficit which, being already rather high, rose abruptly when economic growth slowed down. Thirdly, a dramatic rise in the uncertainty over the country's solvency led, from the last quarter of 2009 onwards, to a rapid rise in the interest rates that the Greek state faced in the primary market. This culminated eventually in the exclusion of Greece from international capital markets. Furthermore, the initial freezing and subsequent reversal of the capital inflows directed towards the real economy left the latter in stagnation and disarray (Varoufakis and Tserkezis 2014). However, no account of the causes of the economic crisis in Greece can be complete without recognis-ing the adverse role of the economic policies (fiscal austerity and internal devaluation) that were followed after Greece was compelled to request offi-cial financial assistance from the International Monetary Fund (IMF) and the EU member states, as a result of which a debt crisis was transformed into an unprecedented depression which is still ongoing.

Having taken a brief look at the developments in the (former) debt-led private demand boom countries, we can identify some common charac-teristics of the transmission of the crisis, but also some differences, which relate mainly to the handling of the crises by the respective governments. We have seen that the debt-led private demand boom economies were most vulnerable to contagion effects from the financial crisis originating in the USA, either directly – like the UK – due to substantial holdings of toxic US financial products, or indirectly – as was the case for Spain, Estonia, and Greece – due to widespread global panic and uncertainty affecting the terms of lending of domestic banking sectors, and finally through the collapse of economic activity in the USA and the effects on international trade. Furthermore, in all cases the prolonged deleveraging due to exces-sive build-up of debt by the private sector before the crisis postponed the process of recovery, and the countries have had to suffer from high unem-ployment rates for a longer time period.

As for the differences within this group, we have observed that the eco-nomic crisis was harsher and more prolonged in those countries where austerity policies were implemented, and this has been the case in particu-lar in the EMU countries of Greece and Spain. Here, high public sector deficits resulting from the attempt of the governments to rescue domestic banking sectors during the crisis ultimately led to the euro crisis, which was mainly due to the lack of a lender of last resort for the governments, backing and guaranteeing government debt. Economic policy responses, linking the stabilisation of government debt of crisis countries with strict austerity policies fundamentally undermined the recovery. These policies, in the context of the institutional framework of the EMU, have pushed Spain, and to a large extent Greece and Estonia, towards an export-led mercantilist type of development. However, the major driving force for this was the depression of domestic demand and thus imports and not increasing exports. Taking a look at the annual data on sectoral financial balances, we see a dramatic decline in the financial balance of the external sectors from 2008 onwards, accompanied by the improvement of private households' financial balance and achievement of surpluses in the cases of Spain and Estonia. Contrary to these developments, the USA, the UK and South Africa have turned towards domestic demand-led growth, with the government – and not the private sector – as the main deficit sector.

The Crises in the Export-led Mercantilist Countries

The export-led mercantilist group distinguishes itself from the others particularly in terms of the effects of the crises on growth. Figure 1.2 shows that the recovery from the Great Recession 2008/09 happened rather quickly.

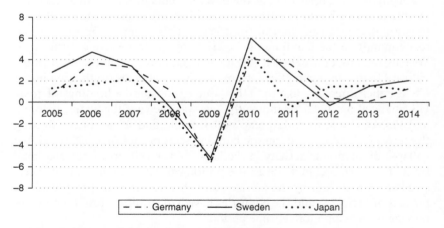

Source: European Commission (2015), authors' calculations.

Figure 1.2   Real GDP growth in Germany, Sweden and Japan, 2005–2014, in per cent

On the one hand, this was due to the fact that these countries benefitted from the recovery of the world economy driven by high growth in emerging market economies like China or India, but also, on the other hand, because domestic policy responses were immediate, especially in terms of dealing with the financial sector, rescuing banks in trouble and successfully preventing/containing a financial system breakdown, as well as due to fiscal stimuli. All three countries came close to a recession for the second time, Japan in 2011, Sweden in 2012 and Germany in 2013. Japan did, in fact, experience a double-dip recession, having suffered severely from a decline in its net exports in 2011 due to the Fukushima event and the following rise in energy imports (Shabani and Toporowski 2015). In the case of Sweden, although the onset of the Euro area crisis had a dampening effect on Swedish growth, the economy still outperformed the Euro area, likely due to the fact that Sweden entered the global financial crisis with strong public finances, i.e. with one of the lowest government debt-to-GDP ratios in Europe (Stenfors 2014).

Ultimately, despite recovering rather quickly, this group of countries has since returned to only low growth. We will see below that this is also due to the fact that their export-led growth strategies have not changed, the only thing that did was the dynamics of their trade partners.

Tables 1.11 and 1.12 show the sectoral financial balances and the growth contributions on average over the last six years for the export-led mercantilist group of countries. All three countries continued with their model, with Germany even strengthening its export-led mercantilist position, while the private sector kept positive financial balances. Growth, however, has been very weak, with the exception of Sweden where private consumption was the major contributor to the Swedish recovery.

The main channels of transmission of the crises to Germany were the financial contagion and the international trade channels. In particular, the

Table 1.11   *Sectoral financial balances as a share of nominal GDP, in per cent, average values for the trade cycle, for Germany, Japan and Sweden*

	Germany	Japan	Sweden
	2009–2014	2009–2014	2009–2014
External sector	−6.6	−1.8	−6.1
Public sector	−1.2	−8.5	−0.9
Corporate sector	2.6	7.7	0.7
Private household sector	5.2	2.5	6.2

Source: European Commission (2015), authors' calculations.

*Table 1.12   Real GDP growth, in per cent, and growth contributions,
in percentage points, average values for the trade cycle, for
Germany, Japan and Sweden*

	Germany	Japan	Sweden
	2009–2014	2009–2014	2009–2014
Real GDP growth	0.6	0.5	1.1
Contribution to the increase of GDP of:			
Private consumption	0.5	0.6	0.9
Public consumption	0.2	0.3	0.4
Investment	0.1	0.0	0.0
Balance of goods and services	0.0	−0.3	−0.2

Source: European Commission (2015), authors' calculations.

latter was relevant with a sharp decline in exports to the rest of the world in 2008/09, especially to European countries. Germany recovered rather quickly from the financial and economic crises. Overall, four reasons can be identified for the swift German recovery (Detzer and Hein 2014). First, the financial crisis was quickly contained by strong government intervention; secondly, the three pillars of the German financial system, with two strong non-profit pillars (public and mutual banks) aided in avoiding a credit crunch; thirdly, there was an exceptionally strong and immediate government intervention in the real economy in the form of stimulus packages; and fourthly, foreign demand picked up rather quickly thus supporting German export performance. In the following years, Germany also benefitted from the depreciation of the euro and from very low interest rates, due to the policies of the ECB, on the one hand, and German government bonds being considered a safe haven in the course of the euro crisis, on the other hand.

In the case of Japan there is little evidence of financial contagion from the USA. The Japanese banking system had not really been involved in the acquisition of subprime financial products and was thus not directly affected by the crisis in the USA. However, the Japanese stock market suffered due to panic caused by the crisis, especially by foreign investors (Shabani and Toporowski 2015). The main channel of transmission of the crisis to Japan lies, however, in exports, which declined substantially in 2009. Japan's government has since been trying to stimulate the economy with both substantial fiscal packages as well as with massive monetary easing, but after a short recovery in 2010 Japan slipped into recession again in 2011 but has been growing at a low pace again since 2012.

The Swedish banking system also had little exposure to US subprime financial products and was therefore not really affected by the financial crisis that broke out in the USA. A minor disturbance came via contagion from the Baltic countries where the presence of Swedish banks is high. Ultimately, only one bank needed government rescue (Stenfors 2014). As with the previous two countries, the main transmission channel of the crisis was the trade channel. Sweden experienced a downturn in the last quarter of 2008 and in 2009, but, as in Germany, the recovery began rather quickly, aided by its role – again like Germany – as a safe haven for foreign financial wealth, leading therefore to a beneficial reduction of the interest rate once the euro crisis started.

Overall we can conclude that the export-led mercantilist economies were affected by the crisis primarily via the trade channel, that is, through falling exports due to a contraction in foreign demand, and only partially by the financial contagion channel. However, recovery came much faster than it did in the debt-led domestic demand boom economies: On the one hand, the financial crisis was dealt with immediately and successfully by the respective governments, if required, and the long process of deleveraging did not need to take place since the indebtedness of the private sector had been low relative to the other group of countries. On the other hand, foreign demand picked up from other global players, in particular China and other emerging market economies, and export performance was strong despite the lack of demand from debt-led private demand boom economies. In Europe, both Germany and Sweden benefitted from the safe haven effect and thus very low interest rates.

Of these three countries, which in the trade cycle before the crises were clearly following an export-led mercantilist pattern, only Germany has remained firmly on this path. Japan as well as Sweden have become weakly export-led economies, Sweden with still high current account surpluses, but both with overall negative growth contributions of net exports in the crisis/post-crisis period.

The Crises in the Domestic Demand-led Countries

The catching-up domestic demand-led countries
Figure 1.3 shows the real GDP growth of Turkey, Poland and Hungary. Despite the highest growth rates in our set of countries in the years leading up to the crisis, none of these countries managed to return to pre-crisis growth rates. Overall, we observe a slow and weak recovery. Poland is an exception here, as it seems to have avoided the worst effects of the crises; its growth has slowed down but the country never entered a recession. The economies of Turkey and Hungary have been more volatile, with Hungary experiencing a second recession in 2012.

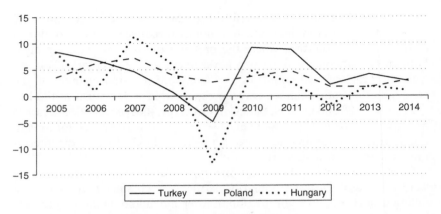

Source: European Commission (2015), authors' calculations.

Figure 1.3   *Real GDP growth in Turkey, Poland and Hungary, 2005–2014, in per cent*

Table 1.13   *Sectoral financial balances as a share of nominal GDP, in per cent, average values for the trade cycle, for Turkey, Poland and Hungary*

	Turkey	Poland	Hungary
	2009–2014	2009–2014	2009–2014
External sector	6.3	1.7	−4.4
Public sector	−2.6	−5.5	−3.7
Corporate sector	−3.8*	4.9	4.5
Private household sector		−1.0	3.6

Note: * Financial balance of the private sector (corporate and private household sectors).

Source: European Commission (2015), authors' calculations.

Looking at sectoral financial balances of these countries since 2009 (Table 1.13) several interesting features emerge. Relative to the trade cycle before the crises, Poland has managed to decrease its current account deficits, while Hungary has become a net exporter with quite substantial current account surpluses. Turkey, on the other hand, saw its current account deficits widen. Both Turkey and Hungary have also seen their public sector deficits decrease, unlike in Poland, and whereas Poland and Hungary saw a significant increase of the corporate sector surplus, in

Table 1.14   Real GDP growth, in per cent, and growth contributions,
                 in percentage points, average values for the trade cycle, for
                 Turkey, Poland and Hungary

	Turkey	Poland	Hungary
	2009–2014	2009–2014	2009–2014
Real GDP growth	3.7	2.9	−0.1
Contribution to the increase of GDP of:			
Private consumption	2.1	1.4	−0.8
Public consumption	0.7	0.3	0.1
Investment	0.8	0.4	−0.3
Balance of goods and services	0.0	1.0	1.2

Source: European Commission (2015), authors' calculations.

Turkey the private sector as a whole went from surplus in the pre-crisis period to deficit over the following six years.

In terms of growth contributions (Table 1.14), private consumption in Turkey and Poland has continued to be the main driver of growth, whereas Hungary now exhibits a major growth contribution from the balance of goods and services, mainly because of weak domestic demand and thus imports. The importance of net exports as a growth contributor features prominently in the case of Poland as well.

The transmission of the crises to Turkey occurred via three main channels, namely an expectations channel, the trade channel and the financial channel. First, the expectations channel became effective, which meant a substantial deterioration in consumer and investor confidence, particularly in early to mid-2008, ultimately resulting in a fall in investment and then consumption expenditures. Secondly, the trade channel of crisis transmission became relevant and Turkey experienced a strong and negative export shock. The cumulative effect was a massive drop in production. Finally, the crisis also affected Turkey through the financial channel, in the form of a sudden stop in capital inflows, which had a contractive effect on credit conditions. However, the decline in financial inflows was relatively short lived (registered only in two quarters). The combination of these factors, however, resulted in Turkey experiencing one of its worst economic downturns since World War II (Bahçe et al. 2015). However, unlike during previous crises, Turkish financial markets did not collapse. This can be attributed to the fact that the financial shock was small and short in duration. The government and the central bank attempted to take significant policy measures in response to the crisis. However, these measures were either relatively late or/

and not very effective. A first fiscal package was announced in March 2009, with tax cuts targeted at stabilising demand. Employment measures were introduced to alleviate the impact on unemployment and a range of measures targeting the attraction of capital inflows were adopted. Interestingly, after the initial problem of capital outflows, later in the crisis the concern shifted to destabilising inflows, caused by the enormous liquidity injection of major developed countries' central banks (Bahçe et al. 2015).

Poland was affected only mildly by the crises and shows signs of a healthy recovery based on increasing private consumption and an improvement in the trade balance. Why has the Polish economy coped with an impact of the global crisis better than any other EU country? Financialisation did not play an important role in Poland, and despite a housing bubble developing in the years leading up to the crisis, housing prices did not increase as much as in Hungary or the Baltic countries, meaning the end of the bubble did not have such a significant impact on the Polish financial sector or the performance of individual banks. Dymarski (2015) specified several factors, which jointly may provide an explanation. First, Poland, like Turkey and Hungary, retained its own currency, allowing the Polish central bank more freedom to pursue internal policy objectives. Secondly, in the years leading up to the crisis, the floating exchange rate helped to prevent the economy from getting into a deep current account deficit. Thirdly, unlike in Turkey and in Hungary, the majority of Poland's domestic sector debt was denominated in national currency, thus reducing the country's vulnerability to the crisis. Moreover, the Polish financial system is mainly bank based, with the banking sector being the least concentrated among the Central and Eastern European (CEE) countries. It is important to underline here that the state exercised effective supervision over the banking sector before the crisis; for instance, to curb the accelerating growth in mortgage and consumer loans, and foreign currency loans. In 2006, the Polish Financial Supervision Authority issued the *Recommendation S* on good practices related to credit exposures, enforced by *Recommendation S II* of 2008, which required banks to apply stricter credit underwriting standards and to disclose foreign currency risks when providing foreign currency loans (Dymarski 2015). As a result, in 2008 new foreign currency loans in Poland accounted for only 25 per cent of total new loans (in Hungary, for instance, they were around 55 per cent).

The crisis hit Hungary very hard, but this was not due to the problems in the domestic financial sector, but rather had to do with the fact that Hungary was extremely dependent on, and exposed to, large external public and private debt in foreign currency (Badics and Szikszai 2015). In addition, due to its high accumulation of private debt and public external debt, Hungary needed to request IMF financial assistance in 2008.

Austerity policies that were attached to the IMF assistance and which Hungary was obliged to implement prolonged the recession and turned Hungary from a domestic demand-led economy towards an export-led mercantilist economy, building up current account surpluses since 2010.

Overall, the crisis transmission experienced by this group of countries was mainly via financial flows – that is via the balance of payments channel – although this channel only affected the countries briefly. Therefore, the financial contagion channel was dominant here, as it was for the debt-led private demand boom countries. In the latter group, however, we had Spain and Greece where this transmission was rendered more severe and translated into the euro crisis, which is a specific crisis due to the EMU institutional framework. In the non-EMU countries of the catching-up domestic demand-led type, however, the countries experienced to a certain extent a balance of payments crisis. The economic crisis developed then as a result of contracting domestic demand, which became more severe when combined with only weak (Turkey) or even adverse (Hungary) government responses.

The mature domestic demand-led countries
France, Italy and Portugal were hit by the global financial crisis and experienced a recession in 2009 (Figure 1.4). After a brief recovery in 2010, both Portugal and Italy fell again into a recession, in 2011 and 2012, respectively. Of this country group, Portugal was most affected by the euro crisis, whereas the crisis in France was least severe. In the aftermath of the crises, none of the three countries has returned to the pre-crisis growth rates.

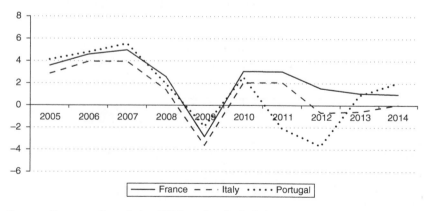

Source: European Commission (2015), authors' calculations.

Figure 1.4   Real GDP growth in France, Italy and Portugal, 2005–2014, in per cent

Table 1.15   Sectoral financial balances as a share of nominal GDP, in per cent, average values for the trade cycle, for France, Italy and Portugal

	France	Italy	Portugal
	2009–2014	2009–2014	2009–2014
External sector	2.0	1.0	3.4
Public sector	−5.4	−3.6	−7.3
Corporate sector	−0.7	1.2	−0.4
Private household sector	4.1	1.5	4.3

Source: European Commission (2015), authors' calculations.

Whereas Italy and in particular Portugal have managed to reduce their current account deficits since the crisis, France saw an increase in the financial balance of the external sector (Table 1.15). In all three countries government deficits have increased relative to the previous trade cycle. Furthermore, private households in both Portugal and France have increased their net saving. Expectedly, net exports have been the main driver of growth in the case of Italy and Portugal, although they have not been sufficient to offset the negative contributions of the domestic demand components (Table 1.16). Of the three countries, France has been the only one with a positive real GDP growth averaged over the period from 2009 until 2014, to which the main contributor has been public consumption.

Table 1.16   Real GDP growth, in per cent, and growth contributions, in percentage points, average values for the trade cycle, for France, Italy and Portugal

	France	Italy	Portugal
	2009–2014	2009–2014	2009–2014
Real GDP growth	0.3	−1.3	−1.1
Contribution to the increase of GDP of:			
Private consumption	0.2	−0.7	−0.9
Public consumption	0.4	−0.1	−0.3
Investment	−0.3	−0.9	−1.3
Balance of goods and services	0.0	0.6	1.6

Source: European Commission (2015), authors' calculations.

The crises affected the French economy via two channels: Firstly, via a consumption and investment demand slowdown, due to the international financial crisis and increased uncertainty (expectations channel), and secondly, via a decline in foreign demand due to problems abroad which worsened the French trade balance (trade channel) (Cornilleau and Creel 2014). With some help from government stabilisation policy, the French banking system weathered the crisis; there have been no major bankruptcies since 2008 nor has a credit crunch developed. Additionally, France has been negatively affected by the austerity measures implemented since the outbreak of the euro crisis while trying to meet the European Stability and Growth Pact targets.

As in France, the Italian banking system did not particularly suffer during the crisis. This was largely due to its low leverage ratios by international comparison. However, the stability of Italian banks has been undermined in the course of the crisis, because of the negative feedback loops between fiscal sustainability concerns, banks' exposure to the Italian sovereign bonds and weakening real economic activity. High uncertainty and deterioration in expectations have caused Italian debtors to suffer from high interest rates in international comparison since then. The Italian recovery has suffered from fiscal austerity measures as has the French; in the Italian case this was due in particular to tax hikes (Gabbi et al. 2014).

Portugal's banking sector was not affected by the crisis since it was not involved in buying subprime financial products from the USA, and it was also not involved in excessive lending to support bubbles, because Portugal did not have a house price boom. The global financial crisis affected Portugal's economy through the uncertainty and expectations channel, via increasing perceived credit risk, which pushed up interest rates and thus adversely affected consumption and investment (Lagoa et al. 2014). Ultimately, the problem in Portugal was the high public debt, with debt-GDP and deficit-GDP ratios worsening after the government's attempt to stabilise the economy, which finally resulted in the need for Portugal to ask for assistance from the IMF and the European Financial Stability Facility (EFSF) in 2010. Conditionalities of the rescue packages which included austerity policies have then worsened the crisis in Portugal.

In sum, France and Italy have both been negatively affected by austerity measures implemented since the outbreak of the crises. Portugal was hit even harder and earlier, because it experienced the strongest financial market pressures among the countries within the group. Also, in terms of economic policies, Portugal, due to the fact it had requested a bail-out, suffered from more extensive and harsher austerity measures. What we can conclude for the group of advanced, mature domestic demand-led economies is that when the global financial crisis broke out, they were primarily affected through rising borrowing costs and rising uncertainty. However, given the low exposure of domestic banks to subprime financial products from the USA, no major or prolonged problems in the banking sector occurred. It was with the euro crisis that a slowdown in private consumption and investment became more marked – largely a result of 'soft' (in the cases of France and Italy) or severe (in the case of Portugal) austerity policies. All three countries have been growing weakly since.

France, which was least affected by the euro crisis, has remained a domestic demand-led economy even in the aftermath of the crises. In Portugal and Italy, however, a shift towards export-led mercantilism can be observed, driven by the collapse of imports due to austerity policies. Italy has been building current account surpluses since 2013, accompanied by private sector surpluses and government deficits, and the situation is similar in Portugal, which saw a sharp reduction in current account deficits and as of 2013 has a roughly balanced current account.

Current Account (Im)balances before and after the Crises

Before concluding, we briefly look at the global development of current account (im)balances since the crises. Figure 1.5 shows current account

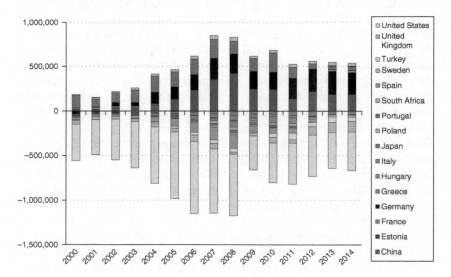

Source: IMF (2015), authors' illustration.

Figure 1.5   Current account balance, selected countries, 2000–2014, in billions of US dollars

balances for all the countries we considered in this chapter, and it also includes China, which of course is one of the biggest contributors to global current account surpluses. Several issues should be pointed out.

First, all of the export-led mercantilist countries of the pre-crisis period have remained current account surplus countries. However, the surpluses of Japan have significantly declined and those of Sweden have remained roughly constant, whereas the German surpluses have even increased. Therefore, while Germany has continued with the radical export-led mercantilist regime, Japan and Sweden seem to have turned towards a weakly export-led regime with current account surpluses, but negative growth contributions from falling net exports.

Secondly, a distinction should be made between those debt-led private demand boom economies, and also those domestic demand-led economies of the pre-crisis period with respect to whether or not they have monetary policy autonomy. The USA, the UK and South Africa have largely remained current account deficit countries. However, it is now the government, rather than the private sector, that is running deficits, indicating that these countries have moved towards a domestic demand-led configuration. Unlike these three countries, the six EMU countries (Spain, Greece, Estonia, France, Italy, Portugal) suffered from the euro crisis and the lack of a proper lender of last resort for the government, due to the lack of an own autonomous central bank acting as a lender of last resort to the government and a proper substitute at the Euro area level. Additionally, they were subject to more or less extensive austerity measures, and policies to increase competitiveness and stimulate exports (internal devaluation). In particular, in those countries where such measures were more extensively adopted, namely in Greece, Spain, and Portugal, which received financial assistance in exchange for reforms, but also in the case of Italy, we can observe the shift towards export-led mercantilism, mainly through dampening domestic demand and imports. Spain and Italy have registered current account surpluses since 2013, while Portugal sharply reduced its deficits and its current account has been roughly balanced since 2013. Greece saw a substantial reduction in current account deficits related to a sharp drop in imports, but continues to register current account deficits, although on a much smaller scale. France, on the other hand, is the only country of the group that remained domestic demand-led, while Estonia – coming from a group of debt-led private demand boom countries – has now become domestic demand-led. Estonia initially shifted to having current account surpluses in 2009 and 2010 but has since registered current account deficits, accompanied by positive financial balances of the private sector and government deficits.

Thirdly, regarding the group of catching-up domestic demand-led

economies, we can see that both Turkey and Poland continued registering current account deficits, however these were accompanied by negative
financial balances of the private household sector (Poland) or the private
sector as a whole (Turkey). We can say that these countries now show characteristics of a debt-led private demand boom type of development. In the
case of Hungary the opposite has occurred, namely the country shifted
towards current account surpluses in 2010 and has registered increasing
surpluses ever since. This development has been accompanied by positive
financial balances of the private household and of the corporate sectors,
thus turning Hungary towards an export-led mercantilist economy.

1.5   CONCLUSIONS

In this chapter we have firstly outlined three types of regimes under the
conditions of financialisation, namely a debt-led private demand boom,
an export-led mercantilist and a domestic demand-led regime. We have
then taken a look at the sectoral financial balances of the main macroeconomic sectors and at the growth contributions of the demand aggregates
of 15 countries, focusing in particular on the trade cycle before the crises.
This has allowed us to cluster these countries according to the typology of demand regimes. We found that a debt-led private demand boom
regime was experienced by the USA, the UK, Spain, Estonia, Greece, and
South Africa, while an export-led mercantilist type could be found for
Germany, Japan, and Sweden. These two types of regime contain internal
contradictions, with respect to household debt and with respect to foreign
debt of the counterpart current account deficit countries, which may
finally undermine the sustainability of these regimes and lead to financial
and economic crises. We also found that France, Hungary, Italy, Poland,
Portugal, and Turkey, all exhibited indicators of a domestic demand-led
type of development.

In the second part of the chapter we focused on the period following the
outbreak of the crises and, by considering transmission mechanisms and
the main obstacles to recovery, we analysed how countries in each of these
clusters were affected. Countries belonging to the export-led mercantilist group, in particular Germany and Sweden, recovered quickly because
their domestic balance sheets were largely in order, the financial crisis
was contained by immediate government responses, and these countries
also benefitted from the recovery of the world economy. In the post-crisis
period it is, however, only Germany that has effectively remained an
export-led mercantilist economy. But such a 'beggar thy neighbour' strategy cannot be considered as a role model for the world economy, because it

requires counterpart current account deficit countries. Japan and Sweden have become weakly export-led, with continuing (high) current account surpluses, but on a declining trend. Average growth contributions of net exports in the crisis/post-crisis period have been negative.

Debt-led private demand boom, as well as domestic demand-led, economies with monetary policy autonomy have been successful in stabilising the financial sector and the economy by government deficits. However, they have had lower growth rates than before the crises. For the debt-led private demand boom countries in this group, the US, the UK, and South Africa, there are some indications of a shift towards domestic demand-led growth accompanied by an improvement of the financial balances of the private sector. For the catching-up domestic demand-led countries in this group, consisting of Turkey, Hungary and Poland, we observed a rather quick recovery of financial flows. However, such economies – with their own but not leading currencies – should be wary of accumulating private and/or public debt in foreign currency during a boom. In the debt-led private demand boom, as well as in the domestic demand-led economies without monetary policy autonomy, on the other hand, macroeconomic stabilisation was terminated first by financial market pressure and then by fiscal austerity. This refers to the six EMU countries (Estonia, France, Greece, Italy, Portugal, and Spain) which have been showing a movement towards export-led mercantilist economies, mainly through a contraction of domestic demand and imports, in the crisis/post-crisis period. However, it remains to be seen whether this regime can be maintained when domestic demand will rise again.

What conclusions can we draw from these developments for the perspectives of the world economy? The tendency towards balanced or surplus current accounts in several former current account deficit countries seems to be based to a large extent on the contraction of domestic demand and imports, and thus on 'stagnation policies' (Steindl 1979). This has a depressing effect on global economic activity. And to the extent that export-led mercantilist strategies will be maintained in the medium run, they face a fallacy of composition problem. Therefore, if pre-crisis export-led mercantilist economies continue to stick with their model and some previously debt-led private demand boom and domestic demand-led economies turn towards these strategies, counterpart current account deficit countries are required by definition. Currently it seems that these will either be some mature economies, which have now become domestic demand-led and which are relying on sustained public sector deficits, as well as some catching-up economies relying on a combination of public sector and private sector deficits and the counterpart capital inflows.

Of course, this constellation suffers from two risks: First, high government deficits and debt in mature domestic demand-led economies as stabilisers of national and global demand may be reversed for political reasons (debt ceilings, debt brakes), although there may be no risks of over-indebtedness of governments, if debt can be issued in the own currency. Second, capital inflows into catching-up domestic demand-led economies may be unstable and face 'sudden stops' because of changes in expectations and/or (perceived) over-indebtedness in foreign currency. Therefore, if this global constellation cannot be overcome by a more balanced development based on expansionary contributions by the current account surplus countries, economic policy making in two areas would have to be re-thought and re-assessed. First, the role of public deficits and debt in order to provide global demand at a reasonable growth rate would have to be accepted, in particular for governments being able to go into debt in their own currency. Second, the stable recycling of current account surpluses towards the high-growth catching-up countries financing their current account deficits would have to be provided in order to avoid unsustainable booms, 'sudden stops' and capital flight.

NOTES

1. See Badics and Szikszai (2015) on Hungary, Bahçe et al. (2015) on Turkey, Cornilleau and Creel (2014) on France, Detzer and Hein (2014) on Germany, Dymarski (2015) on Poland, Evans (2015) on the USA, Ferreiro et al. (2014) on Spain, Gabbi et al. (2014) on Italy, Juuse and Kattel (2014) on Estonia, Lagoa et al. (2014) on Portugal, Lepper et al. (2015) on the UK, Newman (2014) on South Africa, Shabani and Toporowski (2015) on Japan, Stenfors (2014) on Sweden, and Varoufakis and Tserkezis (2014) on Greece.
2. The beginning of a trade cycle is given by a local minimum of annual real GDP growth. Consequently, it ends in the year preceding the subsequent local minimum. This method is applied for each of the country groups for the pre-crisis period. The trade cycle after the crises is incomplete, beginning in 2009 and ending with latest available data.
3. In other words, the net saving of the household sector is financing the investments of the corporate sector.
4. We do not consider Estonia before the dissolution of the Soviet Union.
5. The adjusted wage share is calculated here as: (Compensation of employees / Total employees) / (Gross domestic product at current market prices / Total employment) (European Commission 2005).

REFERENCES

Badics, T. and S. Szikszai (2015), 'Financialisation and the financial and economic crises: the case of Hungary', FESSUD Studies in Financial Systems, No. 31, University of Leeds.
Bahçe, S., H. Cömert, S. Çolak, N. Erdem, E. Karaçimen, A. H. Köse, Ö. Orhangazi, G. Özgür and G. Yalman (2015), 'Financialisation and the financial and

economic crises: the case of Turkey', FESSUD Studies in Financial Systems, No. 21, University of Leeds. For a shortened version see Chapter 12 of this book.

Barba, A. and M. Pivetti (2009), 'Rising household debt: its causes and macroeconomic implications – a long-period analysis', *Cambridge Journal of Economics*, **33**, 113–137.

Boone, L. and N. Girouard (2002), 'The stock market, the housing market and consumer behaviour', *OECD Economic Studies*, **35**, 175–200.

Cornilleau, G. and J. Creel (2014), 'Financialisation and the financial and economic crises: the case of France', FESSUD Studies in Financial Systems, No. 22, University of Leeds. For a shortened version see Chapter 9 of this book.

Cynamon, B. and S. Fazzari (2008), 'Household debt in the consumer age: source of growth – risk of collapse', *Capitalism and Society*, **3** (2), 1–30.

Cynamon, B. and S. Fazzari (2013), 'Inequality and household finance during the consumer age', Working Paper, No. 752, Annandale-on-Hudson, NY: Levy Economics Institute of Bard College.

Detzer, D. and E. Hein (2014), 'Financialisation and the financial and economic crises: the case of Germany', FESSUD Studies in Financial Systems, No. 18, University of Leeds. For a shortened version see Chapter 7 of this book.

Duménil, G. and D. Levy (2011), *The Crisis of Neoliberalism*, Cambridge, MA: Harvard University Press.

Dymarski, W. (2015), 'Financialisation and the financial and economic crises: the case of Poland', FESSUD Studies in Financial Systems, No. 29, University of Leeds.

European Commission (2005), AMECO – List of Variables, available at: http://ec. europa.eu/economy_finance/db_indicators/ameco/documents/list_of_variables. pdf.

European Commission (2015), *AMECO Database*, May 2015, available at: http:// ec.europa.eu/economy_finance/db_indicators/ameco/index_en.htm.

Evans, T. (2015), 'Financialisation and the financial and economic crises: the case of the U.S.A.', FESSUD Studies in Financial Systems, No. 32, University of Leeds. For a shortened version see Chapter 2 of this book.

Ferreiro, J., C. Galvez and A. Gonzalez (2014), 'Financialisation and the financial and economic crises: the case of Spain', FESSUD Studies in Financial Systems, No. 19, University of Leeds. For a shortened version see Chapter 4 of this book.

Gabbi, G., E. Ticci and P. Vozella (2014), 'Financialisation and the financial and economic crises: the case of Italy', FESSUD Studies in Financial Systems, No. 23, University of Leeds. For a shortened version see Chapter 10 of this book.

Guttmann, R. and D. Plihon (2010), 'Consumer debt and financial fragility', *International Review of Applied Economics*, **24**, 269–283.

Hein, E. (2012), *The Macroeconomics of Finance-dominated Capitalism – and its Crisis*, Cheltenham: Edward Elgar.

Hein, E. (2014), *Distribution and Growth after Keynes: A Post-Keynesian Guide*, Cheltenham: Edward Elgar.

Hein, E. (2015), 'Finance-dominated capitalism and re-distribution of income – a Kaleckian perspective', *Cambridge Journal of Economics*, **39**, 907–934.

Hein, E. and T. van Treeck (2010), 'Financialisation and rising shareholder power in Kaleckian/Post-Kaleckian models of distribution and growth', *Review of Political Economy*, **22**, 205–233.

Hein, E. and M. Mundt (2012), 'Financialisation and the requirements and potentials for wage-led recovery – a review focussing on the G20', Conditions of Work and Employment Series, No. 37, 2012, Geneva: ILO.

Hein, E. and N. Dodig (2015), 'Financialisation, distribution, growth and crises – long-run tendencies', in E. Hein, D. Detzer and N. Dodig (eds), *The Demise of Finance-dominated Capitalism: Explaining the Financial and Economic Crises*, Cheltenham: Edward Elgar.

Hein, E., N. Dodig and N. Budyldina (2015), 'The transition towards finance-dominated capitalism: French Regulation School, Social Structures of Accumulation and post-Keynesian approaches compared', in E. Hein, D. Detzer and N. Dodig (eds), *The Demise of Finance-dominated Capitalism: Explaining the Financial and Economic Crises*, Cheltenham: Edward Elgar.

Herr, H. (2012), 'International monetary and financial architecture', in E. Hein and E. Stockhammer (eds), *A Modern Guide to Keynesian Macroeconomics and Economic Policies*, Cheltenham: Edward Elgar.

Horn, G., H. Joebges and R. Zwiener (2009), 'From the financial crisis to the world economic crisis (II). Global imbalances: Cause of the crisis and solution strategies for Germany', IMK Policy Brief, December 2009, Dusseldorf: Macroeconomic Policy Institute (IMK) at Hans-Boeckler Foundation.

IMF (2015), *International Monetary Fund World Economic Outlook database*, April 2015, available at: https://www.imf.org/external/pubs/ft/weo/2015/01/weodata/index.aspx.

Juuse, E. and R. Kattel (2014), 'Financialisation and the financial and economic crises: the case of Estonia', FESSUD Studies in Financial Systems, No. 20, University of Leeds. For a shortened version see Chapter 6 of this book.

Lagoa, S., E. Leao, R. Paes Mamede and R. Barradas (2014), 'Financialisation and the financial and economic crises: the case of Portugal', FESSUD Studies in Financial Systems, No. 24, University of Leeds. For a shortened version see Chapter 11 of this book.

Lepper, J., M. Shabani, J. Toporowski and J. Tyson (2015), 'Financialisation and the financial and economic crises: the case of United Kingdom', FESSUD Studies in Financial Systems, No. 30, University of Leeds. For a shortened version see Chapter 3 of this book.

Ludvigson, S. and C. Steindel (1999), 'How important is the stock market effect on consumption?', *Federal Reserve Bank of New York Economic Policy Review*, July, 29–51.

Mehra, Y. P. (2001), 'The wealth effect in empirical life-cycle aggregate consumption equations', *Federal Reserve Bank of Richmond Economic Quarterly*, **87** (2), 45–68.

Newman, S. (2014), 'Financialisation and the financial and economic crises: the case of South Africa', FESSUD Studies in Financial Systems, No. 26, University of Leeds.

Onaran, Ö., E. Stockhammer and L. Grafl (2011), 'Financialisation, income distribution and aggregate demand in the USA', *Cambridge Journal of Economics*, **35**, 637–661.

Orhangazi, Ö. (2008), 'Financialisation and capital accumulation in the non-financial corporate sector: a theoretical and empirical investigation on the US economy: 1973–2003', *Cambridge Journal of Economics*, **32**, 863–886.

Shabani, M. and J. Toporowski (2015), 'Financialisation and the financial and economic crises: the case of Japan', FESSUD Studies in Financial Systems, No. 28, University of Leeds.

Steindl, J. (1979), 'Stagnation theory and stagnation policy', *Cambridge Journal of Economics*, **3**, 1–14, reprinted in: Steindl, J., *Economic Papers, 1941–88*, Basingstoke: Macmillan, 1990.

Stenfors, A. (2014), 'Financialisation and the financial and economic crises: the case of Sweden', FESSUD Studies in Financial Systems, No. 27, University of Leeds. For a shortened version see Chapter 8 of this book.

Stockhammer, E. (2004), 'Financialisation and the slowdown of accumulation', *Cambridge Journal of Economics*, **28**, 719–741.

Stockhammer, E. (2010), 'Income distribution, the finance-dominated accumulation regime, and the present crisis', in S. Dullien, E. Hein, A. Truger and T. van Treeck (eds), *The World Economy in Crisis – the Return of Keynesianism?*, Marburg: Metropolis.

Stockhammer, E. (2012), 'Financialization, income distribution and the crisis', *Investigación Económica*, **71** (279), 39–70.

Stockhammer, E. (2015), 'Rising inequality as a cause of the present crisis', *Cambridge Journal of Economics*, **39**, 935–958.

UNCTAD (2009), *The Global Economic Crisis. Systemic Failures and Multilateral Remedies*, New York, Geneva: UNCTAD.

Van Treeck, T. (2008), 'Reconsidering the investment-profit nexus in finance-led economies: an ARDL-based approach', *Metroeconomica*, **59**, 371–404.

Van Treeck, T. (2014), 'Did inequality cause the US financial crisis?', *Journal of Economic Surveys*, **28**, 421–448.

Van Treeck, T. and S. Sturn (2012), 'Income inequality as a cause of the Great Recession? A survey of current debates', Conditions of Work and Employment Series, No. 39, Geneva: ILO.

Varoufakis, J. and L. Tserkezis (2014), 'Financialisation and the financial and economic crises: the case of Greece', FESSUD Studies in Financial Systems, No. 25, University of Leeds. For a shortened version see Chapter 5 of this book.

World Bank (2015), World Bank Database, July 2015, available at: http://data.worldbank.org./.

2. The crisis of finance-led capitalism in the United States*

Trevor Evans

2.1 INTRODUCTION

For some 25 years after the Second World War, the US economy experienced an unprecedented period of growth in which wide sectors of the population shared in rising prosperity. Fordist techniques of mass production, which had been pioneered before the war, were widely introduced and facilitated a steady rise in the productivity and intensity of labour. At the same time, following successful struggles to organise unions in the 1930s, workers were able to secure a steady rise in real wages, ensuring – unlike the pre-war period – a strong growth of domestic demand, which rose broadly in line with labour productivity. Industrial and commercial firms sustained a strong growth of fixed investment which was financed to a large extent out of retained earnings. External finance was obtained from a financial sector that was subject to tight constraints, introduced in the aftermath of the 1929 crisis, and which seriously limited the possibilities for financial speculation. These constraints involved a strict separation between commercial and investment banks, and a legal limit on interest rates. The period also witnessed a strong growth of international trade between the US and other developed capitalist states, facilitated by a stable international monetary regime based on the US dollar and fixed exchange rates. Finally, while the US was involved in organising or supporting numerous armed interventions in Africa, Asia and Latin America, developing countries could, for the most part, be relied on to ensure a steady – and cheap – supply of primary commodities.

In the late 1960s, as the US army faced defeat in the jungles of South-East Asia, the virtuous constellation that had underpinned the post-war boom began to unravel. Perhaps most significantly, the Fordist model appeared to be approaching its limit and, despite continued investment, the growth of labour productivity began to slow. Younger workers

* This is a shortened version of Evans (2015).

42

who had not lived through the mass unemployment of the 1930s were not willing to moderate their demands for rising wages and, as industrial conflicts intensified, profitability began to decline. At the same time, as the business cycle in the US and the other advanced capitalist countries became more closely attuned, a synchronised expansion in the early 1970s led to a strong increase in demand for primary commodities and, as their price was pushed up, this further eroded profitability. Furthermore, firms in the US, which had once been the technological leaders, began to be challenged by competitors in Europe and Japan. Following a steady deterioration in the US trade balance, in 1971 the country experienced its first current account deficit since the beginning of the century and, as foreign central banks accumulated ever larger quantities of dollars, the US government unilaterally announced it would no longer convert these for gold. Shortly after, in 1973, the US abandoned the system of fixed exchange rates in a move designed to allow it to devalue the dollar and so cheapen its exports in relation to those of key competitors. But none of this was sufficient. From 1973 to 1975 the US economy – along with all the other advanced capitalist economies – experienced the deepest recession since the 1930s, thereby marking the end of the post-war boom.

In the second half of the 1970s US governments sought to raise domestic demand through the adoption of highly expansive fiscal policies, and to promote exports by allowing the dollar to weaken. This succeeded in reviving economic growth for a time but, as inflation began to rise sharply, it could not be sustained. In the autumn of 1979, foreign investors responded to the steady decline in the value of the dollar by abandoning their holdings en masse. As the value of the dollar threatened to plummet, the Federal Reserve, led by Paul Volcker, seized on the arguments of monetarist economists to justify a dramatic rise in the US lead interest rate. Higher returns successfully attracted short-term capital back to the dollar, which subsequently staged a major recovery in its value. But the unprecedented level of interest rates led to a collapse in investment and provoked a deep and lengthy period of recession between 1980 and 1982. A steep increase in unemployment successfully broke the back of union demands for wage increases. However, the rise in interest rates, together with a sharp fall in commodity prices, resulted in many developing countries being unable to service their debts to big US banks and, with the threat of major bank failures, in the autumn of 1982 the US authorities quietly abandoned their monetarist experiment.

This chapter is concerned with the new phase of US capitalism that emerged from the deep recession at the start of the 1980s. This period, sometimes characterised as finance-led capitalism, was marked by a serious weakening in the bargaining position of waged workers. At the same time, innovation and deregulation led to a major expansion of the financial sector, which exercised a remorseless pressure on non-financial companies to raise returns. Non-financial companies, meanwhile, themselves became increasingly involved in generating returns from financial investments and this was associated with a corresponding weakening in investment in fixed capital. Most of the benefits of economic growth accrued to top earners – the notorious 1 per cent – who appropriated an increasing share of national income. Wages no longer rose in line with labour productivity, and economic growth became dependent on a continual expansion of credit-financed consumption. This unstable constellation faltered in 1990, and again in 2001, generating short recessions that the authorities sought to combat by pumping yet more money into the economy. But the expansion was precarious and in 2007 and 2008 the failure of highly complex financial securities based on house mortgages detonated the most serious financial crisis since 1929.

2.2   FINANCE-LED CAPITALISM IN THE US

The phase of capitalism that began in the US in the early 1980s was characterised by a significant weakening in the position of labour and a marked strengthening in the position of financial capital. The position of labour was weakened, first, by the monetarist offensive launched at the end of 1979. As interest rates were raised to unprecedented levels, investment collapsed, and unemployment increased from 5.8 per cent in 1979 to 9.8 per cent in 1982 (Bureau of Labor Statistics, Historical Data, Table A-1). Although high inflation was eroding the value of wages, workers' primary concern was to keep their jobs. Second, in 1981, the newly elected President, Ronald Reagan, responded to a strike of air-traffic controllers by sacking the staff involved, and using supervisors and military personnel until new civilians could be trained (McCartin 2011). As intended, other unions reigned in their ambitions. Third, a wave of corporate takeovers, 'downsizing' and the outsourcing of tasks in the 1980s left many workers deeply cautious of risking their jobs by raising demands for better wages or working conditions, a process described by Alan Blinder and Janet Yellen (2001) as 'the frightened worker effect'. One indicator of the weakening position of labour is the percentage of non-agricultural employees covered by union contracts. In 1980 this stood at 25.7 per cent but, as the position of unions was weakened, and as non-unionised sectors of the economy expanded, by 2007 it had fallen to 13.3 per cent (Hirsch and Macpherson 2013).

Financial capital had been subjected to strict controls by the Banking

Act of 1933 whose provisions included the enforced separation of commercial banks and investment banks, and the imposition of legal ceiling on interest rates. In the 1960s, however, banks began to introduce innovations that enabled them to circumvent these restrictions. A key step was the creation of certificates of deposit, which allowed banks to offer interest rates above the legal ceiling. The growth of off-shore banking in the late 1960s, predominantly in London, also enabled US banks to circumvent tighter restrictions on the export of capital that had been introduced in 1965. Then the end of fixed exchange rates in 1973, and the subsequent growth of the foreign exchange markets, provided the big banks with a major new source of profitable activity. The US government responded by abolishing controls on international capital flows in 1974 and from the 1980s the process of financial innovation and deregulation gathered pace.

In 1980, as official interest rates were raised to combat rising inflation, the Carter government abolished the legal ceiling on deposit interest rates that had been introduced in 1933.[1] The process of financial liberalisation then accelerated after the Reagan government took office in 1981. In 1982, a new banking law lifted many of the restrictions on the activities of savings and loans associations (S&Ls), financial institutions that allowed households to save and subsequently obtain financing to purchase a home. This allowed the S&Ls to expand rapidly and many embarked on financing more speculative activities until huge losses led to a serious crisis in the sector in the late 1980s and early 1990s, requiring government support that eventually amounted to some $150 billion. In 1987, the Reagan government appointed Alan Greenspan as head of the Federal Reserve and in the following years the Fed adopted an increasingly flexible interpretation of the 1933 Banking Act, allowing commercial banks to slowly expand into activities that previously had been prohibited. Finally, in 1999 under the Clinton government, the legal separation between commercial and investment banks was entirely lifted, allowing the re-emergence of giant financial conglomerates.

The financial sector had grown roughly in line with the rest of the US economy between the 1950s and 1970s, but from the 1980s its growth accelerated. First, there was a major expansion of financial institutions, including banks, institutional investors (in particular mutual funds where better-off middle-class households could invest their savings) and, somewhat later, smaller but highly speculative hedge funds and private equity funds, which operated to a large extent with borrowed money. Second, there was a rapid growth of financial markets, including the foreign exchange market, and the markets in bonds, shares and other securities. Finally, there was a rapid process of innovation, which gave rise to the creation of a whole range of new financial instruments, including exotic forms of derivatives and highly complex instruments, such as collateral debt obligations, which were designed so as to obscure the risks which they involved.

Developments in the financial sector had a significant impact on non-financial corporations. Institutional investors, which had previously played a relatively passive role, began to exert pressure on non-financial companies to give priority to raising their short-term profitability, so as to push up dividends and share prices. Companies that failed to meet profit projections were threatened with the prospect that investors would sell their shares, and that the resulting fall in share prices would leave the top management vulnerable to a hostile takeover. Indeed, non-financial firms began to buy back their own shares so as to strengthen their price, in part to guard against the risk of takeovers. In order to meet profit targets, firms were under constant pressure to rationalise and cut costs by closing the least profitable units and by outsourcing tasks, either within the US or abroad. Because of the constant pressure to obtain high returns, non-financial firms also began to invest in financial markets themselves when this appeared to offer a higher return than investing in production or commerce.

The Contours of Economic Growth

The broad contours of US economic growth from 1980 to 2014 are shown in Figure 2.1.[2] The first phase of expansion, from 1983 to 1989, was dependent on a highly expansionary fiscal policy as the Reagan government increased military spending and cut business taxes. Unusually, this

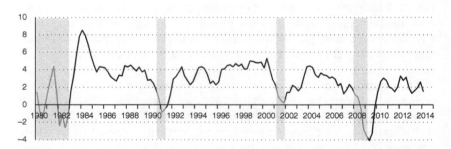

Note: Shaded areas show NBER designated recessions. The NBER classifies the period from 1980 to 1982 as a double recession with a brief expansion between July 1980 and July 1981.

Source: BEA, *National Income and Product Accounts*, Table 1.1.3 (2015a).

Figure 2.1   US real GDP, % change over four quarters

was combined with a restrictive monetary policy that kept interest rates high. The high return attracted foreign capital to the US and this financed an important part of the government's deficit. However, fixed investment by the business sector remained low for a period of expansion. Instead, non-financial corporations embarked on a major round of mergers and takeovers, made possible by greater financial deregulation which enabled firms to raise finance by issuing so-called junk bonds.[3] Takeovers were followed by a process of rationalisation and plant closures, which left many workers willing to accept real wage cuts if they could keep their jobs. The expansion came to an end in 1989 when, after several years of over-lending, the banking system abruptly curtailed the expansion of credit, leading to a short recession in 1990.

The next expansion, from 1992–2000, was initially rather weak. The Federal Reserve had responded to the credit crunch and recession by reducing its main interest rate, and it remained low until 1994. As dollar assets became less attractive for international investors, the dollar weakened and US exports began to rise. Because of the large government debt inherited from the Reagan era, the governments of both Bush (senior) and Clinton felt they could not use fiscal policy to boost the economy, but the automatic effect of increased welfare and unemployment payments together with a decline in the tax take did help stimulate the economy. Following a period of weak 'jobless' growth in the early 1990s, in the second half of the decade the US experienced its strongest sustained growth since the 1960s as a result of the boom in information technology. During this period, tax payments were so strong that the government, unusually, had a budget surplus. Furthermore, as unemployment fell, real wages began to rise for the first time since the 1970s. But the expansion was highly dependent on borrowing by non-financial corporations. This was partly to finance strong fixed investment; but it was also used by companies to buy back their own shares. Share buy-backs helped push up share prices, to the benefit of institutional investors and of top managers, who had themselves acquired substantial holdings in the 1990s through the exercise of share option. In the late 1990s, the stock market developed all the signs of a classic bubble, as share prices soared way beyond the rise in company earnings. When the bubble burst in early 2000, companies slashed their fixed investment, and the economy entered a recession in 2001.

The following expansion, which began in 2002, was also weak at first. The Federal Reserve reacted to the recession especially strongly, repeatedly cutting the lead interest rate between 2001 and 2003. In addition, on taking office in 2001, the Bush government introduced a big package of tax cuts. These had been originally proposed before the recession broke and were heavily skewed in favour of the top 20 per cent of earners, but it served to strengthen demand in the economy. The low rate of interest helped promote a new wave of mergers and takeovers, in many cases initiated by private equity firms, which took advantage of so-called leveraged loans to raise much of the capital required. Mortgage lending also increased strongly and, despite a boom in construction, a bubble in house prices developed in large parts of the country. With incomes for most people stagnant in real terms, many households borrowed against the rising value of their homes in order to finance additional consumption. Nevertheless, although economic growth increased from 2004, by US standards it remained relatively weak until 2007, when the expansion ended and the US economy was faced with the onset of the deepest financial and economic crisis since the 1930s.

The average annual growth of GDP in each of the business cycles since 1980 is shown in Table 2.1. The figure for the period from 1980 to 1990 is depressed due to the long double recession at the start of the decade. Even so, it is notable that average growth in the period from 2001 to 2007 is significantly weaker than in the previous two cycles. In the final cycle, which began in 2008 and had not been completed at the time of writing, growth was a mere 1.0 per cent, reflecting the acute decline in output at the end of 2008 and the start of 2009, and the weakness of growth in the initial years of the subsequent recovery.

Table 2.1 shows that, in every cycle, economic growth was driven predominantly by personal consumption expenditure. Over the whole period from 1980 to 2007, when GDP growth averaged 3.0 per cent, consumption accounted for 2.2 per cent growth. By contrast, private investment made only a modest contribution to the growth of GDP and, although it was somewhat stronger in the 1990s, it was especially weak in the early 2000s.

Table 2.1   Contributions to the growth of US GDP

	1980–1990	1991–2000	2001–2007	2008–2013
GDP, average annual % change	3.0	3.5	2.5	1.0
Contribution to change in GDP				
Personal consumption	2.03	2.43	1.99	0.78
Fixed investment	0.42	1.11	0.31	−0.18
Change in private inventories	0.00	0.07	−0.03	0.07
Net exports of goods and services	−0.07	−0.36	−0.24	0.35
Government consumption and investment	0.66	0.22	0.42	−0.02

Source: BEA, *National Income and Product Accounts*, Table 1.1.2 (2015a).

Over the whole period from 1980 to 2007, government spending contributed slightly less than private investment to overall growth while, due to the persistent trade deficit, the contribution of net exports to growth was negative.

The Dynamics of the Crisis

The onset of the crisis, as is widely known, was triggered by the failure of complex securities based on so-called subprime mortgages.[4] The standard or 'prime' mortgage in the US was introduced by the Roosevelt government in the 1930s in order to enable middle-class households to acquire a home. In the post-war period this generally involved a mortgage that would cover 70–80 per cent of the price of a home. It was repayable over a period of up to 30 years at a fixed rate of interest that was set when the mortgage was granted, usually at around 1 per cent above the central bank's lending rate. For home owners it was a good deal. From the 1990s, banks increasingly used a system of credit scoring based on applicants' income and previous credit record to simplify the process of granting mortgages.

With the end of the legal limit on interest rates, it became possible for banks and other financial institutions to offer mortgages to households that did not meet the credit scores required to obtain a prime mortgage but the interest rate they charged for these 'subprime' mortgages was some 5 or 6 per cent above the central bank's lending rate.[5] There was an especially strong expansion of subprime mortgages in the early 2000s as banks sent sales personnel into low income neighbourhoods, encouraging households to buy their home, and by the peak in 2006 subprime mortgages accounted for 23 per cent of US mortgage lending (Financial Crisis Inquiry Commission 2011, p. 500). Most subprime mortgages had adjustable interest rates, which would be reset periodically in line with changes in the central bank interest rate and, in order to make such mortgages attractive, 'teaser rates' were offered for the first one or two years, in which repayments did not even cover interest payments, although the cost was added to the outstanding debt.

Banks did not have a strong incentive to check the credit record of applicants for subprime mortgages because they did not plan to keep the loans on their own books. As a result of the Basel Accords, introduced in 1988, banks were required to hold a certain minimum amount of capital against assets, such as mortgages, to provide a safety cushion against bankruptcy in the event that the assets declined in value. In order to avoid tying up their capital in this way, banks would package several thousand mortgages and create a security which they could sell on the capital market to a financial investor. By this process of securitisation, banks could generate fees from selling mortgages, but then remove them from their balance sheets and so free up their capital for further loans.

In order to place the securities, the originators had to pay a rating agency to assess the security, which employed a system of grading to indicate the risk that debt service payments on the security might fail. Securities based on subprime mortgages were awarded relatively low ratings as many of the mortgages had been extended to households with low incomes and precarious employment and were seen as being at risk of defaulting on their repayments. This meant that institutions such as pension funds could not buy the securities, since they were legally required to invest their funds in securities with the very highest ratings.

The big New York investment banks intervened in this situation by transforming mortgage backed securities into extraordinarily complex securities known as collateralised debt obligations (CDOs). This involved combining a number of riskier securities, including mortgage backed securities, and breaking down the right to the repayment streams into a series of slices or *tranches*. It was assumed that not everyone would default on their repayments and that the holders of the rights to the first tranches would therefore be sure to receive their payments; those with the right to repayments in the intermediary or *mezzanine* tranche would be at slightly greater risk, and accordingly were offered a higher return; the greatest risk would be borne by those holding the lowest tranche, who were therefore paid the highest returns. The investment banks negotiated with the ratings agencies to ensure that their constructions would obtain the very highest rating – AAA – for the senior tranches of a CDO. Because these paid higher returns than other AAA rated securities, they were considered attractive investments, including by institutions that were legally required to invest only in top rated instruments. The construction of CDOs proved highly profitable, generating huge fees for investment banks and a strong rise in the income of the big ratings agencies.[6]

Because the returns on CDOs proved so attractive, major banks actually maintained significant holdings themselves. These were generally held in off-balance sheet entities known as structured investment vehicles (SIVs), where minimum capital requirements did not apply. The holdings of CDOs were financed by issuing shorter-term commercial paper which, before the onset of the crisis, could readily be refinanced at maturity. After the crisis broke and the commercial paper market collapsed, banks were obliged to dramatically reduce their holdings of CDOs. This provoked a major decline in their value and, as SIVs failed, was a major source of financial losses for the banks.

A major expansion of mortgage lending in the early 2000s fuelled a big rise in house prices and a boom in house construction. However, the construction boom came to an end in 2005 and, according to official figures, house prices peaked in April 2006 at 201 per cent of their value in January 2000.[7] At almost the same time, the number of households facing problems in servicing subprime mortgages began to rise sharply as interest rates were adjusted in line with increases in the central bank rate and as initially low 'teaser rates' expired. The serious delinquency rate (mortgages that are more than 90 days in arrears) on adjustable rate subprime mortgages, which had fluctuated around 5 per cent, began to increase in early 2006; by 2007 the rate had risen to 20 per cent and it eventually rose to just over 40 per cent in 2009.[8] A first signal of the forthcoming financial crisis occurred in July 2007, when Bear Stearns, a Wall Street investment bank, announced that due to losses it was closing a mortgage fund.

The onset of the crisis can be dated to 9 August 2007 when BNP Paribas announced that it was halting withdrawals on three investment funds that had large holdings of subprime-based securities. Since major banks were unsure which other banks might also have made large losses, lending on the unsecured inter-bank money market abruptly declined. This led to a sharp rise in the inter-bank interest rate and, in order to prevent a breakdown of the market, the Federal Reserve was obliged to inject reserves into the banking system. Over the next 12 months the situation steadily deteriorated. In March 2008, Bear Stearns, the smallest of the big five New York investment banks, failed and the Fed arranged for it to be taken over by JP Morgan. In July, the two large semi-official mortgage institutions, Fannie Mae and Freddie Mac began to report rising losses and in early September the government was obliged to effectively nationalise the two institutions.

The most dramatic deepening of the crisis began in mid-September 2008. On Monday, 15 September the fourth biggest Wall Street investment bank, Lehman Brothers, failed after a frantic weekend attempt by the authorities to find another bank willing to take it over proved unsuccessful. The next day, on Tuesday, 16 September, the largest insurance company in the US, the American International Group (AIG) was faced with failure and effectively nationalised at a cost of $85 billion after making huge losses from holdings of Credit Default Swaps (CDSs). Then, on Friday, 19 September, as money market mutual funds were faced with massive withdrawals they were obliged to sell commercial paper – one of the key short-term credit instruments used extensively by companies in the US – and the commercial paper market came close to closing. A meltdown was only avoided because the Treasury drew on the Exchange Stabilisation Fund – established in the 1930s to stabilise the *foreign* exchange market – to guarantee existing money market fund deposits.

On Sunday, 21 September, following runs on the two remaining Wall Street investment banks, Morgan Stanley and Goldman Sachs, these successfully applied to become bank holding companies, i.e. commercial banks that are supervised by the Fed and, consequently, eligible for its financial support. In the course of the following week there also followed two major commercial bank failures. On 25 September the Washington Mutual, the largest savings and loan bank in the US and the sixth largest bank in the country, was closed by the Fed, making it the largest bank failure in US history. Shortly after, on 29 September, it was announced that another major bank, the Wachovia, would be taken over by Citibank, although a few days later, on 2 October, following further negotiations it was actually taken over by Wells Fargo.

In response to the increasingly alarming financial situation, the Treasury Secretary, Hank Paulson, announced plans for a $700 billion Troubled Assets Relief Program, which would relieve pressure on financial institutions by buying bad assets. The initial proposal, which was only three pages long, gave the Treasury Secretary sole discretion over how the funds would be deployed, and, despite the gravity of the situation, was rejected by Congress. The programme was eventually approved on 2 October after it had been expanded to 451 detailed pages, but even this was not sufficient to stem the crisis. In the course of the following week, the value of shares on the US stock market fell by some 30 per cent. On Friday, 10 October, the International Monetary Fund's Managing Director informed the international press corps, gathered in Washington for the organisation's annual conference, that the world was facing the danger of a financial collapse. Over the weekend the Treasury let it be known that it was working on proposals to use part of the Troubled Asset Relief Programme for capital injections into banks. The following Monday, the heads of nine of the largest US banks were summoned to a meeting at the US Treasury where they were requested to sign a one-sheet document giving their approval for the government to take shares in their institutions – in effect, a partial nationalisation.[9]

On Monday, 13 October 2008, when financial markets opened for the first time since the collapse of Lehman Brothers, the financial crisis did not deepen. The decision to partly nationalise the banking system appeared to have broken the spiral of financial collapse; the acute level of interest rates in the money market began to decline and share prices even recovered somewhat. The Fed had cut its lead interest rate repeatedly, from 5.25 per cent in September 2007 to an unprecedentedly low range of 0–0.25 per cent by December 2008; it had also introduced a host of new facilities for lending to banks in an attempt to overcome the breakdown of traditional lending channels. There was, nevertheless, a major contraction of lending by commercial banks, even to the best known firms, and in the final quarter of 2008 and the first quarter of 2009 the US economy registered a major slump in output. The situation in the financial system, meanwhile, continued to be viewed as highly precarious. According to Alan Blinder it was not until May 2009, when the results of bank stress tests proved largely positive and most banks' share prices began to rise, that a turning point was reached and the acute stage of the financial crisis came to an end (Blinder 2013).

2.3   MACROECONOMIC DEVELOPMENTS IN THE AGE OF FINANCE-LED CAPITALISM

Income Distribution

There has been a major shift in the distribution of income in the US since the 1980s, as shown in Figure 2.2. Although the share of employees' compensation increased in each business expansion, there was a clear downward trend with the value falling at each successive peak (1992, 2001 and 2008). The share of corporate profits, by contrast, tended to increase. The peaks occur slightly before the onset of the cyclical downturn but each peak is higher than the previous peak. Strikingly, the share of profits in 2013 is even higher than at the peak in 2006.

According to Gérard Duménil and Dominique Lévy (2011), the US national income figures actually mask a more serious decline in the share of income for all but the highest paid 5 per cent of employees since the 1980s. They estimate that, for the corporate sector, if the top 5 per cent is excluded, the share of wages for the remaining 95 per cent fell from

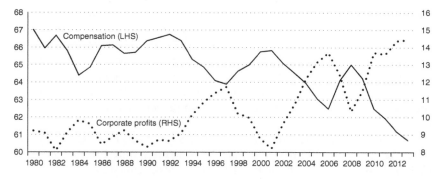

Source: BEA, *National Income and Product Accounts*, Table 1.12 (2015a).

Figure 2.2   *US employee compensation and corporate profits, % national income*

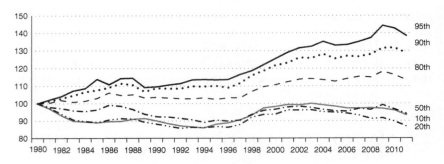

Source: Mishel et al. (2012), database, Figures 4c.

Figure 2.3   US real hourly wages of men by wage percentile, 1980 = 100

62.2 per cent of income in 1980 to 51.5 per cent in 2009, a decline of some 10 per cent. They also note that the share of profits distributed as dividend payments has risen since 1980 and, if dividend payments are added to the income of the top 5 per cent of employees, the total increased from around 18 per cent of net income in the corporate sector in the early 1980s to some 28 per cent in 2007.

The marked divergence in the evolution of real wages at different levels of income from the early 1980s onwards is shown for men in Figure 2.3. The hourly real wage for workers at the 50th percentile and below all declined in the 1980s and the first half of the 1990s and, despite an increase during the late 1990s, at the peak in 2009 they remained below the value in 1980. It is only for workers at the 80th percentile and above that real hourly wages registered an increase through from the 1980s up to the onset of the crisis. The largest increase accrued to those at the 95th percentile, who registered a rise of 45 per cent between 1980 and 2009. The pattern is similar for women workers although, while their income increased somewhat more than that of men, at the peak in 2009 men continued to be paid more than women at every level of income, with the gap rising from 12 per cent at the 10th percentile to 38 per cent at the 95th percentile (Mishel et al. 2012, database, Figure 4d).

The strong rise of top incomes in the US has been highlighted by the much cited research initiated by Thomas Piketty and Emmanuel Saez (2003). This shows that the share of top incomes declined in the 1930s and 40s and then remained comparatively low until the 1970s, when it began to rise again, returning to levels last seen in the 1920s. According to updated figures (Alvaredo et al. 2014, *Database*) the share of the top 1 per cent roughly doubled between 1980 and 2007, rising from 8.2 to 18.3 per cent

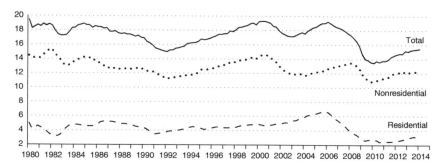

Source: BEA, *National Income and Product Accounts*, Table 1.1.5 (2015a).

Figure 2.4   US private fixed investment, % GDP

of income; if capital gains are included it increased from 10.0 per cent to 23.5 per cent. Including capital gains, the share of the top 0.1 per cent roughly trebled, from 3.4 per cent to 11.3 per cent of income, while that of the top 0.01 per cent roughly quadrupled from 1.4 per cent to 5.5 per cent.

Investment Expenditure

Fixed investment in the US economy is strongly cyclical, principally due to the pattern of nonresidential investment. As shown in Figure 2.4, nonresidential investment declined as a share of GDP during the business expansion in the 1980s – principally because corporations were involved in a major wave of mergers and takeovers. In the business expansions in the 1990s and in the early 2000s the share of nonresidential investment in GDP did register a cyclical increase, but against a declining overall trend, and this decline is even more marked in the cycle that began in 2008. Residential investment increased strongly from the mid-1990s to 2006, but then fell dramatically, contributing significantly to a marked fall in total fixed investment between 2006 and 2010.

The Federal Reserve's Financial Accounts (Table F102, Board of Governors of the Federal Reserve System, 2015) indicate that, in addition to fixed investments, non-financial corporations have also incurred considerable expenditure on what is categorised as 'other financial investments' since the early 1980s. This tended to fluctuate quite strongly but, at the business-cycle peaks in 2000 and 2007, these amounted to some 50 per cent or more of fixed investment. According to the statistical authorities at the Federal Reserve, this is a residual category, but it reflects the importance which financial investments have come to play for non-financial corporations.

Table 2.2   *US non-financial corporations' interest payments, dividends and retained earnings, % operating surplus*

	1980–1990	1991–2000	2001–2007	2008–2013
Net interest	29.2	23.1	21.2	22.0
Corporate profits	66.0	71.2	72.0	72.2
Taxes on corporate income	22.1	21.9	19.8	17.7
Profits after tax	43.9	49.4	52.2	54.5
Net dividends	20.3	29.8	34.1	33.2
Undistributed profits	23.6	19.6	18.2	21.3

Source: BEA, *National Income and Product Accounts*, Table 1.14 (2015a).

The pressure on non-financial companies to reward shareholders is indicated by the distribution of the sector's operating surplus, shown in Table 2.2. The share of interest payments declined from cycle to cycle.[10] By contrast, the share of the operating surplus paid out as dividends increased steadily, from some 20 per cent in the 1980s, to around 30 per cent in the 1990s, and it reached almost 40 per cent in the years immediately prior to 2007. Over the same period, the share of taxes and even more markedly, that of retained earnings, declined.[11]

The figures shown in Table 2.2 actually understate the pressure on nonfinancial corporations to reward shareholders. Partly for tax reasons, and partly so as not to establish expectations of continued high dividend payments, non-financial corporations have since the 1980s also rewarded shareholders through the use of share buy-backs on an ever increasing scale. The Federal Reserve's Financial Accounts (Table F102) show that, while dividend payments increased from some 1.8 per cent of GDP in the early 1980s to 3.6 per cent at the peak in 2006, the amount returned to shareholders as a result of share buy-backs increased even more strongly, most notably during the expansion leading up to the crisis. By 2007 the sum of dividends and share buy-backs was equal to 8.8 per cent of GDP – only just short of non-financial corporations' spending on fixed investment, which stood at 9.4 per cent of GDP.

For most of the period since 1980, non-financial corporations' internal funds have been sufficient to finance the sector's fixed investment.[12] In fact, from 2002 to 2006 and again from 2009 to 2013, fixed investment was actually below the value of internal funds. However, because of the takeover boom in the 1980s, and the increasing importance since then of financial investments and of share buy-backs, it was necessary for the sector to raise funds in the credit markets, something that it realised predominantly through selling bonds. Consequently, non-financial corporations' credit market debt increased strongly, rising from 32 per cent of GDP in the early 1980s to 51.4 per cent in 2008. After declining slightly in the next two years it then increased yet again, and had reached 56.1 per cent of GDP by 2013 (Federal Reserve's Financial Accounts, Table L102).

Household Consumption

Economic growth in the US since the 1980s has been driven primarily by household consumption spending, which increased from some 60 per cent of GDP in 1980 to 68 per cent in 2008 (BEA, NIPA 2015a, Table 1.1.5). Since median incomes have scarcely risen during this time, various explanations have been put for this growth of consumer spending.

In the 1990s, when US stock market values increased strongly, it was argued that the growth of consumption could be explained by a wealth effect. At the time, a paper by the Federal Reserve estimated that a rise in stock values of one dollar led to a rise in consumption of some 4 cents (Ludvigson and Steindel, 1999). However, as is well known, share ownership in the US is extremely concentrated. In the late 1990s, when the significance of the wealth effect was most emphasised, the top 1 per cent of households owned some 50 per cent of shares while the bottom 80 per cent owned just 4.1 per cent.[13] While a wealth effect might help to explain the very strong rise in luxury consumption spending of top income groups, for the majority of households who own very few shares it is unlikely to have played a very significant role.

One important factor that accounted for the steady rise in consumer spending despite the stagnation of median incomes was a decline in the savings rate. This fell steadily, from around 11 per cent at the start of the 1980s to a mere 3 per cent in 2007, although it began to rise again after the onset of the crisis (BEA, NIPA 2015a, Table 2.1).

The other significant factor that explains the growth of consumption spending was a steady rise in borrowing – a development that Raghuram Rajan (2010) presents as being, in effect, a policy choice by successive governments in the face of stagnant incomes. One important form of borrowing, particularly in the final phase of expansion, was for households to borrow against the rising value of their homes. Some households took advantage of lower interest rates to refinance their mortgages – a procedure that is permissible at relatively little cost in the US – and borrowed more than was required to pay off their existing mortgages; others simply took out a new loan against the increase in value of their home. According to estimates published by the Federal Reserve, this form of borrowing rose from $157 billion in 2000 to $485 billion at its peak in 2005 – sufficient to finance some 65 per cent of the increase in consumption spending that year.[14]

The scale of the borrowing led to a marked rise in the outstanding debt of the household sector. At the start of the 1980s this was equal to around 47 per cent of GDP. It then began to rise in the course of the 1980s and the 1990s, but it registered an especially marked rise from the start of the 2000s and, at its peak in 2007, reached 95.5 per cent of GDP (Federal Reserve, Financial Accounts, Table L100). The increase was almost entirely due to increased mortgage debt as debt from consumer credit remained relatively stable at just under 20 per cent of GDP.

Unit Labour Costs and International Competitiveness

The monetarist offensive in the early 1980s led to a sharp rise in unemployment and succeeded in breaking the ability of workers to raise wages in line with inflation. This was reflected in unit wages costs, which had increased by 12 per cent in 1980, but then rose by only 4 per cent a year from 1984 and, following the recession in the early 1990s, by around 2 per cent a year up to 2007. Following the onset of the crisis, there were several years in which unit labour costs did not rise at all.

From the 1950s to the 1970s, unit wage costs had risen at roughly the same rate as the consumer price index. From the 1980s, however, this ceased to be the case and the evolution of unit labour costs fell steadily behind the rise in the consumer price index (OECD, Unit labour costs and consumer price index).

The US dollar's nominal exchange rate has registered significant swings since the early 1980s, as shown in Figure 2.5. In the early 1980s exceptionally high interest rates in the US succeeded – as intended – in attracting

Source: Bank for International Settlements, effective exchange rate indices (2015).

Figure 2.5   Nominal effective exchange rates, 2010 = 100

short-term capital back to the US, and the value of the dollar soared to unsustainable levels. In order to avoid the disruption that an uncontrolled fall in the dollar might have caused, the other major capitalist states collaborated in facilitating a so-called 'soft landing', and the dollar registered a rapid decline in value between 1985 and 1987 (Marris 1987). There followed a lengthy period when, thanks to low interest rates in the US, the dollar tended to weaken against other currencies. In the late 1990s, when the US experienced its strongest phase of expansion in some 20 years, higher interest rates attracted capital to the US and the value of the dollar again increased strongly. However, following the onset of the recession in 2001 and the adoption of low interest rates in the US, the dollar again tended to weaken through until 2008. Since 2008 the dollar has begun to strengthen somewhat, reflecting the irony that – although the crisis began in that country – the US was seen as a safer bet, especially since it had greater success than European countries in regenerating growth in the aftermath of the crisis. These large shifts in the nominal exchange rate were largely reflected in the real effective exchange rate, and had a significant impact on the pattern of US international trade.

International Payments

US international payments have been characterised since the early 1980s by a deficit on the current account and net inflows of capital on the financial account. The country's trade balance registered a rising deficit in the first half of the 1980s, principally due to the sharp rise in the value of the dollar and a notable decline in exports. Although the trade deficit declined in the second half of the 1980s as the dollar weakened and exports began to recover, from the early 1990s the deficit steadily increased again, reaching a peak of almost 6 per cent of GDP in 2006. While a weakening of the dollar from 2002 onwards was followed by a strengthening of exports, this was not sufficient to counter the strong rise in the demand for imported goods and services. It was only with the dramatic deepening of the crisis at the end of 2008 that US imports fell sharply, and – although exports also declined – the trade deficit was reduced to around 3 per cent of GDP.

The trade deficit since the 1980s has been slightly offset by a positive balance on US receipts and payments of income from abroad. The balance on international interest payments registered a deficit as a result of the rising foreign holdings of US bonds, but this was more than offset by the balance of income from foreign direct investment, where the US has consistently generated a surplus.

The evolution of the US current account has been determined primarily by the trade balance. As a result, the current account deficit increased to

*Table 2.3   US international investment position, period averages as %
            GDP*

	1980–1990	1991–2000	2001–2007	2008–2013
US assets	34.5	57.6	93.8	139.3
US liabilities	−31.0	−64.4	−110.8	−164.5
Net US international investment	3.5	−6.7	−17.0	−25.2

Source: Based on BEA, *International Economic Accounts*, Table 1.1 (2015b), US net
international investment position at end of period.

over 3 per cent of GDP during the 1980s and, following a decline during
the recession at the start of the 1990s, it then increased steadily to reach
6 per cent of GDP in 2006. Following the onset of the crisis, the current
account deficit fell quite sharply, and since 2010 it has fluctuated just
below 3 per cent of GDP.

The persistent deficit in the US current account since the 1980s has been
financed by large net inflows of capital, most notably by inflows into US
government bonds. As a result, the US's net international investment position, which had for long registered a positive balance, was steadily eroded
in the course of the 1980s. As shown in Table 2.3, it shifted from a positive
average balance equal to 3.5 per cent of GDP in the 1980s, to a negative
average balance equal to 17 per cent of GDP in the period from 2001 to
2007, and to 25 per cent of GDP in the period following the onset of the
crisis.

2.4   THE INTERNATIONAL TRANSMISSION OF THE CRISIS

Financial Transactions

One of the key channels by which the crisis in 2007–2008 was transmitted
from the United States to other countries was through bank transactions.
The full picture is complex and involves sudden shifts in both the assets
and liabilities of banks. The scale of these shifts is indicated in Figure 2.6,
which shows changes in US banks' holdings of foreign financial assets.
There was a strong rise in the volume of transactions with other countries
between 2003 and the first two quarters of 2007, when quarterly outflows
amounted to almost $300 billion a quarter. However, these transactions
virtually ceased in the second half of 2007, and in 2008 there was a very

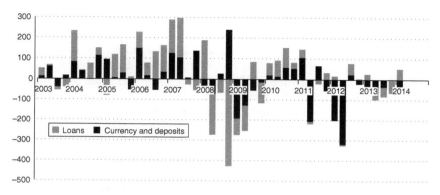

Source: BEA, *International Economic Accounts*, Table 1.2 (2015b).

*Figure 2.6 US banks' acquisition of foreign assets: loans and deposits,
$billion*

large flow back to the US, particularly of foreign loans, amounting to over
$400 billion in the fourth quarter of 2008 at the height of the crisis. Since
the second half of 2009 the pattern of transactions has been less consistent, but there has clearly not been a return to the large outflows of foreign
loans seen before the crisis.

The European Union is by far the largest counterpart of US banks' international transactions. In the first quarter of 2007 when outflows from US
banks were at a peak, outflows to the EU accounted for $243 billion of the
total outflows of roughly $300 billion, while, in the final quarter of 2007,
there was an outflow of assets from the EU amounting to $296 billion out
of a total US withdrawal of foreign bank assets of just over $400 billion
(BEA 2015b, International Economic Accounts, Table 1.3).

International Trade

The deep downturn in output in the US at the end of 2008 and the beginning of 2009 was also transmitted to other countries through international
trade, particularly trade in goods.[15] The value of US imports of goods in
current dollars roughly doubled between 2002 and 2008. However, the
deepening of the financial crisis in late 2008, and the consequent contraction of the US economy, resulted in an abrupt decline in imports, which fell
by 33.6 per cent between the fourth quarter of 2008 and the first quarter of
2009.[16] In the same period US exports of goods fell by 26.8 per cent. These
abrupt declines were reflected in trade with the EU: imports from the EU
declined by 32.7 per cent while exports to the EU fell by 24.4 per cent.

2.5   ECONOMIC RESPONSES TO THE CRISIS

In February 2008, even before the crisis had reached its most acute moment, the government of George W. Bush introduced the Economic Stimulus Act, which involved tax rebates amounting to some $150 billion (about 1 per cent of GDP). In fact, this measure was part of the government's tax-cutting agenda and had been planned even before the onset of the crisis, but it was now repositioned as a response to the deteriorating economic situation.

The main fiscal response to the crisis was initiated by the government of Barack Obama, which assumed office in January 2009 when the danger of financial collapse was still paramount and the level of economic output was plummeting. The American Reinvestment and Recovery Act was approved in February 2009, and was originally intended to provide an expansionary impulse of $787 billion (5.5 per cent of GDP), although subsequent estimates by the Congressional Budget Office put the actual figure at $830 billion (Blinder 2013, pp. 227–235). This involved in roughly equal proportions tax cuts, new spending and aid to state and local governments. While Obama sought to obtain bipartisan support for the measures, this was completely unforthcoming from Republican members of Congress.

The impact of the programme is disputed. While conservative opponents such as John Taylor argue that it had little effect, Alan Blinder (2013, pp. 346–355) points out that the rate of job loss began to decline following the introduction of the measures, even though employment continued to fall until February 2010. Some high-profile economists such as Bradford de Long and Lawrence Summers (2012) argued for an investment programme, particularly in infrastructure, that could mobilise resources that would otherwise be idle. But, in a political context where there was widespread Congressional opposition to further expansionary fiscal measures, subsequent initiatives stemmed primarily from the Federal Reserve.

The Federal Reserve's response to the onset of the recession involved a series of initiatives known by the euphemism of quantitative easing (QE) (for fuller details, see Blinder 2013, pp. 248–256). The first of these, now known as QE1, was implemented between November 2008 and March 2010, and involved purchases of $600 billion of mortgage backed securities (MBS) issued by other financial institutions. The aim of the intervention was to reduce the spread between such MBS and the rate on Treasury securities. The second programme, QE2, was implemented between December 2010 and June 2011, and involved the Fed in purchases totalling $600 billion of medium and long-term Treasury securities. It aimed to bring about a reduction in the interest rate on these securities and, with them, the rate on other securities. The final programme, QE3, was initiated in late 2012 and involved the Fed in purchasing $40 billion of securities a month, a sum which was raised in December 2012 to $85 billion a month, but which the Fed reduced or 'tapered' in the course of 2014 as economic growth began to strengthen. These measures led to a major rise in the Fed's holding of Treasury securities, which increased from just under $900 billion in 2008 to some $2.4 trillion by 2014. At the same time, the Fed's holdings of mortgage backed securities, first introduced on a small scale in 2009, increased to $1.7 billion by 2014. In total, the credit provided by the Fed increased from $866 billion in early September 2008 to $4.4 trillion in September 2014. There is considerable agreement that the Fed's policies have had some impact on long-term interest rates, but Martin Wolf (2014, pp. 263–264), a commentator who supported the Fed's initiatives, notes that their impact has, nevertheless, been limited: it brought about only a modest recovery and the extent of the impact is difficult to measure; at the same time it may keep unviable 'zombie' companies alive for too long while the US's aggressive monetary expansion has been particularly destabilising for many developing countries which were confronted with very large inflows of capital.

The major regulatory response to the crisis in the US was the Dodd-Frank Wall Street Reform and Consumer Protection Act, which was signed into law by President Obama in July 2010, and which introduces the most significant change to financial regulation since the Glass-Steagall Act of 1933 (see Pollin and Heintz 2013, Chapter 3). One of its key proposals is the introduction of a so-called Volcker rule, intended to impose restrictions on the propriety trading activities of large banks which were a major cause of the financial bubble whose bursting detonated the crisis in 2008–09. The Dodd-Frank Act is extremely wide-ranging and runs to 2,300 pages but, even so, it only lays out the broad framework for new regulations. Implementation will depend on the formulation of detailed regulations, and Wall Street firms have been mounting a massive lobbying effort in an attempt to influence how these rules are set.

2.6 CONCLUSION

The prolonged economic boom in the US after the Second World War came to an end in the 1970s and, following a period of economic and political malaise, the basis was established for a new phase of capitalism from the 1980s. This new phase was characterised by a significant weakening in the bargaining position of labour while the position of financial capital was greatly strengthened as a result of innovation and deregulation. Non-financial corporations were subjected to intense pressure to prioritise so-called 'share-holder value' and raise their rate of return which, in addition to the persistent pressure to cut labour costs, promoted a significant growth in investments in financial assets to the detriment of investments in productive assets.

Since the 1980s the pattern of growth in the US has been highly cyclical, with periods of economic expansion strongly dependent on the growth of credit. As each expansion came to an end, the Federal Reserve adopted highly expansionary policies which ensured that periods of recession were relatively short, but at the expense of accumulating tensions. The first expansion, from 1983–1989, was characterised by a wave of mergers and takeovers financed by bonds and a major expansion of bank credit. The second, from 1993 to 2000, led to strong investment in information technology, financed by bond issues and a further major expansion of bank lending, but was accompanied by a stock market bubble which burst in 2000. The third expansion from 2002 to 2007 was characterised by a new wave of mergers and takeovers and a major boom in house prices. When house prices began to falter, and many of the complex instruments created to finance the housing boom began to fail, the US was faced with the prospect of a collapse of the financial system. This was narrowly averted through massive government intervention, but in late 2008 and early 2009 it led to the most serious downturn in output and employment in the US since the 1930s.

The period since the 1980s has been marked by a significant shift in the distribution of income. The share of profits in national income has steadily risen; the share of wages, by contrast, has steadily declined. Furthermore, large sectors of the working population have experienced either no, or very little, increase in their real incomes, and most of the increase in income has been appropriated by those at the top, in particular the now infamous top one per cent.

Fixed investment in the US since the 1980s has, as always, been strongly cyclical but it has tended to decline, and the expansion from 2002 to 2007 was particularly dependent on the boom in housing. Economic growth in the US since the 1980s has, consequently, been driven primarily by consumption spending. This was possible despite the stagnation in incomes of large sectors of the population due to a decline in the savings rate and a very significant rise in household indebtedness. International trade, by contrast, has made a consistently negative contribution to US growth. Since the 1980s, the US has had a trade deficit, and this increased particularly strongly in the years leading up to the crisis. The counterpart of the deficit was large inflows of both private and official capital, and since the late 1980s the net international investment position of the US has registered an increasingly negative balance.

Economic growth in the US resumed in the second half of 2009 but it was not until 2012 that output recovered to the pre-crisis level of 2007. By 2014, the share of profit in national income, which fell very sharply during the crisis, was even higher than before the crisis, while the share of wages, correspondingly, is lower. Fixed investment remains very low for a period of expansion, but after a period in which households sharply reduced their spending, consumption is beginning to expand. The country's trade deficit has been almost halved, but demand remains dependent on a government deficit which, although down from 11 per cent of GDP in 2009, was still equal to almost 5 per cent in early 2014. The Dodd-Frank Act has introduced wide-ranging legal changes to the regulation of the financial sector, but banks have lobbied intensively to ensure that the actual impact of the measures will be limited. And following the failure of numerous financial institutions, the position of the biggest banks is even more dominant than before the onset of the crisis.

NOTES

1. The following paragraphs are drawn from Evans (2014).
2. The following paragraphs are drawn from Evans (2009).
3. Junk, or high-yield bonds, refers to bonds that have a higher risk of default, but which also pay a significantly higher return than industrial-grade bonds issued by large, well-known companies that have a very low risk of default.
4. This section draws substantially on Evans (2009). For more detailed accounts see Financial Crisis Inquiry Commission (2011) and Blinder (2013).
5. There was also an intermediary category between prime and subprime mortgages known as Alt-A mortgages.
6. Investment banks also engaged in yet further engineering, constructing what were known as CDO^2, in which the repayments on the lowest and riskiest tranches of a number of CDOs would be combined and subjected to a further process of *tranching*.
7. Financial Crisis Inquiry Commission (2011), Figure 6.2, p. 87. According to the Case-Shiller index of house prices, based on 20 major US cities, the peak was in May 2006; a broader index maintained by the Federal Housing Finance Agency dates the peak one year later (Blinder 2013, pp. 17–18).
8. Financial Crisis Inquiry Commission (2011), Figure 11.2, p. 217. Serious delinquencies for fixed rate subprime mortgages, and for adjustable prime mortgages began to rise in 2007 and reached a peak of around 20 per cent in 2009. Traditional fixed rate prime mortgage delinquencies increased, but only slightly, from 2008 following the onset of the deep recession and the sharp rise in unemployment.
9. The intention of obliging all the banks to accept an infusion of capital was to avoid any stigma attaching to those banks that did need it. Immediately after the meeting, however, three of the participating banks let it be known that they neither needed nor wanted the infusion of capital (Blinder 2013, p. 202).
10. This was despite a rise in the level of the non-financial corporate sector's debt, which is discussed below, and reflects the steady decline in interest rates from the high levels in the early 1980s.
11. The annual figures indicate that even during cyclical downturns, non-financial

corporations maintained dividend payments and absorbed the decline in income in their retained earnings.

12.   The only exception was the period between 1998 and 2000, when fixed investment was unusually strong and exceeded internal funds by some 20 per cent.
13.   Poterba (2000). If indirect holdings through pension funds were excluded, the figure for the bottom 80 per cent fell to 1.7 per cent. More recent figures, including the years 2007 and 2010, are available in Bricker et al. (2012).
14.   Figures from Greenspan and Kennedy (2005) and updated figures kindly provided by Jim Kennedy.
15.   For a detailed analysis of the downturn in US trade see Levchenko et al. (2010). They find that sectors of the US economy with larger reductions in domestic output had larger drops in trade, but that trade credit did not play a major role in the collapse of trade.
16.   Seasonally adjusted US imports fell from $568.8 billion in the third quarter of 2008 to $377.7 billion in the first quarter of 2009; exports fell from $347.2 billion to $254.2 billion. In relation to US GDP, imports of goods fell from 24.1 per cent in the third quarter of 2008 to 18.0 per cent in the first quarter of 2009, a decline of some 6 per cent of GDP. Exports fell from 9.4 to 7.1 per cent of GDP, a decline equal to 2.3 per cent of GDP.

REFERENCES

Alvaredo, F., T. Atkinson, T. Piketty and E. Saez (2014), *The World Top Incomes Database*, available at: http://www.wid.world/.
BIS (2015), Effective exchange rate indices, Basel: Bank for International Settlements, available at: http://www.bis.org/statistics/eer.htm.
Blinder, A. (2013), *After the Music Stopped. The Financial Crisis, the Response, and the Work Ahead*, New York: Penguin Press.
Blinder, A. and J. Yellen (2001), *The Fabulous Decade: Macroeconomic Lessons from the 1990s*, New York: The Century Foundation.
Board of Governors of the Federal Reserve System (2015), Financial Accounts, available at: http://www.federalreserve.gov/apps/fof/DisplayTable.aspx?t=f.102.
Bricker, J., A. B. Kennickell, K. B. Moore and J. Sabelhaus (2012), 'Changes in U.S. family finances from 2007 to 2010: Evidence from the survey of consumer finances', *Federal Reserve Bulletin*, **98** (2), June.
Bureau of Economic Analysis (2015a), National Income and Product Accounts (NIPA) Tables, available at: http://www.bea.gov/national/nipaweb/DownSS2.asp.
Bureau of Economic Analysis (2015b), International Economic Accounts, available at: http://www.bea.gov/international/.
Bureau of Labor Statistics, Historical Data, Table A-1, available at: http://www.bls.gov/webapps/legacy/cpsatab1.htm.
De Long, B. and L. Summers (2012), 'Fiscal policy in a depressed economy', *Brookings Papers on Economic Activity*, Spring, 233–297.
Duménil, G. and D. Levy (2011), *The Crisis of Neoliberalism*, Cambridge, MA: Harvard University Press.
Evans, T. (2009), 'The 2002–2007 US economic expansion and the limits of finance-led capitalism', *Studies in Political Economy*, No. 83, Spring, 33–59.
Evans, T. (2014), 'The impact of financial liberalisation on income inequality', *International Journal of Labour Research*, **6** (1), 129–142.

Evans, T. (2015), 'Financialisation and the financial and economic crises: the case of the U.S.A.', FESSUD Studies in Financial Systems, No. 32, University of Leeds.

Financial Crisis Inquiry Commission (2011), Final Report of the National Commission on the Causes of the Financial and Economic Crisis in the United States, available at: http://fcic-static.law.stanford.edu/cdn_media/fcic-reports/fcic_final_report_full.pdf.

Greenspan, A. and J. Kennedy (2005), 'Estimates of Home Mortgage Originations, Repayments, and Debt on One-to-Four Family Residences', Federal Reserve Working Paper, No. 2005-41.

Hirsch, B. and D. Macpherson (2013), Union Membership and Coverage Database from the CPS, US Historical Tables: Union Membership, Coverage, Density and Employment, 1973–2013, available at: www.unionstats.com.

Levchenko, A., L. Lewis and L. Tesar (2010), 'The collapse of international trade during the 2008–09 crisis: In search of the smoking gun', *IMF Economic Review*, **58** (2), 214–253.

Ludvigson, S. and C. Steindel (1999), 'How important is the stock market effect on consumption?', *Federal Reserve Bank of New York Policy Review*, July, 29–51.

Marris, S. (1987), *Deficits and the Dollar: The World Economy at Risk*, Washington: Institute for International Economics, 2nd edition.

McCartin, J. (2011), *Collision Course: Ronald Reagan, the Air Traffic Controllers, and the Strike that Changed America*, New York: Oxford University Press.

Mishel, L., J. Bivens, E. Gould and H. Shierholz (2012), *The State of Working America, 12th Edition*, Ithica: Cornell University Press.

Piketty, T. and E. Saez (2003), 'Income inequality in the US, 1913–1999', *Quarterly Journal of Economics*, **118** (1), February, 1–39.

Pollin, R. and J. Heintz (2013), *Study of U.S. Financial System*, FESSUD Studies in Financial Systems, No. 10, available at: http://fessud.eu/studies-in-financial-systems/.

Poterba, J. (2000), 'Stock market wealth and consumption', *Journal of Economic Perspectives*, **14** (2), Spring, 99–118.

Rajan, R. (2010), *Fault Lines. How Hidden Fractures Still Threaten the World Economy*, Princeton: Princeton University Press.

Wolf, M. (2014), *The Shifts and the Shocks*, London: Allan Lane.

3. Monetary adjustment and inflation of financial claims in the UK after 1980

John Lepper, Mimoza Shabani, Jan Toporowski and Judith Tyson

3.1 INTRODUCTION

This chapter explores two ways in which the UK financial system developed out of step with the real economy after 1980. It argues that companies and households took advantage of the easing of financial regulation by securing credit against assets with decreasing regard to the underlying value of those assets. Hence, in the UK, financialisation[1] largely involved inflation of financial claims and this followed directly from business strategies adopted in response to deregulation. We explain why these strategies meant that significant business and financial system risks went unmanaged and why monetary authorities did not foresee and forestall systemic failure.

We summarise the UK policy background that existed in 1980 and how monetary regulation developed thereafter. We then outline the two main avenues of UK financialisation. After that we describe some of the systemic impacts of them, which leads to a short discussion of the 2007–08 Crisis. Conclusions then follow.

3.2 POLICY BACKGROUND

By early 1980, UK monetary policy included the following features:

(a) Unanimity among leading politicians that low inflation in goods and services prices is the pre-eminent target for economic policy;
(b) Sterling floating against all currencies and largely fully convertible so that the Government no longer assumed responsibility for managing overseas reserves;
(c) No restrictions on capital movements to and from the UK;

(d)   A large, active Eurodollar market located in London but beyond the jurisdiction of any monetary authority;

(e)   Monetary policy instruments confined to Special Deposit Regulation and manipulation of the Minimum Lending Rate on borrowing by the London discount market;

(f)   Sterling's role as a reserve currency was limited to the remnants of the Sterling Balance System and minor elements of reserve balances of other countries.

In addition, clear directions for future policy development had been established. These largely followed from official faith that markets develop naturally, are not owned (Lepper 2012) and their formation offers new opportunities for citizens to maximise utility. So, if left alone, markets lead to stable and optimal outcomes. As early as 1980 there was increasing emphasis on monetary policy conducted through 'market means' via manipulation of interest and exchange rates. It has subsequently become clear that the UK authorities had started to progressively withdraw from making markets in Government securities and to increasingly rely on the self-interest of individual institutions to provide adequate contingency reserves.

The Conservative Government, elected in 1979, progressively permitted the economy to be shaped by market dynamics. It reduced Government expenditure in real terms, sold some public assets (such as social housing) and corporatised some public functions. Private enterprise was allowed to compete for some Government contracts and with existing state concerns. Active industrial policy was largely withdrawn. Trades unions were systematically disempowered and increasingly unequal distribution of income and wealth was accepted. At the same time, targets for the growth in the money stock were established but not met.

Regulation of interest rates was progressively withdrawn and greater reliance placed upon Open Market Operations from November 1980 and by auctions of gilts between 1987 and 1988 and after 1991. Throughout the early 1980s, traditional British credit and capital market institutions like stock jobbers and brokers, discount and acceptance houses and clearing banks merged with, or were acquired by, international financial companies and the long-standing separation of their functions ended. By 1986, stock market commissions had become negotiable (the Big Bang) and day-to-day regulation of financial company balance sheets ceased. After October 1988, the Bank of England was prepared to deal in Sterling securities with any organisation, not just discount houses.

Together, these changes opened the UK financial system to the world and the UK economy to the world's finances. They meant that any company could become a financial institution and that financial institutions were free to create financial claims and to make markets in them outside organised exchange structures. The British authorities paid less attention to the internal management of financial companies and withdrew from making and enforcing detailed rules of market conduct. The changes were particularly important to US-based companies, which were still subject to financial regulation (e.g. Regulation Q, which determined interest rates until 1986). Many UK-based financial conglomerates were subsidiaries of US companies.

3.3 THE STRATEGIC RESPONSE

UK-based financial institutions faced significant change. The tradition of specialist institutions operating in regulated exchange structures was clearly going to end with the coming of competition in unregulated markets. Business solutions usually adopted involved entry into overseas markets, cultivation of mass markets for consumer products, and financial innovation to extend arbitrage and hedging in financial markets by developing products such as derivatives. Investment banks, finance companies, building societies and clearing banks started to enter each other's traditional markets. The 1980s saw the emergence of financial service conglomerates and strategic moves by manufacturing and service companies into the financial sector. Increasingly, international capital movements were dominated by the activities of multinational corporations (MNCs) on the Eurodollar market. As corporations became more active in financial markets, the traditional distinctions between financial and non-financial companies began to disappear.[2]

The new conglomerates exploited significant economies of scale and scope in the management of information. They made extensive use of computerised financial management systems, which facilitated arbitrage and hedging across different markets. Calculation of average default rates on different types of lending allowed computerised systems to make decisions on loans without benefit of local knowledge. This implied that no lending proposition was *per se* unacceptably risky (e.g. because of illiquidity considerations) provided lenders could charge a sufficiently high interest rate to compensate for the risk they believed they were carrying. This calculation ignored the possible positive relationship between risk of default and interest rate charged and the possibility that institutions often suffer from optimism bias which can lead to underestimation of the long-term risks of lending. Such standardisation encouraged rationalisation and simplification of branch banking systems and eventually led to retail banking becoming a sub-sector of retail trade in financial services.

Further, the Efficient Markets Hypothesis (EMH) assumes that the market price of an asset represents the best guess of the discounted future income yielded by that asset so any asset no matter how complex or wherever located, can be valued on the same basis as any other. Widespread adoption of EMH enabled assets to be 'marked to market' or 'marked to model' irrespective of the actual conditions governing their viability. However, in practice, the calculations involved relied heavily on subjective judgements about prospective risks and rewards which, in turn, were heavily influenced by so-called 'market sentiment' and individual perceptions of corporate reputation.

Corporate finance, which was once largely the preserve of stock brokers and investment banks, became dominated by new financial conglomerates. Highly centralised, they dealt with finance directors who centrally managed company assets. Much business was directed at helping non-financial MNCs take advantage of corporate welfare, tax concessions or tax loopholes. Much was conducted 'off balance sheet' in semi-autonomous subsidiaries presided over by computerised management systems. Increasingly, companies found that profits could be more readily enhanced by takeover than by fixed investment. In the case of financial intermediaries, operations were financed by money market liabilities while non-financial corporations made capital issues in excess of their requirements for fixed investment. Capital issues and bank loans packaged as assets were on-sold to pension funds and other long-term investors.

The resulting increase in liquidity as turnover of credit increased at every point of the yield curve, was unprecedented in Britain since the First World War, and the US since 1929. There was no relevant history to guide risk management by regulators or market participants and little reliable information on which to base the complex computerised systems for centrally managing assets and liabilities. Centralised balance sheet management systems in banks, financial institutions and large corporations created new, albeit largely unrecognised, uncertainties. High levels of capital market liquidity went unquestioned. Credit transactions were undertaken without understanding how vulnerable balance sheet valuations were to interdependencies with other firms (including other banks), general economic conditions and the state of sentiment in the financial system. Thus, many banks and financial conglomerates grew rapidly in the 1980s and 1990s but without full appreciation of the risks they undertook. Inevitably, requirements for contingency reserves were under-estimated if only because cautious balance sheet expansion meant renouncing apparently profitable arbitrage opportunities which competitors took with apparent safety.

During the 1980s, structural foundations were laid for London markets to rival those of New York at the centre of the international financial system during the boom of the long 1990s. The liquidity of the UK financial system depended on anonymous short-term money market liabilities. The abolition of capital controls made attractive off-shore financing through the Euro-markets in London. At the same time, the abandonment of Keynesian counter-cyclical policies made market economies more prone to instability which increased arbitrage and hedging opportunities. After the international debt crisis in 1982, banks redirected their lending to MNCs rather than to governments and overseas investment took the form of more direct investment and fewer loans or other debt. Similar forces were at work to enhance the relative positions in the international financial system of the Frankfurt and Singapore markets. Since 1980, UK markets and institutions secured a disproportionately large share of international financial flows. By 2014, the Fair and Effective Markets Review estimated that the UK was the venue for 70 per cent of international bond trades, nearly 50 per cent of OTC interest rate derivatives and 40 per cent of foreign exchange markets (Bank of England 2015). In addition, two thirds of European revenues amassed in fixed interest, currency and commodity markets accrue in the UK.

Corporate Financialisation: Banking the Globe

Until the 1970s, UK markets for long-term securities relied on the Bank of England to provide liquidity through the Bank's open market operations in government bonds. In effect, this meant that larger mergers and takeovers made such calls on capital market liquidity that they had to be accommodated by the Bank's open market operations if they were to eventuate. Abolition of exchange controls made such liquidity management impractical because it implied providing liquidity to a truly international market. Moreover, the focus of the Bank's open market operations shifted to trying to regulate the reserves held by British-registered commercial banks at the Bank (the so-called 'reserve position doctrine'). Hence, after 1980, companies found new freedoms in merger and acquisition activities. Ultimately, it became easier to enhance their size and profitability by buying other companies than by creating new products or enhancing productivity through fixed capital investment (see Figure 3.1 for an illustration). This was particularly so because firms could issue debt and equity at negligible short-term marginal cost with which to make such purchases and so earn a kind of private seigniorage.

The ability to purchase other companies by the issue of debt and equity relied heavily on establishing vibrant markets for the securities. Companies were managed to ensure that share prices were buoyant and their debt was highly rated. They dealt in their own shares and paid generous dividends. Managerial remuneration was closely linked to share market performance. In many cases, financial subsidiaries of large MNCs became the dominant source of company profits. However, this could not persist for any length of time unless the corporation exercised a significant measure of market power that could be mobilised to underpin the value of the debt and equity it issued.

Merger and acquisition activity involving British companies increased rapidly after 1980. This meant that the viability of corporate financial structures became more reliant on the future income flows of the newly merged entities (Barwell and Burrows 2010) or continuing inflation in the capital market into which merged companies could be sold on deglomeration (Toporowski 2010).

Hitherto non-financial corporations now became more focused on financial activities with the result that their leverage increased. Non-financial gross corporate debt increased nearly three-fold after 1997 reaching a peak of £1,661 billion in 2008. Increasing leverage is not, in itself, a major concern if borrowings are used productively so that, over time, they generate enough resources, not only to meet financial obligations but also to contribute to economic growth[3] and welfare. However, high levels of debt may induce instability by inflating asset prices (in markets for shares or commercial real estate) rather than facilitating productive investment.

There was also a shift in emphasis away from production (including investment in capital stock and R&D) towards finance so that non-financial companies invested heavily in financial assets. In the UK, between 1996 and 2008, productive business investment remained at a constant 10 per cent of GDP. However, the role of banks in financing investment declined. The proportion of bank lending devoted to productive investment fell from 30 per cent to 10 per cent. This showed that, far from supporting business investment, the new financial order made productive investment more precarious. Companies came to rely more and more on retained profits to finance investment in current production and future innovation.

New types of security were devised including a wide variety of instruments called derivatives. They were compiled from complex combinations of swaps, forwards and options and were designed to afford a company protection against its unique business risks. They were often so difficult to price that their promoters supplied buyers of them with computer programmes to provide estimates of their value. Inevitably, such securities tended to be illiquid because so few institutions were capable of finding prices for them. Moreover, many buyers of derivatives relied upon the good name of their

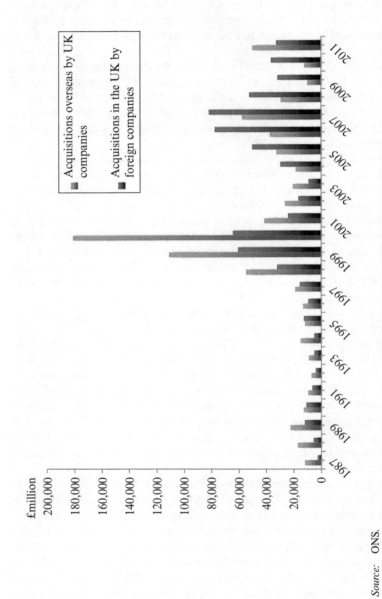

Source: ONS.

Figure 3.1 International mergers and acquisitions involving UK companies

promoters rather than an assessment of the value of the assets that underlay them. This practice was perhaps excusable when securities traded among a few highly capitalised and well-managed institutions. However, as derivatives came to be traded beyond such a charmed circle, markets became more ignorant of the risks entailed. More precisely, the menu of risks undertaken through market activity became significantly greater than the inventory of available information that could accurately inform the choices about market opportunities. As a consequence, in some cases, trades took place beyond the limits of information required to correctly price them. In other words, market participants entered a Zone of Ignorance.

Domestic Financialisation: The My Bank Era

Just as capital market inflation allowed large firms to issue claims in amounts that exceeded the earning potential of the underlying assets they commanded, so the expansion of credit in the housing market allowed UK households to borrow beyond their possibilities of servicing their debts from actual income. Normally, such borrowing took the form of loans from financial institutions secured against the value of domestic dwellings (mortgage loans). Starting with the stimulus in demand for house mortgages generated by the 1979 Conservative Government's sale of social housing to existing tenants, financial companies sought to make a mass market in home loans. Householders were enabled, through aggressive consumer marketing, to borrow mortgages in multiples of their past earnings and in anticipation of future capital gains. On occasion in the 1980s and 1990s some customers were permitted to borrow in excess of 100 per cent of the current valuation of the property they offered as security.

These developments were aided in the 1990s by the securitisation and syndication of lending assets by which housing loans of varying quality were bundled together and, accompanied by derivative-based risk hedging, distributed as one asset issued by well-respected institutions to a syndicate of purchasers. If that institution is of first quality, then logic decrees that the assets it issues are also of first quality. Hence, the over-arching security can be taken onto a buyer's balance sheet as if it were first class. However, when mortgages on real estate are packaged for on-sale in this way a number of processes occur, the prudence of which potential buyers cannot readily verify. First, mortgages with a high risk of default are combined with those carrying lower risk so that although the average risk of the whole package is acceptable the risk of default is not negligible. Second, mortgages included in the package may themselves be part of another securitised mortgage package. Third, the ultimate buyer of a securitised asset has no claim on the real estate security upon which the original mortgages were based. Fourth, many of the mortgages that were securitised were agreed by salespersons only interested in achieving sales targets and not trained in prudent lending. Sometimes mortgages were lent to people who could not afford to service them. Holders of securitised instruments based on house mortgages could not make an accurate assessment of the risks attached to them or of their underlying value. Moreover, risks involved could not always be adequately managed through the derivative-based hedging operations which usually accompanied securitisation.

Throughout the long 1990s, as the number of participants in the UK financial system increased, it was no longer possible for the Bank of England to ensure system stability by regulating the balance sheets of a few key financial institutions. The new financial institutions went beyond the traditional UK list of clearing banks, discount houses, acceptance houses and bond dealers. It included the activities of building societies, finance houses, investment banks, stockbrokers, MNCs and the treasuries of investment funds, pension funds and large domestic non-financial companies. Thus, for example, in the retail financial market credit cards (although issued by only a small number of international companies) came to be operated by a wide variety of traditionally non-financial organisations which actively marketed them.

With the failure of monetarism in the 1980s, the Bank of England reverted to operating monetary policy through interest rate manipulations ostensibly to maintain inflation at low levels. The first inflation target was set in October 1992 but it was not until 1997 that UK monetary policy was officially conducted by setting Bank Rate (i.e. the rate at which the Bank of England is prepared to repurchase financial securities, hence its common name the 'repo' rate) in an attempt to keep future inflation within desired bounds. With the establishment of the Financial Services Authority (FSA) in October 1997 to regulate banks and financial institutions, the Bank of England withdrew from direct oversight of financial companies and markets. In so doing, it cut itself off from some information that only continuous market participation can generate; a situation that some financial companies subsequently sought to exploit by manipulating flows of market intelligence. The FSA adopted an approach of risk-based supervision, which was conducted by examining individual institutions taken in isolation from each other. Financial markets had come to be regarded as inherently stable and financial institutions as just another commercial undertaking so that no more than light-touch monitoring and intervention was thought necessary to ensure system integrity and dynamic stability. Trust in stable market equilibria was reinforced by the unprecedented economic boom. Hence, there appeared to be little need to intervene directly in the commercial activities of financial companies. In the absence of official oversight, many companies took on new types of financial business without the aid of adequate information about the rewards, risk and uncertainties involved. Many of these firms sought to retail financial securities on a mass scale to customers not previously served by the financial system. In 2013, the FSA was abolished and the Bank of England became responsible for financial stability. The role of the FSA was split between the Prudential Regulation Authority, a subsidiary of the Bank of England, which regulates institutions and the Financial Conduct Authority that regulates financial market behaviours.

The My Bank era popularised house ownership and was, for many, a time of massive rise in personal wealth via house purchase. From 1978 to 2014, UK house prices rose by 2.7 per cent per annum faster than consumer prices. In the 1990s, a rapid rise in mortgage lending drove up house prices. By adoption of innovative financial instruments (e.g. securitisation) and more liberal lending criteria, as competition in retail markets intensified, the market for house purchase was extended. This trend accelerated as public housing was sold to its tenants and the traditional building societies were de-mutualised to become retail banking chains. Loans secured on dwellings (mortgage loans) are the most significant component of the sector's debt (see Figure 3.2). Mortgage debt increased steadily during 1997–2013. In 1997, it accounted for around 69 per cent of total financial liabilities, reaching a peak in 2010 of about 75.5 per cent of total liabilities. Leverage of the household sector also rose. UK household debt rose continually from the mid-1990s, from approximately 55 per cent to 100 per cent of GNP.

Between 1994 and 2007 household net worth increased primarily due to increases in the value of the housing stock from £1.4 trillion to £4.9 trillion and from 53 per cent to 66 per cent of net assets. The price of residential property became an increasingly important component of household spending and saving plans. Pensions and deposits also increased in value but remained relatively constant percentages of total net worth. Mirroring these changes in housing assets were increases in debt, which tripled from £0.5 trillion to £1.5 trillion in the same period.

UK consumption grew faster than real earnings (Barwell and Burrows 2010). This was partially financed through a decline in savings. From over 9 per cent of disposable income in 1997 savings became negative between 2006 and 2008. They then rose to over 5 per cent of disposable income only to fall again to under 1 per cent by 2013. Declines in savings were augmented among property owning classes by borrowing for consumption secured against unrealised gains in house prices. Termed 'equity withdrawal', it was particularly prevalent during the 1980s and between 2000 and 2007. Such borrowing grew every year from 1997 to 2007, peaking at £140 billion annually in 2006 before sharply declining during the financial crisis (Reinold 2011).

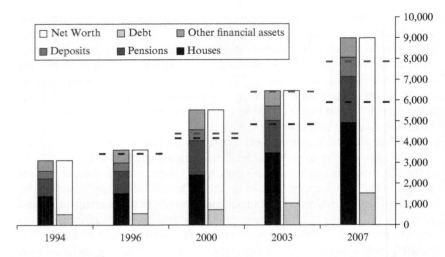

Source: Barwell and Burrows (2010) (Secondary source: post 2007 data not available).

Figure 3.2   Household balance sheets (1994–2007), in £billions

3.4   SYSTEMIC IMPACTS

Interdependence and Contagion

Banking intermediaries of a financial system are intimately inter-related. They depend on each other for access to short-term liquidity and for market information. A weakness in a single institution potentially affects many companies that have claims on it. Normally, each institution in a financial system matches large flows of debits with almost equally large flows of credits. The difference between total debits and total credits is small in most cases. Risk to the financial system lies not in these relatively small net amounts. Rather, the whole system is put at risk when a particular institution cannot meet its obligations. Then, the gross obligations it has with the rest of the system will not be met. Hence, a very large volume of debits become worthless. The gross flows between institutions are, therefore, an indication of potential risk to the system as a whole (i.e. systemic risk). In a typical money market the failure of one firm to meet gross obligations is sufficient to undermine the liquidity of all. All participants in a highly integrated money market, like that of the UK, are likely to fail if one does. This is systemic liquidity risk.

Systemic liquidity risk means that a financial institution operating in money markets must know what other participants are doing and must be able to trust that their prospective actions and strategies will not adversely affect its own business. (Alternatively, it must deal with intermediaries that can guarantee payments.) Frequent contacts occur between institutions and between the markets that the institutions make. Much of the inter-institutional communication concerns nominal interest rates and exchange rates. It is the way that each institution informs its fellows about what it is doing and shows that it can be trusted without revealing details of its own business or that of its customers. Thus, the institution reveals itself as part of the financial 'flock'; and does not incur large imbalances with the rest of the system that could presage a threat to system stability. Concerted behaviour of this kind is a response to systemic risk, credit risk, maturity risk and exchange risk. However, it does not address uncertainty that might arise from large-scale shifts in liquidity in long-term markets which can unexpectedly increase demand for short-term funds. Consequently, in the face of unmanageable uncertainty or large-scale change that threatens the financial system, there is a danger that concerted action ensures that all parts of the system fail together.

Aside from pension funds and insurance companies, financial institutions rely on each other for access to funding, particularly short-term funding. They are, therefore, particularly prone to liquidity risk (i.e. the risk that accommodation cannot be had at any price). The emergence of such risk led to the collapse of Northern Rock in the UK and the subsequent liquidity crisis in interbank markets.

Institutions also rely on each other for assessments of credit worthiness. Credit instruments overseen by derivatives and other contracts create direct counterparty credit risks between financial institutions. The values placed on these risks are intimately linked to perceived valuations by market participants, which rely on 'mark-to-market' and 'mark-to-model' values. Valuations reflect market sentiment and affect liquidity risk because other institutions are influenced by them when deciding whether or not to lend short-term funds. This process led to contagion which caused panic on interbank markets during the 2007–08 Crisis, before the collapse of Lehman Brothers, because it was impossible for institutions to assess the creditworthiness of counterparties. The result was a vicious cycle of collapsing asset markets and further falls in confidence.

Interdependence of this type means that each financial institution faces similar incentives and must expand or contract at a similar speed to others in the system. Thus, financial institutions implicitly act in concert even when they do not explicitly agree to adopt a set pattern of unified behaviour. Such behaviour may not conform to classical models of monopoly, oligopoly or small-group monopolistic competition. It may also not qualify legally as a cartel. (Nevertheless, there have been instances of explicit price fixing in the UK including collusion to fix LIBOR and exchange rates.) It is driven by alignment of incentives within private financial institutions and market interconnectedness. Financial institutions tend to behave in very similar ways in similar circumstances. Moreover, this behaviour pattern, together with the market rules associated with it, discourages alternative competing behaviours that might conceivably act as a viable antidote when markets fail.

In theory, a particular institution can assure itself against the possibility of failure by holding a sufficient reserve of assets liquefiable at minimum cost at very short notice in any conceivable state of financial markets. In practice, such reserve assets are wholly backed by fully subscribed equity. However, such holdings impose considerable opportunity costs on the organisation. It is likely, therefore, that managers would conclude that holding such reserves would not be a profitable use of the organisation's resources because risk of system failure is low and it is highly likely that the government could be induced to ensure that all citizens meet the costs of forestalling potential failure of the financial system. In any case, for the system as a whole, holding liquid assets implies over-capitalisation and a growing interdependence between the state of the money market and the reported value of the assets and liabilities of each institution. Before 2007, some firms took an alternative approach involving active risk management. However, all too often this took the form of derivatives or inter-institutional lines of credit the value of which proved as vulnerable to market disruption as other financial assets.

Accumulation

Positive real interest rates that emerged after 1980 in the US and the UK were supposed to encourage asset accumulation by companies by reducing the present value of given future revenue flows and corresponding asset prices. Instead, high real interest rates and the inflation that persisted through the 1980s encouraged inflation of financial claims which became a strategy for survival of large firms. Hence, the value of claims created bore only an indirect relationship with the value of corporate assets. Traditional capital market disciplines (e.g. shares trade at the present value of the prospective income flow to which they are a claim) broke down. Since the late 1980s, gross fixed capital formation in the UK has declined steadily as a percentage of real GDP (shown in Figure 3.3). Significant falls from the long-term trend were recorded in the late 1980s and early 1990s and in the aftermath of the 2007–08 Crisis.

The downward trend in fixed investment reduced the cash flow from

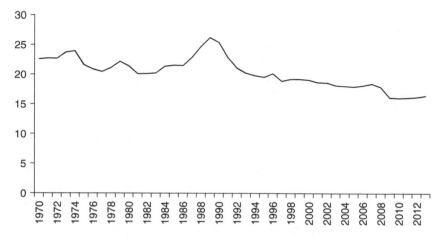

Source: ONS, National Accounts.

Figure 3.3 Gross fixed capital formation as a percentage of GDP

commercial operations just as the capital market exhibited growing liquid-ity and rising asset prices. So capital restructuring became a more reliable and more rapid way of generating corporate income than the long-term business of fixed investment. However, it also meant that if a company fell short of liquidity postponement or cancellation of investment plans, selling subsidiaries or issuing new equity represented the most effective avenues of adjustment. Hence, liquidity shortages had an immediate, nega-tive impact on the real economy.

A company unable to mobilise sufficient liquidity to meet its current financial obligations, and unable to refinance its debts, will not cut current production as long as it generates cash flow. Instead, the company will reduce fixed investment. Even merely approaching its liquidity constraint may lead to an emasculation of the company (e.g. the case of ICI). If many companies make the same adjustment simultaneously, as they did in 2008, then there is a significant negative income multiplier effect, with falling output and employment. Moreover, it may be necessary for a particular corporation to repeatedly re-adjust its plans as falling spending by other companies reduces its future revenues.

Financialisation and Income Distribution

UK financialisation was accompanied by growing inequality of income and wealth, particularly since 2000. Nevertheless, the links between rising inequality and financialisation are unclear and require further analysis. Rising inequality has been attributed to the spread of markets, globalisation and technical change, all arguably accompaniments to financialisation. Yet, evidence supporting this proposition remains ambiguous. However, there is a consistent finding that institutional and regulatory structures (or lack of them) are critical to income disparity (OECD 2011).

Inequality of households' disposable income and market income has increased since the mid-1980s (see Table 3.1). Because the rich save more of their income than the poor, greater income inequality implies that an increasing proportion of current income is saved rather than spent. The result is that sales revenues are lower than would otherwise be the case. Accumulation on the basis of income inequality translates into inequality of wealth, which is further accentuated over time through inheritance. Growing disparities of income and wealth after 1980 were important in inducing widespread acquiescence to the policy stance among property owners who enjoyed appreciating assets. The systematic dismantling of labour protections this permitted, allowed capitalists to increase the proportion of surplus acquired by capital at the expense of labour. This reinforced political support for growing inequality and formed an obstacle to social welfare policies that distribute income or wealth more equally.

The financial sector and some corporations provided high-skilled, high wage employment especially for top earners. By contrast, protective structures for the low-paid and low-skilled were largely destroyed. This included the undermining of labour unions during the 1980s and the progressive adoption of 'flexible labour markets' under legislation of successive governments since.

Wealth is usually more unequally distributed than income. In 2010, aggregate total wealth of all private households in the UK was £10.3 trillion. The top decile of households held £4.5 trillion or 44 per cent of wealth,

Table 3.1   Gini coefficient for market income and disposable income

Year	1985	1990	1994	2000	2005	2010
Gini coefficient for households' disposable income						
	0.309	0.354	0.336	0.352	0.334	0.341
Gini coefficient for households' market income						
	0.468	0.490	0.506	0.512	0.503	0.522

Source: OECD.

making it 4.3 times wealthier than the bottom 50 per cent of households (see Figure 3.4). The top two deciles owned 62 per cent of all wealth or £6.4 trillion and held 92 times the wealth of the bottom two deciles, which amounted to a mere £0.06 trillion (Office for National Statistics (ONS)). In addition, and masked by the above aggregates, in 2010, nearly a quarter (24.3 per cent) of UK households had negative net financial wealth.

The commanding heights of societies whose growing wealth is increasingly held in financial assets, are generally politically reactionary and ignorant of the conditions under which most people live. This makes them vulnerable to unforeseen political and social change, the reality of which is not fully reflected in prices and yields quoted on financial markets upon which their personal wealth depends.

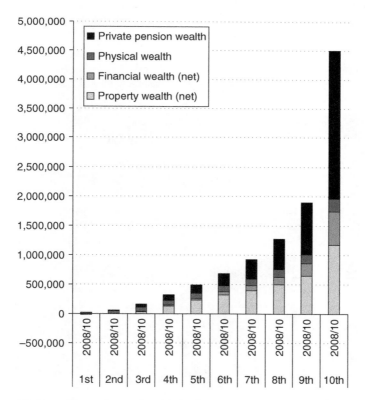

Source: Wealth and Assets Survey (latest 2010 shown), Office for National Statistics.

Figure 3.4   Total aggregate wealth: by deciles, 2010, in £million

The Financial Crisis of 2007–08

From the summer of 2007, financial pressures escalated beyond the global financial system (illustrated in Figure 3.5). Housing markets became less liquid in economies, like the UK, that had experienced house price booms. Mark-to-market losses and liquidity strains escalated in the corporate sector. Key financial markets of the world became paralysed after the US-based bankruptcy of Lehman Brothers. The UK was affected immediately because of its importance as an international financial centre. Massive government-backed and government-funded recapitalisations of banks followed, and central banks in the USA and UK provided unprecedented liquidity support. Base rates were pushed to historical lows and substantial quantitative easing (i.e., central bank buying of long-term securities) was implemented. The official view was that illiquidity in the housing market (rather than weak corporate balance sheets) caused the financial crisis.

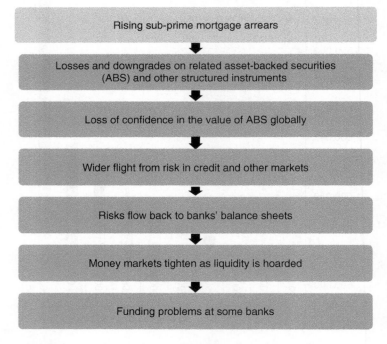

Source: Financial Stability report, Bank of England, October 2007.

Figure 3.5   The phases of the crisis, 2007

Two factors ensured that contagion was particularly widespread in UK financial markets:

- Opaque and complex innovation in financial instruments with high embedded leverage; and
- Widespread use of an 'originate and distribute' business model, in which banks believed themselves relieved of responsibility for due diligence because securitisation was accompanied by credit derivatives that were designed to assure the value of the loans.

Much funding relied on short-term money market instruments and sustained demand for credit instruments in capital markets. This funding combination was particularly susceptible to a fall in liquidity in the market for long-term instruments where mortgage-backed securities were supposed to find a home in the portfolios of long-term investors. When that liquidity failed, banks found themselves unusually dependent on money markets to finance growing portfolios of mortgage-backed securities. Interest rate spreads widened substantially. There was a rapid increase in hoarding of liquidity and increased aversion to accepting counterparty risks.

In the UK, this crisis reached a critical point at Northern Rock, which relied heavily on money market funding and securitisation to manage its assets. In July 2007, the bank was unable to pay its depositors and the Government was eventually obliged to guarantee all retail deposits and subsequently nationalise the bank (Bank of England 2009). However, by the spring of 2008 it was clear that dislocation of financial markets was continuing with increasing illiquidity and higher interest rate spreads in many markets. Financial institutions, including heavily financialised companies, rapidly deleveraged, sold assets or reduced investment plans.

Central banks, including the Bank of England, responded by lowering interest rates and providing longer-term funding based on increasingly low quality collateral. Yet as 2008 progressed, further intervention was needed and the Bank of England announced measures which included raising capital for UK banks, the Special Liquidity Scheme and guarantees for UK debt issuances. There was a government-supported recapitalisation scheme for UK banks and building societies, to which all major UK institutions had access although in which only HBOS, Lloyds TSB and Royal Bank of Scotland participated. These institutions promised to increase Tier 1 capital and accept government-funded capital in the form of preference shares or ordinary equity. In addition, participants in the programme were given a Government guarantee for senior unsecured debt instruments for terms up to three years, commercial paper and certificates of deposit. The Bank of England's Special Liquidity Scheme was extended to include

£200 billion to banks and again allowable collateral was extended, including debt issues guaranteed by the Government.

Yet even these measures proved inadequate for some institutions. There were many nationalisations, mergers and takeovers across Europe and North America. In the UK, Bradford & Bingley was partly nationalised, Alliance & Leicester was taken over by Banco Santander and Lloyds TSB acquired HBOS. The UK Government was also forced to support UK retail depositors in Icelandic banks following institutional collapses in Iceland. There was concern that focus on capital and liquidity requirements had not been an adequate regulatory approach. The Bank of England commented that events have 'highlighted the need for a fundamental rethink of internationally appropriate safeguards against systemic risk, including through the development of macro prudential polices to dampen the financial cycle' (Bank of England 2008).

By the end of 2009, provision of liquidity in all the important banking markets of the world was such that financial markets were calming. Funding and liquidity concerns eased and asset markets stabilised. This continued into 2010 despite the Euro area crisis. UK banks reduced net lending through reductions in loans to households and non-financial companies and by reducing holdings of non-government debt securities.

In addition to continued deleveraging, the overall capital position of the major UK banks improved, with issuances of substantial amounts of term debt in 2010 and 2011. However, the rebuilding of capital strength continued to be impaired by losses or weak profits. By the end of 2010, core Tier 1 capital ratios, on a Basel II basis, rose by 0.85 percentage points to 9.9 per cent in 2010, the highest level since 1992, although notable divergences between banks remained.

3.5   CONCLUSIONS

Perhaps the most surprising result of the 2007–08 Crisis is that nothing much has changed. Governments espouse retrenchment while running budget deficits; companies still buy other companies with equity and debt; house lending and house prices still rise; the share of GDP accruing to wages and salaries falls; income and wealth inequalities have increased. It is true that banks have been forced to carry larger reserves but banking appears as well-remunerated and as profitable as ever. There are two possible explanations. Either the financialisation processes we analyse are accepted as part-and-parcel of rapid development of an economic system based on capital accumulation or they represent a proliferation of uncontrolled financial structures that renders the whole economy vulnerable to illiquidity in obscure and opaque financial markets. Our judgement is that these processes are always present and the stability of the economy cannot be left unattended at the mercy of financial bubbles.

Although the financial always affects the real and the real affects the monetary, financialisation dislocates real economic factors from monetary ones. Money capital can be created and re-created relatively quickly compared to production facilities. Thus, a disassociation between the real and the monetary makes possible rapid alterations of income distribution, economic structure and ownership and the adoption of new patterns of accumulation without alteration to income generated by underlying assets. However, the development of all economies depends on the income earning investments that companies make. That investment determines company cash flow and future capacity to support the debt structure of the economy. In the long run, the eternal challenge, therefore, is to build a financial system which smoothly transforms savings into productive investment without increasing the level, reach, opacity and longevity of the risks involved. In particular, this requires financial institutions that will support real investment, rather than depressing it with complex and opaque financial obligations.

The widespread discussion on financial reform has identified a number of constraints that may limit the financialising process. They include:

- An inability to make or maintain a market in debt and equity;
- Erosion of reputation and perceived counterparty risk;
- Insufficient liquidity to meet dividend payments and debt interest;
- Inability to continue with capital accumulation;
- House prices stagnant or falling; and
- Disposable income insufficient to support product demand.

But the most effective constraint is the regulation of liquidity in asset markets. Unconstrained liquidity inflates prices of residential real estate, makes it easy to feed more credit into the housing market through securitising bank debt and encourages corporations to use debt finance to restructure because it brings more profit in the short-term than fixed investment. Until liquidity is regulated to support investment at a level sufficient to provide high levels of employment and cash flow adequate to make payments on the debt incurred, economies will remain vulnerable to crises like that which occurred in 2007–08.

NOTES

1. The term 'financialisation' has no universally agreed meaning. However, it is widely accepted that it refers to the growing economic, mercantile, political and social significance of financial motives, markets, actors and institutions.
2. Even as early as the 1970s the Finance Division of IBM was so large that it was referred to as 'The Bank' in the argot of Eurobond dealers.
3. By means of increasing employment, infrastructure, profits, improve productivity etc.

REFERENCES

Bank of England (2008), Financial Stability Report, Issue No. 24, October 2008, available at: http://www.bankofengland.co.uk/publications/Pages/fsr/2008/fsr24. aspx.

Bank of England (2009), Financial Stability Report, Issue No. 26, December 2009, available at: http://www.bankofengland.co.uk/publications/Documents/fsr/2009/ fsrfull0912.pdf.

Bank of England (2015), Fair and Effective Markets Review: Final Report June 2015, available at: http://www.bankofengland.co.uk/markets/Documents/ femrjun15.pdf.

Barwell, R. and O. Burrows (2010), 'Growing fragilities? Balance sheets in the great moderation', *Bank of England Financial Stability Paper*, No. 10.

BIS (2011), *The UK and the Single Market*, Trade and Investment Analytical Papers, Topic 4 and 18, Department for International Development, Basel: Bank for International Settlements.

BIS (2009), 'The supply of equity finance to SMES: Revisiting the 'equity gap'', A Report to the Department for Business, Innovations and Skills (BIS), SWQ Consulting, Basel: Bank for International Settlements.

Lepper, J. (2012), *An Enquiry into the Ideology and Reality of Market and Market System*, Basingstoke: Palgrave Macmillan.

OECD (2011), *An overview of growing income inequality in OECD countries*, s.l., available at: http://www.oecd.org/els/socialpoliciesanddata/49499779.pdf.

Reinold, K. (2011), 'Housing equity withdrawal since the financial crisis', *Bank of England Quarterly Bulletin*, May 2011, available at: http://www.bankofengland. co.uk/publications/Documents/quarterlybulletin/qb110205.pdf.

Toporowski, J. (2010), 'Response to consultation', London: Independent Commission on Banking, available at: http://ec.europa.eu/internal_market/ consultations/2012/hleg-banking/individuals/toporowski-mr-jan_en.pdf.

4. Financialisation and the economic crisis in Spain

**Jesús Ferreiro, Catalina Gálvez and
Ana González**

4.1 INTRODUCTION

The aim of this chapter is to analyse the relationship between the financial crisis and the real economic crisis in Spain. The main hypothesis put forward by this chapter is that financialisation, which lies at the root of the financial crisis, has also implied changes in the real and financial behaviour of private (and public) agents, which explain the extent and prolonged duration of the crisis in European and other advanced economies, in general, and in Spain in particular.

With this aim in mind, we will first analyse the financialisation process of the Spanish economy, and then its effects on households, non-financial corporations, and the external sector. Finally, we will focus on the mistakes in the management of fiscal policy and in the management of the Spanish banking crisis that have helped to deepen the economic crisis.

4.2 THE FINANCIALISATION PROCESS OF THE SPANISH ECONOMY

Like most developed countries, the Spanish economy has financialised intensely in recent decades (Altuzarra et al. 2013). When we take the size of the financial sector as a percentage of GDP as a proxy for financialisation (Sawyer 2014), we see that it is a quite recent phenomenon in Spain, starting in the nineties, that is, later than in other European and advanced economies: between 1980 and 1990 outstanding financial liabilities in Spain increased from 222 per cent to 325 per cent of GDP, but they amounted to 647 per cent of GDP in 2002, and they peaked at 1,006 per cent of GDP in 2012. Although financial assets and liabilities have both grown in a sustained way, the growth of the financial liabilities has been much faster than that of assets. As a result, the net debit balance against the rest of the world has been increasing since the eighties. Thus, net financial assets of the Spanish economy have moved from −9.9 per cent of GDP in 1990 to −31.6 per cent of GDP in 2000 and to −95.5 per cent of GDP in 2013.

This excessive indebtedness is one of the key elements that explain the extent of the economic crisis in Spain. The financial turbulence that has affected the world economy after 2007 led to severe constraints in access to the international financial markets for all economic sectors, but mainly for the banking sector. These problems were exacerbated by the sovereign debt crisis in the Euro area and its contagion effects. Furthermore, the excessive indebtedness of private non-financial (non-financial corporations and households) agents forced an intense deleveraging process that has negatively affected economic activity, at least until 2013.

The increase in the financial liabilities in Spain can be explained entirely by the larger debt incurred by private agents, which in 2007 amounted to 886 per cent of GDP. All private agents saw an increase in their financial liabilities: between 1997 and 2007 the financial liabilities of households rose from 43 per cent to 89 per cent of GDP; while those of non-financial corporations changed from 191 per cent to 386 per cent of GDP, and those of financial institutions rose from 246 per cent to 411 per cent of GDP. Conversely, the general government's financial liabilities fell from 79 per cent in 1998 to 48 per cent of GDP in 2007.

The economic crisis, which, in Spain, started at the end of the year 2008, marked a turning point in the financialisation of the Spanish economy. Non-financial corporations and households have deleveraged intensely, and in 2013 their outstanding financial liabilities (339 per cent and 83 per cent of GDP, respectively) were lower than those seen in 2007. In the case of financial institutions, their financial liabilities went on rising until 2012 (480 per cent of GDP), but in 2013 a sudden adjustment of the liabilities of the financial system took place, and its financial liabilities fell to 433 per cent of GDP.

Given that this deleveraging process has taken place within the context of a major economic crisis (Spanish GDP at current prices in 2013 was 6 per cent lower than in 2008), the above figures underestimate the process of nominal deleveraging that has taken place in Spain since the onset of the crisis: between 2007 and 2013 non-financial corporations reduced their financial liabilities by 598 billion euros (−14.7 per cent). In the case of the household sector, financial liabilities fell by 90 billion euros (−9.6 per cent). If we focus on financial institutions, their financial liabilities increased to 98 billion euros (+2.3 per cent), but the deleveraging process of the financial sector started later than for other sectors: thus, only in the year 2013, financial institutions diminished their financial liabilities by 519 billion euros (−10.5 per cent).

4.3 ECONOMIC ACTIVITY IN THE FINANCIALISATION ERA

The Spanish economy has gone through three different phases since 1980. In the first phase (1981 to 1993) Spain enjoyed noticeable economic growth. This phase ended abruptly with the crisis of the European Monetary System. The most intense and lasting phase of growth of recent decades commenced after 1993. This second phase came to an end in 2007. In 2008 the current phase of recession and economic stagnation began (lasting until 2013), which meant that real GDP in 2013 was 6.7 per cent lower than in 2008.

During these four decades, the composition of Spanish GDP has undergone a deep change. Although final consumption of households amounted to 60.7 per cent of GDP in 1980 (GDP measured at chain-linked volumes, reference year 2005), since the mid-eighties it remained quite stable, at around 57 per cent of GDP. This situation changed with the current crisis, and household consumption commenced a downward trend after 2011, falling to 55.3 per cent of GDP in 2013.

Conversely to household consumption, final consumption of the general government (public consumption) has gained relevance. During the first phase, public consumption increased very quickly, from 13.1 per cent of GDP in 1980 to 17.6 per cent of GDP in 1993. After this year, public consumption declined, reaching 16.5 per cent of GDP in 1999. Although public consumption returned to an upward tendency in 2000, public consumption gained a new impulse in the 2006–2008 period, rising from 18 to 19.3 per cent of GDP. With the crisis, public consumption kept on rising, peaking at 21.2 per cent of GDP, but the fiscal austerity measures implemented since 2010 have made public consumption fall to 20.2 per cent of GDP in 2013.

Gross capital formation (GCF) has been the component of GDP that has gained the most weight. Although GCF fell in the early eighties, both as a percentage of GDP (from 22.4 per cent of GDP in 1980 to 18.9 per cent of GDP in 1984) and in absolute (real) terms, GCF started to rise after 1985, and since then it has always been above 20 per cent of GDP. Indeed, GCF rose from 22.7 per cent to 30.9 per cent of GDP between 1993 and 2007. This tendency dramatically changed with the current crisis: in 2013 GCF only amounted to 20.5 per cent of GDP.

The depth of the structural change of the Spanish economy was more clearly reflected in the evolution of the size of the trade flows. Spain's trade openness rose between 1980 and 2013 from 18.8 per cent to 62.5 per cent of GDP. During this period a negative sign on net exports of goods and services has prevailed, with an annual average balance of goods and services amounting to −1.7 per cent of GDP. However, the trade balance is highly cyclical: the phases of expansion have always gone hand in hand with high external trade deficits, which are corrected during the downward phases of the business cycle. This pattern has also taken place in the current stage of recession and economic stagnation. Thus, in 2013 the balance of goods and services reached an unparalleled surplus of 2.4 per cent of GDP.

Although the current improvement in the trade balance could be (partially) explained by the poor economic situation and its consequent (declining) impact on imports of goods and services, in contrast to previous crises the goods and services surplus is nowadays driven by higher exports and not (so much) by lower imports. Between 2007 and 2013, the balance of goods and services moved from a deficit of 6.7 per cent of GDP to a surplus of 2.4 per cent of GDP due to lower imports (−1.9 per cent of GDP) and higher exports (+7.2 per cent of GDP). The export-led improvement in the trade balance is more evident if we focus on the period 2010–2013: the trade balance has moved from −2.1 per cent of GDP to +2.4 per cent of GDP thanks to higher exports (+6.7 per cent of GDP). Therefore, exports have been the main driving force of the Spanish economy in more recent years, avoiding an even greater decline of the economic activity. As far as this rising trend in exports being maintained, this could involve a change in the model of growth of the Spanish economy, less dependent on domestic demand, in general, and private consumption, in particular.

In order to explain the model of economic growth in Spain during the last decades it is useful to analyse the contribution of the main components of the aggregate demand to real economic growth. During the first period, from 1981 to 1993, the average annual GDP growth rate was 2.5 per cent. In this period we cannot find a clear-cut growth model, because both at the beginning (1981) and at the end (1993) of the period economic growth was negative. Therefore, the period reflects a business cycle, which includes a first period with an upward trend that began with negative growth, a plateau, where high rates of growth (above 2 per cent) were recorded, and, finally, a downward trend that began in 1992 and ended in 1993 with a negative growth.

At the beginning (1981–1984) and the end (1992–1993) of the period, external demand contributed positively to economic growth due to the decline of imports, which helped to improve the balance of goods and services. Conversely, in the intermediate years (1985–1991), the contribution of external demand to economic growth was negative, due to the weak growth of exports of goods and services and, mainly, the strong growth of imports.

Regarding the components of domestic demand, we can highlight the role played by public consumption and gross capital formation as the driving forces behind growth. As an average for the whole period, the contributions of public consumption and GCF to the GDP growth rate amounted to 0.7 and 0.6 per cent, respectively. Although the largest absolute contribution to GDP growth came from private consumption (1.2 p.p.), this is because private consumption is the biggest component of GDP. Between 1981 and 1993, household consumption actually fell from 60.1 per cent to 58.2 per cent of GDP.

In sum, in this first period, the growth model of the Spanish economy was based on higher domestic demand, where the driving forces of economic growth were public consumption and gross capital formation.

The second phase (1994–2007) was characterised by a high and sustained growth, with the average growth rate of GDP amounting to 3.7 per cent. Domestic demand was again the driving force behind the Spanish economy, with a contribution to GDP growth amounting to 4.4 p.p. Conversely, external demand increased its negative contribution (−0.7 p.p.): although exports of goods and services rose from 16.1 per cent to 27.1 per cent of GDP, with a contribution to economic growth amounting to 1.7 p.p., imports of goods and services saw an extraordinary increase, from 15.9 per cent to 34.2 per cent of GDP. As a result, the balance of goods and services moved from +1 per cent of GDP to −6.8 per cent of GDP.

If we focus on the components of domestic demand, the driving forces in this period were household consumption and gross capital formation. The contribution of public consumption to economic growth (0.7 p.p.) was similar to that of the previous phase. Nonetheless, it is important to note that although until 1999 the size of public consumption had declined, after 1999 it started to rise, reaching 18.4 per cent of GDP in 2007, above the level seen in 1994 (17.3 per cent of GDP). The contribution of household consumption to economic growth in this period amounted to 2.1 per cent. Thus, the growth of private consumption enabled its size to remain unchanged as a percentage of GDP during these years. Gross capital formation was the component with the highest rise. Its contribution to GDP growth amounted to 1.6 per cent. This strong growth of GCF implied that its size rose from 22.7 per cent of GDP in 1993 to 30.9 per cent of GDP in 2007.

In sum, the growth model of the Spanish economy in this phase (1993–2007) was domestic-demand driven, with the main driving forces of economic growth coming from household consumption and, mainly, gross capital formation.

The current financial and economic crisis has led to a radical change in the Spanish economy. Between 2008 and 2013, the average GDP rate of growth was −1 per cent. This collapse in economic activity is entirely explained by the collapse of domestic demand, whose contribution to GDP growth was −2.8 per cent, and, as a result, the size of domestic demand has fallen between 2007 and 2013 from 107 per cent to 96.1 per cent of GDP. Conversely, during the crisis the contribution of external demand to economic growth has been positive (+1.8 per cent). The external sector has become the only driving force behind the Spanish economy during the current crisis. Both exports and imports of goods and services have contributed positively to economic growth (+0.7 per cent and +1.1 per cent, respectively): between 2007 and 2013 exports rose from 27.1 per cent to 33.1 per cent of GDP, and imports fell from 34.2 per cent to 29.5 per cent of GDP.

Since 2008, until 2013, both household consumption and gross capital formation have negatively contributed to economic growth: −1 per cent and −2 per cent, respectively. Regarding public consumption, its contribution to GDP growth was limited but positive (+0.1 per cent), a proof of the stabilising role played by the public sector in the crisis.

However, when we analyse the behaviour of domestic demand since 2008 we can detect the existence of two sub-periods: 2008–2010 and 2011–2013. Although average GDP growth rates in these periods were similar (−1 per cent and −0.9 per cent, respectively), the contributions of the components of domestic demand to economic growth significantly changed: contributions in these periods of household consumption were −0.8 per cent and −1.1 per cent; contributions of public consumption were +0.7 per cent and −0.5 per cent; and, lastly, those of GCF were −2.6 per cent and −1.3 per cent.

Therefore, the main decline in investment took place at the beginning of the crisis, that is, before 2011, contrary to what happened to household consumption, whose deterioration accelerated after 2011. Lastly, in the case of public consumption, fiscal austerity measures implemented since 2010 have turned the contribution of this component to economic growth negative, thus aggravating the economic recession.

Figures 4.1, 4.2 and 4.3 show the financial balance sheets of the different economic sectors. The study of the financial balances, joined to the analysis of the contributions of the different components of aggregate demand to economic growth will help us to identify the type of long-run development of the Spanish economy: debt-led consumption, domestic demand-led, weak export-led or export-led mercantilism (Hein 2012). Again, we will analyse the type of long-run development for the three phases of growth previously defined: 1980–1993, 1994–2007 and 2008–2013.

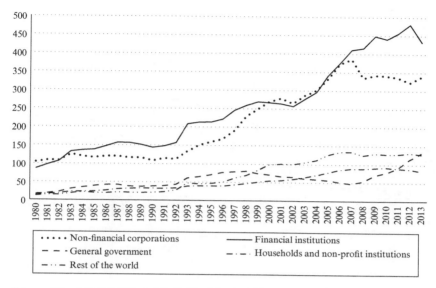

Source: Our calculations based on Bank of Spain, Boletín Estadístico, Financial Accounts of the Spanish Economy, Financial Accounts.

Figure 4.1 Financial liabilities (per cent of GDP)

During the period 1980–1993, the financial balance of non-financial corporations was very stable, with only small changes in the size of their financial liabilities and assets. In the case of financial institutions, the most relevant fact is that, after 1992, they maintained a low and stable annual growth of their financial assets and liabilities close to 5 per cent of GDP.

The behaviour of the general government's financial balance is closely related to the business cycle and the public budget balance. The stability of financial assets, at least until the current crisis, made financial liabilities become the most volatile component of financial balance, thus being the main determinant of the variations in net financial assets. In this first phase, the high fiscal deficits of the early eighties explain the increase in the outstanding general government's financial liabilities. The adjustment of fiscal imbalances that took place after the mid-eighties meant that the size of financial liabilities and net financial assets remained stable until the crisis in 1993.

Spanish households saw an increase in the size of their balance sheet, although the higher increase of the assets led to a higher size in net financial assets of households. This process ended abruptly in the late eighties, at the same time as a strong increase of household consumption. In this

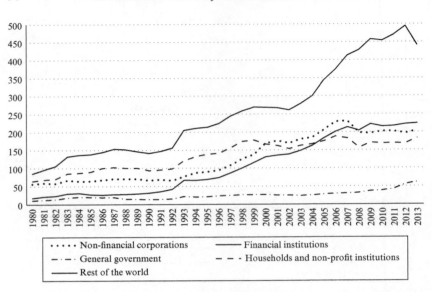

Source: Our calculations based on Bank of Spain, Boletín Estadístico, Financial Accounts of the Spanish Economy, Financial Accounts.

Figure 4.2   Financial assets (per cent of GDP)

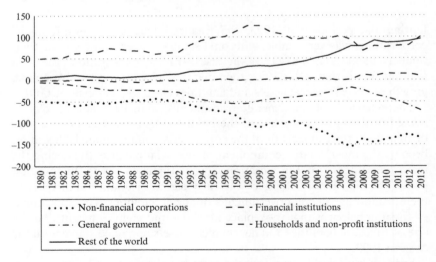

Source: Our calculations based on Bank of Spain, Boletín Estadístico, Financial Accounts of the Spanish Economy, Financial Accounts.

Figure 4.3   Net financial assets (per cent of GDP)

period, household financial assets fell slightly at the same time as their liabilities rose. The result was a fall in household net financial assets, which only recovered in 1993 due to the major increase in financial assets.

In the case of the external sector, its financial balance was positive, with a very small current account deficit. Nonetheless, the acceleration of economic growth and the increase in the trade deficit mentioned above led to an increase in the positive financial balance of the external sector.

Therefore, the type of development of the Spanish economy in this first period might be referred to as a domestic demand-led type, given the existence of a positive financial balance of the household sector and a negative contribution of the external sector to economic growth.

During the second phase (1994–2007), non-financial corporations saw a considerable increase of financial assets and liabilities, although the greater increase in the latter led to a strong decline of their financial balance, which fell from −57.7 per cent of GDP in 1993 to −155.9 per cent of GDP in 2007.

In the case of financial institutions, the most relevant fact is related to the evolution of the size of their financial balance. With financial liabilities taken as a proxy, the size of the financial balance of the sector rose from 205 per cent of GDP in 2003 to 412 per cent of GDP in 2007. This financial expansion accelerated after 2003: between 1993 and 2002 the size of the financial balance of financial institutions increased annually by 5.6 p.p. of GDP, but between 2003 and 2007 this growth increased by up to 26.7 p.p. of GDP.

During this second phase, households' financial assets saw a significant increase. However, between 1999 and 2002 they fell 24 p.p. of GDP. Later, the size of financial assets increased again, although it fell by 5.1 p.p. of GDP in 2007. Financial liabilities grew in a sustained manner, accelerating between 1996 and 2006, when they moved from 40.1 per cent to 85.6 per cent of GDP. Resulting from larger liabilities, net financial assets, which peaked at 126.6 per cent of GDP in 1998, began a decline, falling to 93.7 per cent of GDP in 2007.

Regarding the general government, the growth of its financial liabilities remained positive until 1998, when their size reached 80.7 per cent of GDP. Since then, the improvement in public finances led to a fall in the outstanding financial liabilities to 48 per cent of GDP in 2007. Thus, the general government's negative financial balance fell from −54.7 per cent to −17.8 per cent of GDP between 1997 and 2007.

Lastly, in the case of the financial balance of external sector, since 1996, but mainly since the year 2000, the positive financial balance of this sector increased significantly (from 19 per cent of GDP in 1993 to 78.7 per cent of GDP in 2007) as a consequence of the rising current account deficits.

The type of long-run development in this second phase is more ambiguous. The high contribution of domestic demand to economic growth, both of private consumption and investment, and the negative contribution of the external sector point to a domestic demand-led growth, given the positive financial balance of households. However, the deterioration of households' financial balance led to a strong deterioration of the financial balance of non-financial private sector (households and non-financial corporations) since 2002, and net financial assets of non-financial private sectors became negative: −62.2 per cent of GDP in 2007. Therefore, we could talk of a debt-led private expenditure type of growth.

During the third phase (2008–2013), non-financial corporations saw an improvement in their financial balance, which moved from −155.9 per cent of GDP in 2007 to −134.3 per cent of GDP in 2013. This noticeable improvement can be entirely explained by the decline in financial liabilities, which fell between 2007 and 2013 from 386 to 339 per cent of GDP.

The financial balances of financial institutions significantly declined in 2013: financial assets and liabilities fell 52.9 and 47.9 per cent of GDP, respectively. But the most relevant fact is that the financial balance of the sector became positive, oscillating between 8.8 per cent of GDP in 2013 and 14.4 per cent of GDP in 2010.

In the case of the general government, its financial assets increased to an unparalleled degree due to the impact of the banking rescue on Spanish public finances. As a result, the outstanding financial assets of general government rose between 2007 and 2013 from 30.7 to 61.7 per cent of GDP. The deterioration of public finances led to a skyrocketing public debt, leading to an unparalleled size of the financial liabilities of the general government (132.1 per cent of GDP in 2013). As a result, net financial assets have fallen from −17.8 per cent of GDP in 2007 to −70.4 per cent of GDP in 2013.

The financial behaviour of Spanish households differs substantially from that of other agents. Financial assets fell 25.8 p.p. of GDP in 2008, but started to rise again in 2009, reaching 183.2 per cent of GDP in 2013, a size similar to the levels of 2006 and 2007. Financial liabilities kept rising until 2010, when they reached 92 per cent of GDP. However, afterwards Spanish households began a process of heavy deleveraging, and their outstanding financial liabilities fell to 82.8 per cent in 2013 (9.2 p.p. of GDP lower than in 2010). As a result, between 2008 and 2013 the financial balance of Spanish households improved, and their net financial assets rose from 68.1 to 100.4 per cent of GDP.

As we analysed above, the current account balance has improved substantially in this period, and in 2012 and 2013 Spain had a surplus in the current account balance. This helped to slow the downturn and stabilise the positive financial balance of the external sector.

In sum, given that in this phase the external sector worked as the only driving force of the economic activity, and that the financial balance of households and non-financial corporations saw significant improvement, although the overall financial balance of the non-financial private agents remained negative, we can state that during the crisis the type of development of the Spanish economy has been one close to the export-led mercantilist type.

4.4 LONG-RUN EFFECTS OF FINANCIALISATION ON THE SPANISH ECONOMY THROUGH DIFFERENT CHANNELS

Financialisation and Distribution

The objective of this section is to check the hypothesis that financialisation contributes to redistribution of income from wages to profits and to higher income inequality for Spain (Hein 2010, 2011, 2012; Hein and van Treeck 2010). However, any conclusion must be viewed with caution. Our analysis is descriptive, and cannot provide a conclusive causal relationship between financialisation and changes in income distribution in Spain. These changes can be explained by other elements or economic policy measures that took place parallel to financialisation, such as fiscal policies or labour market reforms. Moreover, income redistribution could be explained by long-run elements that were operating in the Spanish economy well before the beginning of the financialisation process. This opens up the possibility that changes in income distribution could be the driving forces behind financialisation in Spain.

Given that financialisation began in Spain in the nineties, and gained momentum since 2000, our analysis of income redistribution will focus on this period. The data on the adjusted wage share (coming from the AMECO database) show that this share increased from 61.7 per cent of GDP in 1960 to 67.1 per cent of GDP in 1981. Since then, with the exceptions of the years 1991–1993 and 2007–2009, adjusted wage share has shown a declining tendency, amounting to 53.3 per cent of GDP in 2013, the lowest figure since 1960.

The declining wage share would suggest a potential relationship between financialisation and (functional) income redistribution from wages to profits. From the mid-nineties until 2007, Spanish wage moderation was considerable (in 2007 real wages were 1 percentage point lower than in 1993), which is difficult to explain given the economic growth and the performance of the labour market in the period (between 1995 and 2007, 7.8 million jobs were created, and the unemployment rate fell from 20 per cent to 8.3 per cent). Although financialisation may have affected real wages, wage moderation was also influenced by the voluntary wage moderation agreed between employers' associations and trade unions (Ferreiro and Gómez 2006, 2014a) and by the depressing impact on wage growth resulting from the temporary employment contracts, whose spread can be explained by the need of corporations to reduce wage costs in order to offset the negative effects of the high real interest of the late eighties and the nineties (Ferreiro and Serrano, 2001).

Table 4.1 shows the evolution of income property and their components:

Table 4.1   Property income (as percentage of Gross National Income)

	Property income	Interest	Distributed income of corporations	Other income
1985	24.83	22.76	1.94	0.13
1986	24.25	22.07	1.91	0.27
1987	25.83	23.44	1.98	0.41
1988	25.76	22.47	2.65	0.64
1989	28.19	25.15	2.44	0.60
1990	29.89	27.11	2.37	0.42
1991	30.25	27.11	2.75	0.39
1992	30.11	27.34	2.39	0.38
1993	32.14	28.66	3.03	0.45
1994	26.21	23.16	2.57	0.48
1995	33.62	28.70	3.53	1.38
1996	31.98	26.17	4.27	1.54
1997	26.76	21.28	4.50	0.98
1998	22.32	17.26	3.47	1.60
1999	19.33	13.88	3.64	1.81
2000	20.76	14.65	4.24	1.87
2001	21.36	15.28	4.68	1.40
2002	18.24	12.59	4.30	1.34
2003	16.47	10.45	4.54	1.47
2004	16.53	10.22	4.87	1.45
2005	17.65	11.14	5.07	1.44
2006	22.29	13.94	5.93	2.41
2007	28.13	18.95	6.27	2.91
2008	30.33	21.70	6.66	1.97
2009	21.66	13.55	6.43	1.69
2010	19.70	11.51	6.42	1.77
2011	22.13	14.03	6.25	1.85
2012	22.02	14.23	6.00	1.78

Source: Our calculations based on Spanish National Statistics Institute and AMECO database.

interest, distributed income of corporations (i.e., dividends) and other income (rents, reinvested earnings on direct foreign investment, and property income attributed to insurance policy holders). Interest is the main component of property income. Its series shows the existence of four phases: until 1995, with the exception of 1994, the share of interest in gross national income (GNI) had an upward tendency, peaking at 28.7 per cent in 1995. Between 1995 and 2004, its share fell sharply, reaching a minimum in 2004 (10.2 per cent). Between 2005 and 2008 interest started to rise again, reaching 21.7 per cent in 2008, but since then it started a new downward phase, reaching 14.2 per cent in 2012.

The sustained growth of the size of financial assets and liabilities implies that the changes of the volume of interest are mainly explained by the changes in the interest rates, i.e., in the profitability of financial assets. Until 1995 the rise in size of interest payments was driven by the joint effect of high interest rates and a larger size of financial assets-liabilities. Since 1995, the fall in interest payments would be explained by the fall in interest rates. However, since 2004 low interest rates were not enough to offset the big increases of financial assets-liabilities, thus leading to a phase of high growth on this component. This new phase ended in 2008, when the fall in interest rates led to the fall in interest payments.

Regarding the item 'other income', its value remained stable until 2005. Henceforth, there was a strong rise in the item 'reinvested earnings on foreign direct investments', which rose from 2.1 to 11.5 billion euros between 2005 and 2006. Since 2006, the volume of this income has fallen, although it stabilised at around 6 billion euros. Furthermore, in the case of households there is an important increase in the volume of 'property income attributed to insurance policy holders' in 2007, which rose from an average annual size close to 10 billion euros, to 14.3 and 15.6 billion euros in 2007 and 2008, respectively. Lastly, dividends, i.e., distributed income of financial and non-financial corporations, have grown continuously from the mid-nineties onwards, and as a result dividends are above 6 per cent of GNI since 2007.

Next, we shall focus our attention on the changes noted in the personal income distribution. According to data from Eurostat (Income and Living Conditions), the Gini coefficient of equivalised disposable income fell from 34 to 31 between 1996 and 2002, a fall related to the intense rise in employment and the fall in unemployment rate. However, since 2004 the inequality in income distribution increased very quickly, and it even accelerated at the beginning of the current crisis, peaking at 35 in 2012, although it fell to 33.7 in 2013.

Another indicator of the changes in income distribution is the ratio median-to-mean income: a declining ratio would imply a larger inequality

Table 4.2   Share of national equivalised income by deciles (per cent)

	D1	D2	D3	D4	D5	D6	D7	D8	D9	D10
1995	2	5	6	7	8	9	11	13	16	25
1996	2	5	6	7	8	9	10	12	15	26
1997	2	4	6	7	8	9	10	13	16	26
1998	2	5	6	7	8	9	10	13	16	25
1999	3	4	6	7	8	9	11	13	15	25
2000	3	5	6	7	8	9	10	12	15	25
2001	3	5	6	7	8	9	11	12	15	25
2004	2.6	4.7	5.9	7.1	8.3	9.5	10.9	12.6	15.1	23.3
2005	2.5	4.6	5.8	6.9	8.1	9.4	10.8	12.7	15.4	23.8
2006	2.4	4.6	5.8	7.0	8.2	9.5	10.9	12.7	15.2	23.7
2007	2.4	4.7	5.8	6.9	8.1	9.5	10.9	12.7	15.4	23.6
2008	2.2	4.7	5.9	7.1	8.3	9.4	11.0	12.8	15.4	23.3
2009	1.5	4.6	5.9	7.1	8.2	9.5	11.0	12.9	15.7	23.5
2010	1.3	4.3	5.7	7.0	8.2	9.5	10.9	12.9	15.8	24.4
2011	1.5	4.2	5.6	6.8	8.1	9.5	11.1	13.1	16.0	24.2
2012	1.5	4.2	5.6	6.8	8.0	9.3	11.0	13.0	16.0	24.8
2013	1.9	4.4	5.7	6.8	8.0	9.4	10.8	12.8	15.7	24.5

Note: Data for 2002 and 2003 are not available.

Source: Eurostat, Income and Living Conditions.

in income distribution, and vice versa. Using data from Eurostat (Income and Living Conditions), this ratio climbed from 82.1 per cent in 1996 to 88.9 per cent in 2004. In 2005 the ratio fell to 87 per cent and started to rise again until 2008 when it amounted to 88.8 per cent. Since then the ratio has fallen, and in 2013 amounted to 86.5 per cent. This evolution suggests a larger equality in income distribution up until 2008. However, with the current crisis, income distribution in Spain has become more unequal.

Table 4.2 shows the evolution of income distribution by deciles since 1995. The data do not show a significant change in income distribution, with the exception of the first decile, which shows a downward tendency, a sign of the worsening economic situation of the poorest people. Nonetheless, the current crisis has generated a less egalitarian income distribution. Thus, the share of national income corresponding to the two first deciles has declined whilst that of the two last deciles has increased.

The existence of an income redistribution process from the lowest to the highest incomes is more evident when we analyse the ratios between different income deciles: D10/D1, D9/D5, D5/D1 and (D9+D10)/(D1+D2). As Table 4.3 shows, in all cases we can detect an income redistribution process

Table 4.3   *Ratios between income deciles*

	D10/D1	D9/D5	D5/D1	(D9+D10)/(D1+D2)
1995	12.5	2.0	4.0	5.9
1996	13.0	1.9	4.0	5.9
1997	13.0	2.0	4.0	7.0
1998	12.5	2.0	4.0	5.9
1999	8.3	1.9	2.7	5.7
2000	8.3	1.9	2.7	5.0
2001	8.3	1.9	2.7	5.0
2004	9.0	1.8	3.2	5.3
2005	9.5	1.9	3.2	5.5
2006	9.9	1.9	3.4	5.6
2007	9.8	1.9	3.4	5.5
2008	10.6	1.9	3.8	5.6
2009	15.7	1.9	5.5	6.4
2010	18.8	1.9	6.3	7.2
2011	16.1	2.0	5.4	7.1
2012	16.5	2.0	5.3	7.2
2013	12.9	2.0	4.2	6.4

Note: Data for 2002 and 2003 are not available.

Source: Eurostat, Income and Living Conditions.

from the lowest incomes to medium and high incomes (above the fifth decile). At the beginning of the crisis, income distribution changed in favour of medium and high incomes and to the detriment of lowest incomes, and although after 2010 inequality declines, it is still higher than before the crisis.

The impact of the current crisis on income redistribution is more evident when we compare the income share of the poorest 5 per cent with that of the richest 4 per cent. Between 2007 and 2013, the income share of the poorest 5 per cent fell from 0.8 per cent to 0.5 per cent, but the income share of the richest 4 per cent has risen from 14.1 per cent to 14.6 per cent.

Financialisation and Investment

In Section 4.3 we ascertained that since the mid-nineties the gross capital formation increased substantially, becoming one of the main driving forces behind economic growth. In this sense, it is difficult to argue that financialisation in Spain has damaged the capital accumulation process. However, this does not mean the financialisation process has not affected the size and the financial sources of investments of non-financial corporations.

Table 4.4   *Net operating surplus and property income resources of non-financial corporations (per cent of GDP)*

	Net operating surplus	Property income	Net operating surplus + property income	Property income		
				Interests	Dividends	Other property income
1985	10.6	1.0	11.6	0.8	0.1	0.0
1986	11.5	1.4	12.8	0.7	0.2	0.4
1987	12.1	1.5	13.6	1.0	0.3	0.2
1988	12.2	1.6	13.8	0.9	0.4	0.4
1989	11.7	1.7	13.4	1.0	0.3	0.3
1990	10.8	1.6	12.4	1.2	0.3	0.1
1991	10.2	1.5	11.7	1.2	0.3	−0.1
1992	9.7	1.6	11.3	1.2	0.2	0.2
1993	10.6	1.5	12.0	1.5	0.2	−0.2
1994	11.9	1.7	13.6	1.2	0.2	0.3
1995	11.7	2.0	13.7	1.1	0.8	0.1
1996	11.2	2.0	13.2	1.0	0.8	0.2
1997	11.5	2.1	13.6	0.9	0.9	0.3
1998	11.4	2.0	13.4	0.8	1.0	0.2
1999	11.0	2.0	13.0	0.6	1.0	0.4
2000	10.4	2.7	13.1	0.9	1.2	0.6
2001	10.2	2.2	12.5	0.9	1.2	0.1
2002	10.1	2.3	12.3	0.9	1.3	0.1
2003	9.8	2.5	12.3	0.7	1.6	0.2
2004	9.8	3.5	13.3	0.7	1.8	1.0
2005	9.1	2.9	12.0	0.7	1.9	0.3
2006	8.7	3.9	12.6	0.8	2.1	1.0
2007	8.3	4.3	12.6	0.8	2.3	1.3
2008	8.5	3.6	12.1	0.9	2.5	0.3
2009	8.5	3.4	11.9	0.5	2.5	0.4
2010	9.5	3.4	12.9	0.5	2.4	0.5
2011	9.8	3.4	13.2	0.6	2.3	0.5
2012	10.3	3.2	13.5	0.6	2.1	0.5

Source: Our calculations based on Spanish National Statistics Institute, Annual National Accounts, Total economy and institutional sectors accounts.

One of the main features of financialisation is that the resources generated by non-financial corporations are increasingly dependent on income generated by the financial operations of the firm (property income), which is detrimental to the income coming from productive activity (net operating surplus).

Table 4.4 shows the evolution during the period 1985–2012 of the net operating surplus and property income of non-financial corporations. The volume of these resources has remained very stable, oscillating between 12 and 14 per cent of GDP. Nonetheless, there is a significant change in the size of each resource: net operating surplus fell from 10.6 to 8.3 per cent of GDP between 1985 and 2007, and property income rose from 1 per cent to 4.3 per cent of GDP. The current economic crisis has contributed to a partial reversion of this tendency, and in 2013 property income fell up to 3.2 per cent of GDP, whilst the net operating surplus increased up to 10.3 per cent. As a consequence, since 1985 property income represents a higher share of the sum of net operating surplus and property income of non-financial corporations: 18.5 per cent in 1997 and 52.2 per cent in 2007. Although the current crisis has implied a decline in this share, in 2012 it still amounted to 31.3 per cent, twice the average share of the nineties.

If we focus on the evolution of the components of property income resources, namely interest payments, distributed income of corporations (dividends) and other property income (rents, property income attributed to insurance policy holders and reinvested earnings on direct foreign investment), it is interesting to note that while other property income (mainly because of the increase in reinvested earnings on direct investment) and dividends have increased in size as a percentage of GDP, interest has had a sustained downward tendency, despite the rise in the size of financial assets of non-financial corporations, denoting the fall in the average profitability of these assets. As a consequence, Spanish non-financial corporations have reduced their dependency on resources coming from net operating surplus and interest, while dividends and profits resulting from their direct investments abroad have gained weight.

Financialisation may also have involved a change in the use of the resources of non-financial corporations. Table 4.5 shows the distribution of these resources between interest paid, dividends and retained profits. Until the beginning of the crisis, dividends paid by non-financial corporations grew. Contrary to what could be expected, the crisis has not implied a fall in dividends but merely a stabilisation.

In the case of interests paid, these began to fall in the year 1992, although after 2000 they climbed due to skyrocketing financial liabilities. This process ended abruptly in 2008 with the reduction of interest rates.

Retained profits rose sharply until 2004. Subsequently, they declined until 2008. With the beginning of the crisis, retained profits recovered and after 2010 were at the same levels as one decade ago. Therefore, in the last decade the greater payment of interest and dividends has gone at the expense of lower retained profits. The declining retained profits, in a context of increasing investments, implied a rising dependence on external

Table 4.5   *Use of resources coming from net operating surplus and property income of non-financial corporations (per cent of GDP)*

	Interest	Dividends	Retained profits	Other uses
1985	6.50	1.30	3.65	0.13
1986	5.62	1.45	5.61	0.13
1987	5.95	1.71	5.81	0.13
1988	5.62	2.18	5.87	0.18
1989	5.67	1.84	5.71	0.18
1990	5.97	1.56	4.67	0.19
1991	5.96	1.65	3.90	0.20
1992	6.14	1.19	3.76	0.20
1993	6.29	1.06	4.52	0.17
1994	5.79	1.58	5.99	0.28
1995	5.31	2.02	6.26	0.10
1996	4.66	2.36	6.11	0.09
1997	4.19	2.61	6.75	0.09
1998	3.68	2.84	6.80	0.07
1999	3.29	2.77	6.84	0.06
2000	2.88	3.41	6.73	0.06
2001	3.44	3.55	5.33	0.14
2002	2.93	3.40	5.96	0.06
2003	2.65	3.57	6.05	0.05
2004	2.82	3.89	6.50	0.04
2005	2.98	4.34	4.61	0.04
2006	3.65	4.79	4.11	0.04
2007	4.94	4.63	2.99	0.05
2008	5.51	4.48	2.07	0.04
2009	3.15	4.77	3.96	0.04
2010	2.91	4.42	5.57	0.04
2011	3.47	4.36	5.30	0.04
2012	3.14	4.19	6.16	0.04

Source: Our calculations based on Spanish National Statistics Institute, Annual National Accounts, Total economy and institutional sectors accounts.

funding to finance investments. This pattern changed with the financial and economic crisis. The crisis has led to higher retained profits, which can be explained by the deep constraints on the access to external (banking and non-banking) funding suffered by non-financial corporations. The recovery of retained profits did not happen at the expense of cuts in dividends, whose size has remained nearly unchanged, with small variations. Higher dividends were fuelled by the fall in paid interests and larger net operating surpluses.

Financialisation and Household Consumption

Although household consumption was one of the main driving forces of the Spanish economy since the nineties, its size, as a percentage of GDP, did not increase during the financialisation process. This does not mean that this process has not affected the real and financial behaviour of Spanish households. Figures 4.1 and 4.3 have shown the fast growth of household financial liabilities and the resulting decline in the size of their net financial assets until the beginning of the crisis. But, besides altering the size of household financial balance sheet, financialisation has also changed its composition. As Figure 4.4 shows, until the onset of the current financial and economic crisis, there had been a fall in the share of currency and banking deposits, which fell from 60 per cent in the eighties to 36.2 per cent in 2006. The declining deposits were offset by the greater insurance technical reserves (related to the larger size of pension funds) and, mainly, by the larger size of shares and other equities. With the current crisis, however, the fall in shares and other equities has gone hand in hand with an equivalent rise in currency and deposits.

Banking loans are their main component of household financial

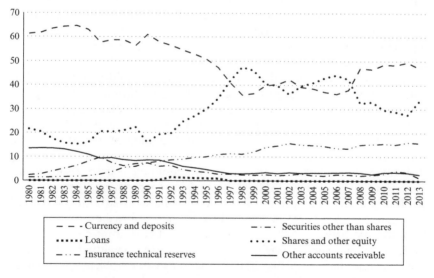

Source: Our calculations based on Bank of Spain, Boletín Estadístico, Financial Accounts of the Spanish Economy, Financial Accounts.

Figure 4.4   Household financial assets (as percentage of total household financial assets)

liabilities. Although their size remained constant around 75 per cent of total financial assets during the eighties, their share began an upward tendency since the mid-eighties, and after 2004 they have represented more than 90 per cent of total liabilities.

The bulk of credit to Spanish households is related to the purchase of housing: these credits amounted to 71.4 per cent of total loans and credits to households in 2007 and 75.4 per cent in 2013. Consumer credit has a minority and declining share: they only amounted to 12.4 per cent in 2007 and 8 per cent in 2013. When we measure banking credit to households as a percentage of GDP, similar results are obtained: the sum of loans to households for financing productive activities, consumer credits, and other purposes rose between 1997 and 2009 from 12.7 to 20.4 per cent of GDP. Since then, they have fallen to 16.2 per cent of GDP in 2013. Conversely, loans for house purchase rose sharply from 19.4 per cent of GDP in 1997 to 60.5 per cent of GDP in 2010, dropping to 56.8 per cent of GDP in 2013.

In this sense, we can argue that financialisation fuelled a housing bubble in Spain, stimulating the purchase of houses by the combination of lower interest rates and greater available external funding. The fall in nominal interest rates meant that despite the increase noted in household financial liabilities, the burden of this borrowing has fallen since the early nineties: in 1992, interest paid by households amounted to 11.4 per cent of their gross available income, but only 1.9 per cent in 2004. Although, interest paid increased after 2004 (reaching 5.3 per cent in 2008) it subsequently fell to 3 per cent in 2013.

The availability of abundant and cheap external funding went hand in hand with a declining savings rate after 1995, and, thus, in 2006 the gross savings rate amounted to merely 10.4 per cent. The financial crisis led to a huge rise in the household savings rate, peaking at an unparalleled 18 per cent in 2009. This increase in the savings rate at the beginning of the crisis could be explained by the deleveraging of Spanish households, who aimed at reducing their financial liabilities, and the uncertainty resulting from the rising unemployment that would have led to higher precautionary savings (Estrada et al. 2014). Since then, the savings rate has declined and in 2012 the household savings rate (10.5 per cent) was similar to that seen before the crisis. It should be noted that between 2009 and 2012 household gross available income fell by 5.5 per cent. The low savings rate of 2012 may therefore be related to declining resources of Spanish households and greater problems with saving.

Financialisation and the Current Account

In Section 4.3 we were able to ascertain that external imbalances in Spain rose increasingly since the nineties. In the first decade of the current century, the goods and services and current account balances reached unparalleled deficits: 6.7 and 10 per cent of GDP, respectively, in 2007. After 2008, Spanish external imbalances have rapidly adjusted, and in 2013 both current account and goods and services balances exhibited surpluses (0.8 per cent and 2.4 per cent of GDP, respectively).

The constant deficits in the balance of payments have led to a sustained increase in Spain's external debt, with the net international investment position skyrocketing to −982 billion euros in 2009. Actually, this deficit continued rising until 2013, when it amounted to 1,004 billion euros. However, the increase in the deficit that has been taking place since 2010 is explained by the larger debtor position of the Bank of Spain with the Eurosystem. Excluding the Bank of Spain, the net debtor position of Spain has shown a significant adjustment: from 1,026 billion euros in 2009 to 863 billion euros in 2013.

The rising external debt of the Spanish economy can be explained by the worsening of the current account balance, a reflection of the declining competitiveness of the Spanish economy. The competitiveness problems are related to the inflation differential with the main trade partners, mainly those belonging to the Euro area, resulting in a loss of price competitiveness of Spain: whilst between 1993 and 2013 the CPI for the Euro area (EU-18) increased 54 percentage points, in Spain it increased 77 percentage points.

The higher inflation rates, combined with a lower growth of productivity, have meant that the growth of the nominal unit labour costs (NULCs) was higher in Spain than in other countries in the Euro area. Between 1999 and 2009, NULCs increased in the Euro area by 22.7 per cent, while in Spain they increased by 37.7 per cent. However, this does not mean that wage growth is the only reason of the lower competiveness. If we analyse the evolution of real unit labour costs (RULCs), we can see that real ULCs have fallen in Spain more than in the Euro area: despite the acceleration in RULCs, Spanish RULCs were 9.3 percentage points lower in 2013 than in 1999 (1.3 p.p. lower in the case of the Euro area).

4.5 TRANSMISSION CHANNELS OF THE FINANCIAL CRISIS INTO THE SPANISH ECONOMY

As we have previously argued, the economic and financial crisis has affected Spain more intensely than most European countries. Excessive levels of private debt have transformed Spain into an economy highly dependent on external funding. The collapse of international financial and inter-banking markets since summer 2007 showed the weaknesses of the pillars that supported the Spanish growth model, and showed the need for financial and non-financial private agents to adopt measures to delever-age and reduce their indebtedness, which resulted in an abrupt decline in private demand. In this sense, the Spanish crisis is very similar to what happened in the other European economies, and has common roots. However, these elements alone do not explain the greater extent and prolonged duration of the crisis in Spain.

The liabilities of the Spanish private sector were not larger than in other European economies. Moreover, the size of the banking crises (in terms of the dimension of the affected institutions or the amount of the public support to the banks with problems) has also been greater in other countries, such as the United Kingdom, the Netherlands or Germany. The size of the external imbalances and the external debt were larger than in other countries, but it is not evident that they alone explain the larger impact of the economic crisis in Spain.

Although we are unable to conduct an in-depth analysis for reasons of space, we should like to point out two particular elements of the economic crisis in Spain that make it different from other crisis episodes. The first element has to do with the restructuring process of the Spanish financial system. The impact of the public support for credit institutions on public debt has not been greater than in other European Union countries (see European Commission 2014). However, the impact of public budget balance has been substantially greater. The delay in the acknowledgement of the existence and depth of the crisis in certain segments of the credit system contributed to an increase in the size of the public support needed in comparison to if the banking rescue had happened earlier.

Furthermore, the public rescue of Spanish banks took place later than in other European countries. In most European countries the banking rescue took place before the burst of the Greek crisis. The result was that there was no contagion effect from the banking crisis to the sovereign debt crisis. This was not the case with Spain. The banking crisis in Spain went hand in hand with a sovereign debt crisis that forced the Spanish Government to request the financial support of European Union institutions in July 2012 due to its inability to ensure that the resources required to support the failing banks entered the financial markets.

The delay in the bank bailout led to major uncertainty as to the true situation facing Spanish credit institutions, which transferred to the whole financial system and to the funding of the sector to non-financial agents, deepening the crisis because of the credit constraints suffered by non-financial agents (International Monetary Fund 2014).

The second element is related to the conduct of fiscal policy, mainly in the years before the crisis (Ferreiro, Gómez and Serrano 2013, 2014b, 2014c; Ferreiro and Serrano 2012a, 2012b). Although Spanish fiscal policy adopted a countercyclical restrictive stance in the years 2005 and 2006, given the dimension of the domestic (inflation) and external (current account deficit) imbalances, fiscal policy should have adopted a more restrictive stance. Moreover, the design of fiscal policy did not take into account the excessive indebtedness faced by households and non-financial corporations. In fact, the tax cuts adopted since 2006, mainly in the personal income tax, lent impetus to private borrowing by rising household available income in a context of low (nominal, but also real) interest rates.

Furthermore, fiscal policy adopted a procyclical expansionary fiscal policy in the years 2006 to 2008, based on a combination of expenditure increases and direct tax cuts implemented in 2006 and 2007, which meant that the public budget balance fell from a surplus amounting to 2.4 per cent of GDP in 2006 to a deficit amounting to −4.5 per cent in 2008, the year before the onset of the crisis in Spain. Besides leading to an over-heating of the Spanish economy, which fuelled private agents' debt, this faulty fiscal policy exhausted the space for an effective expansionary fiscal policy during the crisis. Actually, the implementation of expansionary fiscal measures meant that public deficit peaked at 11.2 per cent of GDP in 2009, an unsustainable figure that led to the necessary measures of fiscal consolidation after 2010, and that, undoubtedly, increased the negative impact of the financial and economic crisis.

4.6   SUMMARY AND CONCLUSIONS

The financialisation process of the Spanish economy came later than in most other advanced economies: it began in the mid-nineties and gained momentum after 2000, until the onset of the financial crisis in 2007.

This process has led to greater indebtedness of private agents, changing their financial and non-financial behaviours. In the case of households, there has been a change in the composition of their financial assets, with shares and other equities gaining weight to the detriment of banking deposits, at least until the current crisis. In the case of financial liabilities, the share of loans has remained nearly unchanged. The main purpose of these loans has been housing purchases. Thus, we can argue that financialisation in Spain indeed contributed to the housing bubble of the 2000s.

Greater household borrowing, therefore, has not gone hand in hand with an increase in the share of household consumption in GDP, despite the creation of many jobs, which could be explained by the stagnation of real wages.

In fact, although since the mid-nineties domestic demand has been the main driving force behind the Spanish economy, investment has been the component with the highest growth, which in turn has led to an increase in the share of GCF in GDP. However, this has not been the only effect of financialisation on the behaviour of non-financial corporations. The process has gone hand in hand with a change in the balance sheet of non-financial corporations. On the one hand, it has increased the size of property income in the primary resources of non-financial corporations. On the other hand, there has been a shift in the composition of primary incomes of these firms, with an increase in the size of interest paid and dividends, to the detriment of retained profits.

The greater availability of external financial resources has allowed an excessive increase in the external imbalances of the Spanish economy, both in terms of the current account deficit and the external debt. This high dependency of Spain on external funding has meant that the collapse of international financial markets has had more serious real consequences than in other neighbouring economies.

Lastly, we should like to emphasise the responsibility of the mistakes made in the management of the crisis for the extent and prolonged duration of the crisis.

REFERENCES

Altuzarra, A., J. Ferreiro, C. Gálvez, C. Gómez, A. González, P. Peinado, C. Rodríguez and F. Serrano (2013), 'Report on the Spanish Financial System', FESSUD Studies in Financial Systems, No. 6, available at: http://fessud.eu/wp-content/uploads/2012/08/the-spain-financial-system.pdf.

Estrada, A., D. Garrote, E. Valdeolivas and J. Vallés (2014), 'Household debt and uncertainty: Private consumption after the great recession', *Documentos de Trabajo Banco de España*, No. 1415.

European Commission (2014), *Eurostat supplementary table for the financial crisis. Background note (April 2014)*, Eurostat.

Ferreiro, J. and C. Gómez (2006), 'New incomes policy in Spain', in E. Hein, A. Heise and A. Truger (eds), *European Economic Policies – Alternatives to Orthodox Analysis and Policy Concepts*, Marburg: Metropolis.

Ferreiro, J. and C. Gómez (2014a), 'Implementing a voluntary wage policy: lessons from the Irish and Spanish wages policy before the crisis', *Panoeconomicus*, **61** (1), 102–127.

Ferreiro, J., C. Gómez and F. Serrano (2013), 'Mistakes in the fiscal policy in Spain before the crisis', *Panoeconomicus*, **60** (5), 577–592.

Ferreiro, J., C. Gómez and F. Serrano (2014b), 'Sustainable future fiscal and debt policies: lessons from and for Spain', in P. Arestis and M. Sawyer (eds), *Fiscal and Debt Policies for the Future*, Basingstoke: Palgrave Macmillan.

Ferreiro, J., C. Gómez and F. Serrano (2014c), 'Conditions for a sustainable counter-cyclical fiscal policy: the case of Spain', *Journal of Economic Issues*, **48** (2), 341–348.

Ferreiro, J. and F. Serrano (2001), 'The Spanish labour market: reforms and consequences', *International Review of Applied Economics*, **15** (1), 31–53.

Ferreiro, J. and F. Serrano (2012a), 'When the solution is part of the problem: The fiscal policy in Spain', in H. Herr, T. Niechoj, C. Thomasberger, A. Truger and T. van Treeck (eds), *From Crisis to Growth? The Challenges of Debt and Imbalances*, Marburg: Metropolis.

Ferreiro, J. and F. Serrano (2012b), 'The economic crisis in Spain: Contagion effects and distinctive factors', in P. Arestis and M. Sawyer (eds), *The Euro Crisis*, Basingstoke: Palgrave Macmillan.

Hein, E. (2010), 'A Keynesian perspective on "financialisation"', in P. Arestis and M. Sawyer (eds), *21st Century Economics*, Basingstoke: Palgrave Macmillan.

Hein, E. (2011), '"Financialisation", distribution and growth', in E. Hein and E. Stockhammer (eds), *A Modern Guide to Keynesian Macroeconomics and Economic Policies*, Cheltenham, UK and Northampton, MA, USA: Edward Elgar Publishing.

Hein, E. (2012), *The Macroeconomics of Finance-Dominated Capitalism and its Crisis*, Cheltenham, UK and Northampton, MA, USA: Edward Elgar Publishing.

Hein, E. and T. van Treeck (2010), '"Financialisation" in post-Keynesian models of distribution and growth: a systematic review', in M. Setterfield (ed.), *Handbook of Alternative Theories of Economic Growth*, Basingstoke: Palgrave Macmillan.

International Monetary Fund (2014), *Spain. Financial Sector Reform: Final Progress Report*, International Monetary Fund, April 2014.

Sawyer, M. (2014), 'Financial development, financialisation and economic growth', FESSUD Working Papers Series, No. 21, available at: http://fessud.eu/wp-content/uploads/2013/04/Financialisation-and-growth-Sawyer-working-paper-21.pdf.

5. Financialisation and the crisis: the case of Greece

Yanis Varoufakis and Lefteris Tserkezis

5.1 INTRODUCTION

Finance became unleashed as the Bretton Woods system dissolved in 1971. The end of capital controls and the breakdown of the fixed exchange rates regime allowed finance to effectively decouple from industry and trade, creating violent flows of capital, as well as new forms of paper assets. It was within that environment that Europe's audacious experiment with monetary union was designed and implemented. For a small deficit country like Greece, these two momentous phenomena (financialisation and monetary union) were to prove pivotal.

Although there is hardly a consensus in the literature as to the exact definition of financialisation, changes in the relationship between the financial and the real sector, leading to the strengthening of the former at the expense of the latter, undoubtedly constitute a central and critical aspect of this process. The objective of this chapter is to examine the available data[1] with a view to establishing what can be discerned from it, regarding the linkages between Greece's real economy and the developments in the world of finance, and with a special interest, naturally, in their macroeconomic effects. This objective cannot be conceived in isolation from the economic turmoil of the last few years, not only because the recent crisis is per se too important to be left out of the discussion, but also in the sense that it constitutes, at least in part, the culmination of these developments.

Section 5.2 offers a general description of the long-run macroeconomic developments of the past three decades. Section 5.3 analyses these developments by focusing on the exact effects of financialisation on four fields of the macroeconomy: income distribution, investment in capital stock, consumption, and the current account. Section 5.4 returns to the question of the relationship between financialisation and the recent financial and economic crisis. In this context, the macroeconomic imbalances that the era of financialisation brought about are highlighted and linked to the onset of the crisis, while the latter is analysed in detail with respect both to its underlying and to its immediate causes. Finally, Section 5.5 concludes.

5.2   LONG-RUN DEVELOPMENT IN THE ERA OF FINANCIALISATION

The long-run development of the Greek economy over the period 1980–2013 can be examined through the dynamics – and the growth contribution – of the basic categories of effective demand, as well as of the financial balances of the main sectors. In this manner, the type of long-run development that prevailed in Greece prior to the crisis can be identified on the basis of the taxonomy employed by Hein (2012)[2] as a debt-led consumption boom.

The general growth performance of the Greek economy throughout the last three decades can be divided into three separate phases. The first one lasted from 1980 to approximately the mid-1990s and is characterised by a rather unstable long-run development, with the economy alternating often between positive and negative rates of growth. The second phase lasts from 1995 to 2007 and constitutes a period of constant growth in real GDP with a rate higher on average than 3.5 per cent per year, while the third phase consists obviously in the deep recession that resulted from the financial and economic crisis of 2008.

As far as the composition of total expenditure in the Greek economy is concerned, public investment and public consumption do not appear to have a clear trend, although the evolution of their shares throughout the period under examination is far from uninteresting. The share of public investment in GDP was between 2 per cent and 3 per cent throughout approximately the first half of the relevant period, but started rising after 1997, constantly surpassing 3 per cent and reaching as high as 3.7 per cent of GDP immediately before the onset of the present crisis. The reductions in the public investment budget in the context of the austerity policy that was adopted led to a rapid decline in public investment's share in GDP, the latter falling in 2011 and 2012 below 2 per cent for the first time since 1980. The behaviour of public consumption is characterised by a similar pattern, although the fluctuations involved are significantly less marked.

More interesting, and certainly more marked, are the fluctuations that have taken place in the other three demand components, namely private consumption, private investment and net exports. Private consumption's share in GDP shows a clear upward trend in the period under examination, starting at 63 per cent in 1980 and reaching almost 75 per cent in 2011, its average value being higher than 70 per cent during the years 1990–2013.

Although private consumption at constant prices has been falling in absolute terms since 2010 at rates greater than 6 per cent per annum, its share in GDP exhibits only a mild decline from the aforementioned maximum, while it remains significantly higher than 70 per cent.

On the contrary, the economic crisis has had a devastating effect on the share of private investment in GDP, reducing it from around 23 per cent in 2007 to just over 10 per cent in 2013. Private investment accounted for more than a quarter of GDP in 1980, but this share declined rapidly, falling to 14.8 per cent in 1995. The period of fast growth that followed was characterised by a rise in the share of private investment, which fluctuated around 20 per cent, without, however, approaching its historically maximum value.

Finally, the share of net exports in GDP has been negative throughout the entire period under consideration, although it has been subject to substantial fluctuations. The share was equal to 6.2 per cent in 1980 but deteriorated dramatically reaching −11.9 per cent ten years later. After a small improvement in the mid-1990s, the share of net exports declined again, reaching −14.5 per cent at the very onset of the international crisis. From then on, it exhibited a marked improvement as a result of the sharp reduction in the demand for imports, rising to −8.1 per cent in 2011 and to −2.2 per cent in 2013.

The contribution of demand components in the growth of GDP, shown in Figure 5.1, constitutes a crucial indicator of the economy's long-run development, although the available data do not distinguish between public and private investment. According to the data, the recessions during

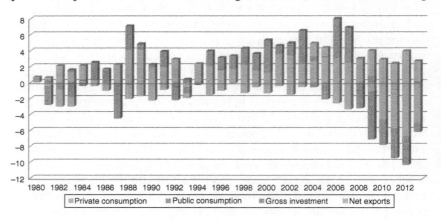

Source: European Commission (2014).

Figure 5.1   Contribution to the GDP growth of main demand aggregates

the 1980s were associated with the negative effects of gross investment and net exports. However, this pattern changes from the mid-1990s onwards, net exports becoming the main, if not the only, factor that had a negative impact on GDP growth. From that point, until the emergence of the crisis, economic growth was based primarily on the advance of private consumption, accounting, for several years, for more than half of the growth in real GDP.

The onset of the crisis led to a dramatic reversal in the pattern that the Greek economy followed. From the rather irregular pattern of the 1980s and the steady-growth of the period 1994–2007, due, primarily, to private consumption, the years of the crisis are characterised by a recession caused by the collapse of private consumption and gross investment, while net exports become the only demand component that led to small but consistently positive contributions to GDP growth.

What can be observed, in a nutshell, is that the pre-crisis pattern has been turned upside down, without, however, any significant changes with respect to the relative importance of the several components. Private consumption is still the dominant component, while the effect of net exports is still not strong enough to counterbalance the effects of the other components that point in the opposite direction. An interesting observation is that gross investment was the first component to be affected by the crisis, contributing massively to the recession in 2008 and 2009. On the other hand, the contribution of private consumption to GDP growth was positive, and quite strong, in 2008, turning mildly negative in the next year. Only from 2010 onwards did private consumption collapse, dragging the economy to unprecedented rates of real GDP reduction.

On the basis of the above data, the historical experience of the Greek economy could be categorised either as a debt-led consumption boom or as a case of domestic demand-led development. The existence of chronic deficits in the current account, the positive growth contribution of domestic demand (especially private consumption), and the negative growth contribution of net exports are characteristics that both these regimes share. However, the two regimes reflect different configurations of the main sectors' financial balances.

The evolution of the main sectors' financial balances for the period 2000–2013 portrayed in Figure 5.2 validates the view that the long-run development of the Greek economy should be characterised as a debt-led consumption boom.[3] The balances of both the household sector and the general government are negative across the board, thus counteracting the consistently large positive balances of the external sector. As far as the balances of the corporate sector, financial and non-financial, are concerned, they display a certain irregularity during the greatest part of the period

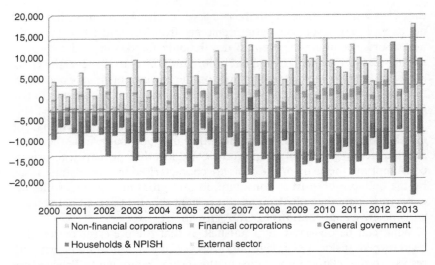

Source: Hellenic Statistical Authority (2014).

Figure 5.2   Sectoral financial balances (millions of euros) – net lending (+) / net borrowing (–)

under examination. It should be mentioned, however, that the overall indebtedness of the private household sector never proceeded too far in the case of the Greek economy, at least in comparison to the respective state of affairs in most members of the Euro area.[4]

A final comment that deserves to be made with respect to the time-path of sectoral balances relates to the new pattern that seems to emerge during the years of the crisis, characterised by consistently positive balances of the corporate sector, presumably due to the corporate sector's engagement into a process of deleveraging. This movement of the corporate sector into a net lending position has taken place mainly at the expense of the external sector, whose balances have been significantly reduced, and even turned negative on some occasions. In the immediate future, it is possible that the pressure exerted upon the external sector will become even larger, given both the further reduction of the general government's fiscal deficit and the attempt by households to deleverage. However, given the rather medio-cre export performance of the Greek economy, it is far from clear whether the entire domestic economy can move, at the same time, into a net lending position at the expense of the external sector alone.

5.3 EFFECTS OF FINANCIALISATION ON THE REAL ECONOMY

This section reports on data concerning the several channels through which the process of financialisation affects the real economy. The analysis will focus on those fields of the economy that have been highlighted in the relevant literature as prone to the onset of financialisation, namely income distribution, investment in capital stock, consumption and the current account.

Income Distribution

One of the most important effects of financialisation is to be found in its tendency to facilitate a redistribution of income at the expense of the relatively low wage incomes (Hein 2012). This redistribution is usually brought about through the decline in the bargaining power of organised labour, the rise in overhead costs, or shifts in the economy's sectoral composition. Irrespective of the exact channel through which such redistribution may take place, its effects should be observed in the time-path of both the functional and the personal distribution of income.

The adjusted wage share[5] had risen temporarily in the early 1980s, reaching a maximum of 72.6 per cent in 1983, followed by secular decline at the beginning of the following decade. It stabilised at a level just above 60 per cent during the years 2006–2011, and then declined again, falling to 54 per cent in 2013 (European Commission 2014).

However, the interpretation of this decline as an outcome of financialisation is neither straightforward, nor possible to be determined econometrically. Attempts towards such a determination can be found in the relevant literature, usually with reference to a subset of advanced industrial economies.[6] Nevertheless, the lack of sufficient official data on the time-path of variables that are used as a measure of the process of financialisation in the literature precludes the possibility of a similar econometric estimation with respect to the Greek case.

However, the hypothesis of a shift in the distribution of income due to the declining bargaining power of labour seems to be at least compatible with developments that have taken place in the Greek economy over the past decades. Although the Greek labour movement was quite strong during the late 1970s and early 1980s, this strength and the consequent bargaining power of organised labour started to weaken in the following years, considerably so after the mid-1990s. This gradual erosion of labour's bargaining power was probably the delayed result of the end of the post-war 'Golden Age' in the early 1970s and the subsequent emergence of low, or negative, growth rates and substantial unemployment, while the reasons for the significant time lag involved should probably be sought at the peculiarities of post-war Greek political history. Although no reliable data exist on this account, the significant decline in union density after the mid-1980s or early 1990s is quite straightforward to anyone having even a superficial knowledge of the Greek economy. Moreover, this weakened position of labour led to, and was at the same time reinforced by, the proliferation of part-time employment as well as other similar schemes from the late 1990s onwards, while the effects of the on-going crisis and of the recent legislative reforms undertaken in the context of the Greek adjustment programme are probably only too obvious.

On the other hand, the hypothesis of a declining wage share due to shifts in the economy's sectoral composition does not seem to provide an adequate explanation. From 2000 onwards, the share of general government has been trendless until the onset of the current crisis[7] (Hellenic Statistical Authority 2014). However, the fact that available data only cover the period after 2000 implies that the hypothesis cannot be entirely ruled out. This is especially so if it is taken into account that the most successful instances of government downsizing and of opening up possibilities for corporate activity, i.e. the banking sector and telecommunications, had already proceeded substantially before the turn of the century.

It would also be of interest to examine whether this redistribution of income also corresponds to a rise in rentier share in net national income, following the methodology proposed by Duenhaupt (2012), in the context of which the rentier share is essentially defined as the ratio of the household's sector net property income to net national income. In terms of official statistics however, the tendency for the rentier share seems rather to be a declining one, falling from almost 13 per cent in 2000 to just 5.3 per cent in 2011, although it does exhibit some slight increase during the last two years.[8] The share of retained earnings does not exhibit any clear trend, although it does display some marked fluctuations, while the share of employees' compensation was steadily rising until 2010, but falling ever since. However, it should be taken into account that the rentier share in net national income was probably already too high in the beginning of the period examined, presumably as a result of the stock market bubble of the time. In this respect, what appears to be a declining trend may actually constitute simply a return to normalcy after the most fervent phases of the rise in stock market prices (Hellenic Statistical Authority 2014).

Turning to the issue of the personal distribution of income, both the Gini coefficient and the ratio of median to mean income display a remarkable constancy throughout the entire period, although the latter does increase significantly in the last two years. The Gini coefficient also increases in these same years, rising from 32.9 per cent in 2010 to 34.3 per cent in 2012, without, however, exceeding values that should be considered consistent with historical experience. Overall, the data seem to suggest that the period of significant growth that preceded the crisis seems to have suppressed income inequality, albeit in small and certainly not decisive steps. Unsurprisingly, the crisis led to a reversal of this path, pushing inequality back to its initial levels (Eurostat 2014).

In conclusion, the data show the existence of a significant shift in functional income distribution at the expense of labour, although the lack of sufficient data precludes the possibility of an econometric testing of whether this shift can be attributed to the process of financialisation. As far as the personal distribution of income is concerned, no evidence of a similar redistribution at the expense of lower wage incomes during the years of financialisation can be detected, although the lack of data on top incomes implies that no decisive answer can be given.

Investment in Capital Stock

Two main channels have been proposed (Hein 2010; Hein and van Treeck 2010), through which the process of financialisation affects gross investment. The first is related to the internal financing of gross investment (the *'internal means of finance channel'*), while the second pertains to the substitution of the 'more uncertain' investment in physical capital with investments in financial 'assets' (the *'preference channel'*).

Specifically, the first channel affects real investment through the imposition of a greater distribution of profits to the firms' shareholders, implying a modified distribution of the non-financial corporate sector's gross operating surplus and a relative decline in the share of total investment that is internally financed. The second channel correlates with short-run profits stemming from financial investments and should therefore, be accompanied by a rising contribution of financial profits to the operating surplus of non-financial corporations.

The respective data for the Greek economy cover only an admittedly small period of time, since no available data exist for the period prior to 2000. Concerning the distribution of the gross operating surplus of the non-financial corporate sector, the data are rather hard to interpret on the basis of the 'internal means of finance' channel. No indication of a rising share of dividend payments in gross operating surplus can be detected for the period 2000–2004, while the period 2005–2013 starts with a substantial share of dividend payments which becomes extremely large in 2007 and declines rapidly from 2009 onwards. The data seem to suggest that there had been, during the pre-crisis years, a certain tendency towards a higher share of dividends, as well as interest payments, which however seems to have lasted just for a few years (Hellenic Statistical Authority 2014).

An alternative method of assessing the validity of the 'internal means of finance' channel for the Greek economy is through the identification of the net sources of finance for non-financial corporations. These were calculated according to the approach developed by Corbett and Jenkinson (1997), implying that all values represent annual flows, while internal financing is defined as the gross savings of the non-financial corporate sector.

According to these calculations, internal financing showed no sign of retreat in the period 2000–2004, while its relative contribution was at very low levels during the years 2005–2008, before rising dramatically after the onset of the financial crisis. In 2013, internal sources have come to represent 93.8 per cent of non-financial corporations' finance, from merely 49.2 per cent in 2008. Net bank financing displayed exactly the opposite behaviour, accounting for 34.2 per cent of total financing in 2008, while moving into negative territory from 2012 onwards. The conclusion is that while some evidence of non-financial corporations' declining reliance on internal financing does show up, they are on the inconclusive side (Hellenic Statistical Authority 2014; Bank of Greece 2014).

Turning to the 'preference channel', financial profits' contribution to the gross operating surplus of the non-financial corporate sector declined dramatically from 8.6 per cent in 2000 to only 3.8 per cent in the following year, probably as a result of the stock market bubble that burst during the same period. Beyond that stock exchange crash, it remained steadily low until 2004. Post-2004, the contribution of financial profits was in general higher, exhibiting a sharp rise in 2007, but continuously declined once the recession began in 2008, falling below 3 per cent by the end of the period under consideration. In conclusion, no decisive answer can be given to the question of financialisation's effect on investment in capital stock in the Greek economy (Hellenic Statistical Authority 2014).

What is certainly clear, however, is the fact that the last two decades have been characterised by a marked increase in the gross indebtedness of the non-financial corporate sector. This increase is plainly obvious in the time-path of non-financial corporations' financial liabilities, expressed in current prices and representing end-of-year stocks. These liabilities rose quite spectacularly from a total magnitude of 25.2 billion in 1994 to over 160 billion in 2009, before the onset of the crisis led to an equally fast process of deleveraging, as a result of which financial liabilities were reduced to just under 118 billion by the end of 2013. It should be mentioned, nevertheless, that despite the rapid increase of these liabilities between 1994 and 2009, it is doubtful whether their absolute values can be considered exceptionally large, especially when compared with the respective magnitudes for other European economies (Bank of Greece 2014).

As far as the internal composition of these liabilities is concerned, long-term loans have consistently been the most important category, comprising close to or higher than half of total financial liabilities throughout the entire period examined, this fraction rising substantially in the last four years due to the corporate sector's attempts at deleveraging. Short-term loans rose from 9.8 billion in 1994 to 53.6 billion in 2008 and then declined again to 35.7 billion by the end of 2013, while securities, though they had always constituted but a small fraction of the total, have reasonably collapsed after the crisis, their total value being equal to only 2.7 billion in 2013 from 29.2 billion in 2008 (Bank of Greece 2014).

Household Consumption

The relationship between financialisation and consumption offers a plausible interpretation of the dramatic rise in private debt that is observable in many developed economies over the past few decades, while it helps explain a long-run, consumer-driven development, despite the observed reductions in labour's share in national income.

According to the most influential theories, the advance of financialisation has led to declining wage shares and, at the same time, facilitated the constant growth of private consumption, even for households in the lower income categories. A combination of new financial instruments and a socially or psychologically induced persistence of consumption patterns are often cited as contributors to this dynamic (Barba and Pivetti 2009; Cynamon and Fazzari 2008).

It is, alas, not straightforward to assess the validity of these theories as far as the Greek case is concerned. Although it is true that economic growth in Greece in the past two decades relied heavily on private consumption, and even though the Greek economy did see a dramatic proliferation of new financial instruments over the past 10–15 years, the levels of private debt are still quite low in comparison to other developed nations. It could probably be said that the process of financialisation arrived late in Greece in comparison to Northern America and Western Europe, as well as that it was abruptly interrupted by the financial crisis of 2008. If this is the case, then the data should be expected to indicate the existence of the aforementioned phenomena related to financialisation, but not their dominance.

The data concerning the distribution of households' income among its basic components, i.e. wages and salaries, net property income and current transfers, do not even indicate that. The sum of wages and current transfers never stopped constituting the bulk of households' income, its minimum contribution being equal to 79.3 per cent in 1995. The share of property income was roughly equal to one-fifth until 2001, when it started declining quite significantly. Moreover, if it is assumed that this share's elevated values in 2000–2001 are related to the stock market bubble of this relatively short-lived period, the decline in the contribution of net property income could probably be said to commence even earlier, namely from 1997 onwards. If that is correct, then this declining tendency of net property income seems to have been interrupted by the stock market mania of the following years, only to re-emerge once the bubble burst in 2000 and the economy returned to its normal path (European Commission 2014).

The national savings rate rose dramatically from 1960 until the early 1970s, reaching a maximum value of 35.7 per cent of GDP in 1973. From that point onwards, it displays a very clear declining tendency that lasted until the onset of the crisis, reaching the exceedingly low value of 4.2 per cent in 2009, before bouncing back during the crisis years surpassing again 10 per cent of GDP. As far as households' savings in particular are concerned, the diminution of the propensity to save is obvious in the data, with the exception of the period 2005–2007, which was characterised by a steep but temporary rise that caused no upward trend to re-emerge (European Commission 2014).

The decline of the savings rates after the commencement of the crisis, and especially their movement into negative territory, should probably be attributed to households' attempts either to retain, at least to the extent possible, a standard of living they had grown accustomed to or, more likely, to continue to service their debts through running down their deposits. On the other hand, the sharp decline observed for the period 1995–2002 does lend significant support to the hypotheses concerning financialisation's effect on consumption, since it probably reflects a combination of increased availability of credit and a declining share of labour in national income (Frank et al. 2010; Iacoviello 2008).

The analysis of households' financial assets shows a sharp rise in shares and other equity in the late 1990s (the period of rapid stock exchange inflation) both in absolute terms and as a percentage of households' total assets. Once the stock exchange bubble had burst, the stock of shares and other equity fell substantially (after 2001) (Eurostat 2014).

Once the global financial crisis began, stock and equity values shrank violently, falling from 108.6 billion in 2007 to only 22.7 billion in 2012. Securities other than shares followed a partly opposite pattern, in the sense that they were significantly reduced during the period of the stock market boom, but rose later on, presumably in an attempt by households to form a less risky asset portfolio. Their total stock reached a maximum of 34.8 billion in 2006, from 10.2 in 1999, before declining to nearly half that value as a result of the crisis. The data concerning households' financial assets seem to resonate with the idea expressed in the beginning of this section, namely that the process of financialisation arrived rather late in Greece and did not have the time to unfold fully due to the financial crisis of 2008. The same conclusion can be drawn from the time-path of households' financial liabilities (expressed again in stocks) and their distribution between short-term loans, long-term loans and other accounts. Short-term loans increased, in absolute terms, more than 17 times in the course of the period examined, rising from merely 1.4 billion in 1995 to 23.9 billion in 2010 (Eurostat 2014).

The rise in long-term loans has been even more dramatic, in both absolute and relative terms, since they increased no fewer than 26 times in the course of the same period, from 4.3 to 114.1 billion. From 2011 onwards stocks enter a downward path, implying negative flows of loans, which is understandable given the deep recession in the Greek economy and the capitalisation problems of domestic banking institutions.

The Current Account[9]

Financialisation is intimately linked to the developments in a macro-economy's current account, as well as in the whole gamut of its international economic relationships. These links are forged by both the liberalisation of trade flows, under floating exchange rates, and, primarily, the deregulation of international capital markets. As a result of 'freer' trade, less competitive economies find it increasingly harder to mitigate their chronic imbalances with the rest of the world.

From the point of view of surplus nations, whose oligopolistic industries enjoy a comparative advantage in key export markets, this state of affairs has enhanced their current account surpluses and the deficits of their trading partners. Under these circumstances, it is theoretically possible that the process of financialisation leads to greater regional and global imbalances, the result being a greater potential for financial instability. When crises are triggered, irrespectively of their immediate cause, they are next to impossible to contain without both short and long-term losses in social welfare.

It could be argued that this aspect of financialisation's effects in the real economy may be much more relevant for the case of the Greek economy in comparison to the aspects examined in the previous subsections. The reason is that although the direct implications of financialisation for the domestic economy came to Greece relatively late, financialisation's effect

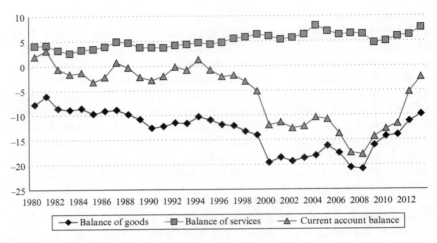

Source: European Commission (2014).

Figure 5.3   Trade balances, in per cent of GDP

on the nation's current account was large and important. One reason for this was that other developed nations, whose economies were 'usurped' by financialisation in a way that does not apply to Greece, happen to constitute Greece's most important trading partners.

As can be seen in Figure 5.3, the time-path of trade flows of the Greek economy over the last three decades demonstrates the existence of a more or less sustainable current account until the mid-1990s, exhibiting surpluses in the balance of services (mainly as a result of tourism and shipping), counterbalancing and in some years even overcoming the deficits in the balance of traded goods. Throughout the first half of the period under consideration, the current account deficit never surpassed 3.24 per cent of GDP (1985), being usually lower than 2 per cent. In the second half of the period, the current account deficit reached 3.2 per cent of GDP in 1998 and 5.1 per cent in the following year, rising precipitously to 12 per cent (or 16.4 billion euros) in 2000, as the rapid increase of deficits in the balance of goods could no longer be restrained by the surpluses in the balance of services.

As far as the years of the crisis are concerned, the data show a tendency to return to the balanced current accounts of the 1980s and early 1990s through a rising surplus in the balance of services and, mainly, a declining deficit in the balance of goods. Moreover, both developments seem to depend primarily on the declining demand for imports, although it is true that the exports of goods did rise significantly during 2009–2012 (from 20.3 to 29.9 billion euros).

The balance of goods had been in deficit throughout the entire period that is examined, but the size of these deficits changed dramatically, from 7.8 per cent in 1980 to 12.6 per cent in 1990 and finally to an incredible 19.6 per cent of GDP ten years later. How was this financed? Put simply, through capital flows from Northern Europe. Until 2010, when the demand for imports started to decline as a result of the Greek State's effective insolvency, and the deep recession that followed after the Greek State and banks lost access to international money markets, the goods deficit never fell below 16 per cent of GDP, leading to a current account deficit persistently higher than 10 per cent of GDP and, during 2007–2008, higher than 17 per cent. The huge imbalances created over the years started to be restrained only after the onset of the crisis and as a result of the austere fiscal policy which killed off demand for imports thus reducing the current account deficit to 11.8 per cent of GDP in 2011 and to merely 2.3 per cent in 2013 – its lowest value since 1997.

The countries of EU-15 constituted by far the most important destination of Greek exports before the crisis, the fraction of total exports being directed towards them being, with the exception of some years in the late 1990s, roughly equal to two-thirds. This situation seems to change quite sharply after 2009, the allocation of exports shifting in favour of extra-EU-15 destinations. It is not clear whether this shift was primarily due to the economic hardships in the rest of the EU or due to Greek corporations' attempts to expand to new markets in order to offset their losses in the domestic economy, but the fact that exports to EU-15 member states have risen back to their pre-crisis levels after 2009 suggests that the latter factor is more likely to be the dominant one.

Imports of goods from EU-15 nations amounted to a total value of €36.2 billion in 2008, but only to €22.1 billion five years later, while the decline in imports originating from third countries, though significant (from €28.7 billion to €24.6 billion), is nowhere near as marked. Therefore, the allocation of imports by category of origin also shifted in favour of extra-EU-15 countries, a development that should probably be attributed to the higher, on average, cost of goods imported from EU-15 member states.[10]

Both the intra-EU and the extra-EU balance of goods exhibit the same behaviour, with deficits rising precipitously before the crisis and being increasingly restrained ever since. However, the extra-EU-15 deficit was kept at relatively sustainable levels for another decade, before it also started to rise out of control in the last years prior to the country's participation in the monetary union.

The terrible external imbalances of the Greek economy during the period that preceded the crisis are reflected in the evolution of the real effective exchange rate of the Greek economy, calculated on the basis of

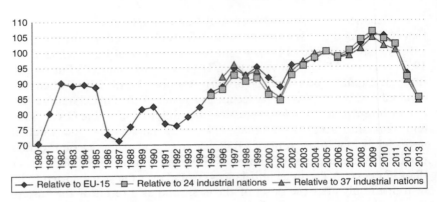

Source: European Commission (2014).

Figure 5.4   Evolution of Greek real effective exchange rates (2005=100)

unit labour costs, and expressed using 2005 as a basis year (Figure 5.4). After the fluctuations that the real exchange rate exhibits during the 1980s and the early 1990s, it follows a clear upward path, leading to a continuously reduced competitiveness of the Greek economy. This upward trend is restrained and temporarily reversed during the period 1998–2001, but reappears afterwards, severely undermining the economy's competitiveness throughout the period 2002–2009, before it is utterly reversed due to the crisis.

If, instead of the unit labour cost, Greek real effective rates are calculated on the basis of the Consumer Price Index, the general picture does not change much, although it is true that the most abrupt changes are somewhat smoothened. As far as the after-crisis period is concerned, a depreciation of the real exchange rate is also observed when CPI is used as a deflator, though it is far less dramatic. This result should probably be expected, in view of the fact that inflation remained positive, at non-negligible levels, throughout the first few years of the crisis. It was only after the deepening of the crisis and the complete collapse of domestic demand that the price level started to decline.[11]

The data seem therefore to validate the conjecture that in the field of international economic relationships, the effects of financialisation outside of Greece's borders on the evolution of the Greek real economy have been considerably stronger and more influential, as compared with the effects of the much slower financialisation happening within Greece. Moreover, the chronic lack of competitiveness and the ensuing deficits in the current account seem to provide a more appealing explanation of why the 2008 global crisis affected the Greek economy so severely. It is mainly this issue that the following section is going to delve into.

5.4   FINANCIALISATION AND THE CRISIS

The analysis presented in the previous section implies that the overall effect of financialisation on the Greek real economy has been rather uneven and in general probably small in comparison to the excesses that financialisation had led to in other European countries. However, there was one aspect of the Greek economy, i.e. the one related to the economy's current account, in the context of which the aforementioned comments do not apply.

In this context, there are three important pieces making up the puzzle of the Greek economy's collapse in the aftermath of the global financial crisis. The first refers obviously to the way in which this global crisis was transmitted to Greece, including its transformation to a public debt crisis. The second refers to the pre-existing weaknesses of the Greek economy, as a result of which the latter proved totally incapable of withstanding the pressure exerted by the crisis. And the third lies in the economic policies that were adopted in the context of the Greek adjustment programme.

Starting from the first element, the international financial crisis of 2008 was transmitted to the Greek economy through two main channels. The first operated through the domestic banking system which was adversely affected by the ensuing credit crunch and the almost total collapse of interbank financing, although it was not particularly exposed to toxic financial assets. The second operated through the fiscal deficit of the general government which, being already rather high, rose abruptly when economic growth slowed down as a result of both uncertainty and the deceleration of credit expansion.

The effect operating through the Greek banking system had a critical effect on the Greek economy through three different channels. First, it made public debt refinancing exceedingly difficult and expensive. Taking into consideration that the nation's public debt was well over 100 per cent of GDP before the outbreak of the crisis, as well as that the Greek State had been enjoying exceptionally low interest rates, it should come as no surprise that the reduced liquidity in international capital markets and the increased risk aversion of the investors led to substantial increases in the cost of debt refinancing. Secondly, even profitable Greek companies were cut off from the circuits of credit, a phenomenon that was going to be continued and reinforced in the following years. Thirdly, a similar pressure on consumer credit deprived the real economy of what had been its main engine of growth throughout the previous decade.

Concerning the nation's fiscal finances, their already precarious position was transformed to an outright derailment in 2009, when the recession automatically acted so as to expand the gap between tax revenues and public expenditure. Although it is true that the economy had been in recession since 2008, it was this derailment of the fiscal deficit of general government during the third and fourth quarters of 2009 that made abundantly clear the full implications of the crisis for the Greek economy. As a result of it, worries about the solvency of the Greek State, which had already emerged in the context of the international financial crisis and had already been reflected in a modest rise of Greek bonds' spreads in the secondary market, were both validated and reinforced, pushing the public debt further down its non-sustainable path.

This dramatic rise in the uncertainty over the country's solvency led, from the last quarter of 2009 onwards, to a rapid rise in the interest rates that the Greek State faced in the primary market, culminating eventually in the expulsion of Greece from international capital markets, while the initial freezing and subsequent reversal of the pre-crisis era capital inflows directed towards the real economy left the latter in stagnation and disarray.

Of course, the credit and liquidity crunch was a common phenomenon in Europe in 2009, and so was the rise in public deficits and the negative growth rates of real GDP. This, therefore, begs the question: Why was Greece affected so much more severely than other European states? The answer to that question must naturally be sought at the pre-existing weaknesses of the Greek economy, as a result of which Greece constituted, at the time when the crisis was triggered off, the only Euro area member state that had (a) an excessive debt to GDP ratio, (b) a large fiscal deficit and (c) a record current account deficit. Therefore, the question must be reduced to the question of the causes behind these imbalances.

The answer to that question can be found in the financial inflows in the domestic economy prior to the crisis, and specifically to the exact nature, causes and consequences of these inflows. The roots of this phenomenon are to be traced in the country's participation in the monetary union, which constituted essentially the vehicle through which financialisation arrived, or at least entered a new and more advanced phase, in the context of the Greek economy.

This was certainly the case with respect to the trade imbalances that the Greek economy exhibited, since the latter constituted initially the effect of the country's participation in a single market dominated by chronically surplus-generating nations that were typified by oligopolistic, capital intensive industries. The surpluses of the latter were always going to flood back to deficit nations like Greece, Portugal etc. causing bubbles whose bursting would, on the one hand, restrain the balance of payments deficit while, on the other, wreck, at least in the medium-term, whatever productive capacities the deficit nations possessed. Hence, while Greece's participation in the Euro area led, as we have already seen, to the derailment of the current account deficit, it also provided with the necessary capital inflows that were needed in order for this deficit to be financed.

A very important aspect of the Greek economy's development in the years preceding the crisis was that these inflows did not take the form of foreign direct investment, but rather the form of – both private and public – debt, mainly due to the peripheral nature of the Greek economy and the lack of a solid, industrial productive base, in comparison at least to Western European nations. Given the relatively low interest rates that the monetary union ensured, these inflows led to the increased indebtedness of the private sector and sustained the high deficits of the public sector, while they also led to the easy and cheap refinancing of the public debt in international capital markets.

This process constituted, however, a vicious cycle in terms of the economy's vulnerability. Despite leading to growth and prosperity, fuelled by the constant rise of domestic demand, it also implied a rising current account deficit, both due to the rise in imports demanded by indebted households and due to the inflationary effects of these inflows with respect to both wages and prices. Thus, the very process through which the economy was growing led at the same time to a continuous deterioration of its net financial position and to the rapid accumulation of fiscal deficits. Moreover, it continuously undermined the competitiveness of the Greek economy, thus making it even more difficult for it to escape this vicious cycle. As a result, when the international financial crisis broke out, the country's position was already precarious due to the large twin deficits and the excessive debt to GDP ratio.

A rather important question with respect to the argument outlined above concerns the reasons why capital flows into Greece were translated primarily to public rather than to private debt, whereas in countries like Spain and Ireland they were channelled into private, rather than public, debt. This fascinating question probably lies outside the scope of the present chapter, as it pertains to the political economics of different Euro area member states. What is important is that given the relatively moderate – despite its clear rising tendencies – indebtedness of the household sector, and the almost consistently positive financial balances of the corporate sector, the external debt-financing of the current account deficits led inescapably to higher net borrowing requirements for the general government. In the unofficial social contract that seemed to prevail in pre-crisis

Greece, the state had essentially assumed the responsibility to keep economic growth going through the accumulation of fiscal deficits, since the competitiveness of the Greek economy (which deteriorated further due to the inflationary effects of the money flows that were directed towards Greece) was too low to open up different possibilities.

The traces of the process described in the previous paragraph can easily be seen in the fact that Greece experienced a rapid economic growth period for more than a decade without managing to reduce its already high public debt and without even being able to contain the deficit within the boundaries set by the Stability and Growth Pact. With the share of private investment in GDP being consistently and significantly lower than its maximum values of the early 1980s, it should come as no surprise that, when the crisis finally broke out, fiscal finances were already on the verge of non-sustainability. One year of recession, under the circumstance, was enough to lead to a total derailment of the government's annual budget.

Finally, no account of the causes of the economic crisis in Greece can be complete without recognising the adverse role of the economic policies that were followed, as a result of which a debt crisis was transformed to an unprecedented depression. When Greece was effectively expelled from the capital markets and had to request official financial assistance in order to avoid a catastrophic default, the solution that was decided consisted of a combination of loans and a consistent policy of internal devaluation meant at eliminating both the fiscal and the current account deficit.

Although a list of the measures adopted would be too vast to be included, some brief comments on the main directions of the adopted policy should be made. Concerning public expenditure, whose ratio to GDP was comparable to the EU average before the crisis, the policies that were followed were focused on the reduction of wages in the public sector, pensions and government expenditures on health and education. Concerning taxation, they focused on increases in value added tax and other indirect taxes, on the reform of the income tax scheme leading to the adoption of higher rates, the drastic decline of the level of non-taxable income and the almost total elimination of tax allowances and deductions, as well as to the introduction of new forms of taxation of an allegedly temporary nature on both households and corporations. Finally, as far as structural reforms are concerned, they were centred around the opening up of formerly regulated professions, on the reform of labour relations leading to the substantial decline of wages in the private sector, on the reform of the social insurance legislative framework, and on an extended privatisation policy that has failed, nevertheless, to arouse much interest.

These policies led, quite naturally, to a deep recession, implying not only the necessity of further austerity measures in order for the Greek State to achieve the rather optimistic deficit reduction targets that had been set, but also the continuous implementation of several different forms of debt restructuring meant to ensure the public debt's sustainability, or rather to contain to the extent possible its obviously non-sustainable development. These forms of restructuring ranged from the rather innocuous, like interest rate reductions in the official sector's loans or the introduction of grace periods for their repayment, to the really drastic ones that implied an actual diminution in the nominal value of public debt securities, like the enforced scheme of debt buyback and, mainly, the PSI (Private Sector Involvement), which led to a higher than 50 per cent diminution of the face value of the greatest fraction of Greek debt that was still in the hands of the private sector.

Hence, not only was the default finally not avoided, but the adjustment programme that Greece was obliged to follow achieved deficit reduction only by bringing about a triple insolvency (of the state, the banks and the non-financial business sector). The debt to GDP ratio, which is currently over 170 per cent[12] despite the aforementioned restructurings, the huge financing problems faced by, even otherwise competitive, Greek corporations and the excessive cost of the banking sector recapitalisation scheme that is estimated at just below €40 billion, constitute rather clear indications of this.

And although the current account deficit has fallen to seemingly sustainable levels, its eradication is a purely Pyrrhic victory. As the structure of the Greek economy remained untouched during Greece's troubled times, any future pick up in aggregate demand will restore, together with GDP, the current account deficit. Despite the improvement of the country's competitiveness, in terms of unit labour costs, the continuing credit crunch facing potentially efficient and productive firms means that structural productivity will remain in the doldrums throughout the Greek economy, with the possible exception of tourism.

Judging therefore from the results to which the implementation of the adjustment programme has led, it can be concluded that the absence of any corrective mechanisms within Europe's monetary union left Greece with a stark choice between an early default and the adoption of the programme funded by the official lenders. The 'official version', according to which Greece was meant to rebound on the basis of internal devaluation, had always been a red herring, in the sense that such a form of devaluation, even if implemented, offers no possibility of avoiding serial defaults on external, private and public, debts (which, unlike prices and wages, stubbornly refuse to shrink during phases of internal devaluation). What actually happened, on the contrary, was that the Greek economy was forced to enter a debt-deflationary cycle, whereby efforts towards the attainment of debt sustainability are continuously frustrated by the considerable GDP reductions caused by these very efforts. And while these deflationary tendencies did not appear, with respect to the price level at least, in the early stages of the implementation of the adjustment programme due to the increased indirect taxation and the effect of prices of imported raw materials, their presence has started to be felt during the last two years, both in the real economy and in the CPI statistics.

5.5   CONCLUSIONS

In the context of the present essay, an attempt has been made to account for the influence that financialisation exerted upon the Greek economy throughout the last decades and to inquire into the links, if any, between this process and the current financial and economic crisis, both in general, and in connection to the extremely harsh form that this crisis has taken in the case of Greece.

The results that have been presented seem to suggest that the overall effect of globalisation on the real economy of Greece, though certainly existent, should be considered rather small, especially when compared to the historical experience of most Western European nations. However, there is one field, i.e. the evolution of the Greek current account and of international economic relations in general, in which these effects were considerable, to the extent that it would not be an exaggeration to say that they actually determined, to a great degree at least, both the course of the Greek economy prior to the recent crisis and the immense vulnerability of this economy when the crisis finally hit.

To sum up the argument of the previous sections, Greece did not experience financialisation like other developed countries did. Greece experienced financialisation via the European Monetary Union that it chose to enter into back in 2000. Thus a chronically deficit nation, with a weak and fragile state apparatus, entered into a monetary union that removed Greece's internal shock absorbers while guaranteeing that the impending shock, when it hit, would be impossible for the meek Greek economy to sustain. At that time, as Greece's macro-economy began to unravel, the same wizards who had designed the instruments of private sector financialisation were gainfully employed by the EU to design the public financial instruments that would allow the Greek government to 'extend and pretend'; to claim that default was avoided through gigantic loans to a deeply insolvent state on condition of fiscal austerity that reduced the nominal national income by one-third from which old and new loans would have to be repaid.

NOTES

1. All data used in this chapter have been obtained from the European Commission (2014), from the Hellenic Statistical Authority (2014) and from the Bank of Greece (2014).
2. According to this taxonomy, the possible types of long-run development consist of the categories of a debt-led consumption boom, of a domestic demand-led development, of a weak export-led development and of an export-led mercantilist development, while the inclusion of an economy in one or the other category depends on the sign of the main sectors' financial balances and of its current account, as well as on the relative growth contributions of the several components of demand.
3. The data on the main sectors' balances are obtained from the Hellenic Statistical Authority's non-financial accounts of the main sectors. This source was chosen over AMECO, since in the latter case no distinction is made between the financial and the non-financial corporate sector, while the Eurostat database contains no available data for the Greek economy.
4. This is true both when the magnitude of households' liabilities is compared with GDP and when it is compared with deposits. Some data concerning the total indebtedness of Greek households are provided in Section 5.3.
5. The share of wages is adjusted so as to reflect solely the changes in relative incomes and not the changing composition between employees and self-employed individuals.
6. For instance, Hein and Schoder (2011) examine the effect of rising long-term real interest rates on income distribution in Germany and the US, while in the studies by Kristal (2010) and Stockhammer (2009) variables related to the process of financialisation are included in the estimated equations' right-hand sides for a set of 16 and 15 industrial economies respectively, the Greek economy being excluded in both cases. Finally, the study by Tomaskovic-Devey and Lin (2011) examines the effect on income distribution of the increased dependence on earnings through financial channels, where the ratio of financial receipts over business receipts is used as the measure of this dependence.
7. The rise in general government's share, mainly at the expense of the household sector, during the crisis years should probably be attributed to the austerity policy adopted in the country's attempt to reduce its fiscal deficit.
8. According to the Hellenic Statistical Authority, data for the periods 2000–2004 and 2005–2013 are not comparable due to the revision of the basis year of annual national accounts that took place in 2011. This weakness of the available data is also relevant for the data that will be presented in the next subsection.
9. All data referred to in the present section are drawn from the AMECO database.
10. More precisely, this development should be attributed to the fact that products imported from EU-15 member states are probably characterised by a greater participation of luxury goods, or goods that would be considered as luxurious in the context of a catastrophic depression. The drastic fall in the market for automobiles, which are, by and large, imported by Western European nations, may provide an apt example.
11. This phenomenon provides a partial explanation of the inability of the internal devaluation policies that were followed after the crisis to lead to a substantial improvement of the Greek economy's export performance. However, this logic should not be over-stressed. On the one hand, because this rather mediocre performance is to some extent the natural outcome of the structure of the Greek economy, i.e. of the prevalence of small and too small enterprises characterised by an insufficient division of labour in their interior, as well as by an almost total lack of access to international trade and distribution channels. On the other hand, because the CPI has actually been declining during the last two years, without leading to an acceleration of Greek exports. Some further comments on the causes of Greek exports' poor performance in relation to the policies that have been adopted since the outbreak of the crisis can be found in Section 5.4.
12. According to the draft of the 2016 Budget, the gross debt of general government reached 177.1 per cent of GDP in 2014, while it is estimated at 181.8 per cent for 2015 and at 192.4 per cent for 2016.

REFERENCES

Bank of Greece (2014), Statistical database, available at: http://www.bankofgreece.
gr/Pages/en/Statistics/default.aspx.

Barba, A. and M. Pivetti (2009), 'Rising household debt: its causes and macro-economic implications – a long-period analysis', *Cambridge Journal of Economics*, **33** (1), 113–137.

Corbett, J. and T. Jenkinson (1997), 'How is investment financed? A study of Germany, Japan, the United Kingdom and the United States', *Manchester School*, **65** (S), 69–93.

Cynamon, B. and S. Fazzari (2008), 'Household debt in the consumer age: source of growth – risk of collapse', *Capitalism and Society*, **3** (2), 1–30.

Duenhaupt, P. (2012), 'Financialisation and the rentier income share – evidence from the USA and Germany', *International Review of Applied Economics*, **26** (4), 465–487.

European Commission (2014), AMECO Database, available at: http://ec.europa.
eu/economy_finance/db_indicators/ameco/index_en.htm.

Eurostat (2014), Statistical database, available at: http://ec.europa.eu/eurostat/data/
database.

Frank, R. H., A. S. Levine and O. Dijk (2010), 'Expenditure cascades', SSRN paper, available at: http://papers.ssrn.com/sol3/Delivery.cfm/SSRN_ID1690612_
code1553888.pdf?abstractid=1690612&mirid=1.

Hein, E. (2010), 'A Keynesian perspective on financialisation', in P. Arestis and M. Sawyer (eds), *21st Century Keynesian Economics, International Papers in Political Economy*, Basingstoke, UK: Palgrave Macmillan.

Hein, E. (2012), *The Macroeconomics of Finance-dominated Capitalism – and its Crisis*, Cheltenham, UK and Northampton, MA, USA: Edward Elgar Publishing.

Hein, E. and C. Schoder (2011), 'Interest rates, distribution and capital accumulation – a post-Kaleckian perspective on the US and Germany', *International Review of Applied Economics*, **25** (6), 693–723.

Hein, E. and T. van Treeck (2010), 'Financialisation in post-Keynesian models of distribution and growth – a systematic review', in M. Setterfield (ed.), *Handbook of Alternative Theories of Economic Growth*, Cheltenham, UK and Northampton, MA, USA: Edward Elgar Publishing.

Hellenic Statistical Authority (2014), Statistical database, available at: http://www.
statistics.gr/el/home/.

Iacoviello, M. (2008), 'Household debt and income inequality, 1963–2003', *Journal of Money, Credit and Banking*, **40** (5), 929–965.

Kristal, T. (2010), 'Good times bad times. Postwar labour share of national income in capitalist democracies', *American Sociological Review*, **75** (5), 729–763.

Stockhammer, E. (2009), 'Determinants of income distribution in OECD countries', IMK Studies 5/2009, Düsseldorf: Macroeconomic Policy Institute (IMK) at Hans Boeckler Foundation.

Tomaskovic-Devey, D. and K. H. Lin (2011), 'Financialisation and US income inequality, 1970–2008', SSRN paper, available at: http://papers.ssrn.com/sol3/
Delivery.cfm/SSRN_ID1954129_code1214661.pdf?abstractid=1954129&mir
id=1.

6. The real sector developments in Estonia: financialisation effects behind the transition process

Egert Juuse

6.1 INTRODUCTION – ESTONIA'S ECONOMIC DEVELOPMENT MODEL SINCE 1991

After regaining independence in 1991, Estonia undertook major economic reforms in order to reinstate institutions necessary for a functioning market economy, some of them being introduced only by the turn of the millennium. More importantly, given the population of 1.29 million, all reforms and institutional arrangements should be seen in the context of a very small country. Also, in contrast to advanced economies with a long capitalist tradition, the legacy of socialism provided a quite different starting point, and influenced the following evolution of capitalist production in Estonia (Myant and Drahokoupil 2011, pp. 299–302; Lane 2007, pp. 13–15). So, it was both institutional and historical-cultural characteristics that yielded a particular result in Estonia, implying a rather peculiar transition process towards a market economy, compared with advanced Western economies and even other Central and Eastern European countries (CEECs). Namely, distinctive institutional approaches such as a *strategic investor* privatisation strategy, neo-liberal radicalism in market reforms, and nationalistic sentiments in socio-economic affairs created path dependencies in the Estonian transformation process (Tridico 2011; Lane and Myant 2007; Knell and Srholec 2007). As it was punctuated by major crises, the period of 1993–1998 saw critical junctures at which key decisions on the shape of the post-socialist regime were taken. However, given the non-presence or immaturity of capitalist institutions and developments, a limited time-range for a full development of economic structures, and inadequate data[1] on some of the issues, it is not such a straightforward matter to undertake an analysis of the Estonian case. The following study endeavours to bring out the peculiarities of the pattern of financialisation in Estonia, with its implications for economic stability and general macroeconomic dynamics, that is, the nature and pattern of income distribution, investment financing and household consumption.

Compared with Western economies, one of the unusual characteristics of Estonia has been the high level of externally financed capital accumulation, through the reliance on foreign direct investments (FDI) and other external funds since the early 1990s.[2] In Estonia, FDI was seen as a supplement to internal resources for financing the growth and restructuring of the economy (Bank of Estonia 1995). A rapid liberalisation of trade and capital flows was the reflection of the neo-liberal political stance of the government(s), which emulated *Washington Consensus* and European Union (EU) policies when constructing the country's institutional framework. Accordingly, Estonia has not relied on intensive intervention into the economy or used any foreign investment management policies beyond macroeconomic reforms oriented towards price stability, balanced public budgets and low taxes (Tiits et al. 2008; OECD 2000a; Thorhallsson and Kattel 2013; Raudla and Kattel 2011). Given such an approach and the perception of Estonia as a potential satellite hub, Swedish and Finnish investors acquired privatised companies in Estonia, but also undertook green-field investments due to the relatively skilled and cheap labour force, while the geographical closeness and cultural ties with Estonia created additional incentives to relocate production to Estonia (Ehrlich et al. 2002; Madureira et al. 2007; EBRD 1994; European Commission 2010; Jevcák et al. 2010). Hence, supported by the liberalisation of the financial system and delegation of powers to foreign actors, the deepening internationalisation of the Estonian economy has had a major impact on the form of capitalist production and ramifications for macroeconomic stability.

Despite an annual real growth rate of 8.7 per cent in 2000–2007, the business models of multinational companies, in both the financial and non-financial sectors, have caused several weaknesses in the productive system. The weakening of the industrial base, affected by the inability of manufacturing industry to withstand intensifying foreign competition (Reinert and Kattel 2007), was worsened further by the decisions of foreign companies to relocate primarily low value added labour-intensive stages of production to Estonia with little spillover effects to the local economy (Drechsler et al. 2006, p. 20). By taking advantage of low labour costs and taxes without notable wider positive effects on the whole economy, foreign-owned companies have entailed the *enclavisation* of a significant part of the industrial sectors by rendering the acquired businesses in Estonia into simple extensions of multinational companies (Reiljan 2006, p. 256; Gallagher and Zarsky 2007 on the concept of enclave economies). The implications have been asymmetrical intra-industry trade relations in the manufacturing sector – Estonia specialising in resource- and labour-intensive activities for subcontracting exports, while Scandinavian countries keep the knowledge- and technology-intensive activities (Tiits et al. 2008; OECD 2000b; Varblane and Ziacik 1999; Ehrlich et al. 2002). Essentially, heavy dependence on FDI has entailed de-linking processes and rendered the Estonian economy into a *satellite-platform* (see Markusen 1999, pp. 21–41 for description of the concept) that reinforces the reliance on external technical expertise and funding, as well as services, but subdues demand for bank-based financing of businesses (Kattel 2010, p. 54). In these circumstances, banks that were acquired by foreign financial institutions gradually shifted their credit policy focus towards households. This is reflected in the main demand aggregates contributing to economic growth (see Figure 6.1 and Section 6.4 in detail).

The consequence of these developments has been a dual structure of the economy. On the one hand, industries in Estonia are led by large and medium-sized companies that in general belong to foreign owners, with the advantage of access to foreign credit and know-how, and which do not depend on local demand conditions due to their focus on export markets. Locally owned micro- and small enterprises, on the other hand, which predominantly operate in the services sector, target the volatile local market and rely on both internal funds and loans from domestic banks (Kangur et al. 1999, pp. 17–20; Mickiewicz et al. 2006, p. 78; Kaarna et al. 2012, pp. 15–16). More importantly, industry leaders have outperformed small enterprises in terms of turnover per employee, creditworthiness and profitability indicators due to economies of scale, which arise from large-scale production and export sales (Golebiowski 2007, p. 26; Männik et al. 2006, p. 283; Varblane and Ziacik 1999).

Thus, the miracle of Estonia's growth has been achieved on the basis of extensive use of foreign savings, as domestic savings have not been sufficient to cover persistently high investment and consumption demand from the 1990s onwards (OECD 2000b; Bank of Estonia 2006a). The financialisation process reveals itself in the reliance on foreign capital in both financial and non-financial sectors (see Figure 6.2) that underpinned rapid but unsustainable economic growth with the culmination of economic crisis in 2007/08. The challenge today is to discontinue this path, set in the economic structure in the 1990s.

As evident in Figures 6.1 and 6.2 below, one can observe a gradual emergence of the *debt-led private demand boom* structure in Estonia's long-term development pattern (Hein 2012; Dodig et al. 2016), where aside from the non-financial corporate sector, debt accumulation occurred rapidly in the household sector (see Section 6.4). Claims of the rest of the world against Estonia steadily increased until 2007. Those were the natural counterparts of the widening current account deficits Estonia ran since 1994, which only

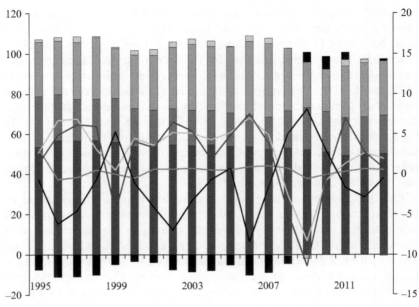

* does not include statistical discrepancy

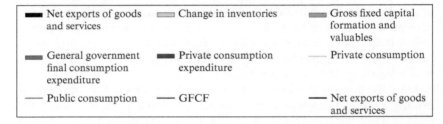

Source: Statistics Estonia (2014).

*Figure 6.1   Contribution to the increase of GDP at constant prices (lines;
              right axis) and share* in GDP in current prices (bars; left
              axis) in Estonia, 1995–2013*

reversed with the crisis in 2009. Despite the continuing trade surpluses, the
current account turned negative again in 2012, revealing the vulnerability
of the economy to increasing investment-related income outflows due to a
development strategy built around the reliance on foreign investments-led
growth (see Figure 6.2).

Thus, financialisation in Estonia has taken a rather different manifestation, characterised by a heavy reliance on foreign savings in financing

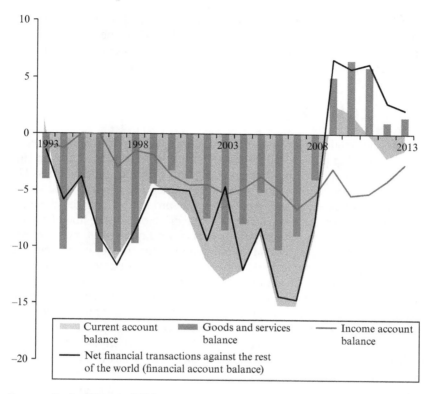

Source: Bank of Estonia (2014).

Figure 6.2 *Net financial transactions against the rest of the world and
balance of goods and services as well as current account
(% of GDP) in Estonia, 1993–2013*

economic growth. In this regard, the FDI-led catching-up process directly
relates to all three studied variables of the Estonian real sector, but also
to the current account dynamics. Moreover, when considering the long-
term effects of financialisation on the real sector variables, one has to
bear in mind that the period in which Estonia has had a market economy
has been very short – around 20 years. In broad terms, Estonia could be
classified as a neo-liberal *peripheral market economy* with structural weaknesses, particularly in the export structure, and reliance on financialised
development that essentially has meant dependence on foreign borrowing
and other financial inflows to cover current account deficits. As Kregel
(2004) has shown, such a development strategy, where imports are paid

for with foreign borrowing is inherently unstable, as it requires that the rate of increase of new capital inflows is larger than the rate of interest on these flows; if that is not the case, the strategy becomes automatically self-reversing.

6.2   INCOME DISTRIBUTION

The developments in the Estonian economy can be portrayed by seemingly conflicting tendencies, evidenced in the rapid economic growth that has been accompanied by deepening regional and social inequalities. The last two decades have revealed social inequalities and a marginalisation of weaker members of society as a natural byproduct of market economy reforms (Lauristin 2011). Adherence to the principles of the liberal market economy, manifest in relatively low social expenditures, weak union movement, low minimum wages and low de-commodification levels, contributed to relatively high income inequality in Estonia (Aidukaite 2011; OECD 2003). Income disparities in the early 2000s were such that the poorest 40 per cent of the population received 20 per cent of total income, while the richest 20 per cent acquired around 40 per cent of the total income. This is further reflected in the average 0.356 Gini coefficient for the 1996–2002 period, but also other analytical indicators such as quintiles' ratios, which indicated Estonia's income inequality in the 1990s to be one of the worst in Europe (Paulus 2003; Kokkota 2000).

However, the general trend has been towards a reduction in income inequality, both when looking at the Gini coefficient (0.313 in 2009), the ratios of income deciles' top cut-off points, or the ratios of average disposable income per household member within deciles. For example, the D10/D1 average disposable income ratio dropped from 13.1 in 1995 to 8.4 in 2009 (author's calculations based on Eurostat 2014 and Statistics Estonia 2014). Despite the improving tendencies in income inequality, one has to bear in mind large initial disparities, which can be attributed to socio-economic turbulences at the beginning of the transition process. Aside from general income inequality, one of the most pressing issues over the years has been gender inequality, as on average the difference in wages between men and women has stood at around 31 per cent, the highest in Europe (Anspal and Rõõm 2011; Nurmela and Karu 2009). In addition, regional disparities exist, such that the average salaries of the capital city region is almost 1.5 times that of the periphery (Anspal and Rõõm 2011; Statistics Estonia 2014).

We can see the development of functional income distribution, by looking at the shares of total employee compensation in Figure 6.3. Even

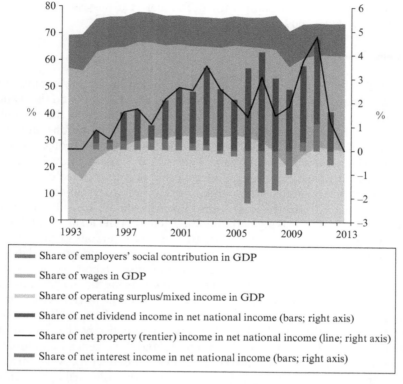

Note: Rentier income is calculated as net property income – interest and dividends – of private households.

Source: Statistics Estonia (2014); OECD Statistics (2014); author's calculations.

Figure 6.3 *Functional income distribution (without net taxes on production and consumption of fixed capital) and rentier income in Estonia, 1995–2013*

though Dünhaupt (2013, pp. 2–3) found that the labour share fluctuates with the business cycle and has been in a general downward trend in advanced economies, in Estonia one can see a decreasing share of wages in the 1990s and then a relative stability of the wage share in total income since 2000. At the same time, the rentier income share in net national income has increased from 0.8 per cent in 1995 to 4.8 per cent in 2011, although with significant drops during the boom years of 2003–2006 that were mostly due to increased servicing of interest liabilities. Net dividend incomes have grown steadily with occasional year-on-year declines (in 1996, 1999, 2005, 2009 and 2012).

Labour Unions

The following sections will look into the potential factors behind the income inequality, in particular, unionisation, privatisation, and fiscal and monetary policy. It is found that the wage share is affected by the bargaining power of labour, which is usually shaped by trade unions' density, unemployment benefit replacement rates, and employment protection legislation (Dünhaupt 2013, p. 18; Stockhammer 2009, p. 14). In the Estonian case, these three last-mentioned dimensions have been affected by the prevailing neo-liberal model with non-corporatist and national-conservative attitudes that is reflected in the government's limited consultation and consensus decision-making with domestic actors in the formation of economic policies. Accordingly, the position of labour unions in the private sector has been weak. While almost all employees belonged to labour unions in the early 1990s, the share of unionised labourers decreased throughout the next two decades. One of the reasons for the small influence of labour unions is their bad reputation from the Soviet period, and the dominance of micro- and small enterprises in Estonia (Hinnosaar 2003, p. 9). By the late 2000s, unionisation and collective bargaining in the Estonian private sector covered only 12 and 9 per cent of employees, respectively (Dabušinskas and Rõõm 2011). Consequently, wage formation takes place mostly at the company level with individual agreements, although some sectoral level minimum wage agreements exist, e.g. in health care and road transportation (Nurmela and Karu 2009). Similarly, employment protection legislation has been liberalised throughout the years in terms of notification procedures and compensation mechanisms (Hinnosaar 2003, p. 22). After a labour market reform in 2009, which made legislation more flexible and considerably lowered layoff costs for employers, Estonian labour regulation was the least strict in Europe (Dabušinskas and Rõõm 2011, p. 60).

Privatisation, Technological Change and FDI

Aside from decreasing workers' bargaining power, the mass privatisation in Estonia in the 1990s could also explain the reduction in the labour income share. In addition, one has to bear in mind idiosyncratic elements in the transition process, e.g. the downsizing part of the *downsize and distribute* approach could be seen as a result of technological and organisational innovations that were envisaged to reduce over manning, typical in socialist economies, and to introduce new labour-saving technologies (Tiits et al. 2006, p. 61).

The impact of technological change on functional income distribution, as argued by the mainstream literature (IMF 2007; European Commission 2007), could be seen in the Estonian case in the developments of the 1990s, but not in a sense of becoming capital augmenting but of a radical restructuring of the economy that was largely FDI-driven and entailed the destruction of existing productive capacities. In other words, the *primitivisation* of the productive base and the reliance on cheap labour as a competitive factor necessitated continuous cost squeezing to keep foreign investors in Estonia, which constrained income growth (Tiits et al. 2006, p. 57). In addition, FDI-companies have entered the Estonian market in relatively resource-intensive and low-tech industries such as food and wood processing, textile and clothing (Tiits 2006, p. 109), which in the long-run do not entail possibilities for increasing returns and hence higher wages. Interestingly, these changes affected incomes of workers with vocational training favourably, whereas increasing supply of those with higher education pushed wages for this type of workers downwards, and therefore income inequalities based on educational background diminished throughout the period of 1997–2006, which is opposite to global trends (Rõõm 2007).

It is also noteworthy that the relatively highly concentrated ownership structure in individual firms together with low turnover of shares has had implications for income distribution. The concentration of ownership started already with the first rounds of privatisation, when in addition to the control of strategic foreign investors, small companies in services, catering and retail were gradually taken over by managers. In light of a relatively poor protection of minority shareholders, the concentration of ownership has increased: the largest owners in Estonia having a stake of over 60 per cent and the second largest more than 20 per cent on average (Pajuste and Olsson 2001; Gerndorf et al. 1999), implying an inequality in capital ownership and wealth concentration to a great extent. The importance of corporate control of local companies is revealed in the preference for external common equity from existing shareholders or target capital providers, as opposed to bonds or other forms of incorporation of external investors (Raudsepp et al. 2003, pp. 61–67; Kaarna et al. 2012, p. 52).

Fiscal and Monetary Policies

Incomes have been also affected by fiscal policies, mostly through different taxation of capital and labour. Contrary to other EU countries, Estonia has opted for a flat tax system, based on the principle of proportional and uniform tax rates – the tax reform in 1994 introduced a flat 26 per cent[3] tax rate for both personal and corporate income tax, while from 2000 undistributed profits have been exempted from corporate income tax. Hence, due to the regressive character of flat taxes, a larger portion of income is taken from those with lower incomes. In addition, the amount of basic exemption deductible from the income is relatively low (154 euros per month in 2015), while social security contributions including unemployment insurance premiums are one of the highest in Europe (Ruusalu 2014). In general, labour and consumption taxes have a dominating share in tax revenues with 50.8 per cent and 41.3 per cent, respectively, while the corporate income tax level has been one of the lowest in Europe – with an average implicit tax rate of 5.8 per cent in 2000–2007 and with a share of tax revenues on capital in total tax revenues of 7.9 per cent in 2007 (Võrk and Kaarna 2010).

Moreover, during the crisis years of 2008 and 2009, increases in value added tax and excise taxes hit the poorest segments of the population hardest (ibid.). This reveals the aim of the Estonian tax policies, namely to support entrepreneurship, while no attention has been paid to either vertical or horizontal fairness of the taxes. Propagated flexibility in the labour market has also been a precondition for the operation of a currency board arrangement that has implied a reliance on internal devaluation as an adjustment mechanism and approach to improve international competitiveness (Hinnosaar 2003, p. 3). In light of these developments, governments have adhered to mainstream arguments by relying on the reduction of benefits and taxation as well as improving the flexibility of the labour market (Tiits et al. 2006, p. 51).

In conclusion, it can be said that given the large income disparities at the starting point, income inequality has decreased throughout the years, partly due to changes in the labour market and the structure of the economy. Nonetheless, the problem is still present today, although with a more narrow focus on topics such as gender and regional inequality. Similarly, the share of wages in functional income distribution fell significantly in the 1990s, but stabilised in the 2000s. One of the reasons behind the initial high income inequality and declining wages share was massive privatisation that targeted strategic investors, which explains high ownership concentration in Estonia. In addition, the deteriorating position of employees has been affected by weak labour unions, increasing flexibility in labour market legislation, and basically non-existent collective bargaining systems in the private sector, but also by the reliance on FDI, implying a cost-based competitive advantage of the economy. Finally, incomes have been affected by different taxation of capital and labour, but also by the currency board arrangement, which pressured wages further. Therefore, persistent social inequalities and the overall decline in the wage share have been related to the introduction of market economy institutions, market reforms, the restructuring of the economy and the elimination of over-manning. Similarly, decisions on dividend payments have been driven by other motives than financialisation, as dividend payments increased only in the 2000s, once businesses had matured and surpassed the development and growth phases. Also, dividend and interest payments have fluctuated according to the business cycles in Estonia, with an increasing trend of dividend and interest payments during the 1996–97 and 2005–07 economic boom periods. It is also noteworthy that Estonian businesses have prac-tised the remuneration of top management with dividends, rather than wages or stock options, due to lower taxation level of capital income.

6.3   CAPITAL STOCK INVESTMENTS

In the analysis of patterns in capital stock investments and their financing in Estonia, it is necessary to acknowledge the context and peculiarities of the Estonian development. The research approach to the Anglo-American type of corporate governance that focuses on stock ownership issues is not exactly applicable in a situation where the ownership structure has been in rapid transition. At the same time, market institutions and the whole busi-ness environment do not operate in the same way as in advanced market economies, or began to operate in this way only lately (Tafel et al. 2006). Several of the phenomena often associated with financialisation such as the proliferation of new financial instruments, the rise of financial invest-ment and income, but also the increase in shareholder value orientation and the transfer of earnings from non-financial corporations to financial markets (see Orhangazi 2008; Stockhammer 2004) are non-present or have only recently emerged in Estonia. Even if detectable, the reasons behind the emergence of these manifestations of financialisation have been differ-ent, compared with the ones in advanced market economies. For instance, the *downsize and distribute* approach was an integral part of the privatisa-tion waves during the transition process in the 1990s. This was reflected in the squeezing of labour costs to attract foreign investors, and the destruc-tion of existing productive capital to get rid of the Soviet-time production complexes, which incurred distribution of assets and massive sales.

Similarly, literature has related the spread of the shareholder value approach to the emergence of institutional investors (Orhangazi 2008; Crotty 2002, p. 23). In the Estonian case, however, domestic institutional investors such as investment funds, insurance and pension funds have played an insignificant role on the local market because they mainly invest abroad.[4] Moreover, since shareholder value orientation and changes in corporate governance refer to listed companies, that is, large corporations (Stockhammer 2004, pp. 728–729), Estonia is again an outlier in terms of having only a few public limited companies that are listed on the stock market – 15 in total as of 2014 – which explains a modest role of foreign institutional investors as well. Also, hostile takeovers with junk bonds or stock options in the pay structure of managers, associated with the *shareholder revolution* (Lazonick and O'Sullivan 2000), have not been characteristic features of the Estonian business landscape. Rather, what is typical in Estonia is the dominance of owner controlled and managed small enterprises (SMEs[5]), *core owners* and active involvement of foreign investors (Alas et al. 2010, p. 39; Juhkam 2000), which indicates a different financing pattern of Estonian firms, compared to conventional corporations (Raudsepp et al. 2003, pp. 58–59). Furthermore, contemporary professional managers emerged in the Estonian business organisations around 2000 or slightly earlier (Kooskora 2008, p. 203; Alas et al. 2010, pp. 30–35). As a result, the manager-shareholder dichotomy as found in the financialisation literature has not been on the agenda from the domestic capital's point of view. On the other hand, substantial presence of FDI-companies and the central role of foreign investors in the Estonian stock market[6] have had implications for corporate governance, which has been adapted to the strategies of foreign (Nordic) owners (Juhkam 2000). The enormous importance of foreign funds could be seen in the dynamics of the primary income balance of the current account that shows negative net investment income flows of the magnitude of 5 to 8 per cent of GDP between 2003 and 2013 (see e.g. Figure 6.2).

Investment Financing in Estonia

As Estonian businesses gained improved access to foreign capital, accompanied by a high level of FDI inflows in the 1990s (Randveer 2000, p. 13), both foreign capital inflows and internal funds from accumulated profits increased the ability to finance investments. Between 1994 and 1998, reinvested profits of Estonian businesses accounted for 49 per cent of all funds used for capital investments (Kangur et al. 1999). In general, the preferred source of financing of Estonian enterprises has been internal equity capital, while external funds such as bank loans or funds from intra-group foreign parent companies have been used in case of dire necessity or when internal resources were insufficient (Kõomägi and Sander 2006; Sander and Kõomägi 2007; Raudsepp et al. 2003, pp. 61–67). For instance, between 1996 and 1999, the average leverage ratio of the Estonian non-financial corporations stood at 1.12 as one of the lowest in CEECs and the share of long-term liabilities was also one of the lowest in international comparison, while almost half of short-term liabilities were inter-enterprise arrears (Randveer 2000, pp. 4–5). Nonetheless, the net financial position of enterprises has become more negative over time. This is partly due to the increasing reliance on bank financing that was used for real estate purchases before the 2008 crisis (Juks 2004, p. 17; Bank of Estonia 2010a). All in all, the shares and other equity category that saw a gross growth from 2.3 to 25.3 billion euros and loans that increased from 0.8 to 17.5 billion euros from 1995 to 2008 have made the most significant contributions to changes in the structure of financial liabilities (OECD Statistics 2014).

Table 6.1 indicates a negative correlation between internal finance and bank lending, but also the increasing contribution of internal funds during the low investment period, while low investment is linked with the low use of external funding. Aside from dynamics in investment demand, the financing patterns in Estonia have been significantly affected by tax policies. The corporate income tax reform in 2000 that lowered the income tax on reinvested profits to zero[7] supported the reliance on internal funds further (Sander 2003). Concerning the effects of the tax reform, one can observe an increase in investment volumes and reinvested profits, in particular, in case of small businesses (Kuusk and Jürgenson 2010; Kaarna et al. 2012). Similarly, Hazak (2009) has found that the tax reform decreased dividend payouts, but also the utilisation of external financing (loans), while liquid assets and the share of retained earnings in total assets have been found to increase (see also Masso et al. 2011). For instance, accumulated retained earnings of the non-financial corporate sector increased from 7 per cent of GDP in 2000 to 113.5 per cent of GDP in 2009 (author's calculations based on the Statistics Estonia 2014). Hence, the availability of internal resources, that is, increased deposits and high excess capacities, has thwarted credit demand in the non-financial sector, even though slower growth in profits after the crisis and the need to finance current expenses with accumulated financial assets curtailed internal buffers.

With regard to bank loans, these were discouraged for a long time by macroeconomic volatility, high interest rates, insufficient collateral, the lack of credit histories of enterprises, and inadequate accounting standards. Bank lending got an impetus only in the 2000s in light of a thriving real estate market – the share of loans granted to commercial real estate companies has been the largest, accounting for almost 40 per cent in the banks' corporate loan portfolio at the peak of the boom in 2006. It is also interesting that since joining the EU in 2004, the growing volume of EU structural funds[8] has induced the demand for bridge financing, that is, bank loans for required self-financed contribution of subsidised investment projects. The main issue with bank lending, however, has been the

Table 6.1   Net sources of finance and gross fixed capital formation in Estonia, 1995–2012 (percentages)

	1995	1996	1997	1998	1999	2000	2001	2002	2003	2004	2005	2006	2007	2008	2009	2010	2011	2012
Internal (net savings + consumption of fixed capital)	65.6	58.5	50.2	63.1	85.4	85.9	68.9	66.9	49.6	69.5	87.5	71.4	56.5	67.3	104.2	113.7	50.6	71.6
Bank (loan) financing (loan liabilities – loan assets – currency and deposits)	14.4	25.4	17.6	40.5	–7.5	17.8	20.2	17.7	20.3	20.9	5.3	25.5	28.5	13.0	–14.0	–50.1	7.1	0.5
Bonds (net securities other than shares, except financial derivatives)	–0.2	3.9	12.5	–15.2	5.0	1.7	2.1	15.3	0.2	1.0	4.3	0.8	4.2	–5.9	0.1	2.2	5.0	4.5
New equity (net shares and other equity, except mutual funds shares)	27.6	13.6	29.0	6.3	10.0	4.4	9.4	6.2	21.6	3.4	4.2	–1.2	2.5	4.6	–20.5	19.7	5.6	0.8
Trade credit	0.7	–4.1	3.0	9.8	–1.2	–7.8	6.0	–2.6	4.9	3.4	–0.8	2.2	2.6	8.8	16.3	–6.8	18.8	15.1
Capital transfers	3.0	1.9	2.5	3.3	2.7	1.3	0.9	1.8	1.8	5.4	2.6	4.2	3.7	7.1	17.3	14.0	6.2	8.6
Other	–11.1	0.9	–14.8	–7.9	5.6	–3.3	–7.4	–5.3	1.6	–3.5	–3.1	–2.8	1.9	5.1	–3.4	7.1	6.8	–1.1
Physical investments (gross fixed capital formation) as % of GDP	17.1	17.1	18.8	21.3	16.7	18.5	18.4	20.0	22.3	21.5	21.3	22.0	22.0	19.1	11.9	10.9	15.0	15.0

Source: OECD Statistics 2014, author's calculations.

priority given to the banks' home-country customers, as the inflow of foreign capital into the non-financial sector was one of the reasons for Scandinavian banking groups to enter the Estonian market (De Haas and Naaborg 2006).

All in all, the financing of capital investments in the Estonian businesses has mostly relied on internal funds and has been accompanied by bank loans, as typical for a bank-based financial system. Reliance on own funds has been supported by the relatively low dividend payments and the corporate income tax reform in 2000. Moreover, high ownership concentration in business entities and the related reluctance of owners to share profits explain the preference for the use of internal funds. Modest credit demand, on the other hand, could be explained by the restructuring of the economy that has entailed the destruction of parts of the production base and the increasing share of the service sector in the economy. Thus, one can observe increasing accumulated retained earnings (savings) in the non-financial corporate sector until the 2008 crisis. This in turn has spurred increased investments in financial assets, even though a relatively large and positive contribution of gross fixed capital formation to GDP growth existed throughout the years, except for 1999 and the 2008–2010 period (see Figure 6.1). The prevalence of non-listed SMEs, whose investment rate and growth increased in the post-reform period, further puts into doubt the negative effect of increased financial investments on real investments. It is important to acknowledge that increasing investments in financial assets have not been the result of the financialisation process in its conventional meaning, but rather incentivised by the fiscal policies and meagre capital investment possibilities due to the small market as well as the *primitive* productive and technological structure as demand- and supply-side constraints in Estonia.

6.4 HOUSEHOLD CONSUMPTION

Private consumption has been the main contributor to GDP growth in Estonia, which has been supported by the increasing net incurrence of financial liabilities by households since the early 1990s, even though the net financial position of the households has been positive; only from 2005 has it started to deteriorate due to the decreasing value of shares and other equity, and the considerably stronger growth of households' financial liabilities compared with assets (OECD Statistics 2014). In the structure of households' assets, shares and other equity (mostly unquoted shares) constitute the largest share, followed by demand and time deposits. Current accounts have been the most popular and liquid channel to save among private persons, despite the introduction of several investment and depositing products by banks. The high share of demand deposits in the asset structure of households can be explained by the fact that employees in Estonia receive their monthly salaries on this account (Sõrg and Tuusis 2008, pp. 12–13). The growth of households' liabilities, on the other hand, where loans have comprised between 80 and 90 per cent of financial liabilities since 2007, has been led by the more than 40 per cent annual increase in the total volume of housing loans and leases between 2000 and 2005 (Bank of Estonia 2006b). Loans to individuals increased from 5–6 per cent in the late 1990s to 53 per cent of GDP in 2009 and the ratio of debt to disposable income grew from 8 per cent in 1996 to 104 per cent in 2009 (author's calculations based on Bank of Estonia 2014 and OECD Statistics 2014). At the dawn of the credit boom in 2004, on average 18 per cent of a household's monthly net income went to service loan and interest payments, while for one-fifth of the debtors loan-servicing costs stood above 29 per cent of the family's net income (Bank of Estonia 2005). By 2010, the average monthly debt servicing had climbed to 26 per cent of households' monthly net income (Bank of Estonia 2011b).

In light of persistent high income inequality, low public social safety nets and relatively low minimum wages (Aidukaite 2011; Eamets 2011), it is not surprising that paid employment as the primary source of income has not been able to uphold growing private consumption without the use of debt financing. More importantly, given that 68 per cent of households have problems with meeting subsistence needs, the majority of people living in Estonia spend their monthly income on everyday needs, while only a few households have managed to accumulate some savings as an additional source to cover costs. Hence, in order to pay for larger lump-sum expenses such as more expensive durable goods, tuition fees etc. or investments such as purchase or renovation of housing, Estonian households have increasingly used bank loans. The share of households with outstanding loan liabilities in all Estonian households grew sharply from 23 per cent in 2001 to 50 per cent in 2011 (Meriküll 2012, p. 2). Hence, bank loans to individuals have been one of the main factors affecting the formation of consumption patterns of households. Expanding credit enabled households to broaden consumption during the boom years, while the credit crunch in the post-2008 period suppressed it (Männasoo 2003).

These increasing mortgage loans caused several vulnerabilities in both the household institutional sector and the economy as a whole. The first stems from the high level of foreign-currency denominated loans up until 2011, when Estonia joined the Euro area. Namely, 90 per cent of the mortgage loans were denominated in euros at adjustable interest rates before the crisis (Bank of Estonia 2010b). This made the repayment capacity of borrowers dependent on their employment situation, the evolution of real estate prices, and to a significant extent on continued low interest rates. Second, the rapid growth in the debt burden, together with the rise in real estate prices that preceded the recession, created the preconditions for a creditless recovery. The sluggish recovery in credit demand can be partly explained by changed household endowments, such as income reduction and lower income expectations, although changed behavioural relations also matter. In addition, Estonia's pre-crisis real estate boom and the subsequent drop in the value of collateral played a role in lowering credit demand (Meriküll 2012). Third, the debt burden of households has increased through the re-financing of previous loans. Irresponsible lending by credit institutions during the boom years in the mid-2000s, coupled by the *e-hype*, paved the way for the emergence of payday loan providers, who have extended high interest rate loans to no-income and no-job borrowers via easily accessible electronic channels, including mobile phones. The propensity to apply for these high interest rate payday loans increased during the post-2008 recession period, as on average the share of expenditures on food and housing in households' budgets increased to 45 per cent due to the fall in real incomes (Bank of Estonia 2011a, p. 13). Therefore, in the Estonian household sector, one can observe a vicious cycle of debt-financed expansion that went together with increasing financial fragility due to greater leverage. In accordance with a typical scenario of the realisation of this fragility, foreign-owned credit institutions tightened credit standards and raised risk premiums that contracted debt and shut down the engine of demand growth. In that sense, bank lending to individuals has behaved in a pro-cyclical manner.

In conclusion, given the persisting income inequalities and overall pressures to squeeze labour costs, thriving private consumption that drove rapid economic growth for years was increasingly financed with debt. To some extent, the increasing borrowing that has been secured on rising real estate values has enabled households to withdraw part of the rise in housing wealth and use the proceeds for additional consumption financing, although the marginal propensity to consume out of housing wealth stood at only 1.1 per cent before the crisis of 2007/08 (Paabut and Kattai 2007), which does not support the financialisation argument in terms of the wealth effects. On the other hand, the explosive increase of different banking products and services – mortgage loans, banking cards and consumer credit – reveals the typical elements of the conventional financialisation process, which was made possible by the inflow of foreign capital, intermediated to households through the foreign-owned banks. In light of skyrocketing bank lending to individuals and a deteriorating ratio of debt to disposable income, savings of households decreased steadily until the dawn of the crisis. In a way, the relative income hypothesis applies to the Estonian case due to meagre living standards that necessitated the use of bank loans and savings, when available. Related to the relative income hypothesis argument, one cannot overrule the workings of demonstration effects in the transition process in terms of catching up with consumption patterns of the Western economies, which was accompanied by the introduction of new financial products and services to households. This in turn reveals the interaction of changing institutional structures and social norms that resulted in the debt-financed consumption boom in the mid-2000s. The portrayed developments in the household sector could be referred to as *privatised Keynesianism* (Bohle and Greskovits 2012, pp. 131–137) that entailed a shift from counter-cyclical state policies to the growth of private credit to households for compensation of low wages. All in all, one can observe soaring loan liabilities, in particular, among higher income earners, and a living beyond one's means that reveals the overall poverty of the majority of population.

6.5 2008 CRISIS AND CONCLUSIONS

In the Estonian case, it is hard to detect long-term trends among the real sector categories and variables that could be attributed to the financialisation process as conceived and perceived of in the West. This has been due to the manifestation of financialisation as a heavy reliance on foreign savings in financing economic growth. In this regard, a FDI-led catching-up process has affected all variables of the Estonian real sector to a great extent. Moreover, when considering the long-term effects of financialisation on the real sector, one has to bear in mind that Estonia's market economy is very young, and has revealed peculiar features, not found in many other economies, if any. Thus, many dynamics in the economy are therefore attributable to the transition process rather than to the financialisation process, which makes it difficult to see the financialisation effects as conventionally understood behind the transition process. For instance, widening current account deficits throughout the last two decades could be ascribed to the status of a catching-up economy that incurred higher demand for capital goods and hence a negative trade balance for most of the years. On the other hand, financialisation also affected external imbalances, given the soaring indebtedness of the Estonian private sector that made it possible to cover the current account deficits. Everything considered, fluctuations in the Estonian economy have depended on developments outside the country, such as EU monetary policy, decisions made by parent companies in the Nordic countries and lately, the overall conditions in export markets.

In the context of the global financial crisis of 2008, the housing market boom in the mid-2000s, followed by the economic recession in Estonia, was the inevitable consequence of deeper structural problems that were created during the restructuring of the economy in the 1990s. Specifically, under the conditions of accelerated deindustrialisation and collapse of complex industries that co-occurred with the marginalisation of R&D and innovation activities, only credit could expand the purchasing power of most of the population. As a result, one can observe a vicious circle of consumer credit, mortgage lending and a housing boom reinforcing each other with dire consequences for export competitiveness due to galloping inflation and an appreciating real exchange rate. In other words, macroeconomic vulnerability has been associated with a structural savings shortfall, evident in current account deficits, excessive loan-to-deposit ratios, and an ongoing funding need from parent banks. This external debt-led growth in Estonia entailed a typical situation of increasing financial fragility that Minsky's (2008) analysis addressed, that is, a growing risk of reversal of capital flows, which was amplified by the extreme openness of the economy, highly leveraged structures and external financing being concentrated in a limited number of economic activities, such as real estate and construction (Kattel 2009, pp. 11–13; Thorhallsson and Kattel 2013). Such domestic market orientation of foreign loans gradually eroded the safety margins by insufficient generation of foreign currency earnings to meet external liabilities, which revealed the *Ponzi* financing position of the Estonian economy when the global crisis of 2008 hit the country.

One of the main channels of the 2008 global crisis that impacted the Estonian economy was the liquidity and funding channel, as in an international comparison, Estonian banks rely less on deposits than other new EU member states, implying foreign external borrowing (Juks 2004, p. 20). A remarkable finding in Danilov (2003) is asymmetric capital flows in relation to stages of business cycles, that is, positive feedback mechanisms between business cycles and capital flows that could increase the danger of financial bubbles during the growth phase of the cycle. Also, given a high share of foreign liabilities on the balance sheets of foreign-owned banks, there has always been the possibility of deleveraging and divestment. In that respect, foreign banks reduced lending first and faster than domestically owned banks in the wake of the global turmoil in 2008 (see EBRD 2013). Moreover, the local banking sector was affected by capital outflows that were materialised through portfolio investment and financial derivatives, and followed by outflows of other investments (Jevcák et al. 2010). Another channel was external trade due to high openness of the Estonian economy that has implied the dependence of its economic performance on trade partners' business cycle and other external events, including shocks.

In particular, the trade channel has a significant role in transmitting the EU's impacts to Estonia as well as in increasing the synchronisation of business cycles. The important role of exports for the local economy in the form of intra-industry subcontracting trade between Estonia and foreign countries is revealed in selling more than half of industrial output on foreign markets (Tiits et al. 2008). Thus, the way Estonia was affected by the 2008 crisis, can be traced to regime-specific economic structure and patterns of international integration. As a result of the global financial crisis and the realisation of its impact through the two main channels, the Estonian economy plummeted by 14 per cent in 2009. The main consequences of the crisis in 2008 were rapidly increasing unemployment, bankruptcies, underutilisation of productive resources, stricter credit conditions, and the drop in assets prices, which undermined investments and private consumption (Bank of Estonia 2010b).

Because of the embeddedness of neo-liberal features in the Estonian political-institutional system, analytical competences to deal with the consequences of crisis were non-existent for policy-makers. At the outset of financial crisis in 2008, there was essentially no experience with alternative macroeconomic policy ideas among politicians or public officials due to the lack of a domestic heterodox economic tradition. The same macroeconomic policy environment in terms of conservatism in fiscal policies and neutrality in monetary policies has been sustained for almost 20 years since the early 1990s with the belief in a simple taxation system, based on the principle of proportional and uniform tax rates, and balanced government budget. Essentially, by creating a condition of *economic Darwinism*, that is, by leaving the survival of enterprises to be determined by the market forces alone without any significant assistance from the government, the economy has been locked into a continuous dependence on foreign capital inflows to keep the economy afloat and maintain the ability to service debt.

NOTES

1. Immature accounting practices and loopholes in the legal framework enabled the manipulation of figures, which undermines the reliability of statistical data from the early 1990s (Terk 1999, p. 160).
2. For a time, Estonia held the second place among CEECs with regard to the cumulative per capita inward FDI stock (Gerndorf et al. 1999).
3. In 2015, personal income tax and VAT rate stood at 20 per cent, but there was no capital gains tax on institutions, while individuals were taxed at a flat rate of 20 per cent.
4. The share of the foreign assets of investment and pension funds has steadily grown, reaching 83 per cent of total assets by the end of 2011 (Bank of Estonia 2012).

5. In 2010, 99.9 per cent of all business enterprises were SMEs, which employed 79 per cent of the labour force, exported 76 per cent total export value and invested 79 per cent of total investments in fixed assets (Kaarna et al. 2012, p.22).
6. By the turn of the millennium, Swedish and Finnish companies controlled 46 per cent of the securities' market capitalisation. Only 20 per cent of the stock market capitalisation belonged to resident investors in 2004, while the share of residents among bond investors reached 92 per cent. However, the share of resident investors in the bond market capitalisation has decreased since 2003, standing at 69 per cent in 2009, while in the case of the stock market, the share of local investors has slowly increased reaching 48 per cent by 2009 (Bank of Estonia 2005; Bank of Estonia 2010b).
7. A peculiar feature of the Estonian corporate income tax system is the provision of list of profit usages that are subject to taxation. However, as the list is non-exhaustive, there are possibilities for tax avoidance, which in turn distorts the profit and rentier income figures.
8. The Baltic States have been among the leaders in absorbing the EU funds for entrepreneurship and social policy measures (see Table 6.1). In particular, the inclusion of banks as intermediary bodies that assess projects, disburse funds, monitor and carry out on-site inspections, is perceived to accelerate the absorption of these funds (Bohle and Greskovits 2012; The European Bank Coordination Initiative 2011).

REFERENCES

Aidukaite, J. (2011), '"Balti heaoluriik" pärast kahtkümmet muutuste aastat', in P. Vihalemm, M. Ainsaar, M. Heidmets, T. Vihalemm, V. Pettai and E. Terk (eds), *Eesti Inimarengu Aruanne, 2010/2011. Inimarengu Balti rajad: muutuste kaks aastakümmet*, Tallinn: Eesti Koostöö Kogu.
Alas, R., T. Elenurm and K. Tafel-Viia (2010), 'Who is driving change? Corporate governance and organizational change in Estonia', *Journal of Baltic Studies*, **41** (1), 23–43.
Anspal, S. and T. Rõõm (2011), 'Sooline palgalõhe Eestis: empiiriline analüüs', *Sooline palgalõhe Eestis, Sotsiaalministeeriumi toimetised*, **2**, 27–67.
Bank of Estonia (1995), *Eesti Pank Annual Report 1994*, Tallinn: Bank of Estonia, available at: http://www.eestipank.ee/en/publication/annual-report/1994/eesti-pank-annual-report-1994.
Bank of Estonia (2005), *Financial Stability Review, November 2004*, Tallinn: Bank of Estonia, available at: http://www.eestipank.ee/en/publication/financial-stability-review/2004/financial-stability-review-22004.
Bank of Estonia (2006a), *Eesti Pank Annual Report 2005*, Tallinn: Bank of Estonia, available at: http://www.eestipank.ee/en/publication/annual-report/2005/eesti-pank-annual-report-2005.
Bank of Estonia (2006b), *Financial Stability Review, November 2005*, Tallinn: Bank of Estonia, available at: http://www.eestipank.ee/en/publication/financial-stability-review/2005/financial-stability-review-22005.
Bank of Estonia (2010a), 'Ettevõtete rahastamine', Majanduse rahastamise ülevaade, November 2010, Tallinn: Bank of Estonia.
Bank of Estonia (2010b), *Financial Stability Review, November 2009*, Tallinn: Bank of Estonia, available at: http://www.eestipank.ee/en/publication/financial-stability-review/2009/financial-stability-review-22009.
Bank of Estonia (2011a), *Lending Review, June 2011*, Tallinn: Bank of Estonia.
Bank of Estonia (2011b), *Financial Stability Review, November 2010*, Tallinn:

Bank of Estonia, available at: http://www.eestipank.ee/en/publication/financial-stability-review/2010/financial-stability-review-22010.

Bank of Estonia (2012), *Financial Stability Review, November 2011*, Tallinn: Bank of Estonia, available at: http://www.eestipank.ee/en/publication/financial-stability-review/2011/financial-stability-review-22011.

Bank of Estonia (2014), Bank of Estonia statistics, available at: http://www.eestipank.ee/en/statistics.

Bohle, D. and B. Greskovits (2012), *Capitalist Diversity on Europe's Periphery*, Ithaka, NY, USA: Cornell University Press.

Crotty, J. (2002), 'The effects of increased product market competition and changes in financial markets on the performance of nonfinancial corporations in the neoliberal era', Political Economy Research Institute Working Paper, 44, Amherst, MA: University of Massachusetts Amherst.

Dabušinskas, A. and T. Rõõm (2011), 'Survey evidence on wage and price setting in Estonia', Working Paper Series, 6, Tallinn: Bank of Estonia.

Danilov, T. (2003), 'Välisarengute ülekandumine ja majandustsüklite sünkroonsus Eesti ja Euroopa Liidu vahel', Eesti Panga toimetised, 2, Tallinn: Eesti Pank.

De Haas, R. and I. Naaborg (2006), 'Foreign banks in transition countries: To whom do they lend and how are they financed?', *Financial Markets, Institutions and Instruments*, **15** (4), 159–199.

Dodig, N., E. Hein and D. Detzer (2016), 'Financialisation and the financial and economic crises: Theoretical framework and empirical analysis for 15 countries', in E. Hein, D. Detzer and N. Dodig (eds), *Financialisation and the Financial and Economic Crises: Country Studies*, Cheltenham: Edward Elgar.

Drechsler, W., J. G. Backhaus, L. Burlamaqui, H.-J. Chang, T. Kalvet, R. Kattel, J. A. Kregel and E.S. Reinert (2006), 'Creative destruction management in Central and Eastern Europe: Meeting the challenges of the techno-economic paradigm shift', in T. Kalvet and R. Kattel (eds), *Creative Destruction Management: Meeting the Challenges of the Techno-Economic Paradigm Shift*, Tallinn: Praxis Center for Policy Studies.

Dünhaupt, P. (2013), 'Determinants of functional income distribution – Theory and empirical evidence', Global Labour University working paper, **18**, November 2013, Global Labour University, Geneva: ILO.

Eamets, R. (2011), 'Tööturg, tööturu paindlikkus ja majanduskriis Balti riikides', in P. Vihalemm, M. Ainsaar, M. Heidmets, T. Vihalemm, V. Pettai and E. Terk (eds), *Eesti Inimarengu Aruanne, 2010/2011. Inimarengu Balti rajad: muutuste kaks aastakümmet*, Tallinn: Eesti Koostöö Kogu.

EBRD (1994), *Transition Report. Economic Transition in Eastern Europe and the Former Soviet Union*. London, UK: European Bank for Reconstruction and Development.

EBRD (2013), *Transition Report 2012. Integration Across Borders*. London, UK: European Bank for Reconstruction and Development.

Ehrlich, L., K. Kaasik and A. Randveer (2002), 'The impact of Scandinavian economies on Estonia via foreign trade and direct investments', Working Paper Series, 4, Tallinn: Bank of Estonia.

European Bank Coordination Initiative (2011), 'The role of commercial banks in the absorption of EU funds', Report by the Working Group, approved by the EBCI Full Forum Meeting 16–17 March 2011, Brussels.

European Commission (2007), 'Chapter 5: The labour income share in the

European Union', *Employment in Europe 2007*, Brussels: European Commission Directorate General for Employment, Social Affairs and Equal Opportunities.

European Commission (2010), 'Introduction, background and the main conclusions of the workshop', *Capital flows to converging European economies – from boom to drought and beyond*, Proceedings to the workshop held on 1 October 2010, Occasional Papers 75, Brussels: European Commission Directorate-General for Economic and Financial Affairs.

Eurostat (2014), Eurostat statistics, available at: http://epp.eurostat.ec.europa.eu/portal/page/portal/eurostat/home/.

Gallagher, P. K. and L. Zarsky (2007), *Enclave Economy: Foreign Investment and Sustainable Development in Mexico's Silicon Valley*, Cambridge, MA, USA: MIT Press.

Gerndorf, K., T. Elenurm and E. Terk (1999), 'Corporate governance in Estonia', background paper to the Seminar on Corporate Governance in the Baltics, Vilnius, Lithuania, 21–22 October.

Golebiowski, G. (2007), 'Financial standing of Estonian and Polish companies – a comparative study', *Kroon and Economy*, **3**, 22–31.

Hazak, A. (2009), 'Companies' financial decisions under the distributed profit taxation regime of Estonia', *Emerging Markets Finance & Trade*, **45** (4), 4–12.

Hein, E. (2012), *The Macroeconomics of Finance-dominated Capitalism – and its Crisis*, Cheltenham, UK: Edward Elgar.

Hinnosaar, M. (2003), 'Eesti tööturu institutsionaalne raamistik rahvusvahelises võrdluses', Eesti Panga toimetised, 7, Tallinn: Eesti Pank.

IMF (2007), 'Chapter 5: The globalization of Labor', *World Economic Outlook*, April 2007, Washington, DC, USA: International Monetary Fund.

Jevcák, A., R. Setzer and M. Suardi (2010), 'Determinants of capital flows to the new EU members states before and during the financial crisis', European Economy – Economic Papers 425, Brussels: European Commission Directorate General for Economic and Monetary Affairs.

Juhkam, A. (2000), *Eesti majandusmudeli eripäradest anglo-saksi ning kontinentaal-Euroopa korporatiivse kontrollisüsteemi taustal*, Tartu: Tartu Ülikooli kirjastus.

Juks, R. (2004), 'The importance of the bank-lending channel in Estonia: Evidence from micro-economic data', Working Paper Series, 6, Tallinn: Bank of Estonia.

Kaarna, R., M. Masso and M. Rell (2012), *Väikese ja keskmise suurusega ettevõtete arengusuundumused*, Tallinn: Praxis Center for Policy Studies.

Kangur, A., T. Rajasalu and M. Randveer (1999), 'Kapitali liikumine ja ettevõtluse rahastamine', Eesti Panga toimetised, 4, Tallinn: Eesti Pank.

Kattel, R. (2009), 'The rise and fall of Baltic states', *Development & Transition*, **13**, July 2009, 11–13.

Kattel, R. (2010), 'Financial and economic crisis in Eastern Europe', *Journal of Post Keynesian Economics*, **33** (1), 41–60.

Knell, M. and M. Srholec (2007), 'Diverging pathways in Central and Eastern Europe', in D. Lane and M. Myant (eds), *Varieties of Capitalism in Post-Communist Countries*, Basingstoke, England: Palgrave Macmillan.

Kokkota, R. (2000), 'Income distribution in Estonia', in B. Lesser (ed.), *Baltic Economic Issues*, Halifax, NS, Canada: Baltic Economic Management Training Program.

Kõomägi, M. and P. Sander (2006), *Venture Capital Investments and Financing in Estonia: a Case Study Approach*, Tartu: Tartu University Press.

Kooskora, M. (2008), 'Corporate governance from the stakeholder perspective, in

the context of Estonian business organizations', *Baltic Journal of Management*, **3** (2), 193–217.
Kregel, A. J. (2004), 'External financing for development and international financial instability', G-24 Discussion Paper 32, October 2004.
Kuusk, K. and A. Jürgenson (2010), 'Ülevaade poliitikakujundajate ootustest ja tänastest hinnangutest maksureformile', in Sotsiaalteaduslike rakendusu-uringute keskus RAKE and Poliitikauuringute Keskus Praxis (eds), *Ettevõtete jaotamata kasumi mittemaksustamise mõju investeeringutele ja majandusaren-gule. Lõppraport*, Tartu, Tallinn: Sotsiaalteaduslike rakendusuuringute keskus RAKE, Poliitikauuringute Keskus Praxis.
Lane, D. (2007), 'Post-state socialism: A diversity of capitalisms?', in D. Lane and M. Myant (eds), *Varieties of Capitalism in Post-Communist Countries*, Basingstoke, England: Palgrave Macmillan.
Lane, D. and M. Myant (2007), 'Introduction', in D. Lane and M. Myant (eds), *Varieties of Capitalism in Post-Communist Countries*, Basingstoke, England: Palgrave Macmillan.
Lauristin, M. (2011), 'Inimareng siirdeajal: Balti riikide ees seisvad väljakutsed', in P. Vihalemm, M. Ainsaar, M. Heidmets, T. Vihalemm, V. Pettai and E. Terk (eds), *Eesti Inimarengu Aruanne, 2010/2011. Inimarengu Balti rajad: muutuste kaks aastakümmet*, Tallinn: Eesti Koostöö Kogu.
Lazonick, W. and M. O'Sullivan (2000), 'Maximizing shareholder value: A new ideology for corporate governance', *Economy and Society*, **29** (1), 13–35.
Madureira, M.A., J.E. Nilsson and V. Gheorghe (2007), 'Structural funds as instru-ment to promote innovation – Theories and practices', VINNOVA Report VR 2007:02, Stockholm, Sweden: VINNOVA – Swedish Governmental Agency for Innovation Systems.
Männasoo, K. (2003), 'The pro-cyclicality of the financial sector: nature, implica-tions and policy options', *Kroon and Economy*, **2**, 32–47.
Männik, K., H. Hannula and U. Varblane (2006), 'Foreign subsidiary autonomy and performance in five central and east European countries', in H. Hannula, S. Radoševic and N. Von Tunzelmann (eds), *Estonia, the New EU Economy. Building a Baltic Miracle?*, Aldershot, England: Ashgate Publishing Ltd.
Markusen, R. A. (1999), 'Four structures for second tier cities', in R.A. Markusen, Y.S. Lee and S. DiGiovanna (eds), *Second Tier Cities. Rapid Growth beyond the Metropolis*, Minneapolis, MN, USA: University of Minnesota Press.
Masso, J., J. Meriküll and P. Vahter (2011), 'Gross profit taxation versus distributed profit taxation and firm performance: Effects of Estonia's corporate income tax reform', Working Paper Series, 2, Tallinn: Bank of Estonia.
Meriküll, J. (2012), 'Households borrowing during a creditless recovery', Working Paper Series, 2, Tallinn: Bank of Estonia.
Mickiewicz, T., K. Bishop and U. Varblane (2006), 'Financial constraints in investment – foreign versus domestic firms: Panel data results from Estonia, 1995–1999', *Acta Oeconomica*, **54**, 425–449.
Minsky, H.P. (2008), *Stabilizing an Unstable Economy*. Reprinted by McGraw-Hill, New York, 2008.
Myant, M. and J. Drahokoupil (2011), *Transition Economies. Political Economy in Russia, Eastern Europe, and Central Asia*, Hoboken, NJ, USA: John Wiley & Sons, Inc.
Nurmela, K. and M. Karu (2009), Estonia: Wage formation, available at: http://www.eurofound.europa.eu/eiro/studies/tn0808019s/ee0808019q.htm.

OECD (2000a), 'Regional economic assessment of the Baltic states, 2000: insights from a decade of transition', Policy Brief, February 2000, available at: http://vvv.oecd.org/dataoecd/22/38/1816965.pdf.

OECD (2000b), *OECD Economic Surveys 1999–2000. The Baltic States: A Regional Economic Assessment*, Paris, France: OECD Publications.

OECD (2003), *Labour Market and Social Policies in the Baltic Countries*, Paris: OECD Publications.

OECD Statistics (2014), OECD Statistics database, available at: http://stats.oecd.org/.

Orhangazi, Ö. (2008), 'Financialisation and capital accumulation in the non-financial corporate sector: A theoretical and empirical investigation on the US economy: 1973–2003', *Cambridge Journal of Economics*, **32** (6), 863–886.

Paabut, A. and R. Kattai (2007), 'Kinnisvara väärtuse kasvu mõju eratarbimisele Eestis', Eesti Panga toimetised, 5. Tallinn: Eesti Pank.

Pajuste, A. and M. Olsson (2001), 'Ownership concentration: the case of the Baltic states', paper for the closing conference of the ACE Project *Corporate Governance and Disclosure in the Accession Process*, CEPR/University of Ljubljana, Portoroz, Slovenia, 23 June.

Paulus, A. (2003), 'Sissetulekute ebavõrdsus ja selle dekomponeerimine Eesti näitel', Bakalaureusetöö, Tartu: Tartu Ülikool.

Randveer, M. (2000), 'Eesti ettevõtete finantsnäitajate dünaamika 1996–1999. aasta I pool', *Eesti Panga toimetised*, 3, Tallinn: Eesti Pank.

Raudla, R. and R. Kattel (2011), 'Why did Estonia choose fiscal retrenchment after the 2008 crisis?', *Journal of Public Policy*, **31** (2), 163–186.

Raudsepp, V., P. Sander and K. Kask (2003), 'Financing problems in Estonian firms', *Current Politics and Economics of Russia, Eastern and Central Europe*, **18** (1), 55–73.

Reiljan, E. (2006), 'Reasons for de-internationalization: An analysis of Estonian manufacturing companies', in H. Hannula, S. Radoševic and N. Von Tunzelmann (eds), *Estonia, the New EU Economy. Building a Baltic Miracle?*, Aldershot, England: Ashgate Publishing Ltd.

Reinert, S. E. and R. Kattel (2007), 'European Eastern enlargement as Europe's attempted economic suicide?', Working Papers in Technology Governance and Economic Dynamics 14, The Other Canon Foundation and Tallinn University of Technology.

Rõõm, T. (2007), 'Haridus ja tööturg Eestis', Eesti Panga toimetised, 12, Tallinn: Eesti Pank.

Ruusalu, R. (2014), 'Väikese palga saaja on Eestis supermaksumaksja', *Eesti Päevaleht*, available at: http://epl.delfi.ee/news/eesti/homses-paevalehes-vaikese-palga-saaja-on-eestis-supermaksumaksja?id=69845053.

Sander, P. (2003), 'Finantshierarhia teooria ja finantseerimisotsused Eesti ettevõtetes', in *Ettevõttemajandus Eestis ja Euroopa Liit. I teadus- ja koolituskonverents*, Tallinn: OÜ Mattimar.

Sander, P. and M. Kõomägi (2007), 'The allocation of control rights in financing private companies: Views of Estonian private equity and venture capitalists', *TRAMES*, **11** (61/56), 189–205.

Sõrg, M. and D. Tuusis (2008), 'Foreign banks increase the social orientation of Estonian financial sector', Wirtschaftswissenschaftliche Diskussionspapiere, 01/2008, Ernst-Moritz-Arndt-Universität Greifswald, Rechts- und Staatswissenschaftliche Fakultät.

Statistics Estonia (2014), Statistics Estonia database, available at: http://www.
    stat.ee/.
Stockhammer, E. (2004), 'Financialisation and the slowdown of accumulation',
    Cambridge Journal of Economics, **28** (5), 719–741.
Stockhammer, E. (2009), 'Determinant of functional income distribution in
    OECD countries', IMK Studies, 5/2009, Duesseldorf: Macroeconomic Policy
    Institute IMK at Hans Boeckler Foundation.
Tafel, K., E. Terk and A. Purju (2006), 'Corporate governance in post-socialist
    countries – Theoretical dilemmas, peculiarities, research opportunities', *EBS
    Review*, **1** (21), 7–26.
Terk, E. (1999), *Erastamine Eestis: ideoloogia, läbiviimine, tulemused*, Tallinn: Eesti
    Tuleviku-uuringute Instituut.
Thorhallsson, B. and R. Kattel (2013), 'Neo-liberal small states and economic
    crisis: lessons for democratic corporatism', *Journal of Baltic Studies*, **44** (1),
    83–103.
Tiits, M. (2006), 'Industrial and trade dynamics in the Baltic Sea region since
    1990s', in T. Kalvet and R. Kattel (eds), *Creative Destruction Management:
    Meeting the Challenges of the Techno-Economic Paradigm Shift*, Tallinn: Praxis
    Center for Policy Studies.
Tiits, M., R. Kattel and T. Kalvet (2006), *Made in Estonia*, Tartu: Institute of Baltic
    Studies.
Tiits, M., R. Kattel, T. Kalvet and D. Tamm (2008), 'Catching up, forging ahead
    or falling behind? Central and Eastern European development in 1990–2005',
    Innovation: The European Journal of Social Science Research, **21** (1), 65–85.
Tridico, P. (2011), *Institutions, Human Development and Economic Growth in
    Transition Economies*, Basingstoke, England: Palgrave Macmillan.
Varblane, U. and T. L. Ziacik (1999), 'The impact of foreign direct investment on
    the export activities of Estonian firms', *Journal of East-West Business*, **5** (1–2),
    173–190.
Võrk, A. and R. Kaarna (2010), 'Eesti maksukoormus areng: jaotus, mõjud ja
    tulevikuväljavaated', PRAXIS Poliitikaanalüüs, 5, Tallinn: Poliitikauuringute
    Keskus Praxis.

7. Financialisation and the crises in the export-led mercantilist German economy*

Daniel Detzer and Eckhard Hein

7.1 INTRODUCTION

This chapter examines the long-run changes in the relationships between the financial and the non-financial sectors of the German economy, and in particular the effects of these changes on the macroeconomic developments, which led or contributed to the financial crisis and the Great Recession in 2008/09. The second section provides an overview of the long-run developments in the era of financialisation. It gives a first impression of the drivers of aggregate demand and growth, which in the case of Germany were mainly net exports, starting in the early/mid 1990s. The macroeconomic development in Germany since then can be classified as 'export-led mercantilist'. The third section will then deal with the long-run effects of financialisation, or the increasing dominance of finance, on the German economy, in more detail, and it will examine to what extent the channels through which financialisation is expected to affect economic development can be found.[1] Here we will examine in detail how financialisation has affected income distribution, investment in capital stock, household consumption, and net exports and the current account. The fourth section will then trace the mechanism through which the financial and economic crises were transmitted into the German economy in a more detailed way. The fifth section will summarise and conclude.

* For a more extensive version of this chapter see Detzer and Hein (2014). Parts of the study were presented at the 16th Annual INFER conference, May 29–31, 2014, in Pescara, Italy, at the 11th International Conference Developments in Economic Theory and Policy, June 26–27, 2014, in Bilbao, Spain, at the FESSUD Conference Understanding and Responding to the Financial Crisis, October 16–17, 2014, in Warsaw, Poland, and at the 18th Conference of the Research Network Macroeconomics and Macroeconomic Policies (FMM), October 30–November 1, 2014, in Berlin, Germany. For helpful comments we are grateful to the participants and to Andrea Boltho, Nina Dodig, Dirk Ehnts and Achim Truger in particular. We are also indebted to Petra Dünhaupt for useful comments and for helping us with data. Remaining errors are, of course, ours.

7.2   LONG-RUN DEVELOPMENTS IN THE ERA OF FINANCIALISATION SINCE THE EARLY 1980s AND THE ECONOMIC AND FINANCIAL CRISES

As analysed in detail in Detzer et al. (2013), the most important changes in the German financial sector which contributed to an increasing dominance of finance took place in the course of the 1990s: the abolition of the stock exchange tax in 1991, the legalisation of share buybacks in 1998, the abolition of capital gains taxes for corporations in 2002, and the legalisation of hedge funds in 2004, among others. While financialisation is often associated with an increase of the share of the financial sector in value added, employment, and profits in the economy, this phenomenon could not be observed in the German economy. The increased dominance of finance, however, was observed in other quantitative and qualitative indicators. Stock market capitalisation and trading activity grew strongly, even though they are still moderate compared with Anglo-Saxon, and other European countries. At the same time, the importance of institutional investors in Germany increased strongly. Rising financial activity of non-financial firms, another feature associated with financialisation, could also be observed in Germany. While real investment of non-financial firms was low, their investment in financial assets and, therefore, the share of financial profits in total profits in those firms, increased rapidly in the course of the 2000s.

This development was accompanied by considerable redistribution of income at the expense of the wage share and of low income households, in particular, as we will show in detail in Section 7.3 of this chapter. Against this background, severe changes in real GDP growth and its composition, as well as in the trends of the financial balances of the main macroeconomic sectors could be observed. Comparing the development of the two trade cycles from the early 1990s until the Great Recession with the previous trade cycles, we find that average real GDP growth over the cycle slowed down considerably with the increasing dominance of finance and the associated redistribution of income (Table 7.1). Furthermore, the relevance of the growth contributions of the main demand aggregates changed significantly. Real GDP growth in the cycles of the 1960s, 1970s and even the 1980s, was mainly driven by domestic demand, and the balance of goods and services only contributed up to 0.25 percentage points to real GDP growth. In the trade cycles of the 1990s and early 2000s, however, the growth contributions of net exports went up to 0.47 and 0.64 percentage points, respectively. In the course of this process the degree of openness of the German economy exploded: the share of exports in GDP increased from 24 per cent in 1995 to 51 per cent in 2013, and the share

Table 7.1 *Real GDP growth in Germany (in per cent) and growth contributions of the main demand aggregates (in percentage points), 1961–2013, cyclical averages*

	1961–1966	1967–1974	1975–1981	1982–1992	1993–2002	2003–2008	2009–2013
Real GDP growth, per cent	4.49	3.82	2.40	2.77	1.40	1.59	0.66
Growth contribution of (percentage points)							
domestic demand including stocks	4.49	3.59	2.36	2.52	0.93	0.94	0.58
private consumption	2.47	2.25	1.55	1.42	0.72	0.28	0.60
public consumption	1.03	0.84	0.70	0.21	0.28	0.17	0.26
gross fixed capital formation	1.28	0.47	0.38	0.69	0.04	0.40	-0.10
change in inventories and net acquisition of valuables	-0.29	0.03	-0.28	0.20	-0.11	0.10	-0.19
the balance of goods and services	-0.01	0.23	0.04	0.25	0.47	0.64	0.08

Notes: The beginning of a trade cycle is given by a local minimum of annual real GDP growth, 1961–1966 and 2009–2013 are incomplete cycles.

Source: European Commission (2014a), our calculations.

166 *Financialisation and the financial and economic crises*

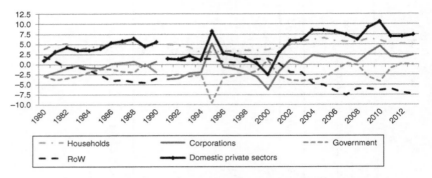

Notes: West Germany until 1990. In 1995 the deficit of the 'Treuhandanstalt' was shifted from the corporate sector to the government sector. In 2000 the payments for UMTS licences from the corporate sector to the government sector are included. RoW is 'Rest of the World'.

Source: European Commission (2014a), our calculations.

Figure 7.1   Financial balances, Germany, 1980–2013 (per cent of nominal GDP)

of imports rose from 23 per cent in 1995 to 44 per cent in 2013 (European Commission 2014a). Growth was thus increasingly driven by net exports and the relevance of domestic demand declined dramatically. This was equally true for private consumption and for investment.

The increasing reliance on net exports as the driver of growth since the early/mid 1990s finds its expression in the development of the financial balances of the main macroeconomic sectors (Figure 7.1). The financial balance of the external sector (RoW), which had turned positive in the 1990s after German re-unification, when Germany ran trade and current account deficits, became negative in the early 2000s, and decreased to 7.5 per cent of nominal GDP in 2007. German growth was thus relying on current account surpluses – the counterpart of the deficits of the external sector – at a level which had never been observed in German history before. The financial balances of the German private households have had a long tradition of being in surplus. But these surpluses even increased in the early 2000s, indicating weak consumption demand, and were accompanied by positive and rising financial balances of the corporate sector in this period, too, which indicates weak investment in capital stock. These large and increasing financial surpluses of the private sector were only temporarily and partly compensated by government sector deficits: the public sector was balanced in 2007, just before the Great Recession. Based on this short description, the German type of development from the early/mid

1990s, and from the early 2000s, in particular, until the Great Recession, can be classified as 'export-led mercantilist'.

7.3   LONG-RUN EFFECTS OF FINANCIALISATION

Financialisation and Income Distribution

The period of finance-dominated capitalism has been associated with a massive redistribution of income.[2] First, functional income distribution changed at the expense of labour and in favour of broad capital income in several countries (Table 7.2). The labour income share showed a falling trend in the developed capitalist economies considered here, from the early 1980s until the Great Recession. As can be seen, the fall in the labour

Table 7.2   Labour income share as percentage of GDP at current factor costs, average values over the trade cycle, early 1980s–2008

	1. Early 1980s – early 1990s	2. Early 1990s – early 2000s	3. Early 2000s – 2008	Change (3. − 1.), percentage points
Austria	75.66	70.74	65.20	−10.46
Belgium	70.63	70.74	69.16	−1.47
France	71.44	66.88	65.91	−5.53
Germany[a]	67.11	66.04	63.34	−3.77
Greece[b]	67.26	62.00	60.60	−6.66
Ireland	70.34	60.90	55.72	−14.61
Italy	68.31	63.25	62.37	−5.95
Netherlands	68.74	67.21	65.57	−3.17
Portugal	65.73	70.60	71.10	5.37
Spain	68.32	66.13	62.41	−5.91
Sweden	71.65	67.04	69.16	−2.48
UK	72.79	71.99	70.67	−2.12
USA	68.20	67.12	65.79	−2.41
Japan[b]	72.38	70.47	65.75	−6.64

Notes: The labour income share is given by the compensation per employee divided by GDP at factor costs per person employed. The beginning of a trade cycle is given by a local minimum of annual real GDP growth in the respective country.
[a] West Germany until 1990.
[b] Adjusted to fit in three cycle pattern.

Data: European Commission (2010a).

Source: Hein (2012, p. 13).

income share was considerable in Germany, in particular from the cycle of the 1990s to the cycle of the early 2000s.

Second, personal income distribution became more unequal in most of the countries from the mid-1980s until the mid-2000s. Taking the Gini coefficient as an indicator, this was true for the distribution of market income, with Germany amongst those countries showing a considerable increase in inequality. In Germany, redistribution via taxes and social transfers was considerable and was not decreasing over time. However, this did not prevent the Gini coefficient for disposable income from increasing as well (OECD 2014). In fact, according to the OECD (2008) applying further indicators for inequality, Germany was one of the countries where the inequality of disposable income increased the most in the early 2000s. And this redistribution was mainly at the expense of those with very low incomes (OECD 2014).

Third, as data based on tax reports provided by Alvaredo et al. (2014) has shown, there has been an explosion of the shares of the very top incomes since the early 1980s in the USA and the UK, which, prior to the financial crisis and the Great Recession, again reached the levels of the mid-1920s in the USA and the mid-1930s in the UK. Although Germany has not yet seen such an increase for the top 1 per cent, top 0.1 per cent or top 0.01 per cent income shares, it should be noted that the share of the top 0.1 per cent, for example, was substantially higher in Germany than in the USA or the UK for longer periods of time and that it was only surpassed by the USA and the UK in the mid-1980s and the mid-1990s, respectively (Hein 2015). Furthermore, if we take a look at the top 10 per cent income share, including capital gains, a rising trend from the early 1980s until 2007 can be observed for Germany, too.

To what extent can these tendencies towards redistribution in Germany be related to the increasing dominance of finance? Integrating some stylised facts of financialisation and neo-liberalism into the Kaleckian theory of income distribution and reviewing the respective empirical and econometric literature for different sets of developed capitalist economies, Hein (2015) has argued that there is some convincing empirical evidence that financialisation and neo-liberalism have contributed to the rising gross profit share, and hence to the falling labour income share since the early 1980s, through three main channels.

First, the shift in the sectoral composition of the economy, from the public sector and the non-financial corporate sector with higher labour income shares towards the financial corporate sector with a lower labour income share, has contributed to the fall in the labour income share for the economy as a whole in some countries.

Second, the increase in management salaries as a part of overhead costs, together with rising profit claims of rentiers, i.e. rising interest and dividend payments of the corporate sector, have in sum been associated with a falling labour income share. Since management salaries are part of the compensations of employees in the national accounts and thus of the labour income share, the wage share excluding (top) management salaries has fallen even more pronounced than the wage share taken from the national accounts.

Third, financialisation and neo-liberalism have weakened trade union bargaining power through several channels: increasing shareholder value and short-term profitability orientation of management, sectoral shifts in many countries away from the public and the non-financial business sector with stronger trade unions to the financial sector with weaker unions, abandonment of government demand management and full employment policies, deregulation of the labour market, and liberalisation and globalisation of international trade and finance.

These channels should not only have triggered falling labour income shares, but should also have contributed to the observed increases in inequality of personal/household incomes. The major reason for this is the (even more) unequal distribution of wealth, generating capital income, which then feeds back on the household distribution of income when it comes to re-distribution between labour and capital incomes.

Checking the relevance of these channels for the German case, with respect to the first channel we find that neither the profit share of the financial corporate sector was higher than the profit share in the non-financial corporate sector in the period of the increasing dominance of finance starting in the early/mid 1990s (Hein and Detzer 2015), nor was there a shift of the sectoral shares in gross value added towards the financial sector. However, the share of the government sector in value added saw a tendency to decline, from 12 per cent in the mid-1990s to below 10 per cent in 2007. Ceteris paribus, this means a fall in the aggregate wage share and a rise in the aggregate profit share, because the government sector is a non-profit sector in the national accounts.

Regarding the second channel, the increase in top management salaries and higher profit claims of financial wealth holders, there are several indicators supporting the validity of this channel for Germany. Dünhaupt (2011) has corrected the wage share from the national accounts for the labour income of the top 1 per cent by assuming that the latter represent top management salaries. The resulting wage share for direct labour shows an even steeper downward trend than the wage share from the national accounts: An increase in the share of top management salaries was thus associated with a decline of the share of wages for direct labour in national income.

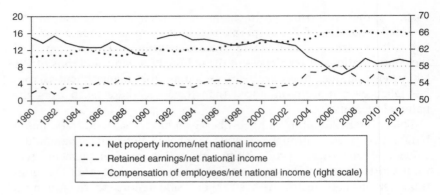

Note: West Germany until 1990.

Source: Statistisches Bundesamt (2014), our presentation.

Figure 7.2   Income shares in net national income, Germany, 1980–2013 (per cent)

Extending another analysis provided by Dünhaupt (2012), we also find that, in the long-run perspective, there is substantial evidence that the increase in the profit claims of rentiers came at the expense of the workers' share in national income (Figure 7.2). In the 1980s, the fall in the wage share was accompanied by an increase of both the share of rentiers' income (net property income consisting of interest, dividends and rents) and the share of retained earnings of corporations. However, from the 1990s, after German re-unification, until the Great Recession, the fall in the wage share benefitted mainly the rentiers' income share. Only during the short upswing before the Great Recession did the share of retained earnings also increase at the expense of the wage share. Decomposing the rentiers' income share (Figure 7.3), it becomes clear that the increase was almost exclusively driven by a rise in the share of dividends, starting in the mid-1990s, when we observe an increasing relevance of finance and shareholder value policies in the German economy.

Regarding the third channel, the weakening of trade union bargaining power, we find that several indicators for this apply to the development in Germany from the mid-1990s until the Great Recession. First, starting in the early/mid 1990s, downsizing the government sector, as shown above, and the switch towards restrictive macroeconomic policies focusing exclusively on achieving low inflation and (close to) balanced public budgets meant low growth and rising unemployment, in particular in the

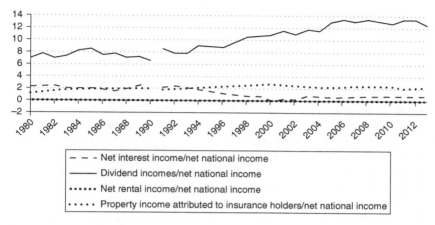

Source: Statistisches Bundesamt (2014), our presentation.

Figure 7.3   *Components of rentiers' income as a share in net national income, Germany, 1980–2013 (per cent)*

stagnation period of the early 2000s, as analysed extensively by Bibow (2005), Herr and Kazandziska (2011) and Hein and Truger (2005, 2007a), for example.

Second, policies of deregulation and liberalisation of the labour market (Hartz-laws, Agenda 2010) explicitly and successfully aimed at weakening trade union bargaining power by lowering unemployment benefits (replacement ratio and duration), establishing a large low-paid sector, as well as reducing trade union membership, collective wage bargaining coverage and coordination of wage bargaining across sectors and regions (Hein and Truger 2005, 2007a).

Third, trade and financial openness of the German economy increased significantly and put pressure on trade unions through international competition in the goods and services markets and through the threat effect of delocalisation. The foreign trade ratio (exports plus imports as a share of GDP) an indicator for trade openness, increased from 39.1 per cent in the mid-1990s to 71.4 per cent in 2007, just before the Great Recession (Statistisches Bundesamt 2011a). The foreign assets/ foreign liabilities-GDP ratios, as indicators of financial openness, increased from 56 per cent/40 per cent in 1991 to 200 per cent/174 per cent in 2007 (Deutsche Bundesbank 2012–14).

Fourth, shareholder value orientation and short-termism of management rose considerably, thus increasing the pressure on workers and trade unions. According to Detzer (2015), two institutional changes were important in this respect. First, ownership of non-financial corporations changed. The share of stock directly held by private investors halved between 1991 and 2007, while the share held by institutional investors increased significantly. Similarly, strategic investors reduced their ownership share and investors who were more likely to have purely financial interests increased it. Furthermore, fewer strategic block holders, which might shield managers from market pressure, were present on corporate boards. Additionally, activist hedge funds and private equity firms, which directly pressure management to favour shareholder value, became more active in Germany. Second, the development of a market for corporate control in Germany since the mid-1990s has put pressure on managers to pursue shareholder value friendly strategies in order to protect themselves against hostile takeovers.

Financialisation and Investment in Capital Stock

In the financialisation literature, the effects of an increasing dominance of finance on investment in capital stock has been discussed extensively and has been reviewed in Hein (2012, Chapter 3) and Hein and van Treeck (2010), among others. Financialisation has been characterised by increasing shareholder power vis-à-vis management and workers, an increasing rate of return on equity and bonds held by rentiers, and an alignment of management with shareholder interests through short-run performance related pay schemes, such as bonuses, stock option programmes, and so on. On the one hand, this has imposed short-termism on management and has caused decreasing management animal spirits with respect to real investment in capital stock and long-run growth of the firm. On the other hand, it has drained internal means of finance for real investment purposes from corporations, through increasing dividend payments and share buybacks in order to boost stock prices and thus shareholder value. These 'preference' and 'internal means of finance' channels should have each had partially negative effects on firms' real investment in capital stock, and hence also on long-run growth of the economy to the extent that productivity growth is capital embodied.

Empirical analyses of the effects of financialisation on investment in capital stock of non-financial corporations have taken the financial profits of non-financial corporations as an indicator for the 'preference channel' of financialisation and increasing shareholder value orientation of managements. Rising financial profits indicate an increased preference

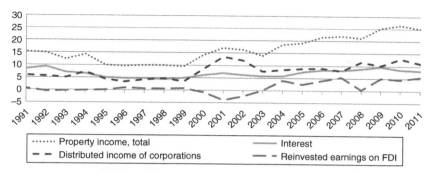

Note: Total property income includes additionally property income attributed to insurance policy and rents.

Source: Statistisches Bundesamt (2012), our calculations.

Figure 7.4   *Sources of operating surplus of non-financial corporations, Germany, 1991–2011 (per cent of sector gross operating surplus)*

of management for short-term profits obtained from financial investment, as compared to profits from real investment. As Figure 7.4 shows, this is exactly what can be found for German non-financial corporations starting in the late 1990s/early 2000s. Property income, consisting of interest, distributed income of corporations (i.e. dividends, property income attributed to insurance policy holder and rents) and reinvested profits from FDI, increased significantly as a share of gross operating surplus. This increase was driven considerably by an increase in interest payments received in a period of low interest rates and by an increase in dividend payments obtained. The increase in the relevance of both types of financial profits indicates an increasing relevance of financial investment, as compared with investment in real capital stock.

Another indicator for the effects of an increasing shareholder value orientation of management on investment in capital stock is the share of profits distributed to shareholders. Retained profits are an important determinant of investment in capital stock, because they lift the finance constraints firms are facing in incompletely competitive financial markets. Therefore, an increasing share of profits distributed to shareholders may hamper real investment through the 'internal means of finance channel'. Figure 7.5 shows that such a phenomenon can be observed for German non-financial corporations, too. The share of distributed property income in the gross operating surplus displays a tendency to rise starting in the mid-1990s. This increase was driven almost exclusively by an increase in

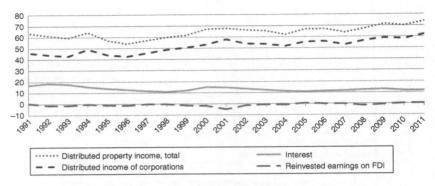

Note: Total property income includes additionally rents.

Source: Statistisches Bundesamt (2012), our calculations.

Figure 7.5   Uses of operating surplus of non-financial corporations, Germany, 1991–2011 (per cent of sector gross operating surplus)

the share of distributed income of corporations, i.e. dividends, whereas the share of interest payments in the gross operating surplus stagnated or even declined.

The decomposition of the sources and the uses of the gross operating surplus of non-financial corporations suggest, therefore, that both the 'preference channel' and the 'internal means for finance' channel have contributed to weak private investment in Germany from the mid-1990s until the Great Recession.

Financialisation and Consumption

Finance-dominated capitalism is said to have generated increasing potentials for wealth-based and debt-financed consumption. In several countries stock market and housing price booms have each increased notional wealth against which households were willing to borrow. Changing financial norms, new financial products, and deterioration of creditworthiness standards triggered by securitisation, as well as 'originate and distribute' strategies of commercial banks, made increasing amounts of credit available, in particular to low income, low wealth households. This allowed households at the bottom to maintain consumption in the face of falling real incomes, and for middle-income households it allowed consumption norms to rise faster than median income, driven by habit persistence, social visibility of consumption, etc. (Barba and Pivetti 2009; Cynamon and Fazzari 2008). But all this does not seem to apply to the development in Germany: As we have already noted in Section 7.2, in Germany private households were running considerable and increasing surpluses in their financial balances. Against the background of redistribution at the expense of the wage share and low income households, growth contributions of private consumption remained modest from the early/mid 1990s onwards and were particularly weak in the trade cycle of the early 2000s.

It is true, after re-unification, the saving rate for united Germany saw a tendency to decline. However, when the 'new economy' crisis hit in the early 2000s, this tendency was reversed and the saving rate increased to well above 11 per cent (European Commission 2014a). Klär and Slacalek (2006) relate this increase to three main causes:

1. redistribution of income at the expense of the labour income share and low income households;
2. increasing precautionary saving since the early 2000s in the face of weak growth, high unemployment, and 'reform policies' aiming at the deregulation of the labour market and a reduction of social benefits (Hartz-Laws, Agenda 2010); and
3. the absence of any wealth effects on consumption.

Saving rates out of profit income are generally higher than out of wages, and the propensity to save out of household income increases with the level of household income. Estimates of propensities to save (or to consume) out of wages and out of profits usually find differentials between 0.32 (Hein and Vogel 2008) and 0.5 (Onaran and Galanis 2012) for Germany. The decrease in the wage share has, therefore, contributed to the increase in the overall propensity to save. There is also considerable evidence that a higher propensity to save is associated with a higher level of household income, irrespective of the source of income. Brenke (2011), drawing on data from the German Socio Economic Panel (GSOEP), reports that households in the bottom half of the distribution have slightly reduced their saving rates after 2000, whereas households in the upper half of the distribution, particularly in the top decile, have slightly increased their saving rates, which has overcompensated for the falling saving rates in the lower parts of the distribution. Van Treeck and Sturn (2012) conclude from this evidence that the relative income model, according to which consumption expenditure is affected by relative income ('keeping up with the Joneses'), has little explanatory power for Germany. Rising inequality rather led to a widespread feeling of insecurity even within the upper part of the middle class.

Wealth effects on consumption have been examined extensively in the econometric literature. Studies have shown that (financial and housing) wealth is a statistically significant determinant of consumption in many countries (Boone and Girouard 2002; Onaran et al. 2011). However, Dreger and Slacalek (2007) argued that the marginal propensity to consume out of financial and housing wealth in capital-market based countries has been significantly higher than in bank-based countries. Therefore, they conclude that these effects are of minor importance in the case of Germany, a typical bank-based country. Furthermore, German households' wealth increases were fairly moderate from the mid-1990s until the crisis, German house prices did not see any significant tendency to rise, and wealth distribution was highly unequal.

Considering both financial and real wealth in Figure 7.6, in the years after the 'new economy' crisis, financial wealth in relation to disposable income of German households stagnated because of positive saving but declining stock market prices, and it started to rise again from 2004 until the Great Recession. The most important assets held by private households were real estate assets. The relation to disposable income continuously increased from the early 1990s until the Great Recession. This development was exclusively driven by new acquisition of real estate, because residential property prices did not increase at all in Germany (BIS 2012).

Finally, real and financial net wealth is extremely unequally distributed among households and individuals in Germany, and the degree of inequality had actually increased prior to the Great Recession. The Gini

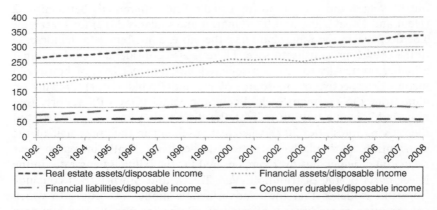

Source: Deutsche Bundesbank and Statistisches Bundesamt (2010), Deutsche Bundesbank (2012–14), our calculations.

Figure 7.6   Assets and liabilities of households, Germany, 1992–2008 (per cent of disposable income)

coefficient for net wealth distribution among adults rose from 0.777 in 2002 to 0.799 in 2007 and decreased again to 0.78 in 2012. Despite the decrease, Germany has the most unequal wealth distribution in the Euro area (Grabka and Westermeier 2014).

Financialisation and the Current Account

As we have seen in the second section of this chapter, Germany can be categorised as an 'export-led mercantilist' country, having generated huge current account surpluses since the early 2000s, in particular. From 2001 onwards net exports increased rapidly until 2007, when it peaked at 7 per cent of GDP, and the current account surplus reached 7.5 per cent of GDP (Figure 7.7). The net international investment position increased rapidly as well and reached 26 per cent of GDP in 2007 (Deutsche Bundesbank 2012–14). This pushed the primary income balance into positive territory from 2004 onwards, contributing to the high current account surpluses. During the crisis net exports decreased but recovered relatively quickly after 2009. Net-primary income also stabilised, after a short decline in 2008, and the current account balance reached pre-crisis levels again in 2012.

Considering the regional dispersion of German trade surpluses (Statistisches Bundesamt 2007–2012, 2013), we find that the largest part of the surplus was with EU countries, particularly with other Euro area countries. Smaller surpluses were achieved against the Americas, and here

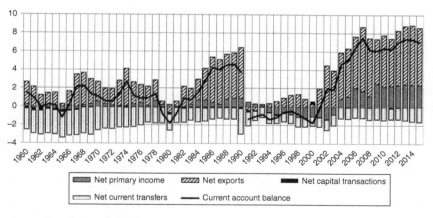

Note: West Germany until 1990.

Source: European Commission (2014a).

Figure 7.7   Current account, Germany, 1960–2015 (per cent of GDP)

in particular the USA. The decline of the overall trade surplus during the 2008/09 crisis was largely due to decreasing net exports to advanced economies, while the deficit with Asia was reduced. The fast recovery after the crisis seems largely to have been driven by increasing surpluses/decreasing deficits against non-EU countries – in particular Asia and the Americas. In contrast, the poor growth performance of many Euro area and EU countries has fed back on Germany through a shrinking surplus with these country groups.

Looking at the potential determinants of German exports we start with the long-run development of price competitiveness since the early 1970s (Deutsche Bundesbank 2012–14). Interestingly, the two periods with rapid increases in German net exports, the 1980s and the 2000s until the Great Recession (Figure 7.7), were not associated with improved price competitiveness against the main trading partners. In the 1980s price competitiveness rather deteriorated. And in the early 2000s it remained constant, because the improvement with respect to the other Euro area member countries was more or less compensated for by a deterioration of German price competitiveness with respect to the non-euro trading partners, mainly because of the appreciation of the euro.

Considering non-price competitiveness, it is remarkable that the German economy, unlike other developed economies, has maintained a relatively high share of manufacturing in net value added (24 per cent in 2007, France: 12 per cent; UK: 12 per cent; USA: 13 per cent) (OECD 2014). Besides large industrial firms, the German economy contains a vibrant sector of small- and medium-sized companies, both focused on the production of high quality, R&D intensive products. Additionally, in international comparison, production is heavily geared towards capital goods.[3] Storm and Naastepad (2015) relate the ability to produce in the high quality segment to the German corporatist model, which they claim still exists, despite policies aiming at 'structural reforms' in the course of the 1990s and the early 2000s. With this high non-price competitiveness German exports can be assumed to be highly sensitive to dynamic growth of export markets and trading partners. Due to the focus on capital goods, German exporters can in particular benefit from high growth in catching-up countries with high rates of investment in capital goods (Storm and Naastepad 2015).

From this perspective, Germany's export performance and its current account position depend heavily on the dynamic development of demand in the rest of the world, and in particular on the development of investment in capital goods. As can easily be seen, comparing Figures 7.8 and 7.7, the acceleration of German net exports in the 1980s and the 2000s indeed highly correlates with an acceleration of worldwide investment expenditures: After a relatively stagnant phase in the beginning of the

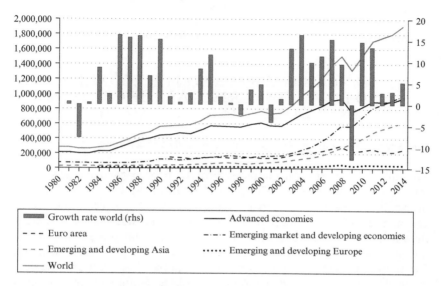

Source: International Monetary Fund (2014), own calculations.

Figure 7.8   *Gross fixed capital formation for different country groups*
(Billion US-Dollar (rhs), growth in per cent (lhs))

1980s, worldwide investment picked up in 1984, which allowed Germany
to strongly increase net exports. A similar pattern can be observed
when worldwide gross capital formation picked up rapidly in 2002. The
extraordinary investment demand growth in this period was dominated
by dynamic demand from emerging and developing countries, which
had only contributed a relatively small part to total investment demand
until then.

To sum up, we would argue that the German economy, because of its
institutional characteristics and its strong industrial sector, can draw on
high non-price competitiveness, which seems to be more important than
competitive gains in nominal unit labour costs and related price competitiveness when it comes to the explanation of export and net export
dynamics. This conclusion is supported by several results in the recent
econometric literature. Storm and Naastepad (2015) and Schröder (2011)
only find very small effects of price competitiveness on the German trade
balance in their estimations for the periods 1996–2008 and 1991–2010,
respectively. The development of the German trade balance is almost completely explained by the dynamics of foreign demand relative to domestic
demand in their estimations. Further evidence is provided by the European

Commission (2010b), which finds a comparatively small price elasticity for German exports using data for the period 1980–2008.

7.4   FINANCIALISATION AND THE ECONOMIC AND FINANCIAL CRISES AS THE CRISIS OF FINANCE-DOMINATED CAPITALISM

The Transmission of the Crisis Starting in 2007 to Germany

The 2008/09 recession in Germany proved to be particularly strong by international comparison. Whereas real GDP in the USA – the country of origin of the financial crisis – dropped by 2.8 per cent, the fall in German real GDP was more than 5 per cent, and it was also clearly larger than in the Euro area as a whole (OECD 2014). This was mainly due to the fact that, as a neo-mercantilist economy driven by export demand, Germany was particularly hard hit by the global slowdown and the dramatically falling export demand. One striking feature of the German slowdown, however, must be stressed: Although the recession was stronger in Germany than in many other economies, the loss in employment and the corresponding increase in the unemployment rate were much smaller (Table 7.3). This can be partially explained by a dramatic rise in short-time work, heavily subsidised by the government, and the extensive use of the so-called working-time accounts, allowing firms to flexibly adjust their labour volume without firing workers (see OECD 2010; SVR 2009b; Will 2011). Another striking feature was the fast recovery in Germany. After the large drop of GDP in 2009, growth picked up strongly in 2010 and 2011 and the unemployment rate fell to levels recently experienced only during the re-unification boom. The main drivers of the recovery were initially (net) exports and then investment. Real exports had already completely recovered in 2010 from the collapse in 2009. Private consumption only accelerated considerably in 2011. Since 2012 this export-led recovery has made German current account-GDP ratios rise even above the pre-crisis ratios of 7.5 per cent of GDP (Table 7.3).

The German Council of Economic Experts (SVR) has identified two important channels by which the crisis was transmitted into the German economy (SVR 2009a): the foreign trade channel and the financial market channel. Of course, the financial transmission channel of the crisis into Germany was closely related to the rapidly increasing German current account surpluses in the course of the early 2000s. Net foreign financial assets held by German wealth owners rapidly increased up to 700 billion euro in 2007 (SVR 2009a, p. 91). Most of these foreign assets were held

Table 7.3   *Key macroeconomic variables, Germany, 2007–2014*
(percentage change if not indicated otherwise)

	2007	2008	2009	2010	2011	2012	2013	2014*
Real gross domestic product	3.4	0.8	−5.1	3.9	3.4	0.9	0.5	1.9
Real private final consumption expenditure	−0.2	0.7	0.3	1.0	2.3	0.7	1.0	1.4
Real government final consumption expenditure	1.4	3.2	3.0	1.3	1.0	1.0	0.7	1.6
Real gross fixed capital formation	5.0	0.6	−11.6	5.2	7.1	−1.3	−0.5	5.7
Real total domestic expenditure	1.9	1.0	−2.2	2.3	2.8	−0.2	0.5	1.6
Real exports of goods and services	8.3	2.3	−13.0	14.8	8.1	3.8	1.0	5.1
Real imports of goods and services	5.6	3.0	−7.8	12.3	7.5	1.8	1.0	4.8
Unemployment rate (per cent of labour force)	8.7	7.5	7.8	7.1	6.0	5.5	5.3	5.0
General government fin. balance (per cent of GDP)	0.2	−0.1	−3.1	−4.2	−0.8	0.1	0.0	−0.2
Short-term interest rate (per cent)	4.3	4.6	1.2	0.8	1.4	0.6	0.2	0.1
Nominal unit labour costs	−0.8	2.3	5.6	−0.9	0.9	3.0	2.2	0.9
Compensation per employee	0.8	2.1	0.1	2.4	3.0	2.6	2.0	2.4
Harmonised consumer price index	2.3	2.8	0.2	1.2	2.5	2.1	1.6	1.1
Current account balance (per cent of GDP)	7.5	6.2	5.9	6.3	6.8	7.5	7.6	7.9

Note: * Forecast by the OECD, nominal unit labour costs and compensation per employee by European Commission (2014a).

Source: OECD (2014), European Commission (2014a).

by German banks such that the ratio of foreign assets to equity of the German banking sector increased tremendously. While the entire foreign exposure stood at about 2.7 times banks' equity in 1995, it had increased to 7.6 times at the end of 2007. Correspondingly, German banks had to bear heavy losses when problems occurred internationally. The write-offs of large German financial institutions (banks and insurance companies) directly related to the financial crisis amounted to 102 billion euros in the period from 2007 to August 2009 (SVR 2009a).

The Bailout of the Financial Sector

The immediate political responses towards the financial crisis were the Financial Market Stabilisation Act (*Finanzmarktstabilisierungsgesetz*, FMStG), as well as the establishment of the Federal Agency of Financial Market Stabilisation (*Bundesanstalt für Finanzmarktstabilisierung*, FMSA) and the Special Financial Market Stabilisation Fund (*Sonderfonds Finanzmarktstabilisierung*, SoFFin) as part of the FMSA in October 2008 (SVR 2009b, Chapter 4). The SoFFin was endowed with 480 billion euros in order to re-capitalise banks and to provide them with guarantees. Later on in 2009, the SoFFin was also empowered to establish wind-down agencies, which could be used to transfer assets from banks' balance sheets to those newly created special purpose vehicles (Detzer and Herr 2014, Chapter 12). The establishment of wind-down agencies was used by two banks, the West LB and the Hypo Real Estate Group. By the end of 2010, the total volume of all these measures peaked at 323 billion euros (FMSA 2014). Guarantees and risk assumptions had been reduced to zero at the end of 2013 (Table 7.4) and according to an interim report, none of the guarantees was used and the SoFFin received fees of 2 billion euros for providing those guarantees. However, substantial risks from the capital provisions, which stood at 17.1 billion euros in June 2014, still exist, along with risks stemming from the bad banks, which still held assets with a nominal value of 233.8 billion euros at the end of 2013. The FMSA estimates that losses on those risks may reach a magnitude of 22 billion euros (Bundesministerium der Finanzen 2013).

All these measures were sufficient to contain the financial crisis and to prevent a financial meltdown in Germany. Despite the stabilisation, there were widespread fears that the damaged financial sector would be curbing loans, thus causing a credit crunch. However, the diverse structure of the German banking sector in which public, cooperative and private banks as well as regionally, nationally and internationally active banks coexist helped to prevent such a scenario and no widespread credit crunch undermined the recovery (Detzer 2014). However, the drawback of the financial

Table 7.4   Stabilisation aid of SoFFin, Germany, 2008–2014 (€ billion)

	Total volume of all measures	Bad banks (nominal asset volume)			Capital injections	Guarantees	Risk assumptions
		Total	FMS-WM	EAA			
31.12.2008	32.1				8.2	23.9	
31.12.2009	166.4				25.7	140.7	5.9 (06/10/09)
31.12.2010	323	238.1	174.3	63.8	29.3	55.6	0
30.06.2011	267.5	217.6	160.5	57.1	17.7	32.2	0
31.12.2011	259.7	211.7	160.7	51	19.8	28.2	0
30.06.2012	227.8	197	151.4	45.6	19.8	11	0
31.12.2012	302.7	280.2	136.9	143.3	18.8	3.7	0
30.06.2013	263	244.8	128.5	116.3	17.1	1.1	0
31.12.2013	233.8	216.7	119.1	97.6	17.1	0	0
30.06.2014	N/A	N/A	N/A	N/A	17.1	0	0

Notes: FMS-WM – FMS Wertmanagement, EAA – Erste Abwicklungsanstalt.

Source: FMSA (2014), our translation.

rescue measures was a considerable contribution to the rise in the government gross debt-GDP ratio, which increased from 65.2 per cent in 2007 to 82.5 per cent in 2010 and only decreased slowly thereafter (European Commission 2014a). This increase was also caused by the expansionary fiscal policies implemented in response to the crisis, which will be discussed in the following section.

Macroeconomic Policies and Recovery from the Crisis

The global financial and economic crisis led to remarkably fast and strong economic policy reactions in many countries (OECD 2009). As an immediate measure, central banks provided extensive liquidity to money markets, thereby meeting their 'lender of last resort' functions. And, to a different extent in different economies, monetary policy and fiscal policy switched to expansion in order to tackle the crisis of the real economy.

Since the start of the euro in 1999, of course, monetary policy has no longer been a German but a Euro area-wide policy in the hands of the European Central Bank (ECB). With respect to its role as a lender of last resort, the ECB acted in a very fast and internationally coordinated manner, thereby saving the financial system from collapse. However, with respect to interest rate policy, the ECB basically followed 'business as usual', which can be described as 'too little too late' (Hein and Truger

2007b) as compared with the US Fed. In July 2008, when the dramatic economic slowdown could not be ignored any longer, the ECB even increased the key interest rate, the main refinancing rate, by 25 basis points to 4.25 per cent with recourse to 'inflationary dangers' (ECB 2014). The ECB started cutting interest rates only after oil prices – and consequently the growth in the harmonised index of consumer prices – had started to fall. The coming dramatic real economic slowdown was completely ignored initially: interest rate cuts came well after GDP had started to fall strongly. This late reaction of the ECB was disadvantageous in particular for those Euro area member countries that were hit hard by the crisis, like Germany. But the consistently low nominal interest rates since then have favoured all Euro area member countries. And this provided an additional impetus for countries like Germany in which economic expansion, driven by net exports, resumed quickly.

Wage policies did not actively help to stabilise the German economy during the crisis (Table 7.3). In the crisis year 2009, the compensation per employee only increased by 0.1 per cent. However, a normalisation of compensation growth in the years 2010–2013, compared with the years before the crisis, contributed to the recovery of private consumption demand. Nominal unit labour cost growth increased in 2008 and 2009 and thus contributed to the rise in German inflation. However, this was due to the usual decrease in labour productivity growth in the course of the crisis because of labour hoarding, in particular, actively supported by the government.

It was therefore fiscal policy that mainly contributed to the quick recovery. In the 2008/9 crisis, fiscal policy reacted in a remarkably counter-cyclical way. After some hesitation and some merely 'cosmetic' measures, in the first months of 2009 a substantial stimulus package for 2009 and 2010 was enacted (Hein and Truger 2010). Overall, the packages together with some additional measures included substantial increases in public investment, as well as tax relief for business and households. The cumulative stimulus for 2009 and 2010 amounted to 3.1 per cent of 2008 GDP, which is certainly above the Euro area average level. However, the US stimulus package had a volume of more than 5 per cent of GDP in the period 2008–2010, and was therefore substantially bigger (OECD 2009).

Figure 7.9 shows the budget balance, as well as the output gap as a measure of the cyclical condition of the German economy. As can be seen, in 2009 the budget balance reacted by 0.49 per cent of GDP per one percentage point drop in the output gap. In 2010 German fiscal policies accepted a further increase in the budget deficits in the face of an improvement of the output gap and the recovery of the economy. With the fast

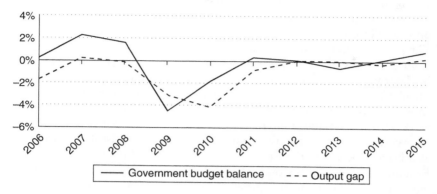

Note: OECD projections for 2014 and 2015.

Source: OECD (2014).

Figure 7.9 *Government budget balance (per cent of GDP) and output gap (per cent of potential GDP), Germany, 2006–2015*

recovery in Germany the output gap closed in 2011 and the government reduced its deficit accordingly.

From the analysis so far it can be concluded that the rapid German recovery since 2009 has been based on three main pillars. First, the successful containment of the crisis in the financial sector and the resilience of the three pillar banking system (public banks, cooperative banks, private banks) prevented a collapse of the financial system and a credit crunch. Second, the German mercantilist type of development, which was a major cause for global imbalances before the crisis and the severity of the crisis in Germany itself, allowed for a rapid recovery via the net export channel as soon as the world economy recovered from the crisis and growth in emerging market economies of Asia and the Americas picked up, in particular. Third, expansionary fiscal policies contributed to the quick recovery of the German economy by means of stabilising domestic demand.

However, this German type of recovery suffers from two major drawbacks. First, to the extent that it is driven by net exports, it has to rely on the export-led mercantilist type of development that considerably contributed to world and regional imbalances and to the severity of the crisis in Germany itself. It therefore contains the seeds for further imbalances, fragilities and future vulnerabilities of the German economy, and it contributes significantly to the persistent euro crisis (see Cesaratto and Stirati 2010; Uxo et al. 2011; Hein 2013/14). Second, as a political precondition for the German stimulus packages, the so-called 'debt brake' was introduced into the German constitution. From 2016 onwards, the federal budget will only be allowed to run a cyclically adjusted deficit of 0.35 per cent of GDP. The federal states' (*Länder*) budgets will have to be structurally balanced from 2020 onwards. As the cyclically adjusted or 'structural' deficit will be determined by a variation of the European Commission's method of calculating structural deficits, it will exhibit the same strong sensitivity to short-term revisions of GDP forecasts, and will therefore prevent the full working of automatic stabilisers. Discretionary fiscal policy will only be allowed under very restrictive conditions. This type of fiscal austerity has also been imposed on the Euro area via a tightened Stability and Growth Pact and the new Fiscal Compact. All this will severely limit the room for manoeuvre for German and European fiscal policies in the future, impede current account rebalancing and constrain aggregate demand management in the Euro area (Hein and Truger 2014; Truger and Will 2012).

7.5   CONCLUSIONS

In this chapter we have studied the long-run changes between the financial and the non-financial sectors in Germany, and in particular the effects of these changes on the macroeconomic developments that led or contributed to the financial crisis starting in 2007 and the Great Recession in 2008/09. In the second section we classified the development in Germany since the early/mid 1990s as 'export-led mercantilist'.

In the third section we then examined the long-run effects of financialisation on the German economy in more detail. First, we explored the effects of an increasing dominance of finance on income distribution and found some indications that the channels of re-distribution in favour of gross profits in the era of financialisation identified in the general literature were operating in Germany.

Second, the effects of an increasing dominance of finance on investment in capital stock were examined. Again, we found some indications that the internal means of finance and the preference channels through which financialisation is said to dampen real investment were operating in Germany as well.

Third, the relationship between financialisation and household consumption was analysed in more detail. In the case of Germany, no indication of significant wealth effects or emulation effects ('Keeping up with the Joneses') on consumption could be detected. Instead, we found that consumption expenditure was dominated by an increasing average propensity to save before the crisis, driven by re-distribution of income, on the one hand, and rising pre-cautionary saving triggered by policies of deregulation of the labour market and downsizing of the welfare state, on the other hand.

Fourth, we more closely examined the development and the determinants of the current account in the period of an increasing dominance of finance. Net exports were the main drivers of German growth, in particular in the trade cycle before the financial crisis and the Great Recession. We argued that Germany, due to the institutional setting and the strong industrial sector, benefitted from high non-price competitiveness, which provides a favourable position when world demand is strong. Price competitiveness only had a minor role to play. Therefore, when global investment demand picked up in the early 2000s, wage moderation policies and restrictive macroeconomic policies as a whole contributed to depress import demand, while growing activity in the rest of the world stimulated export growth, explaining the widely praised export performance of Germany. However, actual growth performance lagged behind most other developed countries.

This specific integration of Germany into the world economy explains to a large extent the transmission of the international financial and economic crisis to Germany. In Section 7.4 we argued that Germany was particularly exposed to the international trade channel and the financial contagion channel of the crisis. However, the specific German export-led mercantilist type of development was also able to provide the condition for a quick recovery, as soon as world demand accelerated again. Active counter-cyclical fiscal policies, as well as expansionary effects of low interest rate monetary policies contributed to this quick recovery. However, we finally argued that this German type of recovery suffers from two major drawbacks. First, it has continued to rely on the export-led mercantilist type of development that has considerably contributed to world and regional imbalances, to the severity of the crisis in Germany itself, and also to the ongoing euro crisis. Second, as a political price for the active fiscal policies during the crisis, Germany – and, under the pressure of Germany, the Euro area member countries – have implemented 'debt brakes' into their constitutions – or agreed to do so. This will mean continuously restrictive fiscal policies for the future, highly constrained room for manoeuvre in future crises, as well as severe obstacles to internal rebalancing and recovery of the Euro area.

NOTES

1. For a macroeconomic approach towards 'financialisation' or 'finance-dominated capitalism' highlighting the four channels mentioned below, see Hein (2012).

2. For a more extensive treatment of the effects of financialisation on income distribution in Germany see Hein and Detzer (2015).
3. The share of investment goods production in total value added for Germany was about 12.5 per cent, Japan was at only 10 per cent, Spain at 7 per cent, the USA at 6 per cent, the UK at 6 per cent (Grömling 2014). See also European Commission (2010b).

REFERENCES

Alvaredo, F., A.B. Atkinson, T. Piketty and E. Saez (2014), 'The World Top Incomes Database', available at: http://g-mond.parisschoolofeconomics.eu/topincomes/.
Barba, A. and M. Pivetti (2009), 'Rising household debt: its causes and macroeconomic implications – a long-period analysis', *Cambridge Journal of Economics*, **33**, 113–137.
Bibow, J. (2005), 'Germany in crisis: the unification challenge, macroeconomic policy shocks and traditions, and EMU', *International Review of Applied Economics*, **19**, 29–50.
BIS Bank for International Settlements (2012), 'Property Price Statistics', available at: http://www.bis.org/statistics/pp.htm.
Boone, L. and N. Girouard (2002), 'The stock market, the housing market and consumer behaviour', *OECD Economic Studies*, **35**, 175–200.
Brenke, K. (2011), 'Einkommensumverteilung schwächt privaten Verbrauch', *DIW Wochenbericht*, August, 2–12.
Bundesministerium der Finanzen (2013), 'Fünf Jahre Finanzmarktstabilisier ungs fonds unter dem Dach der Bundesanstalt für Finanzmarktstabilisier ung, Gastbeitrag der Bundesanstalt für Finanzmarktstabilisierung (FMSA)', Monatsbericht Dezember 2013, Bundesministerium der Finanzen, Berlin, available at: http://www.bundesfinanzministerium.de/Content/DE/Monatsberichte/2013/12/Downloads/monatsbericht_2013_12_deutsch.pdf?__blob=publication File&v=7.
Cesaratto, S. and A. Stirati (2010), 'Germany and the European and global crises', *International Journal of Political Economy*, **39** (4), 56–86.
Cynamon, B. and S. Fazzari (2008), 'Household debt in the consumer age: source of growth – risk of collapse', *Capitalism and Society*, **3** (2), 1–30.
Detzer, D. (2014), 'The German financial system and the financial crisis', *Intereconomics*, **49** (2), 56–64.
Detzer, D. (2015), 'Inequality and the financial system – the case of Germany', *The Pakistan Development Review*, **54** (4), 585–608.
Detzer, D., N. Dodig, T. Evans, E. Hein, and H. Herr (2013), 'The German financial system', FESSUD Studies in Financial Systems, No. 3, University of Leeds.
Detzer, D. and E. Hein (2014), 'Financialisation and the financial and economic crises: the case of Germany', FESSUD Studies in Financial Systems, No. 16, University of Leeds.
Detzer, D. and H. Herr (2014), 'Financial regulation in Germany', FESSUD Working Paper Series, No. 55/2014, University of Leeds.
Deutsche Bundesbank (2012–14), 'Time Series Data Base', available at: http://www.bundesbank.de/Navigation/EN/Statistics/Time_series_databases/Macro_economic_time_series/macro_economic_time_series_node.html.

Deutsche Bundesbank and Statistisches Bundesamt (2010), 'Sektorale und gesamtwirtschaftliche Vermögensbilanzen 1992–2010', Wiesbaden, available at: http://www.bundesbank.de/Redaktion/DE/Downloads/Statistiken/sektorale_und _gesamtwirtschaftliche_vermoegensbilanzen.pdf?__blob=publicationFile.

Dreger, C. and J. Slacalek (2007), 'Finanzmarktentwicklung, Immobilienpreise und Konsum', *DIW Wochenbericht*, **74**, 533–536.

Dünhaupt, P. (2011), 'Financialization, corporate governance and income distribution in the USA and Germany: introducing an adjusted wage share indicator', in T. Niechoj, Ö. Onaran, E. Stockhammer, A. Truger and T. van Treeck (eds), *Stabilising an Unequal Economy? Public Debt, Financial Regulation, and Income Distribution*, Marburg: Metropolis.

Dünhaupt, P. (2012), 'Financialization and the rentier income share – evidence from the USA and Germany', *International Review of Applied Economics*, **26**, 465–487.

ECB (2014), 'European Central Bank, Statistical Data Warehouse', available at: http://sdw.ecb.europa.eu/reports.do?node=1000005.

European Commission (2010a), 'AMECO Database', Spring 2010, available at: http://ec.europa.eu/economy_finance/db_indicators/ameco/index_en.htm.

European Commission (2010b), 'The impact of the global crisis on competitiveness and current account divergences in the euro area', *Quarterly Report on the Euro Area*, **9** (1), 7–48.

European Commission (2014a), 'AMECO Database', Spring 2014, available at: http://ec.europa.eu/economy_finance/db_indicators/ameco/index_en.htm.

European Commission (2014b), 'Eurostat Statistics on Income, Social Inclusion and Living Conditions', September 2014, available at: http://epp.eurostat. ec.europa.eu/portal/page/portal/income_social_inclusion_living_conditions/ introduction#.

FMSA (2014), 'Bundesanstalt für Finanzmarktstabilisierung. Historischer Überblick über die Maßnahmen des SoFFin', Stand 30.06.2014, available at: http://www.fmsa.de/export/sites/standard/downloads/20140630_Historischer_ Ueberblick.pdf.

Grabka, M.M. and C. Westermeier (2014), 'Anhaltend hohe Vermögensungleichheit in Deutschland', *DIW Wochenbericht*, September, 151–164.

Grömling, M. (2014), 'A supply-side explanation for current account imbalances', *Intereconomics*, **49** (1), 30–35.

Hein, E. (2012), *The Macroeconomics of Finance-Dominated Capitalism – and its Crisis*, Cheltenham: Edward Elgar.

Hein, E. (2013/14), 'The crisis of finance-dominated capitalism in the euro area, deficiencies in the economic policy architecture, and deflationary stagnation policies', *Journal of Post Keynesian Economics*, **36** (2), 325–354.

Hein, E. (2015), 'Finance-dominated capitalism and re-distribution of income – a Kaleckian perspective', *Cambridge Journal of Economics*, **39**, 907–934.

Hein, E. and D. Detzer (2015), 'Finance-dominated capitalism and income distribution: a Kaleckian perspective on the case of Germany', *Italian Economic Journal*, **1**, 171–191.

Hein, E. and A. Truger (2005), 'What ever happened to Germany? Is the decline of the former European key currency country caused by structural sclerosis or by macroeconomic mismanagement?', *International Review of Applied Economics*, **19**, 3–28.

Hein, E. and A. Truger (2007a), 'Germany's post-2000 stagnation in the European context – a lesson in macroeconomic mismanagement', in P. Arestis, E. Hein and E. Le Heron (eds), *Aspects of Modern Monetary and Macroeconomic Policies*, Basingstoke: Palgrave Macmillan.

Hein, E. and A. Truger (2007b), 'Monetary policy, macroeconomic policy mix and economic performance in the Euro area', in E. Hein and A. Truger (eds), *Money, Distribution and Economic Policy: Alternatives to Orthodox Macroeconomics*, Cheltenham: Edward Elgar.

Hein, E. and A. Truger (2010), 'Financial crisis, global recession and macro-economic policy reactions – the case of Germany', in S. Dullien, E. Hein, A. Truger and T. van Treeck (eds), *The World Economy in Crisis – The Return of Keynesianism?*, Marburg: Metropolis.

Hein, E. and A. Truger (2014), 'Fiscal policy and rebalancing in the euro area: a critique of the German debt brake from a post-Keynesian perspective', *Panoeconomicus*, **61**, 21–38.

Hein, E. and T. van Treeck (2010), '"Financialisation" in post-Keynesian models of distribution and growth – a systematic review', in M. Setterfield (ed.), *Handbook of Alternative Theories of Economic Growth*, Cheltenham: Edward Elgar.

Hein, E. and L. Vogel (2008), 'Distribution and growth reconsidered – empirical results for six OECD countries', *Cambridge Journal of Economics*, **32**, 479–511.

Herr, H. and M. Kazandziska (2011), *Macroeconomic Policy Regimes in Western Industrial Countries*, Abingdon: Routledge.

International Monetary Fund (2014), 'World Economic Outlook Database', April 2014, available at: www.imf.org/external/pubs/ft/weo/2014/02/weodata/index. aspx.

Klär, E. and J. Slacalek (2006), 'Entwicklung der Sparquote in Deutschland – Hindernis für die Erholung der Konsumnachfrage', *DIW Wochenbericht*, 40/2006, 537–543.

OECD (2008), *Growing Unequal? Income Distribution and Poverty in OECD Countries*, Paris: OECD Publishing.

OECD (2009), *Economic Outlook*, Interim Report, March, Paris: OECD Publishing.

OECD (2010), *OECD Employment Outlook: Moving Beyond the Job-Crisis*, Paris: OECD Publishing.

OECD (2014), 'OECD.StatExtracts', available at: http//stats.oecd.org.

Onaran, Ö. and G. Galanis (2012), 'Is demand wage- or profit-led? National and global effects', ILO Conditions of Work and Employment Series 40, Geneva: ILO.

Onaran, Ö., E. Stockhammer and L. Grafl (2011), 'Financialisation, income distribution and aggregate demand in the USA', *Cambridge Journal of Economics*, **35**, 637–661.

Schröder, E. (2011), 'Trade balances in Germany and the United States: Demand dominates price', paper presented at the 15th conference of the Research Network Macroeconomics and Macroeconomic Policies (FMM), 'From crisis to growth? The challenge of imbalances, debt, and limited resources', Berlin, 27–29 October 2011.

Statistisches Bundesamt (2007–2012), 'Außenhandel – Zusammenfassende Über-sichten für den Außenhandel (endgültige Ergebnisse)', 7 (1), Wiesbaden: Statistis-ches Bundesamt, available at: https://www.destatis.de/DE/Publikationen/ Thematisch/Aussenhandel/Gesamtentwicklung/ZusammenfassendeUebersich tenJendgueltig.html.

Statistisches Bundesamt (2011a), 'Export, Import, Globalisierung. Deutscher Außenhandel', Statistisches Bundesamt, August, Wiesbaden, available at: https://www.destatis.de/DE/Publikationen/Thematisch/Aussenhandel/Gesamtentwick lung/AussenhandelWelthandel5510006127004.pdf?__blob=publicationFile.

Statistisches Bundesamt (2011b), 'Inlandsproduktsberechnung – Detaillierte Jahresergebnisse', Fachserie 18 Reihe 1.4 – 2011, Wiesbaden, Statistisches Bundesamt, available at: https://www.destatis.de/DE/Publikationen/Thematisch/Volkswirtscha ftlicheGesamtrechnungen/Inlandsprodukt/InlandsproduktsberechnungEndgueltig PDF_2180140.pdf?__blob=publicationFile.

Statistisches Bundesamt (2012), 'Sector Accounts – Annual results 1991 onwards – 1991 to 2011', Statistisches Bundesamt, August, Wiesbaden: Statistisches Bundesamt, 1–87, available at: https://www.destatis.de/DE/Publikationen/Thematisch/ VolkswirtschaftlicheGesamtrechnungen/Nationaleinkommen/SectorAccounts AnnualresultsPDF_5812106.pdf.

Statistisches Bundesamt (2013), 'Außenhandel – Zusammenfassende Übersichten für den Außenhandel (vorläufige Jahresergebnisse)', **7** (1), Wiesbaden: Statistisches Bundesamt, available at: https://www.destatis.de/DE/Publikationen/ Thematisch/Aussenhandel/Gesamtentwicklung/ZusammenfassendeUebersichten Jvorlaeufig.html.

Statistisches Bundesamt (2014), 'Genesis-Online Data Base', available at: https://www-genesis.destatis.de/genesis/online.

Storm, S. and C.W.M. Naastepad (2015), 'Crisis and recovery in the German economy: the real lessons', *Structural Change and Economic Dynamics*, **32**, 11–24.

SVR (2009a), 'Deutschland im Internationalen Konjunkturzusammenhang. Expertise im Auftrag der Bundesregierung', Wiesbaden: Statistisches Bundesamt.

SVR (2009b), 'Die Zukunft nicht aufs Spiel setzen', Jahresgutachten 2009/10, Wiesbaden: Statistisches Bundesamt.

Truger, A. and H. Will (2012), 'The German "debt brake": a shining example for European fiscal policy?', IPE Working Paper 15/2012, Institute for International Political Economy Berlin.

Uxo, J., J. Paul and E. Febrero (2011), 'Current account imbalances in the Monetary Union and the Great Recession: causes and policies', *Panoeconomicus*, **5**, 571–592.

Van Treeck, T. and S. Sturn (2012), 'Income inequality as a cause of the Great Recession? A survey of current debates', Conditions of Work and Employment Series, No. 39, Geneva: ILO.

Will, H. (2011), 'Germany's short time compensation program: macroeconom(etr) ic insight', IMK Working Paper 1/2011, Macroeconomic Policy Institute (IMK) at the Hans Boeckler Foundation, Düsseldorf.

8. Swedish financialisation: 'Nordic noir' or 'safe haven'?*

Alexis Stenfors

8.1 INTRODUCTION

This chapter studies the Swedish financialisation process through the lens of the global financial crisis and the subsequent Euro area sovereign debt crisis. The emphasis is twofold. First, by acknowledging the rapid and widespread nature of the Swedish financialisation process since the 1980s, it traces the transformation of Sweden from a 'debt-led consumption boom' country towards an 'export-led mercantilist' regime. Second, by highlighting the country's unique characteristics within these classifications, the report considers its ability to shield itself from some of the turbulence in the international financial markets following the recent crises.

The outline of the chapter is as follows. Section 8.2 provides a summary of key characteristics of the Swedish financialisation process. Section 8.3 studies the effects of the Swedish financialisation process in more detail by examining two channels in particular: household consumption and the current account. Section 8.4 analyses the transmission mechanism of the global financial crisis and the Euro area sovereign debt crisis vis-à-vis Sweden. Section 8.5 concludes.

8.2 THE SWEDISH FINANCIALISATION PROCESS SINCE THE 1980s

The demise of the 'Swedish model'[1] coincides with the deregulation process that was put in motion during the 1980s. This also marks the beginning of a remarkably widespread financialisation process in the country. Once put in motion, the financialisation process gained pace rapidly and

* The author wishes to thank Malcolm Sawyer and Daniel Detzer for valuable help, comments and suggestions – as well as participants at the Financialisation Workshop at Leeds University Business School on 28 July 2014 and the FESSUD Annual Conference in Warsaw on 16–17 October 2014.

has since profoundly changed Swedish society. Part of the transformation can be summarised as follows (Stenfors et al. 2014).

First, the country, traditionally regarded as having had a typical bank-based system, has embraced the more market-based model with gusto, and has in many respects gone further than Anglo-Saxon countries. Neoliberalism has penetrated Swedish society profoundly but also, perhaps surprisingly, with little social and political resistance. Seen from a political perspective, the country has transformed itself from a role model for those wishing to implement reforms often associated with the Swedish Social Democratic Party to a 'poster boy' for European parties on the Right, aiming to pursue an agenda with a limited role of the state.

Second, macroeconomic, as well as monetary, policy has changed remarkably during the period. The central bank adopted inflation targeting relatively early after a long tradition of various fixed exchange rate regimes, whereas government policy has changed to encompass a range of measures seemingly incompatible with the 'old' Swedish model, such as income tax cuts, large scale privatisation programmes, and policies aimed at achieving budget surpluses and government debt reduction.

Third, a high degree of protectionism has been replaced by internationalism and openness to foreign financial interests. Sweden today is truly a small, open, economy. The previously under-developed financial market is barely recognisable. For a country with less than 10 million people, Sweden and the Swedish krona (SEK) rank disproportionally high in terms of stock market capitalisation and turnover in the foreign exchange and derivatives markets. Seen from the perspective of the international financial markets, Sweden has evolved from being perceived as a volatile, unpredictable country during the late 1980s and early 1990s to gaining a 'safe-haven' status.

Fourth, the financialisation process has become highly visible in overall daily life, not least as market mechanisms have been encouraged to enter previously 'sacred' areas, such as housing, education, health care and pensions. The Swedish population has, directly and indirectly, become a collective of individual investors and risk managers highly exposed to the direction and volatility of the financial markets. In addition, the Swedish rate of increase in *in*equality is the highest in the world, albeit rising from very low levels. The consensus-based and solidaristic wage negotiation process has been replaced by mediation in between increasingly fragmented unions.

The financialisation process in Sweden might portray itself as a paradox. How could such a radical reform agenda be implemented without much opposition, either politically (given the political hegemony of the Social Democratic Party for almost a century) or in terms of popularity (given a largely homogenous population having grown accustomed to and prided itself for the Swedish model for several generations)? However, as Stenfors et al. (2014) argue, Sweden should not be regarded so much as a country that suddenly has abandoned the state in favour of the markets, but as a culture that historically has been distinctively consensus-based, pragmatic and also rather individualistic. Financialisation has been embraced widely not as a perceived end-goal in itself, but as a pragmatic choice in an on-going ambition to maintain economic growth, full employment and individual freedom in an increasingly globalised world. In fact, the famous Swedish model contained a number of features that, when put to the test at particular junctions in time, proved unusually fertile for grains of financialisation: an overall belief in market mechanisms and efficiency (as long as quality and security is assured); a relatively corporate-friendly tax system; a conflict-free and non-politicised wage negotiation process; a unique long-term corporate governance structure; a pragmatic adoption of inflation targeting outside the Euro area; a consensus-based agenda against budget deficits and unsustainable government debt; and a widely embraced strategy to increase household financial literacy both directly and indirectly.

However, Sweden has also had a different journey during the very recent era of financialisation, making similarities with other European countries hard to find yet again. Indeed, the global financial crisis and the subsequent Euro area crisis, which have provided the financialisation literature with an abundance of material and insights, have affected Sweden differently. This chapter aims to highlight some of these differences, and to trace their roots within the concept of financialisation.

Hein (2012) distinguishes between two (or sometimes four[2]) types of capitalism under financialisation, when attempting to classify countries in accordance with rising current account imbalances in Europe, as well as in the world economy. During the decade running up to the global financial crisis, 'debt-led consumption boom' countries (Greece, Ireland, Spain and the UK) were characterised by debt accumulation in the private sector, property booms and/or high increases in wealth-income ratios. High growth contributions of private consumption and domestic demand were mirrored in current account deficits. The countries were also characterised by relatively high real GDP growth rates, as well as increases in inflation rates and nominal unit labour costs.

According to this classification, however, Sweden firmly positioned itself within the opposite group: namely among the 'export-led mercantilist' European economies (along with Austria, Belgium, Germany and the Netherlands). These countries were characterised by current account surpluses stemming from weak private consumption and domestic demand,

Table 8.1   *Swedish GDP growth contributions of main demand aggregates*

Growth contribution / cycle	Household consumption	General government consumption	Gross fixed-capital formation	Stock-building	Balance of goods and services	Real GDP growth
1960–1969	2.38%	1.45%	1.20%	–	−0.67%	4.37%
1970–1979	1.59%	1.20%	0.20%	–	−0.55%	2.45%
1980–1989	0.71%	0.62%	1.06%	–	−0.15%	2.23%
1990–1993	−0.65%	−0.27%	−0.26%	−0.31%	0.32%	−0.93%
1994–2000	1.63%	0.12%	1.14%	0.20%	0.56%	3.66%
2001–2007	1.25%	0.26%	0.84%	0.00%	0.66%	3.01%
2008–2009	−0.06%	0.47%	−1.41%	−1.15%	−0.67%	−2.82%
2010–2013	1.18%	0.38%	0.79%	0.41%	0.26%	3.01%

Sources: NIER (2014), Statistics Sweden (2014) and author's calculations.

as well as surpluses in the balances of goods and services. Property booms and/or increases in wealth ratios were prominent in Belgium, the Netherlands and Sweden, but not in Austria and Germany. The countries were also characterised by low increases in inflation rates and nominal unit labour costs. Real GDP growth was consistently weaker among the countries in this group during the early 2000s – with Sweden being the exception.

However, as can be seen from Table 8.1, the three decades *prior* to the Swedish banking crisis of the early 1990s were characterised by high, but gradually slowing, GDP growth. Household and government consumption were key drivers of growth, as was the private corporate sector during the 1960s and 1980s. The balance of goods and services was negative. Thus, it could be argued that Sweden, prior to the financialisation era, could have been classified as a 'debt-led consumption regime'.

By contrast, during the last two decades, the growth contribution of government consumption has been very weak, whereas the balance of goods and services has seen a sharp reversal. Apart from the crisis-eras of 1990–93 and 2008–09 (which have been isolated as separate cycles for the sake of clarity), the growth contributions of household consumption and gross fixed-capital formation have been moderately positive. They have generally been high in comparison with other export-led mercantilist European economies, but lower than for debt-led consumption boom countries. Sweden's radical regime shift also becomes clear if we examine the sectoral financial balances (flows) during the equivalent cycles from 1980. As Table 8.2 shows, Sweden shifted to an export-led regime immediately after the domestic crises in the early 1990s.

As the following sections will demonstrate, Sweden has gone through a

Table 8.2   Swedish sectoral financial balances (flows), % of GDP

Financial balances / cycle	Public sector	Household sector	Corporate sector	External sector
1980–1989	−1.09%	−1.08%	2.10%	0.08%
1990–1993	−3.68%	2.00%	0.11%	1.53%
1994–2000	−2.30%	1.61%	3.98%	−3.52%
2001–2007	1.00%	1.56%	3.72%	−6.65%
2008–2009	0.59%	3.87%	3.16%	−7.69%
2010–2013	−0.53%	4.42%	2.37%	−6.42%

Sources: European Commission (2014).

transformation towards an export-led mercantilist economy that mirrors the demise of the old Swedish model and the rapid and widespread financialisation process during the recent decades. The country's experience during the global financial crisis echoes this transformation.

8.3   LONG-RUN EFFECTS OF THE SWEDISH FINANCIALISATION

Financialisation and Household Consumption

The debt-led consumption boom that prevailed in the run-up to the Swedish banking crisis was almost immediately replaced by an export-led mercantilist regime. Nonetheless, the contribution of household consumption to the Swedish GDP growth during the last decade has been higher than in other comparable European export-led mercantilist regimes. In fact, the financialisation process after the Swedish banking crisis appears to have created a new domestic housing boom that has neither been halted by the global financial crisis, nor the Euro area sovereign debt crisis.

Figure 8.1 shows the asset and debt composition of Sweden in relation to household disposable income from 1971 to 2013. Five broad trends are notable (Stenfors 2014).

First, wages and salaries make up the vast majority (over 80 per cent) of household factor income. At the same time, however, the share of dividend income as a percentage of the total non-wage factor income has increased substantially during the last two decades. Whereas the ratio was around 10 per cent after the Swedish banking crisis, it stood at over 30 per cent in 2013.

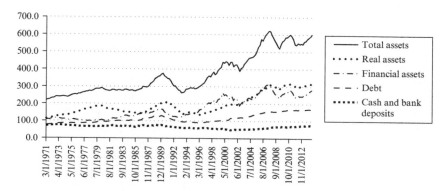

Note: Total assets exclusive collective insurance. Financial assets refer mainly to cash, bank deposits, bonds, mutual funds and shares. Real assets refer to single-family houses, tenant-owned apartments and second homes.

Sources: Statistics Sweden (2014) and Sveriges Riksbank (2014a).

Figure 8.1 Swedish household balance sheet 1971–2014 (% of disposable income)

Second, household financial assets roughly equalled household disposable income in 1980. Following the deregulation process, this ratio has gradually increased from 1 to 2.5. After a dip around the dot-com crisis, it has been fairly stable at around twice the disposable income. It has to be noted that 'financial assets' are of a volatile nature, as they are highly correlated with the development of the Swedish stock market.

Third, the distribution of household financial assets has seen a remarkable shift from what could be seen as relatively risk-free investments towards riskier assets. In addition, the share of insurance savings has increased substantially. Between 1980 and 1995, the share of deposits and savings accounts gradually fell from around two-thirds to one-third. The decrease was largely offset by an increase in individual insurance savings, shares and mutual funds. From 1996 to 2013, collective insurance saving is also included in the household assets as reported by Statistics Sweden. During this period, deposits, savings accounts, but also bond holdings continued to decline – whereas the proportion invested in shares and mutual funds[3] (as well as total insurance savings) increased.

In 2012, around three-quarters of the Swedish population invested in mutual funds (excluding the Premium Pension). It is important to note that mainly as a result of the new pension system, passed by the parliament in 1994, almost all adult Swedes are exposed to mutual funds directly or indirectly. The system separates the capital accumulation phase from the annuity phase in institutional terms, has no guarantees with regards to the rate of return, nor any additional regulations with regards to the funds allowed to act as outlets for the individuals' investments. Although there is a public fund for 'non-choosers' (that holds a mixed portfolio of bonds and domestic and foreign equities), the new pension system has undoubtedly had the overall tendency to transfer risk from state and employers to the individual. Pension saving has hereby been transformed towards a kind of active portfolio and risk management by the individual, with an increasing dependency on the performance and volatility of the financial markets. The incentives to save privately have increased, as have the requirements to gain financial literacy (Belfrage and Ryner 2009). Indeed, as pointed out by Belfrage (2008), the Swedish pension reform is extremely risk-privatising, also by European standards.

The fourth notable change relates to the housing market. Figure 8.1 above clearly shows the impact of the Swedish banking crisis on housing prices (and consequently 'real assets') during the early 1990s. The development of the property market was dramatic during this period (see Figure 8.2). However, the boom years came to an end during the autumn of 1989, with a large price correction. By the end of 1990, the real estate index had fallen by 52 per cent against its peak the previous year. Since 1993, however, real wealth has steadily increased from around 150 per cent of household disposable income to over 300 per cent. Whereas household financial asset returns are closely correlated with the development of the Swedish stock market, household real asset returns are equally dependent on the development of the housing market. Considering the magnitude of

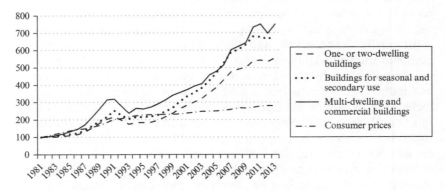

Source: Statistics Sweden (2014).

Figure 8.2   Real estate price index 1981–2013 (1981=100)

the banking crisis, however, the property and mortgage markets managed to recover quickly.

Today, more than 70 per cent of Swedish households own their property. Of these, 96 per cent have a mortgage. This figure is very high in an international comparison. However, it is important to highlight that the cost of living in rental accommodation has risen considerably faster than the cost of living in owned accommodation, let alone inflation, during this period (Bergenstråhle 2006). As such, this process has benefitted property ownership at the expense of tenants in rental housing. As Hedin et al. (2012) point out, tenure neutrality was a cornerstone of the old Swedish housing policy model. This is clearly no longer the case.

Since the early 1990s, a range of neoliberal housing policy reforms began to be implemented – thereby transforming the Swedish housing sector from one of the most regulated in Europe to one of the most market-oriented (Hedin et al. 2012). As Lind and Lundström (2007) note, state engagement is now considerably less pronounced than in the UK and the US, traditionally seen as prominent proponents of market liberalism. Clark and Johnson (2009) argue that this structural shift has come to have had significant consequences in a range of areas: a decline in new construction and a rise in vacancies; an increase in the crowded housing conditions; an increase in privatisation and outsourcing of housing planning; an increasing segmentation in terms of gaps between different forms of tenure; the closing of municipal housing agencies and the abandonment of social housing commitments; an increase in profit-maximising public housing companies; and a social polarisation manifested in growing 'supergentrification' and low-income filtering. Since the end of the banking crisis in the early 1990s, construction has been particularly slow. For instance, production in new dwellings dropped from 70,000 in 1990 to just around 10,000 in 1997, the lowest since World War II (Hedin et al. 2012). Homelessness more than doubled in Sweden between 1999 and 2005 (Socialstyrelsen 2006).

The fifth point relates to household debt. Household debt (in particular mortgages) has increased considerably faster than disposable income. From 1970 to 2000, Swedish households had a debt/disposable income-ratio of around 100 per cent (with the notable exception of around 130 per cent prior to the banking crisis). Since the turn of the Millennium, however, this ratio has steadily increased and now stands at around 170 per cent. A study by Winstrand and Ölcer (2014) shows that the debt ratio of *indebted* households stood at 263 per cent in July 2013, whereas the equivalent ratio for households with mortgages amounted to 313 per cent. Moreover, households with the lowest incomes have a disproportionally high debt ratio.

We can gain additional insights into these changes by using the Swedish mortgage market as a lens. Previously, interest regulations ensured mortgage rates were set below market interest rates. Strict liquidity ratios regulated the amount of mortgage bonds banks and insurance companies were required to hold on their balance sheets. The government had also introduced a range of interest-rate subsidies to households and construction companies in order to encourage the creation of new housing (Sveriges Riksbank 2014b). With a limited array of savings alternatives for the households prior to the deregulation process, household savings were thereby channelled back to the mortgage bond market via the banks. Thus, government policy prior to the deregulation process promoted not only the construction of housing, but it also intervened in the functioning of the closely connected mortgage bond market through a range of direct institutional regulations.

The 'old' model could be seen as having been driven by artificial demand of mortgage bonds, as the government directly promoted funding of mortgage institutions using mortgage bonds, and by forcing banks and insurance companies to invest in those bonds. Both households' ability to take out loans, as well as mortgage institutions' means of funding these loans, were subject to strict control. The channelling of household funds into mortgages in the 'new' model is more indirect, as it often takes place via pension funds and mutual funds. Indeed, household pension and mutual fund saving has increased more in Sweden than in other comparable countries during the recent decades.

The trend in house prices, as well as the increase in mortgages, during the era of financialisation can be attributed to a number of factors. Relatively generous tax rules have contributed to increasing credit demand. During the 1980s, around 50 per cent of interest expenditure was tax deductible. Although this was reduced to 30 per cent, after-tax real interest rates have been low. Similarly, the property tax reform in 2008 has acted to increase confidence in the property market.

Another important factor has been the downward trend in Swedish interest rates (with mortgage bond yields falling from around 9 per cent in 1996 to 1–2 per cent in 2013). Historically, fixed-rate mortgages have been prominent in Sweden. This is no longer the case. Due to low inflation, the central bank has kept repo rates low. This has prompted a gradual increase in demand for floating-rate, rather than fixed-rate, mortgages (from about 10 per cent in the mid-1990s to around 70 per cent in 2013). This trend has markedly increased the exposure of households to the volatility of short-term interest rates.

On the mortgage supply side, the deregulation process was undoubtedly important, as it solved the credit-rationing situation that had existed previously. Moreover, increasing competition with regards to mortgage rates, cash down payments and amortisation requirements has enabled a more 'efficient' mortgage market to emerge. Mortgage institutions and banks have faced increasingly lower funding costs, and found new funding alternatives. Importantly, a significant portion of borrowing takes place in foreign currency: through the international wholesale markets, and then swapped into Swedish krona. Cheaper funding rates have obviously made property purchases more attractive. The housing shortage has contributed to the phenomenal rise in property prices since the market recovered after the banking crisis. Higher prices (i.e. more collateral) have also enabled existing mortgage-holders to increase their borrowing during the last two decades.

To sum up, the Swedish deregulation process during the 1980s was a key ingredient in the subsequent house price bubble and banking crisis during the early 1990s. Since then, five important financialisation trends have been prominent in relation to household consumption. First, household income has become more dependent on the development of the financial markets. Second, financial wealth in relation to disposable income has roughly doubled. Third, the distribution of household financial assets has tended to increasingly include risky and volatile assets. Fourth, Swedish households have become increasingly exposed to a housing market that has not seen a major price correction in over 20 years. Fifth, (particularly low-income) households have become increasingly indebted in relation to disposable income. Thus, despite being an export-led mercantilist regime, the Swedish household also displays some symptoms of a debt-led consumption boom. Noticeably, Sweden has not experienced a major correction in house prices in conjunction with the global financial crisis. By contrast, prices are higher than in 2007, both in the major cities, as well as in Sweden as a whole.

Financialisation, Sovereign Debt and the Current Account

Although Sweden currently positions itself within the category of export-led mercantilist countries according to the classification by Hein (2012), it is important to note that this is a fairly recent phenomenon – particularly when it comes to the current account. During the decades running up to the Swedish banking crisis, the drivers of GDP growth were strikingly different, with significant contributions from household and government consumption. The growth contribution of the balance of goods and services was low and often negative. This section examines the significant policy changes that enabled Sweden to switch from a current account deficit regime to a current account surplus regime during the early 1990s.

During the 1950s and 1960s, Sweden had experienced a 'golden era' with low inflation, high GDP growth and an unemployment rate steadily around 2 per cent. However, after the collapse of the Bretton Woods system in 1971 and the oil crisis soon thereafter, Sweden began to experience similar inflationary pressures as other countries. Following a mixed strategy of incomes policy, fiscal policy and exchange rate policy, the results were not overly successful in lowering inflation. Public expenditure as a share of GDP rose from 45 per cent in 1973 to 65 per cent in 1982. GDP growth fell significantly below that of previous decades and even below the OECD-average. Budget and current account deficits became a new norm, and government debt rose from 20 per cent of GDP to 60 per cent of GDP in just one decade. Inflation remained high and the krona was devalued repeatedly. However, the main policy target at the time – namely unemployment – remained stubbornly low at around 2 per cent.

During the late 1980s, it became clear that the combination of rapid deregulation of the financial sector, removal of exchange rate controls, high inflation expectations and low after-tax interest rates had become unsustainable. The very low unemployment rate, which even dropped below 2 per cent during 1987–90, began to be reflected in higher wage pressures – causing the wage growth to increase from 7 per cent in 1987–88 to 10 per cent in 1989–90. The trade surplus also began to diminish.

The combination of deregulation, low interest rates with generous tax-deductibility rules and high inflation expectations led to a property and asset price boom. With the Swedish exchange rate policy having lost its credibility after a series of devaluations, higher German interest rates and another devaluation by the Bank of Finland (following a post-Soviet export shock), a series of rate hikes followed. Separately, interest rate tax deductibility was cut from 50 per cent to 30 per cent. Within a year, real interest rates rose from below zero to over 5 per cent. Bankruptcies followed in quick succession and banks' credit losses, having been a couple of billion SEK per year, increased to SEK 10 billion in 1990 and SEK 36 billion in 1991 (around 4 per cent of total lending) – leading to one bank being fully nationalised in the summer of 1992, and another going bankrupt and becoming nationalised in September the same year (Flodén 2013). Depositors and creditors were issued with a general guarantee, and banks were rapidly recapitalised. The culmination of the Swedish banking crisis, however, coincided with the ERM currency crisis. After a series of speculative attacks against the krona, and the infamous interest rate hike to 500 per cent by the Riksbank, the Swedish krona became free floating on 19 November 1992.

Domestic demand fell rapidly in the aftermath of the banking and currency crises, and the unemployment rate rose to 8 per cent in 1994 (on top of around 5 per cent of the labour force that were employed in public labour market programmes). Lower tax revenues coupled with higher public spending (to support the banks, unemployed, etc.) led to higher budget deficits and an increase in government debt from 44 per cent of GDP in 1990 to 77 per cent of GDP in 1994.

This episode can be seen as the turning point when Sweden was transformed from a debt-led consumption boom to an export-led mercantilist regime. However, the foundation had already been laid. The collapse of the Soviet Union and increasing European integration had already spurred the military neutral and non-EU members Sweden and Finland to make structural adjustments to a new European landscape. An intention to join the EU was announced in 1990, requiring fundamental changes to macroeconomic policy in order to comply with the Maastricht criteria and to boost confidence in the Swedish economy. In the fiscal plan of 1991, the government declared that low and stable inflation was to be prioritised ahead of 'other ambitions and demands'. Formally, this was the first time that a Social Democratic government had downgraded employment from its list of priorities in economic policy. The new overriding target – price stability – also became widely accepted among the political opposition, the trade unions and the public. The shift came to coincide with the Conservative government having gained power. Subsequently, an ambitious programme with regards to market-oriented reforms (including deregulation, privatisation, public spending cuts and tax cuts) was laid out.

The change from a fixed to a floating exchange rate regime came to have profound effects on foundations of the stabilisation policy in Sweden. Sveriges Riksbank announced an inflation target in January 1993, which came to apply from 1995. To regain credibility, a law was passed to formalise the independence of the central bank. The framework for fiscal policy was also radically changed. The government term was extended from three to four years in order to enhance stability. A top-down budget process, with a nominal expenditure ceiling, was introduced in 1996. A year later, a surplus target for general government net lending came into effect, and in 2000 a balanced-budget requirement was introduced for local governments (Flodén 2013). In 2007, a fiscal-policy council was formed in order '[. . .] to review and assess the extent to which the fiscal and economic policy objectives proposed by the Government and decided by the Riksdag are being achieved [. . .]' (Fiscal Policy Council 2013).

The impact of these policy changes has been dramatic, as can be seen from Figure 8.3 below.

During the early 1980s, Sweden showed a balanced budget, with small income deficits offset by small trade surpluses. From the late 1980s to the early 1990s, Sweden began to record slight deficits mainly due to the

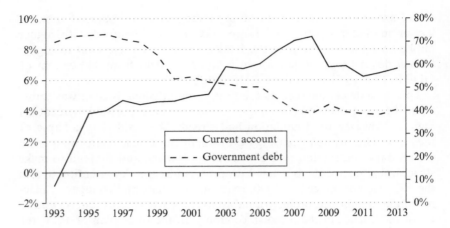

Sources: Statistics Sweden (2014) and NIER (2014, National Institute of Economic Research database, available at: http://konj.se/english.html).

Figure 8.3   *Current account (LHS) and government debt (RHS) 1993–2013 (% of GDP)*

increase in net outflows. Since the mid-1990s, by contrast, the Swedish economy has registered a remarkably solid current account surplus stemming mainly from the trade balance.

The Swedish government sector has registered primary balance surpluses from the mid-1990s onwards, whereas the interest burden has decreased steadily. This, in turn, has been allowed by solid current account surpluses recorded by Sweden since 1994, and relatively stable growth. The three economic downturns experienced by advanced economies since the early 1990s have had only limited impact. Except for 1995–1997, 2002–2003 and 2009, the Swedish government balance has been in surplus.

The fiscal burden has historically been high in Sweden. However, there has been a decreasing trend since the 1990s. Accordingly, the tax revenue ratio has decreased from 52 per cent of GDP in 1990 to 44 per cent of GDP in 2011. The decrease has largely been a result of a corresponding decrease in income and profit taxation, whereas the share of other taxes (indirect taxes, property taxes, etc.) has remained fairly steady. Government expenditure as a share of GDP has been reduced from 64.9 per cent in 1995 to 52.2 per cent in 2011 (Stenfors et al. 2014). The government debt to GDP ratio has decreased sharply during the last two decades, from around 75 per cent of GDP during the mid-1990s to around 40 per cent by the outbreak of the global financial crisis. As can be seen from Figure 8.3 above, the government debt has remained remarkably stable since 2007.

It is difficult to single out the precise factors that caused this regime shift to take place in the aftermath of the Swedish banking and currency crisis. The rapid recovery would most likely have been difficult without the quick recapitalisation of the Swedish banking system, and the upswing in the country's main export markets at the time. At the same time, the export sector benefitted from the sharp depreciation of the Swedish krona following the abandonment of the fixed exchange rate regime in 1992. Since then, Swedish industry has benefitted from high productivity and experienced strong growth. From an international perspective, inflation and the growth in unit labour costs have been low since the adoption of inflation targeting. There is no doubt, however, that measures that are traditionally associated with the promotion of financialisation (such as deregulation of the financial system and the economy, as well as expansion and proliferation of financial markets and market-based solutions) have been equally central to the Swedish policy mix that has led to low government debt and high current account surpluses. Thus, the regime shift stems from the combination of a favourable environment for the export industry, a series of market-friendly reforms and radically altered fiscal and monetary policy frameworks founded in pragmatism and political consensus.

8.4 SWEDISH FINANCIALISATION AND THE GLOBAL FINANCIAL CRISIS

The Money Markets and the Banking System

The Swedish money market risk premium (often measured in the so-called STIBOR-STINA spread[4]) was hardly affected by the initial turmoil of the global financial crisis – not even after the collapse of Bear Stearns in March 2008, which caused major uncertainty in the global money markets. The Lehman bankruptcy in September 2008, however, led to an immediate spike in the STIBOR-STINA by around 100 basis points (bps) and suggested a breakdown of the first stage of the monetary transmission mechanism (Stenfors et al. 2014). Swedish banks also faced specific difficulties in raising US dollars in the interbank markets, like their peers in the rest of Europe. Funding in foreign currencies had increased significantly during the previous decade and now made up 60 per cent of total market funding (Sveriges Riksbank 2011). Nonetheless, the impact was considerably smaller than for risk premia in the major currencies.

The improved sentiment in the global financial markets in 2009 had a fairly rapid impact on the Swedish money market risk premium, whereas it took somewhat longer for the major currencies to reach the more 'normal' levels seen before the outbreak of the crisis. The effects of the Euro area sovereign debt crisis from 2010 on the money markets were also significant. Nonetheless, the Swedish risk premium showed resilience.

Although Swedish banks and investors had minimal direct or indirect exposure to the US sub-prime mortgage market, the global financial crisis was transmitted to the country as the international money markets froze. Importantly, Swedish banks entered the crisis with relatively sound finances, and with the benefit of having relatively recent experience from the domestic banking crisis during the 1990s. The credit default swaps (CDS) market provides a measure of perceived creditworthiness of a particular 'entity' by market participants. The CDS spreads for all European banks increased sharply post-Lehman Brothers, i.e. their perceived creditworthiness deteriorated. Two of the big four Swedish banks, Nordea and Handelsbanken, fared slightly better than their European peers. The other two (Swedbank and SEB), however, were hit significantly harder in comparison with the major European banks. The exposure of the Swedish banks (in particular that of Swedbank and SEB) to the Baltic countries had become a major concern towards the end of 2008. They had expanded aggressively into the three neighbouring countries. At the time, 80 per cent of the Estonian, 60 per cent of the Latvian and 55 per cent of the Lithuanian markets were dominated by SEB and Swedbank with their subsidiaries and branches. The Baltic countries absorbed 15 per cent of the total lending by Swedbank, whereas the corresponding figures for SEB were 13 per cent and Nordea 3 per cent. Consequently, Swedbank had credit losses amounting to 19 billion SEK during the first three quarters of 2009, of which 60 per cent were related to losses in the Baltic countries. The credit losses by SEB were smaller (9 billion SEK). Nonetheless, 75 per cent came from the Baltic region (Sveriges Riksbank, 2010). The extraordinary monetary policy measures introduced by central banks across the globe managed to reverse the sharp decline in perceived creditworthiness of banks, resulting in a significant fall in CDS spreads during 2009. Spreads continued to fall until the advent of the Euro area crisis in 2010, when the perceived creditworthiness of *all* the big four Swedish banks surpassed those of the large European banks.

In sum, seen through the lens of money market risk premia, the transmission of the global financial crisis to Sweden was less pronounced than to the major European economies. However, the large exposure of Swedish banks to the crisis-affected Baltic countries (coupled with a dependency on market funding in foreign currency) prompted a sharp and negative reaction from the international financial markets in 2009. The situation improved quickly, however, and the Swedish banks and money markets largely managed to avoid the subsequent turbulence in conjunction with the subsequent Euro area crisis.

Sovereign Debt and the Real Economy

The Swedish real economy, being heavily dependent on the export industry, was immediately affected by the weakening international economic activity as a result of the global financial crisis. Swedish GDP fell by close to 4 per cent during the last quarter of 2008, and by a further 5 per cent during 2009 (Elmér et al. 2012). However, the severe downturn was rapidly reversed and Sweden overcame the crisis of 2008 faster than neighbouring and other EU countries (except for Denmark). Although the onset of the Euro area crisis has had a dampening effect on Swedish growth, the economy has clearly outperformed the Euro area.

The global financial crisis also resulted in a reduction of the current account surplus in 2009. Trade in goods and services, as well as income, was immediately affected, and thus profits of corporate directly exposed to foreign direct investment (Statistics Sweden 2009). However, the current account surplus has remained high and above 6 per cent of GDP throughout the global financial crisis and the Euro area debt crisis. As Bergman (2011) points out, Sweden entered the global financial crisis with strong public finances – with one of the lowest government debt/GDP ratios in Europe. Government net lending for 2013 was −0.2 per cent of GDP (the second highest in the EU), compared with the EU-average of −3.2 per cent (Jonung 2014).

Another indication of how Sweden fared during the Euro area crisis can be seen in the sovereign CDS spreads. As has already been well documented, the peripheral Euro area countries (Greece, Portugal, Spain, Italy and Ireland) were badly hit, resulting in surging CDS spreads. Consequently, the 'core' Euro area countries (Germany, Finland, Austria and the Netherlands) became regarded as 'safe havens' within the currency area, often showing offsetting dips in their government bonds yields as those of the peripheral countries rose. However, since mid-2009, Sweden has outperformed most other European countries in terms of the sovereign CDS spreads, even those considered to be 'core' Euro area countries. The combination of persistent current account surpluses, low government debt and non-Euro area membership have undoubtedly played a crucial role in portraying Sweden as a potential safe haven in international financial markets.

The sharp bounce in the Swedish GDP in 2010 was certainly aided by the weaker exchange rate. Both the Swedish krona and the Norwegian krone had, up until and including then, for decades been subject to volatility and depreciation in conjunction with turbulence in the financial markets (for instance during the dot-com crisis around 2000). Perhaps not always justified for macroeconomic reasons, their relatively lower liquidity often prompted an exodus by investors and speculators alike in line with general market uncertainty. The reaction to the Lehman bankruptcy was similar, and even amplified. However, the reaction to the Euro area crisis was quite different. It resulted in a general flight to safety *outside* the currency area (such as the US dollar) and *within* the Euro area (for instance to Germany). Moreover, investors desiring an exposure to Western and Northern Europe (without an exposure to the Euro area) flocked to the Swiss franc and Swedish, Norwegian and Danish currencies. Thus, on the whole, the Swedish krona appreciated as a result of the Euro area crisis. Sweden has also been immune to the surge in long-term yields in a range of Euro area countries. Between 1987 and the launch of the euro, the Swedish 10-year government bond yield spread over Germany gradually decreased from around 500 bps to close to zero, with a temporary spike during the aftermath of the currency crisis in the early 1990s. The combination of low inflation, low central bank rates, low government debt, current account surpluses and an own currency has been favourable for Sweden throughout the crisis with regards to bond yields.

Although the Swedish economy has shown signs of slowing down recently, the robust development during the height of the Euro area crisis might be surprising given the sharp appreciation of the currency. However, it has to be noted that although the Swedish export industry is heavily geared towards the Euro area (40.2 per cent in 2011), the country has a fairly diverse export market (Norway 9.3 per cent, Denmark 6.5 per cent, UK 7.4 per cent, US 5.5 per cent and emerging markets 22.8 per cent in 2011). The so-called PIIGS countries stand for less than 6 per cent of the Swedish export market (Konjunkturinstitutet 2012). Moreover, the Swedish non-financial sector had gained price competitiveness ahead of the recession.

Policy Measures

During the height of the global financial crisis, the Riksbank introduced a range of extraordinary measures to alleviate stress in the Swedish banking system (Elmér et al. 2012; Sveriges Riksbank 2012). Between October 2008 and July 2009, the repo rate was cut by 450 basis points in total – to an all time low of 0.25 per cent. The Riksbank also began to offer loans in SEK with maturities up to three and six months, and later offered three fixed-rate loans with a 1-year maturity, totalling SEK 296.5 billion.

The fixed and variable loan volume in SEK amounted to approximately 9 per cent of GDP. The intention of the Riksbank was that these measures would reduce the spread between the record low repo rate and the market rates actually charged to households and companies (Elmér et al. 2012). In addition, temporary reciprocal currency arrangements in the form of foreign exchange swap lines were established with the Federal Reserve in order to channel dollars to banks in other jurisdictions – including Sweden.

The Euro area crisis from mid-2010 expectedly came to result in wider money market risk premia in the Euro area. By contrast, the Swedish financial markets had begun to show signs of recovery during 2010, and access to market funding had once again become possible. The economy as a whole was very strong: GDP increased by 6.1 per cent in 2010 and the unemployment rate began to fall. The reaction by the Riksbank was to gradually phase out the extraordinary schemes it had introduced during the earlier parts of the global financial crisis. Monetary policy was tightened and, most importantly, the final outstanding fixed-rate term loan to banks that expired in October 2010 was not renewed.

Whereas the focus of the Riksbank was on the liquidity squeeze in the financial system, measures adopted by the government in the aftermath of the Lehman bankruptcy were largely aimed at preventing a Swedish credit crunch. A stability plan was presented on 20 October 2008 and the Government Support to Credit Institutions Act was passed by the parliament only nine days later. According to an evaluation by the Financial Crisis Committee in 2013, the overall results were positive. First, a strengthened depositor protection scheme served to maintain confidence in the Swedish financial sector. Second, as the government stepped in as a guarantor of the banks' loans (through the 'guarantee programme'), the ability of banks to borrow for longer maturities and without collateral increased. Third, although only used by one bank (Nordea), a 'capital injection programme' contributed to market confidence and financial stability. Fourth, the Stabilisation Fund,[5] seen as an appropriate budgetary solution, started with a substantial contribution and gave the government a mandate to execute unlimited measures and payments in accordance with the Government Support to Credit Institutions Act. Although these assessments refer more to the indirect impact of the measures, it has to be noted that lending to corporations only showed a marginal decline, whereas household lending continued to increase. Moreover, as the measures largely consisted of risk transfers from the private sector to the public sector (at a fee), the net impact for the Swedish taxpayers is estimated to be positive – amounting to around SEK 10 billion (SOU 2013, p. 6, 2013).

8.5   CONCLUSIONS

Sweden's debt-led consumption boom regime came to an abrupt end in 1993, after the banking crisis and the ERM crisis. Having switched to an export-led mercantilist regime, the global financial crisis and the Euro area sovereign debt crisis affected the country differently. The Swedish economy was hit hard by the global financial crisis, but rebounded quickly. Although the country was not immune to the Euro area sovereign debt crisis, it fared considerably better than most EU member states. At the same time, however, the Swedish economy has come to show symptoms of a renewed debt-led consumption boom through the housing market, and benefitted from the productivity in the non-financial sector and a depreciation of the real exchange rate at 'the right moment in time'.

The regime shift has largely mirrored the Swedish financialisation process – which has been rapid and widespread. State involvement in pensions, education, health care and housing has been replaced or complemented by a range of market-based solutions. Shareholder orientation in the corporate sector has increased, at the same time as inequality, and households have become significantly more exposed to the direction and volatility of the international financial markets. An overriding political ambition to achieve and maintain full employment was replaced in 1991 by that of a low and stable inflation rate. The banking system was quickly recapitalised, and a fiscal framework was put in place that resulted in a budget surplus, rather than deficit, bias. As Bi and Leeper (2010) note, the fiscal policy infrastructure that was put in place after the Swedish banking crisis has come to 'institutionalise a public fiscal discourse'.

Perhaps paradoxically, the Swedish banking and currency crisis, quickly following the deregulation process, and fiscal reform, as well as the ability to conduct a flexible and pragmatic policy outside the Euro area, appears to have shielded Sweden from some of the recent turbulence. To some extent, this has also been aided by the change in the way Sweden is perceived by the international financial markets. Whereas the Swedish financial markets had come to be identified with volatility and crises during the 1980s and 1990s, the picture that is emerging after the global financial crisis and the Euro area sovereign debt crisis is remarkably different. Here, Sweden appears to have weathered the storms very well – to the extent that the country, at least colloquially, has sometimes been referred to as a new 'safe haven'. Evidence does not yet provide conclusive support that such a shift has taken place. However, underlying fundamentals do suggest that Sweden has at least clearly moved in such a direction – in line with the country's transformation towards an export-led mercantilist economy.

Thus, whereas the financial crises since 2008 could be seen as outcomes of financialisation in a number of countries, similar previous experiences appear to have served to *reinforce* the momentum of financialisation in Sweden. As such, the Swedish financialisation process as described in this chapter can be traced to the same pillars of pragmatism, consensus and individualism that were prevalent during the successful era of the 'old' Swedish model.

NOTES

1. Although there is no clear definition of the Swedish model, most scholars would agree that the following characteristics could be attributed to it: a 'decommodified' wage relation, public commitment to full employment, welfare state universalism, a large social service sector, egalitarianism (in particular with regards to women) and a kind of class compromise between capital, labour and farmers (and later including white collar workers) (Ryner 1999, 2007). Broadly speaking, the society could truly be portrayed as egalitarian, with a solid social safety net stretching from free education to universal health care.
2. Between the two extreme groups, Hein also identifies a third (consisting of France, Italy and Portugal) that could be considered as 'domestic demand-led', as well as a fourth comprising 'weak export-led' economies.
3. In 2012, around half of the mutual funds' assets consisted of equities, whereas a quarter was interest rate funds. The remaining part was made up of mixed funds (19 per cent) and hedge funds (around 5 per cent).
4. The difference between the three-month Stockholm Interbank Offered Rate (STIBOR) and the 3-month Stockholm Tomnext Interbank Average (STINA).
5. The main objective of the Stabilisation Fund was to be an effective tool for financing central government support measures in case of a banking crisis. The Government has targeted the size of the Fund to 2.5 per cent of GDP in 2023 (Swedish National Audit Office 2011).

REFERENCES

Belfrage, C. (2008), 'Towards "universal financialisation" in Sweden?', *Contemporary Politics*, **14** (3), 277–296.
Belfrage, C. and M. Ryner (2009), 'Renegotiating the Swedish democratic settlement: from pension fund socialism to neoliberalization', *Politics & Society*, **37** (2), 257–288.
Bergenstråhle, S. (2006), *Boende och välfärd 1986–2003*, Stockholm: Hyresgästföreningen.
Bergman, M. (2011), 'Best in class: public finances in Sweden during the financial crisis', *Panoeconomicus*, **4**, 431–453.
Bi, H. and E. M. Leeper (2010), 'Sovereign debt risk premia and fiscal policy in Sweden', NBER Working Paper Series, No. 15810, March 2010, National Bureau of Economic Research.
Clark, E. and K. Johnson (2009), 'Circumventing circumscribed neoliberalism: The "system switch" in Swedish housing', in S. Glynn (ed.), *Where the other half lives: Lower income housing in a neoliberal world*, London: Pluto.

Elmér, H., G. Guinbourg, D. Kjellberg and M. Nessén (2012), 'The Riksbank's monetary policy measures during the financial crisis – evaluation and lessons learned', *Sveriges Riksbank Economic Review*, 3, 1–24.

European Commission (2014), AMECO database, available at: http://ec.europa.eu/economy_finance/db_indicators/ameco/index_en.htm.

Fiscal Policy Council (2013), 'Swedish fiscal policy – fiscal policy council report 2013', available at: http://www.finanspolitiskaradet.com/download/18.1b89d914 0c56bc4c73b70/1378219272657/Swedish+Fiscal+Policy+2013.pdf.

Flodén, M. (2013), 'A role model for the conduct of fiscal policy? Experiences from Sweden', *Journal of International Money and Finance*, 34 (2013), 177–197.

Hedin, K., E. Clark, E. Lundholm, and G. Malmberg (2012), 'Neoliberalization of housing in Sweden: Gentrification, filtering, and social polarization', *Annals of the Association of American Geographers*, 102 (2), 443–463.

Hein, E. (2012), *The Macroeconomics of Finance-dominated Capitalism – and its Crisis*, Cheltenham: Edward Elgar.

Jonung, L. (2014), 'The Swedish experience of fiscal reform: Lessons for Portugal', Department of Economics Working Papers Series, No. 2014:27, Lund University.

Konjunkturinstitutet (2012), 'En jämförelse av nationell konkurrenskraft i Sverige och Finland', Fördjupnings-PM Nr. 19, 2012, available at: http://www.konj.se/download/18.11e05f6313b817f634f7ee/Fper%20centC3%20per%20centB6rdjup nings-pm+19_Finlands+och+Sveriges+konkurrenskraft.pdf.

Lind, H. and S. Lundström (2007), *Bostäder på marknadens villkor*, Stockholm: SNS Förlag.

NIER (2014), National Institute of Economic Research database, available at: http://konj.se/english.html.

Ryner, M. (1999), 'Neoliberal globalization and the crisis of Swedish social democracy', *Economic and Industrial Democracy*, 20, 39–79.

Ryner, M. (2007), 'The Nordic model: does it exist? Can it survive?', *New Political Economy*, 12 (1), 61–70.

Socialstyrelsen (2006), 'Social rapport 2006', available at: http://www.folkhal-somyndigheten.se/pagefiles/12984/social-rapport-2006.pdf.

SOU 2013:6 (2013), *Att förebygga och hantera finansiella kriser*, Delbetänkande av Finanskriskommittén, Stockholm: Fritzes.

Statistics Sweden (2009), 'Balance of payments – 4th quarter 2009', available at: http://www.scb.se/statistik/_publikationer/FM0001_2009K04B_BR_FM04BR 1001.pdf.

Statistics Sweden (2014), Statistics Sweden database, available at: http://www.scb. se/en_/.

Stenfors, A. (2014), 'Financialisation and the financial and economic crises: The case of Sweden', FESSUD Studies in Financial Systems, No. 27, University of Leeds.

Stenfors, A., E. Clark, I. Farahani, A. L. Hansen and M. Passarella (2014), 'The Swedish financial system', FESSUD Studies in Financial Systems, No. 13, University of Leeds.

Sveriges Riksbank (2010), 'Krisen i Baltikum – Riksbankens åtgärder, bedömningar och lärdomar', available at: http://www.riksbank.se/Upload/Dokument_ riksbank/Kat_publicerat/Tal/2010/tal_100202.pdf.

Sveriges Riksbank (2011), 'Financial stability report 2011:1', available at: http:// www.riksbank.se/Upload/Rapporter/2011/FS_1/FSR_2011_1_en.pdf.

Sveriges Riksbank (2012), 'The Riksbank's monetary policy measures during the financial crisis–evaluation and lessons learnt', *Sveriges Riksbank Economic Review*, 2012:3, available at: http://www.riksbank.se/Documents/Rapporter/POV/2012/rap_pov_artikel_1_121017_eng.pdf.

Sveriges Riksbank (2014a), Statistics, available at: http://www.riksbank.se/en/Statistics/.

Sveriges Riksbank (2014b), 'From A to Z: the Swedish mortgage market and its role in the financial system', *Riksbank Studies*, April 2014.

Swedish National Audit Office (2011), 'The stabilisation fund – Does it live up to its name?', RiR 2011:26, available at: http://www.riksrevisionen.se/PageFiles/16070/12-0226_RiR_Rapport%202011_26_ENG_Customized.pdf.

Winstrand, J. and D. Ölcer (2014), 'How indebted are Swedish households?', *Economic Commentaries*, No. 1, 2014, Sveriges Riksbank.

9. France, a domestic demand-led economy under the influence of external shocks*

Gérard Cornilleau and Jérôme Creel

9.1 INTRODUCTION

Over the past 40 years the growth of the French economy has experienced several downturns and accelerations. It is, however, not possible to talk about actual endogenous cycles. Changes of the economic trend can be explained almost entirely by exogenous shocks, be they geopolitical, technological, banking or financial. The real economy has responded to these shocks in a very classical way, and it is very difficult to identify structural malfunctions since 1990, or a weakening of the growth capacity of the economy in a stable environment.

In the early seventies, the rate of growth of the French economy was high. This period ended with the first oil shock of 1974 and especially the second one of 1980–81. The rise in oil prices was caused by the conflict in the Middle East, which had no connection with the structural functioning of the French and European economies. It took a long time to adapt to the new situation in the energy sector. Furthermore, the effects of the second shock were amplified by the 'Reaganomics' and the sharp rise in real interest rates that accompanied it. In the United States the shock caused by the interest rate hikes was offset by a fiscal policy very favourable to economic growth. It combined tax cuts and a sharp rise in military spending. In contrast, European fiscal policy did not offset the impact of higher rates, so that in France average growth in the years 1982 to 1987 fell to 1.2 per cent. At that time the development of speculation in financial markets and the constraints on the exchange rate forced

*   A longer version of this chapter is available as Cornilleau and Creel (2014). Parts of the study were presented at the 18th Conference of the Research Network Macroeconomics and Macroeconomic Policies (FMM), October 30–November 01, 2014, in Berlin, Germany. For helpful comments and discussions, we are grateful to Gary Dymski, Eckhard Hein, Eric Heyer and Mathieu Plane. Remaining errors are, of course, ours.

European governments and the French government in particular to align their monetary policies to that of the United States and the most rigorous (inflation-averse) governments. These two shocks, with respect to energy and monetary policy, are enough to explain the sharp drop in growth in the early eighties.

However, the period was also characterised by the emergence of a significant imbalance in the distribution of income. The slower growth resulting from the oil shocks and higher interest rates, did not affect the rate of growth of wages as much as labour productivity, which slowed down quite substantially. This resulted in a sharp increase in the share of labour compensation in GDP, and a corresponding decrease in the mark up of firms (Figure 9.1).

The excess of wages during the late seventies resulted from the negative gap between the rate of growth of labour productivity and the rate of growth of real wages. This structural mismatch extended throughout the second half of the seventies. However, the policy of wage restraint implemented in 1982, coupled with rising unemployment, quickly brought wages to a level consistent with a balanced growth of the global supply and demand, i.e. it enabled the return to a situation of equal rates of growth of

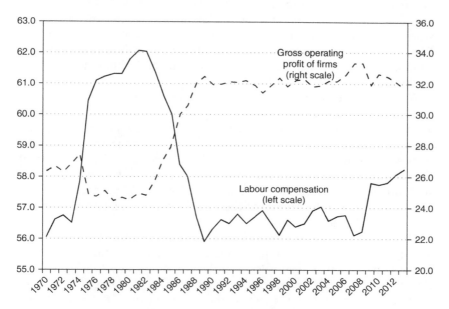

Source: National Institute of Statistics and Economics – INSEE (national accounts).

Figure 9.1 Share of wages and profits in the GDP

productivity and real wages. It should be noted that the shortening of the legal duration of work to 35 hours in 1997 was carried out under neutral conditions such that the distribution of income between wages and profits did not change.

Due to demographic trends, France experienced a steady increase in its workforce. In the seventies the maintenance of a very low unemployment rate would have meant a surge in growth and/or a collapse in labour productivity. The oil shocks and rising interest rates complicated the situation, and the unemployment rate rose from about 3 per cent to about 9 per cent in 1987. Thereafter the unemployment rate changed according to the business cycle: It decreased following the recovery related to the decrease in oil prices; it increased after the European Monetary System (EMS) crisis; and decreased with the introduction of the 35-hour working week and the recovery of the 2000s. It was then stabilised before it increased again after the financial shock of 2008–2009. In 2008, with peaking GNP per capita and with an unemployment rate of 6.8 per cent, France had almost returned to full employment without experiencing inflationary pressures. The financial and economic crisis of 2008–2009 certainly led to a new surge in demand-driven unemployment. The evolutions of GDP and unemployment in France raise doubts about analyses that emphasise the so-called lack of flexibility of the labour market to explain the persistence of unemployment. In situations of high economic growth, the French economy has been able to create jobs and to reduce unemployment without sharp consequences on the income share and without jeopardising the increase in supply.

When the time dimension is taken into consideration, the classification of the French growth regime is generally very difficult. Indeed, France has gone through different situations, from current account deficits to surpluses, and from surpluses to deficits, which prevents the application of a one-category-fits-all diagnosis. Nevertheless, drawing on the cyclicality of the French public deficit and the steady contribution of households' consumption to the GDP growth rate, a mild domestic demand-led economy is certainly the best description of the French economy and its connections with financialisation.

The rest of the chapter is organised as follows. Section 9.2 reviews the long-run development of France in the era of financialisation. Section 9.3 reviews the different channels of influence of financialisation on the French economy, via investment in capital stock, consumption, and the current account. Section 9.4 reviews the management of the global financial crisis by French public authorities. Section 9.5 concludes.

9.2 LONG-RUN DEVELOPMENT IN THE ERA OF FINANCIALISATION SINCE THE EARLY 1980s

France is certainly among the countries that have financialised early. In the 1980s, the French economy opened its capital markets to foreign capital while French non-financial companies were starting to expand abroad.[1] Under the 'Franc fort' policy, a commitment to stabilise the value of the French franc vis-à-vis the German mark within the EMS, France escaped the risk of foreign currency denominated external debt: France was able to issue its own public debt in French francs.

The opening up of the French banking and financial system began in the late 1980s, with the dismantling of foreign exchange controls in 1989 and the removal of almost all administrative barriers to foreign entry in the banking sector. Moreover, the French stock exchange supervisor (i.e. Commission des Operations de Bourse or COB) saw its power and independence strengthened, which enhanced its credibility and therefore the attractiveness of Paris in the eyes of international investors. In a context of higher competitive pressures, a first wave of banking concentration occurred in 1991/1992 to generate productivity gains and to streamline both structures and activities. Later, the internationalisation of French banks gained momentum with the adoption of the euro. This was conducive to a second wave of concentration, in particular in the field of investment banking. The increase in the size of potential markets caused a search for an optimal size and economies of scale. Yet, this was favoured by the modernisation and liberalisation of capital movements, associated with the deregulation of banking and financial activities, in a context of more harmonised regulatory and prudential standards. The result was intensification of international competition on the French market, leading the country's banks to diversify into other regions and into the major foreign financial centres.

France had a weakly concentrated banking sector in the 1990s compared with small countries like the Netherlands or Norway, for instance, but a relatively highly concentrated one in comparison with Germany. In fact, the deregulation and disintermediation processes cut the French banking sector into two sub-sectors: investment banking in which competition is quite low but concentration high (five major groups), and retail banking in which competition is quite harsh but concentration low.

Another important trend towards internationalisation (or at least Europeanisation) of the French financial system has to be mentioned: the participation in mergers and clustering of European stock markets (leading notably to the creation of Euronext).

The disintermediation process in the French financial system has been relatively mild, in comparison with other Western countries: The amount of credit to households and non-financial corporations kept on increasing until the early 2010s, despite the surge in stock and bond market capitalisation. The reliance on loans by non-financial corporate firms has remained high. One reason behind this mild disintermediation process lies in the surge of market-related activities by banks themselves. Moreover, the development of a French shadow banking sector, although it has been mostly active abroad, also testifies to the influence of French banks on the financialisation of the French economy.

In this banking and financial environment, financialisation has affected French daily lives in an ambiguous way. The French have a strong preference for credit cards, which are a product of financialisation. However, they retain a certain caution against new risks: Consumer credit and cash loans are mildly developed, and most public services are still under the aegis of the state. Above all, legislation against financial exclusion and the struggle against over-indebtedness are quite advanced and solidarity seems to be still deeply rooted in the French financial culture through microcredit and solidarity savings.

A common feature of financialisation has been housing bubbles which jeopardise the solvency of households and/or limit their purchasing power. The current situation of France, though prices have grown substantially since the 1980s, appears by no way critical. Consequently, the risks – for the banks – coming directly from the housing sector seem quite limited. The housing market in France is sustained by intrinsic forces, in particular strong demographic growth which fuels demand. If the attractiveness of large cities or regions continues in the future (in Paris for young workers and in the south of France for young retirees), a large fall in housing prices cannot be expected. It furthermore remains the case that the French supervisory and regulatory authorities recommend banks to continue to follow prudent and safe rules when providing credit to households. Finally, the main risk is indirect. If weaknesses in the competitiveness of French firms will persist, the resulting job and income losses will have harmful consequences on the market with some (over)-indebted households facing difficulties in honouring their reimbursements. Negative impacts on banks and on the stability of the banking sector could then materialise.

9.3   GROWTH IN FRANCE SINCE 1980

Examining the sectoral financial balances of the main sectors of the economy, France lies between a domestic demand-led economy and a weakly export-led economy, following the Hein (2012) classification.[2]

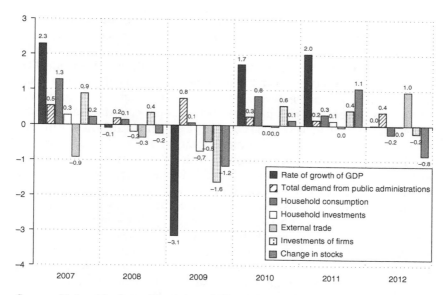

Source: National Institute of Statistics and Economics – INSEE (national accounts).

Figure 9.2 *Decomposition of the rate of growth of the French economy during the crisis*

Between 2007 and 2014, the GDP growth rate can be explained by households' and government's consumption, on the one hand, and by exports, on the other hand (Figure 9.2). The former part amounts to a domestic-related contribution to growth, whereas the latter is a foreign-related contribution. It is noteworthy that periods of recent high growth, between the end of 2009 and beginning of 2012, can be explained by high contributions of households' consumption (until 2011) and exports. Although the contribution of exports was offset by high volumes of imports, the latter faltered earlier (2011) than the former. It may be that imports entered exports as intermediate products and thus permitted a development in the contribution of exports to GDP growth in France.

Income Distribution

France has experienced an increase in inequalities in income and wealth. However, this trend has been much less pronounced than in most comparable countries primarily because of public income support to the poorest. Moreover, it is difficult to link the evolution of inequality with the financialisation of the economy. The major changes are due to the evolution of the primary distribution of wages and, more recently, due to the increase in land prices.

In France poverty has been relatively stable since the end of the nineties. Compared with Sweden, which has long been the model of the most equal distribution of income in developed countries, this stability is surprising. In Sweden the poverty rate increased from 5.3 per cent (measured at the 50 per cent of median income) in 2004 to 8.4 per cent in 2008. The gap with the poverty rate in France, which was 2 points in favour of Sweden, is now 2 points in favour of France. Measured with a threshold of 60 per cent of median income, poverty rates are changing in the same way in Sweden or Germany: In terms of this criterion France was the worst country among the three examined in 1996, but the opposite is the case in 2011. However the (small) difference with Germany is probably not significant. And it remains the case that, measured by the Gini index, the comparison is less favourable to France. Indeed, in 2011 the overall level of inequality was still higher in France than in Germany and Sweden. But the trend towards more inequality is less pronounced. Sweden in particular has seen an explosion of inequality that cannot be found in France.

In France overall inequality has increased, mainly because of the faster growth of high incomes, but without increasing poverty. One must, of course, acknowledge the effect of social protection, which prevents low incomes from falling behind. Figure 9.3 shows the evolution of the share of social benefits to support income (i.e. housing allowance + benefits for families + unemployment benefit and minimum income + various benefits, excluding pensions and reimbursement of health insurance). Since the 1980s this effort in favour of the less fortunate has shown an increasing trend, and it is clear that such benefits have played a counter-cyclical role, with a strong increase in the share of transfer income during crises in 1982–83, 1993 and 2008–2009.

Corporate Income, Productive Investments and their Financing

The corporate investment efforts typically depend on expectations of demand and financial conditions. Financial conditions affect both funding constraints and profitability. Since the mid-1980s it has become difficult to highlight any constraints on the profitability of productive investment. After the first oil shock, the drift of distribution towards wages had weighed heavily on the profitability of investments. However, this drift was contained in the early 1980s and the level of corporate profitability returned to 'normal' (i.e. pre-oil-price-shocks) levels by 1987 (Figure 9.4).

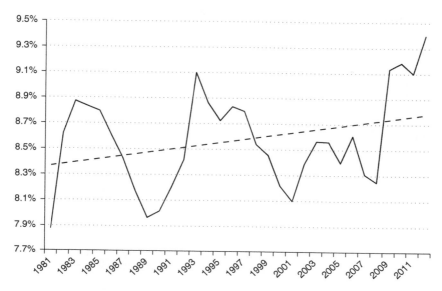

Sources: Insee (National accounts), Drees (Comptes de la protection sociale); computed by the authors.

Figure 9.3 *Share of social benefits that support income in per cent of total disposable income*

The 2009 crisis has reduced corporate mark ups, although in a historical perspective, they remain high, with the share of gross operating surplus in value added remaining higher by one percentage point than the average level of the sixties. The crises of the 1990s and 2000s never cut corporate profitability as did the first oil shock. The idea of a structural deterioration in profitability is therefore not confirmed by macroeconomic data.

This idea is even less founded when one relates profitability and growth and shows that both are moving in the same direction. The depth of the crisis of 2009 has reduced the mark up in the manufacturing sector to the level of 1980, which is of great concern, but it is difficult to speak of a new structural imbalance. It is rather the lack of growth that is clearly the cause of the fall in profitability. As the causal chain from the financial turmoil in the world economy during the late 2000s to the crisis in the real economy at the beginning of the 2010s is well established, there is no reason to reverse this causality to make low mark-up levels in the current period be the cause of the current crisis and stagnation. Conversely, if appropriate macroeconomic policies were able to reinstate a more satisfactory growth process, the profitability of firms would soon return to a 'normal' level.

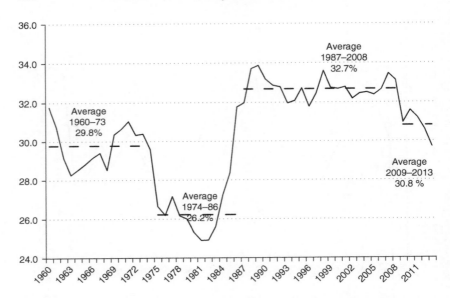

Source: National Institute of Statistics and Economics – INSEE (national accounts).

*Figure 9.4   Profit share for non-financial firms (gross operating surplus /
value added)*

Heyer and Timbeau (2002) estimated the structural rate of unemployment
in France, and showed that in the long period, it is not higher than 5–7
per cent. This is far from the situation prevailing in the 1980s when wages
grew faster than trend labour productivity, while oil crises brought down
the sustainable growth potential of the economy. So there is currently no
structural obstacle to growth on the side of the labour market.

In the statistics the private investment rate has been particularly high
since 2010, even under the conditions of low GDP growth and negative
expectations on future developments. This could reflect the recent increase
in the price of capital goods, or the possibility of a bias in the measurement
of capital stock due to an acceleration of depreciation during the crisis.

Two facts about the financial situation of French companies can be seen
clearly in Figure 9.5:

- From 1985–1986, the rebalancing of the distribution of income
  between capital and labour has helped to restore the financial situation of the firms such that it never deteriorated to the level reached
  directly after the oil shocks. Even during the current crisis the profit

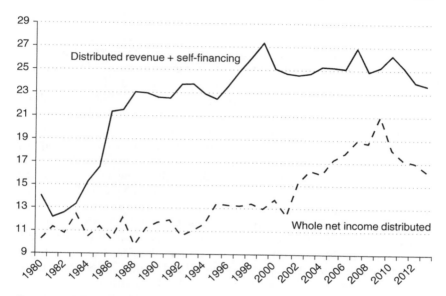

Sources: National Institute of Statistics and Economics – INSEE, National Accounting, base 2010, computations by the authors.

Figure 9.5   *Total of distributed revenue of capital and self-financing in per cent of the value added of non-financial firms*

income distributed or retained and invested accounted for a stable share of value added.

• After the rebalancing of income distribution, internal investment financing was initially given preference over the distribution of dividends. Since the 2000s, however, the structural improvement in profitability has been accompanied by an increase in capital income distributed to shareholders, although this has never cut off internal financing. During the current crisis, internal financing has been preferred to the distribution of profit income again.

Household Income and Expenditure

Since the 1980s household incomes have kept in line with the growth of the economy and the average purchasing power of gross disposable income per consumption unit has increased by 0.9 per cent per year. Two periods, which correspond to the most marked crises, 1980–1987 and 2008–2012, have shown stagnating purchasing power. The distributional imbalance of the 1980s having been cleared by 1987, income growth was relatively steady until the shock of 2008–2009.

The changes in income distribution had a relatively large influence on the structure of household incomes. Labour income (gross salaries including employer contributions + mixed income of individual entrepreneurs) accounted for 85 per cent of disposable income in 1980, and about 80.5 per cent in 2013. Since 1994 the share of labour income has stabilised at around 80 per cent with no significant trend.

As noted above (Section 9.3.1) inequality has increased less rapidly and less strongly in France than in other countries. This moderation in income inequality has essentially been the result of the support of lower income households, in the form of social benefits. The situation is quite different for wealth inequality, which increased through a strong increase in housing prices, itself the result of the increase in land prices, after the decentralisation of decision making regarding the creation of new buildings (Levasseur 2013). With very low inflation, the rise in housing prices may continue because falling interest rates fuel demand without sowing the seeds of accelerating housing construction (Timbeau 2013).

Despite the contribution of property values to the increase in wealth inequality, which can eventually feed through on income inequality (Piketty 2013), there has been no impact so far on the composition and trend of economic growth. The saving rate, traditionally high in France, fell sharply during the process of structural adjustment in the 1980s, but now oscillates around 15 per cent – which means that there is not much concern about the financing of investment, be it public or private, in the long term.

Foreign Trade and Balance of Payments

Foreign trade is generally a weak point of the French economy. Over the last 30 years the balance of trade in goods and services was negative from 1980 to 1991 and positive from 1992 to 2005 before returning to negative from 2006 onwards.

However, this weakness of trade is a relative notion. The openness of the French economy has been increasing since the early 1980s and ratios of exports to GDP and imports to GDP have been at historically high levels despite the crisis. Exports have been stable as a percentage of the GDP since the early 2000s, and though they have been lower than imports since 2005, the imbalance is moderate and has not increased during the crisis.

Expressed in terms of products, the developments are quite comparable to other developed economies. In the agricultural sector, France increased its share of the global market from 1980 to 1990, but it has been declining ever since. Over the entire period though, these losses have been smaller than those of the US, although its market share has since 2005 stabilised. In comparison to Germany, which, like France, gained market share in the 1980s, France lost ground as Germany continued to gain market share after its reunification, so that it now exceeds France in the global agricultural market.

Regarding the manufacturing sector the situation is a bit different, but again the decline in market share does not appear abnormal over long periods. From 1980 to 2013 the decline has been comparable to that of the US, which stabilised between 1980 and 2000, and has dropped sharply since. Germany has the inverse profile of the US, with a very rapid decline until 2000 and stabilisation since. France, whose foreign trade remains high, lost market share in the rapidly expanding global market. There is nothing particularly worrying here, and comparison with the American situation does not require acknowledging an extra structural cause other than the rise of emerging countries.

During the 1980s, the redistribution of income in favour of wages could be evoked to explain the weakness of French exports. There was at the time a situation of absolute structural imbalance. Can the same reasoning be applied today? A priori the situation is very different since there is no longer a massive imbalance in the distribution of income between labour and capital, even after the shock of the years 2008–2009. Globalisation and competition from emerging countries could be invoked in order to explain at least part of the French external trade problem. But, though trade structures might be somewhat different, this argument should also be invoked in the case of Germany, which has run a surplus. A look at the competitiveness of the French economy is therefore legitimate. An economy can suffer from an excessive increase in wages for two reasons. The first one is a reduction of the profit rate to below the level that allows for a smooth financing of investment. This requires a stable allocation of total revenue between wages and profit and, as a consequence, a rate of growth of wages equal to the rate of growth of productivity. The disequilibrium resulting from an excessive increase of wages in this context could be presented as an *internal* wage problem.

The second reason rests on the effect on competitiveness of an *external* differential of wage increases. If the major competitors of a country are on a path of decreasing labour costs, the level of wages could appear excessive even if the internal distribution of wages appears compatible with a sufficient level of profitability. This particular problem of excessive wages vis-à-vis other countries could be presented as an *external* wage problem. Since the end of the eighties the evidence for France suggests the absence of an internal wage problem. Since the middle of the 2000s, France has rather suffered from a problem of *relative* wage costs due to an external

Table 9.1   Annual growth rates of real unit labour costs

	2013/2008	2008/2000	2000/1995
Greece	−2.0%	−0.2%	
Ireland	−1.8%	1.4%	
Spain	−1.3%	−0.3%	
Portugal	−0.7%	−0.2%	0.3%
Denmark	−0.3%	0.5%	−0.1%
Sweden	−0.1%	−0.3%	0.8%
Italy	0.3%	0.3%	−1.2%
Euro area (12 countries)	0.4%	−0.3%	
UK	0.5%	−0.1%	0.5%
Austria	0.6%	−0.4%	−0.9%
France	*0.7%*	*0.0%*	*−0.3%*
Germany	0.7%	−0.8%	−0.2%
Belgium	0.7%	−0.1%	−0.4%
Netherlands	1.1%	−0.3%	−0.6%
Finland	1.2%	0.3%	−1.3%

Source: Eurostat (real unit labor costs, national accounts, annual data [nama_aux_ulc]).

differential of wage increases (Le Bayon et al. 2014), mainly due to the de-synchronisation of economic developments in Europe.

Table 9.1 shows that since the crisis the rise in real unit labour costs in the manufacturing sector has been relatively rapid in France (+0.7 per cent a year), but the same pace was recorded in Germany, Belgium and Austria. In contrast, the southern European countries experienced a rapid decline in real unit labour costs: 1.3 per cent per year in Spain, 0.7 per cent in Portugal, etc. These developments contrast with those recorded before the crisis. Between 2000 and 2008, the decline was much lower in southern Europe and much faster in Germany. The labour costs were completely stable in France, meaning the situation therefore deteriorated especially vis-à-vis Germany. To sum up, competitiveness (measured by the differential change in real unit labour costs between France and its major partners) has deteriorated due to the declining costs in Germany during the 2000s and in the southern countries since the beginning of the great crisis of 2008–2009.

There has not been a uniform trend of real unit labour cost growth over time: Unit labour costs showed a period of steady decline in the 1980s, when it was necessary to correct the imbalance in the distribution between wages and profits; followed by a long period of stability consistent with the hypothesis of structurally balanced growth. Nevertheless, France is now one of the countries with high labour cost. The paradox is that this high level of labour costs does not reflect an internal imbalance of the distribution between wages and profit. Consequently, reducing the cost of labour would not be beneficial in terms of internal balance. Engaging in such a strategy can only lead to lower levels of domestic demand and hence stagnation in production. The firms could have more and more resources to finance investment, and the profitability of these investments would be guaranteed by a high mark-up rate, but these investments would not be feasible due to a lack of demand. The economy would be trapped in a chronic lack of demand. However, the decline in labour costs would be effective to boost external demand. By stimulating exports and limiting imports it would allow, in the long term, the offsetting of the negative impact of wage restraint on domestic demand, provided that the partners of France do not launch a race to lower labour costs. If this were the case, the French economy would slow down in a similar fashion as when it used disinflation policies in the late 1980s: With all European countries implementing the same type of policy, none was able to reap the benefits of limiting wage growth, because wage and price differentials remained (more or less) stable.

9.4 FINANCIALISATION AND THE ECONOMIC AND FINANCIAL CRISES

Since 2008, the deterioration of the financial environment and the resulting impact on the real economy have severely tested the strength and resilience of the French financial system. The financial turmoil arising from the US subprime crisis, which spread to all segments of the financial market, created a difficult operating environment for banks, which also faced a general crisis of confidence. Overall, the French banking system appears to have weathered the crisis: No major bankruptcy has occurred in the banking sector since 2008, and private agents have kept on financing their activity without substantial credit rationing.

Channels of Transmission of the Financial Crisis to France

The first channel of transmission of the crisis to French economic activity was the rise in the cost of financing, which triggered a demand slowdown. The second channel was a bank-lending one that saw banks substitute loans to small and medium-sized enterprises (SMEs) with loans to larger corporations, in a movement of re-intermediation that created credit rationing to SMEs. This put additional downward pressure on internal demand. Furthermore, the decrease in housing and stock market prices also reduced spending, both directly through a negative wealth effect and indirectly through a reduction in the value of collateral, which amplified the asymmetry of information and the cost of external finance. Finally, the rise in uncertainty, generally indicated by a jump in the volatility of the stock index, led firms to postpone important hiring and investment decisions.

Consequently, the rise in the cost of external finance and uncertainty combined with the drop in wealth led French households and non-financial corporations to cut down on spending. The investment rate of non-financial corporations dropped by nearly 2 percentage points between 2008 and 2009. The decrease of housing investment reached 1.4 percentage points. The total contribution of investment to the recession, including public investment, added up to 2.7 percentage points of GDP. Households reduced spending, consumption decreasing slightly for five consecutive quarters, whereas from 2001Q2 to 2007Q4, the average quarterly growth rate of households' consumption had been 0.5 per cent per quarter. The negative wealth effect combined with the increase in uncertainty, and notably the fear of unemployment, produced a rise in the households' saving rate by 1 percentage point (from 15.4 per cent of real disposable income) between 2007 and 2009.

The negative impact of the downward adjustment of domestic demand was dampened by the public sector. From 2008 to 2009, public consumption and investment increased by 2.6 per cent and 2.5 per cent, respectively. The rest of the recession was attributed to net external trade (−1.2 percentage point of GDP) and to changes in inventories (−0.9 percentage point of GDP). In line with the slump in world trade, French exports collapsed. Between the peak and the trough, the fall amounted to 15.6 per cent, whereas during the same period imports decreased by 11.9 per cent. The negative contribution of stocks reflects the larger negative adjustment of supply (GDP) compared with the decrease in demand.

The decline in demand, and then production, has entailed a rapid adjustment of the labour market. The unemployment rate inevitably increased, reaching a first peak at 9.6 per cent and then stepping back temporarily. When decomposing the structure of this unemployment rate, the youngest were hurt most. The further the macroeconomic outlook deteriorated, the harder it became for young graduates to find a job, since before downsizing firms started to reduce new hires. The bulk of the unemployment nevertheless concerned people between 25 and 49 years old. Finally, the unemployment rate of those under 25 years old declined at the beginning of 2010, but in a less marked manner than for those over 50. Thus, the probability of older people being unemployed was less than for the youngest, but the probability of remaining unemployed was higher. As a corollary, the length of unemployment increased with the length of the crisis.

Government Support to French Banks

Soon after the beginning of the financial crisis, the French government undertook various policy actions in support of the banking sector, to avoid negative feedback effects on the real economy. Between late 2008 and early 2009, the government granted loans to the five largest banks for a total amount of €20.75 billion (or 1.1 per cent of French GDP). Loans bore a high interest rate (around 7.5 per cent) and were associated with the constraint that every year the beneficiary banks had to increase their lending to the private sector by 4 per cent. Initially granted for five years, almost all banks repaid these loans within a year after they were granted. A combination of several factors (i.e. a high interest rate, the private credit-growth constraint and the unwillingness to depend on government support) explains why the repayment occurred so early. Grossman and Woll (2014) have also argued that to avoid stigmatising a particular bank, the French government struck a deal with the main institutions, making them simultaneous beneficiaries of loans, although not all of them required it. In the fall of 2009, all major banks, except BPCE (Banques Populaires and Caisses d'Epargne), had already repaid.

Recourse to explicit debt guarantees was another important tool to support French banks, especially at the beginning of the financial crisis. The government de facto 'loaned' its creditworthiness to the beneficiary banks, thereby containing their funding costs and mitigating liquidity risk (Breton et al. 2012). In the case of France, the total amount of guarantees approved by the government (and agreed by the European Commission in compliance with the State Aid Policy) was €320 billion (16 per cent of GDP). Only €93 billion was effectively used (or less than 5 per cent of GDP). Indeed, two French banking institutions (Natixis, Dexia) had to be recapitalised and/or dismantled.

In the context of asset losses due to Euro area debt problems, in particular exposures to the Greek debt, estimations about the needs of recapitalisation for European banks were carried out. The first estimations made in October 2011 by the European Commission was €8.8 billion for the French banks (€106.4 billion for the EU banks), accounting for 8.3 per cent of the EU needs for recapitalisation. The second estimate (in January 2012) was a bit lower for the French banks, at €7.3 billion, or 6.4 per cent of EU needs. Considerable uncertainty has arisen about the quality of the banks' balance sheets, the treatment of sovereign debt and systemic risks (Merler and Wolff 2013). Consequently, estimates by the European Commission are based on stress tests, which should be judged with due caution. For instance, Dexia passed the stress test in July 2011 but needed financial rescue a few months later.

Macroeconomic Consequences of the Crisis

The financial crisis was transmitted to the real economy via a drop of inventories and a freeze of investments of households and private firms. The decrease in production led to a decrease in employment and household income, which caused a reduction of consumption growth.

The immediate consequence of the financial crisis was, in France as well as in other countries, a huge increase of the public budget deficit and public debt. In 2008–2009, fiscal policy was expansionary to limit the fall of production, but very rapidly this policy was reoriented towards debt sustainability. This reorientation was not imposed by the market, as the interest rate on sovereign debt fell to a very low level. The main factor that led to the decision of reorientation was the willingness of government to fulfil, at any price, the Stability and Growth Pact. Table 9.2 shows that without shocks, the economy could have reached a steady growth path of more than 2 per cent a year over the period 2010–2014. However, the effective growth rate

Table 9.2   Obstacles to recovery in France

	2010	2011	2012	2013	2014	*2015*
Actual growth of GDP (1)	1.9	2.1	0.4	0.4	0.4	*1.1*
Impact of :						
Oil prices	0.0	−0.1	−0.3	−0.1	0.0	*0.0*
Prices competitiveness	0.2	0.2	−0.1	−0.1	−0.4	*0.2*
Linked with Euro rate change	−0.1	0.1	0.1	−0.1	−0.2	*0.1*
Linked with intra Euro area position	0.3	0.1	−0.2	0.0	−0.2	*0.1*
Monetary conditions	−0.4	−0.2	−0.3	−0.1	−0.2	*−0.1*
Public finances policy	−0.7	−1.4	−1.6	−1.5	−1.2	*−1.0*
Direct impact of French policy	−0.5	−1.2	−0.9	−0.9	−0.8	*−0.6*
Impact of other European countries (include impact of French policy on others)	−0.2	−0.3	−0.7	−0.6	−0.4	*−0.4*
Total of shocks (2)	−0.9	−1.5	−2.3	−1.9	−1.8	*−0.8*
Acquired and others (3)	0.5	1.2	0.3	−0.1	−0.2	*−0.5*
'potential' rate of growth (1-2-3)	2.4	2.4	2.4	2.4	2.4	*2.4*

Source: Heyer et al. (2014).

was only 0.4 per cent annually during 2012–2014. The difference results mainly from the negative impact of fiscal policy; the latter cut the GDP growth rate by 0.7 percentage points in 2010, 1.4 points in 2011, 1.6 points in 2012 and 1.5 points in 2013. Domestic fiscal policy was thus responsible for 60 per cent to 80 per cent of the cut, whereas the same policies, implemented in the rest of the Euro area, were responsible for 20 to 40 per cent. In sharp contrast, the impact of competitiveness on growth was low.

The stagnation of the French economy since 2012 thus relates to a historical mistake in the management of fiscal and tax policies in the Euro area. The consequences of the financial crisis have been intensified by a wrong analysis of the actual situation of the European economy. As in the 1930s, the initial shock was no doubt a financial one. It could have been offset by appropriate Keynesian stabilisation. However, like during the pre-war years, policy turned the wrong direction and deepened the crisis instead of solving it. Public deficits are certainly not the cause of the crisis; they are its consequence and its cure.

9.5 CONCLUSION

Is the French economy ill and is the current French situation related to its financialisation? The first part of the question is certainly the most difficult, whereas the second one is easier to answer. The most important change that financialisation has brought to the real economy in France came early. At the beginning of the eighties, jointly with the development of French financial markets, the French economy underwent a structural change in the distribution of value added between wages and profits that benefited the launch of the new French stock market.

The current diagnosis is that of a structural disease whose supposed symptoms are an imbalance in public finances, foreign trade imbalances, and high unemployment. Paradoxically, the proposed remedy, 'structural reforms' aimed at lowering wage costs, is ignorant of the historical evolution of the income shares. The French economy undoubtedly had a well-known structural imbalance in the distribution of income, with an increase of wages systematically higher than the rate of productivity growth, which led to structurally high inflation, deterioration of profitability and competitiveness. However, a massive correction occurred during the 1980s and it produced the desired effects: Profitability drove investment, and before the global financial crisis, France had reached a low unemployment rate without inflation.

Before the crisis the growth of the French economy was based on a fairly healthy balance between rising demand permitted by the distribution of the productivity gains to employees, and rising supply guaranteed by largely internally financed profitable investments. At no time has French growth relied on domestic credit, housing or stock market bubbles. Only the recent rise of property prices could have resulted in a cycle of unsustainable growth. This has not been the case, as the unaffected level of the saving rate has testified. The main transmission channel of the financial crisis to the French economy has been external trade.

In the recent period, the French economy thus faces a paradox. While its internal balances remain good, its trade imbalance is far too high, and France can neither restore fiscal balance nor return to full employment. Contrary to what happened in the years 1975–1985, during which an internal structural imbalance prevented the return to growth, it is the external stress resulting from outstanding wage deflation in many European countries that is at stake. The return to growth does not require committing to costly structural reforms. It would be enough to release the budget constraints in all EU countries, such as simulations in the Independent Annual Growth Survey (iAGS) project show for the European economy (see Blot et al. 2014). Consequently the return to growth, which France has never been really far from since 1986, would be once again attainable.

NOTES

1. See the study on the French financial system by Blot et al. (2012).
2. For the pre-crisis trade cycle Hein (2012) classified France as a domestic demand-led economy.

REFERENCES

Blot, C., J. Creel, A.-L. Delatte, K. Durand, A. Gallois, P. Hubert, J. Le Cacheux, S. Levasseur and M. Viennot (2012), 'The French financial system from past to present', FESSUD Studies in Financial Systems, No. 2, University of Leeds.
Blot, C., J. Creel, M. Cochard, B. Ducoudré, D. Schweisguth and X. Timbeau (2014), 'Fiscal consolidation, public debt and output dynamics in the Euro area: Lessons from a simple model with time-varying fiscal multipliers', *Revue d'Economie Politique*, No. 6, November–December, 953–989.
Breton, E., C. Pinto and P-F. Weber (2012), 'Banks, moral hazard, and public debts', Banque de France, *Financial Stability Review*, No. 16, 57–70.
Cornilleau, G. and J. Creel (2014), 'Financialisation and the financial and economic crises: The case of France', FESSUD Studies in Financial Systems, No. 22, University of Leeds.
Grossman, E. and C. Woll (2014), 'Saving the banks: The political economy of bailouts', *Comparative Political Studies*, **47** (4), 574–600.

Hein, E. (2012), *The Macroeconomics of Finance-dominated Capitalism – and its Crisis*, Cheltenham: Edward Elgar.

Heyer, E. and X. Timbeau (2002), 'Le chômage structurel à 5% en France?', *Revue de l'OFCE*, No. 80, 115–151.

Heyer, E., B. Ducoudré, H. Péléraux and M. Plane (2014), 'France: Croissance hors taxes, perspectives 2014–2015 pour l'économie française', *Revue de l'OFCE*, No. 136, 97–168.

Le Bayon, S., M. Plane, C. Rifflart and R. Sampognaro (2014), 'La dévaluation par les salaires dans la zone euro: un ajustement perdant-perdant', *Revue de l'OFCE*, No. 136, 255–291.

Levasseur, S. (2013), 'Éléments de réflexion sur le foncier et sa contribution au prix de l'immobilier', *Revue de l'OFCE*, No. 128, 365–394.

Merler, S., and G.B. Wolff (2013), 'Ending uncertainty: Recapitalisation under European Central Bank supervision', *Bruegel Policy Contribution*, Issue 2013/18, December.

Piketty, T. (2013), *Le capital au XXIème siècle*, Paris: Le Seuil.

Timbeau, X. (2013), 'Les bulles "robustes": Pourquoi il faut construire des logements en région parisienne', *Revue de l'OFCE*, No. 128, 277–313.

10. The transmission channels between the financial and the real sectors in Italy and the crisis

Giampaolo Gabbi, Elisa Ticci and Pietro Vozzella

10.1 INTRODUCTION: LONG-RUN DEVELOPMENTS IN THE ERA OF FINANCIALISATION

Financialisation in Italy has experienced a huge increase since the mid-1980s. From 1960 to 1985, the financial assets to GDP ratio ranged almost smoothly around 300 per cent. This period was mainly characterised by the transformation of the Italian economy, with the industrial sector increasingly taking the place of the primary sector. At the end of this transformation industry made up around 35 per cent of the country's annual GDP, with agriculture only a 4 per cent share.[1] This shift from an agricultural to an industrial economy was accompanied by a massive rise in the Italian GDP, along with a strong dependence of the public deficit on the financial market. One of the reasons behind this trend has been the agreement (the 'divorce'), signed in 1981, between the Bank of Italy and the Italian government to reform the bid system of government bonds, removing the mandatory underwriting role of the central bank in sovereign bond auctions. The rationale of this decision was to increase the accountability of the central bank and its capability to control inflation. Despite the Italian primary balance being one of the highest in the Euro area (OECD 2014), the government has thus lost the power to manage the interest rate in the primary market.

The second phase of financialisation started in the mid-1990s, when the liberalisation of capital movements and then the Euro Monetary Union drove private investments to global markets. The freedom to take exposure in foreign markets and the removal of currency risk within the Euro area caused a strong dependence of the Italian public debt on foreign institutional investors.

One of the reactions to the increasing government debt was the neo-liberal policies, characterised by an extensive privatisation process. From 1992 until 2009 Italy experienced 93 instances of privatisation, for the total proceeds of about 119 billion euros. The state completely lost the control over credit institutions in 1998. Nonetheless, the public debt to GDP ratio increased from 95 to 110 per cent. Comparing the development of the two trade cycles from the early 1990s until the Great Recession with the previous trade cycles, average real GDP growth over the cycle slowed down considerably, with the increasing dominance of finance and the associated redistribution of income (Table 10.1). Real GDP growth in the cycles of the 1960s, 1980s and 1990s was mainly driven by domestic demand.

During the period 1961–1992, the Italian model of development was characterised by a strong contribution of domestic demand to real GDP growth, positive financial balances of the private domestic sector as a whole, a neutral current account, high private consumption (in this period, private consumption accounts for more than 65 per cent of aggregate demand), and relatively high inflation. The 1970s and 1980s also saw the build-up of the public debt to finance expansionary policies. Overall, Italy therefore followed a model of domestic demand-led growth, though the role of the external sector was not marginal. Over the last two decades, Italy's development model has not radically changed but the role of domestic demand, and particularly private consumption, albeit still determinant, has decreased (Table 10.1). Moreover, the economic system has started to face important challenges. Since the mid-1990s, during the acceleration of the financialisation process, Italy has experienced a marked slowdown of productivity growth and a progressive deterioration in competitiveness, leading to a steady loss of export market shares and, since 2000, a significant contraction in manufacturing activity. At the same time, in the 1990s, the Italian government introduced the first attempts of debt stabilisation and consolidation and government's financial deficits were substantially reduced (Figure 10.1). In addition to this, Italy recorded a sharp decline in the saving propensity of households from the cycle of the 1980s onwards. The financial balances of Italian private households had for a long period seen one of the largest surpluses among the industrialised countries, but in the course of the 1990s, they started to decrease (Figure 10.1). This process has been also accompanied by a decline of deficit-finance needs of non-financial companies (Figure 10.1), which, however, should be interpreted as a signal of weak investment in capital stock rather than of economic dynamism and sustainability. Since the mid-1980s, indeed, Italy has experienced an increasing divergence between investment and gross profits (Figure 10.2).

After these macroeconomic developments, on the eve of the 2008 global

Table 10.1   *Real GDP growth in Italy (in per cent) and growth contributions of the main demand aggregates (in percentage points), 1961–2013, cyclical averages*

	1961–1974	1975–1992	1993–2002	2003–2007	2008	2009	2010–2011	2012	2013
Real GDP growth, cyclical averages (in per cent)	5.38	2.60	1.61	1.30	−1.16	−5.49	1.09	−2.37	−1.85
Contribution to increase of GDP of:									
domestic demand including stocks	5.28	2.62	1.34	1.32	−1.20	−4.43	0.55	−5.11	−2.70
private consumption	3.44	1.74	0.80	0.63	−0.47	−0.92	0.38	−2.45	−1.60
public consumption	0.63	0.51	0.09	0.31	0.11	0.16	−0.18	−0.53	−0.16
gross fixed capital formation	1.08	0.41	0.38	0.30	−0.80	−2.46	−0.16	−1.52	−0.85
changes in inventories and acquisitions less disposals of valuables	0.14	−0.09	0.07	0.08	−0.04	−1.20	0.51	−0.62	−0.08
the balance of goods and services	0.10	0.04	0.27	−0.02	0.04	−1.07	0.54	2.75	0.84

Note: The beginning of a trade cycle is given by a local minimum of annual real GDP growth, 1961–1974 and 2008–2013 are incomplete cycles. 2008, 2009, 2012 and 2013 are separately considered for their peculiarity.

Source: European Commission, AMECO Database (2014), authors' calculations.

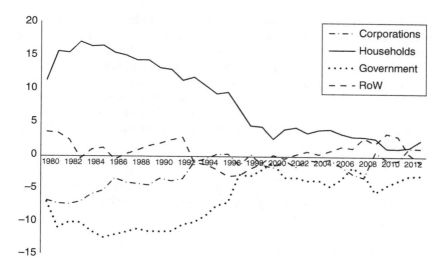

Source: European Commission, AMECO Database (2014), authors' calculations.

Figure 10.1 *Financial balances, Italy, 1980–2013 (per cent of nominal GDP)*

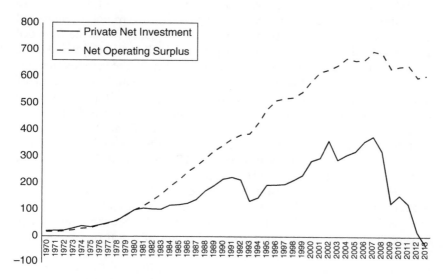

Source: European Commission, AMECO Database (2014), authors' calculations.

Figure 10.2 *Investments and profits, Italy, 1970–2013 (Index 1980 = 100)*

financial crisis, the Italian domestic demand-led model of growth, coupled with a strong profit increase without investments, was as fragile as the debt-led consumption boom type of development in the most financialised countries, such as the US and the UK. The consequence of the collapse of investments, the negative dynamic of real wages, and the neutral demand contributions of the external sector, was a precarious economic condition of the Italian economy when the financial crisis started. In the following sections, we present a more detailed analysis of the long-run developments leading to the crisis.

10.2 LONG-RUN EFFECTS OF FINANCIALISATION ON THE ECONOMY THROUGH DIFFERENT CHANNELS

Financialisation and Distribution

Over the last three decades, Italy has experienced an increase in inequality, as several other developed countries did (OECD 2015). By analysing the Survey of Households Income and Wealth (SHIW) of Bank of Italy (2014), we find that the Gini coefficient of disposable income rose during the 1990s, with a peak in 1998 when it reached 0.413 per cent. From 1998 to 2012 the Gini coefficient showed a U-shape with a remarkable decline until 2008 (Gini: 0.387) and a strong growth of inequality when the financial crisis hit (Gini: 0.398 at the end of 2012). Survey data also show that there has been an income re-distribution at the expense of the very low-income households. In 2012, the average income of the richest 10 per cent of households was more than 12 times that of the poorest 10 per cent, while it was 9 times in 1989. Moreover, from the early 1980s onwards, the share of the very top incomes has rapidly increased: the income share of the top 0.01 and 0.1 per cent practically doubled, while the share of the top 1 and 10 per cent grew, respectively, from 6.9 and 27.2 per cent in 1980 to 9.4 and 33.9 per cent at the end of 2009 (Alvaredo et al. 2014).

Recent economic literature has suggested that the financialisation process can have a role in explaining the recent trends in functional and personal income distribution (Dünhaupt 2013; Stockhammer 2009; Kristal 2010). The most direct effect of financialisation on income distribution is represented by the increase in top officers' remuneration, which has been documented in several countries. Italy confirms this trend. Looking at the composition of the top 1 per cent income share, the main drivers of its increase are wages, salaries and pensions (whose contribution increased from 30 per cent in 1980 to 40 per cent in 2008) followed by business income, defined as sum of self-employment and entrepreneurial income (Alvaredo et al. 2014). Since the top 1 per cent includes top corporate executives, and bonuses and stock options are included in the wage share, then it is plausible that remuneration of top management has also contributed to making income distribution more unequal.

In addition to this dynamics, the economic literature has identified also a deeper potential effect of financialisation on distribution. According to Hein (2015), for instance, financialisation and the neo-liberal paradigm explain the increase in the capital income share and the fall in the labour income share registered in several advanced economies since the early 1980s. We assess this hypothesis by investigating the effects of financialisation on labour share through three main channels: the role of interest and dividends payments of the corporate sector, the shift in the structural output composition from the real to the financial sector and the deregulation of the labour market in the Italian economic system.

In Italy, the last three decades have been characterised by a pronounced income re-distribution from labour to capital income. The ordinary wage share in net national income ratio fell in the period from 1980 to 2012, from 56.15 to 53.7, following a U-shaped development, with a strong decline from the early 1980s to 2000 (around −10 per cent) and a partial recovery from the early 2000s onwards (+6 per cent) (European Commission 2014).

Financialisation might have a role in explaining the trend of fall in the wage share since it can be associated with a growth of the rate of return on bonds, stocks and other financial assets which increase rentiers' income and capital gains compared to labour earnings. In order to assess this potential explanation, we compute the rentier share and the other complementary income shares following the Dünhaupt (2010) methodology. As reported in Figure 10.3 we find no evidence that the fall of labour share was accompanied by an increase in the rentier income share. On the contrary, our estimates show a constant decline of the share of property income over the entire observed period.

To better understand the reasons of the strong downward trend, we split the property income share into its components, namely interests, dividends and rents. The decrease was caused by a fall of the share of interests, which dropped from 12 per cent in 1990 to 3 per cent in 2013 (Figure 10.4). The dividend income share shows a less pronounced trend: it was relatively stable around 12 per cent until the early 2000s, and it fell to 9 per cent in 2013. This evidence, therefore, does not fit with the hypothesis that financialisation, and particularly the increasing adoption of a shareholders' value orientation, leads to an increase in the dividend income share.

To better treat corporate executives' stock options and bonus payments as capital transfers, and not as wage components, as suggested by Lavoie

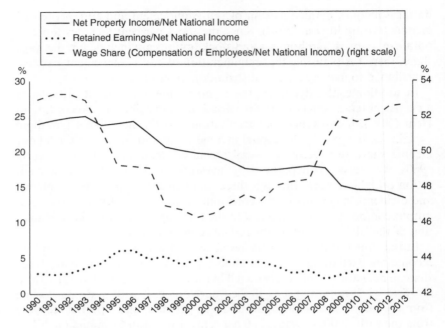

Source: OECD, National Accounts (2014), authors' calculations.

Figure 10.3   Income shares, Italy, 1990–2013

(2009), and Atkinson (2009), we adjusted the wage share as taken from national accounts for the labour income of the top 1 per cent (Alvaredo et al. 2014) following Dünhaupt's (2011) approach. In Italy, during the 1990s this adjusted wage share showed a more pronounced decline than the wage share (−6.5 and −7.2 respectively). From 2000, its recovery was less strong (3.8 per cent and 4.3 per cent, respectively). These findings support the hypothesis that financialisation affected wage inequality, especially when remuneration of financial and top officers is taken into account.

Relating to the shift in the structural output composition in Italy, the gross value added of non-financial corporations (NFCs) has steadily fluctuated around 52 per cent between 1990 and 2013 while it has been stable for financial corporations (FCs), at around 4.5 per cent (OECD 2014). In contrast, the share of the government sector, after an initial phase of decline, shows an upward trend from the end of the 1990s, which peaked in 2009 (about 30 per cent). Given that Italy is a country where public employment, in addition to its standard functions, has also a distributive role (Alesina et al. 2001), this last evidence might contribute to

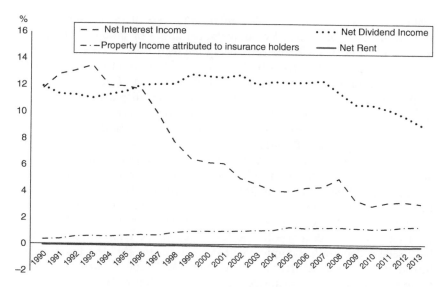

Source: OECD, National Accounts (2014), authors' calculations.

Figure 10.4   Components of rentier income as a share of net national income, Italy, 1990–2013

explain the recovery of the aggregate wage share in the national accounts. The evolution of valued added shares, therefore, does not identify a link between financialisation and the wage share through the channel of sectoral composition of the economy. Data on profit shares, instead, are more consistent with this hypothesis. Using the OECD national accounts data, we have calculated that between 1990 and 2013, the profit share of NFCs, computed as the share of sector gross operating surplus as a percentage of sector gross value added, has been substantially higher than that of FCs. However, starting from the mid-1990s, when the role of finance in the economy became more pronounced, we observe a strong recovery of the profit share of the financial sector and a clear downward trend for the non-financial sector.

Another channel explaining the shift from labour to capital income between 1990 and 2000 is represented by some important reforms of labour market institutions introduced in this period. First, in 1993 the adoption of The Cost of Labour Agreement, which aimed at reducing the public deficit and containing inflation, established that contractual wages were to be negotiated on the basis of the future target of inflation rate set by the government rather than on actual inflation. The result was a slowdown in real wage growth. Second, the deregulation process of the labour markets started in the 1990s which led to an exacerbation of labour market segmentation while at the same time being ineffective to reach employment targets. Italy is characterised by high rates of long-term unemployment, particularly among youth and women, wide diffusion of undeclared work in the underground economy, and deep regional disparities. Moreover, job protection is coupled with central regulation of salaries and working requirements which gives significant power to insiders. Indeed, the extension and enlargement of collective agreements signed by trade unions are generally binding for all employee categories covered by the agreement. In addition, the protection of insiders is not evenly distributed throughout the economy. Since the 1990s, Italian governments have tried to correct these distortions rigorously applying the neo-liberal paradigm. While employment protection for regular contracts has been substantially stable, with only a slight decrease in the last three years, temporary contracts have seen a deep fall in employment protection. In 1997 the Labour Act introduced some structural reforms to increase flexibility, through limited period full-time and part-time contracts, internship contracts for young workers, and private job-placement agencies. The Labour Act of 2003 reinforced this de-regulation process.

The result of this liberalisation trend, however, has been a lower protection of workers in temporary and atypical labour contracts and a deeper segmentation, as well as an increase in the share of unprotected workers. The union density rate dropped from 47 per cent in the early 1990s to 35.5 per cent in 2010, and the strictness of employment protection indicator for temporary contracts fell from 4.8 to 2.0 in the same period. However, at the same time, trade unions were able to protect insiders: bargaining coverage has remained high over the entire period and indicators of unemployment benefits, and both gross and net replacement rates, have shown an upward trend (OECD 2014; Visser 2013).

To sum up, in Italy there has not been a clear increase in overhead costs in the corporate sector, in the form of interest and dividend payments. At the same time, the dynamics of the wage share seems to be largely associated with the developments in the Italian labour market and also with the trend of the government sector's share in terms of value added, while data on the role of sectoral composition of the economy do not provide clear-cut evidence.

Financialisation and Investments in Capital Stock

Financial systems and the provision of payments, insurance, risk-pooling and intermediation services are expected to promote real investments.

Recent theoretical and empirical studies (for a review see Gabbi and Ticci, 2014), however, suggest that the acceleration of financialisation in several advanced economies has crowded out and depressed real investments in capital stock. Most of the related literature does not include analyses of Italy. This section contributes to filling this knowledge gap by comparing the main trends and dynamics in investment financing of Italian NFCs in three periods: in the 1990s, at the beginning of the financialisation era; in the pre-crisis period, when the Italian financial and banking systems had already integrated most of those deregulation and liberalisation reforms which are preconditions and foundations of financialisation; and finally in the recent years of the Great Recession.

During the last two decades, Italian NFCs have been increasingly active on financial markets, have started to invest more in financial assets, and have become more exposed to financial markets. In the period 1995–2006, the ratio of financial assets held by NFCs to GDP grew from 39 to 59 per cent, and remained stable around 60 per cent until 2012 (with the exception of a drop during the 2008 financial crisis). The debt to financial asset ratio of NFCs has grown from 92 in 2000 to 109 per cent in 2005 before climbing to levels higher than 125 per cent during 2008–2012. The debt of NFCs, as a percentage of GDP, has experienced an even stronger growth, with a rise from 99 to 127 per cent between 2000 and 2012. The proportion of short-term financial assets available to cover short-term liabilities follows a similar evolution, increasing from 43 to 68 per cent in the same period. In brief, in the era of financialisation, Italian NFCs have become more able to finance capital investment even in periods of stagnant or weak sales with an improvement in liquidity. Despite this potential strengthening in investment financing capacity, the growth of private investments in capital stock has seen a deceleration. The annual growth rate of investments in gross fixed capital stock of NFCs was, on average, 7.7, 4.4 and −2.2 per cent in the 1995–2000, 2001–2006 and 2007–2013 periods, respectively. Therefore, the growing interactions between NFCs and financial markets have not been effective in boosting real investments.

In fact, an excessive debt burden also represents a constraint on investment expenditure, and can make NFCs more vulnerable to interest rate risk and perturbations in financial markets. There are signs (for example, the ratio of debt to operating surplus has almost doubled from the second half of the 1990s to the recent years) that the debt sustainability of NFCs has deteriorated since the beginning of the 2000s, in the second phase of financialisation, before collapsing in the years of the ongoing economic crisis. In 1995 the debt outstanding of NFCs was 270 per cent of the annual flow of gross operating surplus, growing to 400 per cent in 2006, and more than 500 per cent in 2012.

An explanation of the weakness in real investment is the introduction of a set of trade-offs to the detriment of real investments compared to financial investments. For instance, the adoption of performance-related pay schemes for corporate economic officers (CEOs) can generate a tighter relationship between shareholder and manager interests. Managers might have incentives to drain resources from 'internal means of finance' and redirect them from productive to financial investments. The evolution of the sources of NFCs' operating surplus over the last 20 years reveals that financial investment has become an increasingly profitable alternative vis-à-vis real investment, especially in the pre-crisis period of credit expansion and low interest rates. Not only financial assets of the NFCs account for an increasing GDP share over time, but the share of the resources from property income in the total operating surplus also increased from less than 10 per cent in the 1990s to 18–19 per cent in the 2005–2008 period. The overall trend has been mainly driven by distributed income, the share of which in the total operating surplus constantly grew, from around 3 per cent in the early 1990s to almost 11 per cent in 2007 (Gabbi et al. 2014). Financialisation and the impact of the Great Recession are also reflected in the structure of investment finance of NFCs. Interestingly, the evolution of the composition of internal means of finance and net financial transactions in the pre-crisis period is consistent with the notion that financialisation creates incentives for NFCs to increase debt exposure, invest in financial assets, and reduce internal means of finance (Figure 10.5). Internal means of finance, calculated as corporate saving plus capital consumption allowances, represent the main source of investment finance for Italian NFCs. However, their relevance showed a U-shape over time, with a strong decline from the mid-1990s until the years before the crisis (from more than 80 to 64 per cent, respectively) and a sizeable recovery between 2009 and 2012 (to around 80 per cent). Bank loans are the main source of the external funds and their use rapidly increased until the beginning of the crisis, showing a growth in financial leverage of NFCs. Finally, with the exception of the first half of the 2000s, where negative values of the contribution of equity trades might suggest the use of share buybacks to stimulate share prices, the issue of new shares represents an important source of financing, especially during the crisis.

The credit crunch experienced by Italian NFCs since 2011, after the sovereign debt crisis (Gualandri and Venturelli 2014), has resulted in a collapse of loans, while NFCs have tried to handle this tightening of bank credit by using internal-financing and by increasing bond issuance. At the same time, the crisis, by reducing the access to bank debt, and inducing firms to grant extended payment deferrals, has led to a marked increase in net transactions of other accounts, such as trading credits and advances.

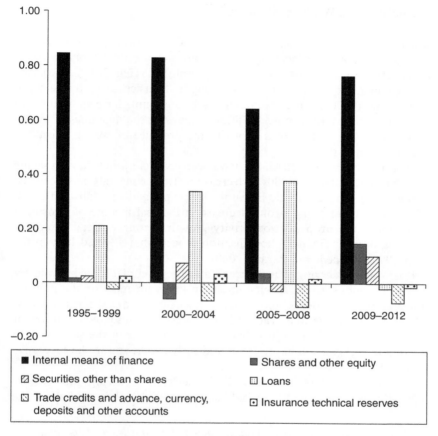

Notes: 'Internal means of finance' are calculated according to the method proposed in van Treeck (2009) as corporate savings plus capital consumption allowances. Items in external finance are calculated as net incurrence of liabilities minus net acquisition of financial assets.

Source: OECD Statistics (2014), authors' calculations.

Figure 10.5 Finance of investment in gross capital stock of non-financial corporations, Italy, 1995–2009 (4- or 5-year averages)

To conclude, in the era of financialisation, Italian NFCs have increased their ability to use financial instruments and to raise financial capital for their investment decisions. However, this change did not translate into particularly positive performances in real investments, even in the pre-crisis period.

Financialisation, Wealth and Consumption

The financialisation process that has affected the economy during the last two decades has been accompanied by an increase in the wealth-based and debt-financed consumption in some countries (Hein 2015). The sharp increase in stock and housing prices along with easier access to the credit market and the loosening of the borrower constraints have allowed credit to expand relative to income. By jointly analysing the dynamics of saving and wealth, this section tries to verify the presence of wealth effects on consumption in Italy.

Historically, Italian households have been characterised by a high saving rate, but since the mid-1980s a decrease in the saving rate has occurred (Table 10.2). The economic literature has explained this fall as a result of different factors: the strong decrease in the real income of consumer households, the drop in productivity growth, stronger social insurance schemes, and the financial liberalisation process that affected Italy in the early 1990s (Jappelli and Pagano 2000).

It is worth observing that the trend and the level of the saving rate are not homogenous across income levels. In line with most of the international empirical evidence, the Italian propensity to save is positively correlated to income as well (Table 10.2). Moreover, households in different income groups did not adjust their saving behaviour in the same way to the financial expansion in the 1990s and early 2000s, and to the successive financial crisis.

Although between 1989 and 2012 the average saving rate fell by 8 percentage points, the households' saving rate in the bottom half of the

Table 10.2   Propensity to save out of income by quintiles of disposable income: Italy, 1989–2012

Income category	1989	1991	1993	1995	1998	2000	2002	2004	2006	2008	2010	2012
Total	0.28	0.30	0.28	0.23	0.29	0.28	0.27	0.26	0.27	0.27	0.24	0.20
I°	0.08	0.13	−0.19	−0.19	−0.17	−0.08	−0.12	−0.10	−0.11	−0.10	−0.14	−0.27
II°	0.15	0.17	0.08	0.05	0.12	0.12	0.10	0.08	0.08	0.09	0.10	0.04
III°	0.19	0.25	0.19	0.12	0.19	0.20	0.21	0.16	0.18	0.18	0.17	0.12
IV°	0.28	0.30	0.30	0.23	0.30	0.27	0.27	0.24	0.25	0.27	0.25	0.21
V°	0.38	0.39	0.42	0.38	0.43	0.41	0.40	0.41	0.41	0.42	0.36	0.33

Note: Quintiles are sorted from the poorest 20% (I°) to the richest 20% (V°).

Source: Bank of Italy (2014), Survey on Household Income and Wealth, Historical Database, authors' calculations.

income distribution fell more steeply and became negative from the early 1990s onwards, while the households' saving rate at the top of the distribution rose, at least until the financial crisis.

Before analysing wealth effects on consumption, it is useful to provide an overview of the composition, level and distribution of net worth as a result from our elaboration on data drawn from SHIW of Bank of Italy. Wealth appears to be more concentrated than income. Between 1987 and 2012, the Gini coefficient for households' net wealth fluctuated, on average, around 0.67. There was a high increase in inequality during the 1990s and a slight slowdown in the 2000s until the financial crisis triggered another increase. The richest 10 per cent households held 47 per cent of total wealth in 2012 (44 per cent in 2008 and 41 in 1991). Net wealth of the poorest 10 per cent was even negative. Interestingly, the ratio between the richest 10 per cent and the bottom 50 per cent, after a downward trend during the 2000s (from 5.3 in 1998 to 4.35 in 2008) grew again during the crisis and reached its peak in 2012 (5.7). In 2012 real assets accounted for around 90 per cent of net wealth, of which around 85 per cent was represented by real estate. During the phase of mature financialisation, namely during the first half of the 2000s, the composition of households' financial wealth changed. The share held in currency and deposits declined from 67 to 50 per cent between 1987 and 2012. In the 1980s and the early 1990s Italian households increased their investments in government bonds until 1995 when the share of financial wealth in government bonds reached the peak of 37 per cent, after which it declined to 11 in 2012. Between 1987 and 2012 the debt securities share moved upwards from 1 per cent to 12 per cent, whereas the ones held in investment funds followed the dynamics of the equity markets, from the dot-com bubble to the 2007 crisis.

Households in the top income quintile (Table 10.3, Panel 1) hold a very large share of both assets and liabilities; concentration has increased in the observed period and has affected most types of assets. In 2012, the richest 20 per cent of households held 50 per cent of real assets and 60 per cent of financial assets, which included almost 80 per cent of risky assets such as equity. Although during the last 20 years the propensity of Italian households to invest in financial assets has substantially increased, most of the financial assets are concentrated at the top of the income distribution.

Referring to the growth of the household net wealth, we find (from SHIW data) that the wealth to disposable income ratio increased from 440 per cent in 1989 to 840 per cent in 2012. This growth has been more pronounced for households at the tails of the income distribution (from 390 to 920 and 480 to 900 per cent, for the bottom and top quintile respectively) and it was mainly driven by the sharp increase in real assets,

Table 10.3 Share of assets and liabilities held by households in the top (Panel 1) and bottom quintile (Panel 2) on the income distribution, Italy 1987–2012

PANEL 1

	1987	1989	1991	1993	1995	1998	2000	2002	2004	2006	2008	2010	2012
Real Assets	0.49	0.44	0.44	0.48	0.46	0.48	0.50	0.47	0.48	0.48	0.49	0.51	0.50
Financial Assets	0.49	0.45	0.46	0.49	0.50	0.52	0.50	0.48	0.48	0.52	0.56	0.58	0.60
Deposits cashable assets	0.45	0.37	0.39	0.38	0.38	0.35	0.34	0.39	0.36	0.44	0.48	0.44	0.46
Government bonds and bills	0.53	0.49	0.47	0.51	0.54	0.50	0.54	0.55	0.51	0.50	0.48	0.57	0.67
Other securities (corporate bonds, stocks, mutual funds, foreign stocks and bonds)	0.69	0.75	0.74	0.70	0.71	0.74	0.69	0.60	0.65	0.63	0.73	0.78	0.77
Total Liabilities	0.42	0.42	0.47	0.48	0.46	0.49	0.57	0.44	0.45	0.47	0.47	0.49	0.46

PANEL 2

	1987	1989	1991	1993	1995	1998	2000	2002	2004	2006	2008	2010	2012
Real Assets	0.07	0.07	0.05	0.05	0.07	0.06	0.06	0.06	0.05	0.05	0.04	0.04	0.06
Financial Assets	0.06	0.06	0.06	0.06	0.04	0.06	0.07	0.08	0.06	0.04	0.03	0.03	0.03
Deposits cashable assets	0.05	0.07	0.08	0.11	0.06	0.09	0.12	0.12	0.09	0.06	0.04	0.06	0.05
Government bonds and bills	0.10	0.04	0.03	0.03	0.03	0.06	0.03	0.02	0.04	0.02	0.02	0.01	0.02
Other securities (corporate bonds, stocks, mutual funds, foreign stocks and bonds)	0.01	0.02	0.03	0.01	0.01	0.02	0.02	0.01	0.01	0.00	0.03	0.03	0.06
Total Liabilities	0.03	0.02	0.02	0.04	0.03	0.03	0.02	0.03	0.03	0.03	0.03	0.03	0.06

Note: Panel 1 shows the population quintile with the highest income; Panel 2 shows the population quintile with the lowest income.

Source: Bank of Italy (2014), Survey on Household Income and Wealth, Historical Database, authors' calculations.

particularly in real estate assets, which account for about 85 per cent of total assets. The two driving factors explaining the rise in the real wealth to income ratio are the increase in the rates of homeownership and the appreciation of the housing stocks starting from 1990 (BIS 2014).

Households' financial assets, instead, after a peak in 2000 (110 per cent of disposable income), recorded a heavy decline during the dot-com crisis. The ratio then saw an upward trend again from 2004 onwards, and continued increasing even when the financial crisis hit.

Since the late 1980s, the issue of wealth effects on consumer behaviour has been widely studied in the economic literature. Financialisation, by facilitating households' participation in financial markets and increasing the value of their wealth, should help consumption smoothing. The relationship between wealth and consumer spending appears to be strong, although its magnitude differs a lot across countries (Paiella 2009; Boone and Girouard 2002). Paiella (2004) finds that in Italy financial wealth effects are close to those in the US and other developed countries, but the marginal propensity to consume out of real wealth is very low. Guiso et al. (2005) estimate that in Italy on average an increase of one euro in housing wealth translates into an increase of consumption of around 2 euro cents, while the substitution effect dominates the income effect when capital gains on financial assets occur. According to Bottazzi et al. (2013), instead, one of the most important drivers of the drop in consumption during the last financial crisis was the decrease in financial wealth. Moreover, they estimated that the impact of a one-euro change in housing wealth caused an effect of between 0.2 and 0.4 cents in non-durable spending.

As suggested by Paiella (2004), one way of looking at the possible influence of wealth accumulation on consumption is by a joined interpretation of the wealth to disposable income ratio along with the saving rate. As we have seen above, the net worth to disposable income ratio shifted from 440 in 1989 to 840 per cent in 2012 with the increase affecting all income groups. Over the same time period the saving rate dropped from 28 to 20 per cent. However, in contrast with the results of Maki and Palumbo (2001) for the US, according to which all of the observed decline in the aggregate saving rate could be attributed to a change in the propensity to save of households at the top of the income distribution, in Italy the wealthiest share of the population continued both to save at a high rate and to invest heavily in stocks. Asset and liability concentration confirms that the main drivers of the increase in the worth to income ratio seem to be real assets for households at the bottom of the income distribution; and financial assets, as well as real assets, for households at the top of distribution.

Financialisation and the Current Account

From 1980 until 2011, the Italian current account balance-GDP ratio averaged around −0.6 per cent. Partly as a consequence of the liberalisation of financial movements in the early 1990s, and the devaluation within the European Exchange Rate Mechanism, the current account balance turned positive between 1993 and 2000, reaching a peak of about 3 per cent of GDP in 1996. After the introduction of the euro, the financial markets assessed the sovereign risk and the risk of bank failures as extremely low, because they did not believe that the no-bail out clause would be enforced.

The current account's relatively neutral contribution to growth in the long run, allows us to categorise Italy as a domestic demand-led economy. How the pattern of external balances was affected by financialisation during the last three decades before the crisis is of interest because it allows us to analyse the link between the real sector and finance.

In the period from the 1960s until the mid-1980s Italy recorded balances within the range [−4; +2] per cent of GDP, showing nine cycles over 25 years (Bank of Italy and Istat). This is consistent with the analysis by Ahearne et al. (2007) who categorise three groups of European countries: those who are structurally in surplus (Germany, Finland, Netherlands, Luxembourg), those which have consistently run current account deficits (Greece, Portugal, Spain, Ireland) and a third group which basically experienced a balanced current account, at least during the last decade before the crisis (France, Italy). After the liberalisation of financial movements, net assets for Italy became more and more negative, with an increasing component of liabilities and other sectors' assets. This process was accompanied by an increasing current account deficit from the mid-1980s to the early 1990s. After a sharp recovery during the early 1990s, however, in 1996 the Italian current account started to dramatically decline until 2010. Indeed, until the mid-2000s, Italy still experienced a significant balance of trade surplus within the European markets, but over the last decade it started to decline becoming a negative component of the current account. In the 1995–2005 period, on average, net exports represented 1.86 per cent of GDP, while during 2006–2013 they fell to −0.37 per cent (Bank of Italy and Istat). During the 1980s, price competitiveness significantly increased, mainly due to currency policy aimed at devaluating the Italian lira, but, after the introduction of the euro, Italy constantly lost in price competitiveness against other Euro area countries until 2008 (Felettigh et al. 2015). According to the Italian government and the EU Commission, the reduction of the cost of labour could contribute to improve the external competitiveness of the Italian economy. Although it is true that the labour tax wedge in Italy is among the highest in the EU, it is worth observing that labour costs are only one dimension of international competitiveness. With the increasing cost-competition from the emerging countries, it has been observed that technological competition and non-price factors, such as quality, innovation, and flexibility have become more important (Tiffin 2014). Institutional, macroeconomic and structural measures affecting these factors are often identified as measures to improve the performance of Italian exporters and of the Italian system as a whole. Examples include interventions to reduce high transportation and network-industry costs, to improve the efficiency of the judicial system, to combat corruption and organised crime, to improve human capital quality, to increase firms' and state's R&D investment, and to establish networks between innovative firms and research institutions.

10.3   UNMASKING THE WEAKNESSES OF ITALY'S ECONOMY: THE IMPACT OF THE CRISIS

The impact of the financial crisis on Italian growth and on the real economy has been the most critical among all the Euro area countries, after Greece. The effects of the global crisis added to the structural and long-standing weaknesses. Averaging real GDP growth rates from 2008 to 2014 (OECD 2014), the Italian decline was −1.2 per cent yearly, while Spain, Portugal and Ireland recorded a GDP fall of about −0.7 per cent per year, and the Euro area of −0.1 per cent. This was mainly due to the fact that, as a domestic demand-led economy, Italy suffered from a collapse of real income and a worsening of income distribution at the expense of the weakest components of the social structure. Along with the collapse of consumption, Italy recorded a drop of private and public investments, caused by a credit crunch originated in the banking sector and in the capital markets. The first phase of the crisis was exacerbated by the collapse of exports, which was partly compensated by social interventions aimed at easing the labour cost for firms. However, during the 2008 financial crisis, in comparison with other EU member states, Italy proved to have a relatively resilient financial sector, despite the constrained policy response due to the burden of public debt. Interestingly, according to the analyses of the European Commission (2013), the capacity of the Italian financial system to withstand the first wave of financial crisis lies on a number of factors linked to its relatively limited market-based characterisation compared with highly financialised countries such as the UK and USA: a traditional intermediation-based business model, a sound regulatory and supervisory regime, the absence of a real estate bubble in the country, and the low level of household debt.

With the second wave of economic crisis, the 2011–12 European sovereign debt crisis, however, the consequences on all economic institutional sectors, households, firms and banks, were more severe. The collapse of consumption was accompanied by a significant and persistent increase of the unemployment and poverty rates and of household indebtedness. At the same time, the loss of access to international wholesale funding markets has increased the vulnerability of Italian banks as demonstrated by the results of the 2014 EU-wide stress test performed by the European Banking Authority (EBA) to assess the resilience of EU banks. Compared with other European countries, Italy displays a weak banking system, with the largest capital loss in the adverse scenario (EBA 2014). Moreover, in a country such as Italy where bank lending is particularly important, the European sovereign debt crisis has generated a severe credit crunch that has deteriorated the availability of bank loans especially for SMEs (Gualandri and Venturelli 2014). Against this background, Italian budgetary policies and reforms essentially inspired by the doctrine of austerity can be evaluated as a weak and inappropriate policy response to the recession and to the structural weakness of the Italian economy.

NOTE

1. Data and statistics of this chapter, if not quoted differently, are based on Gabbi et al. (2014).

REFERENCES

Ahearne, A., B. Schmitz and J. von Hagen (2007), 'Current account imbalances in the Euro area', in A. Aslund and M. Dabrowksi (eds), *Challenges of Globalization: Imbalances and Growth*, Washington, DC: Peterson Institute for International Economics.

Alesina, A., S. Danninger and M. Rostagno (2001), 'Redistribution through public employment: The case of Italy', *IMF Staff Papers*, **48** (3), 447–473.

Alvaredo, F., A.B. Atkinson, T. Piketty and E. Saez (2014), The world top incomes database, available at: http://topincomes.g-mond.parisschoolofeconomics.eu/.

Atkinson, A.B. (2009), 'Factor shares: The principal problem of political economy?', *Oxford Review of Economic Policy*, **25** (1), 3–16.

Bank of Italy (2014), Survey on households income and wealth, historical database, available at: https://www.bancaditalia.it/statistiche/tematiche/indagini-famiglie-imprese/bilanci-famiglie/documentazione/index.html.

BIS (2014), Residential property price, National Sources, Database, available at: http://www.bis.org/statistics/pp_detailed.htm.

Boone, L. and N. Girouard (2002), 'The stock market, the housing market and consumer behavior', *OECD Economic Studies*, **35**, 175–200.

Bottazzi, R., S. Trucchi and M. Wakefield (2013), 'Wealth effects and the consumption of Italian households in the Great Recession', Institute for Fiscal Studies, Working Paper 13/21.

Dünhaupt, P. (2010), 'Financialization and the rentier income share – evidence from the USA and Germany', Macroeconomic Policy Institute (IMK), Working Paper No. 2/2010.

Dünhaupt, P. (2011), 'The impact of financialization on income distribution in the USA and Germany: A proposal for a new adjusted wage share', Macroeconomic Policy Institute (IMK), Working Paper No. 7/2011.

Dünhaupt, P. (2013), 'The effect of financialization on labor's share of income', Institute for International Political Economy (IPE), Berlin School of Economics and Law, Working Paper No. 17.

EBA (2014), Results of 2014 EU-wide stress test, available at: http://www.eba.europa.eu/risk-analysis-and-data/eu-wide-stress-testing/2014/results.

European Commission (2013), In-depth review for Italy in accordance with Article 5 of Regulation (EU) No. 1176/2011 on the prevention and correction of macroeconomic imbalances, SWD Commission Staff Working Document 118 final, Brussels.

European Commission (2014), AMECO Database, available at: http://ec.europa.eu/economy_finance/db_indicators/ameco/index_en.htm.

Felettigh, A., C. Giordano, G. Oddo and V. Romano (2015), 'Reassessing price-competitiveness indicators of the four largest euro-area countries and of their main trading partners', Questioni di Economia e Finanza (Occasional Paper) No. 280, Bank of Italy.

Gabbi, G. and E. Ticci (2014), 'Implications of financialisation for sustainability', FESSUD Working Paper Series, No. 47, Leeds University.

Gabbi, G., E. Ticci, and P. Vozzella (2014), 'Financialisation and economic and financial crises: The case of Italy', FESSUD Studies in Financial Systems, No. 23, Leeds University.

Gualandri, E. and V. Venturelli (2014), 'The financing of Italian firms and credit crunch: Findings and exit strategies' in T. Lindblom, S. Sjogren and M. Willesson (eds), *Financial Systems, Markets and Institutional Changes*, Basingstoke, Hampshire: Palgrave Macmillan.

Guiso, L., M. Paiella and I. Visco (2005), 'Do capital gains affect consumption? Estimates of wealth effects from Italian households' behavior', Banca D'Italia, Temi di discussione, No. 555, June.

Hein, E. (2015), 'Finance-dominated capitalism and re-distribution of income – a Kaleckian perspective', *Cambridge Journal of Economics*, **39** (3), 907–934.

Jappelli, T. and M. Pagano (2000), 'The determinants of saving: Lessons from Italy', in C. Reinhart (ed.), *Accounting for Saving: Financial Liberalization, Capital Flows and Growth in Latin America and Europe*, Washington: Inter-American Development Bank.

Kristal, T. (2010), 'Good times, bad times. Postwar labor's share of national income in capitalist democracies', *American Sociological Review*, **75** (5), 729–763.

Lavoie, M. (2009), 'Cadrisme within a Kaleckian model of growth and distribution', *Review of Political Economy*, **21**, 369–391.

Maki, D. and M. Palumbo (2001), 'Disentangling the wealth effect: A cohort analysis of household savings in the 1990s', Finance and Economics Discussion Series, Federal Reserve Board of Governors, No. 21.

OECD (2014), *Economic Challenges and Policy Recommendations for the Euro Area*, Paris: OECD.

OECD (2015), *In It Together: Why Less Inequality Benefits All*, Paris: OECD.

Paiella, M. (2004), 'Does wealth affect consumption? Evidence for Italy', Banca d'Italia, Temi di discussione, No. 510, July.

Paiella, M. (2009), 'The stock market, housing and consumer spending: A survey of the evidence on wealth effects', *Journal of Economic Surveys*, **23** (5), 947–973.

Stockhammer, E. (2009), 'Determinants of functional income distribution in OECD countries', IMK Studies, No. 5/2009, Macroeconomic Policy Institute (IMK) at the Hans Boeckler Foundation.

Tiffin, A. (2014), 'European productivity, innovation and competitiveness: The case of Italy', IMF Working Paper No. 79/14.

Van Treeck, T. (2009), 'The political economy debate on "financialisation" – a macroeconomic perspective', *Review of International Political Economy*, **16** (5), 907–944.

Visser, J. (2013), ICTWSS: Database on Institutional Characteristics of Trade Unions, Wage Setting, State Intervention and Social Pacts in 34 countries between 1960 and 2012, Version 4 – April, Amsterdam Institute for Advanced Labour Studies, University of Amsterdam.

11. The long boom and the early bust: the Portuguese economy in the era of financialisation*

Ricardo Paes Mamede, Sérgio Lagoa, Emanuel Leão and Ricardo Barradas

11.1 INTRODUCTION

This chapter expands upon our previous work (Lagoa et al. 2013) on the Portuguese financial system's evolution in the past three decades. In that work we extensively documented the various signs of financialisation in the Portuguese economy. For example, by 2007 Portugal had the fourth highest share of finance and insurance in GDP in the EU (after Ireland, the UK and Cyprus), being among the countries in which this indicator increased the most since the mid-1990s. Between 1997 and 2008, the Gross Operational Surplus (GOS) of financial corporations rose from nearly 12 per cent to more than 23 per cent of the total GOS of Portuguese firms (including both financial and non-financial firms). Largely as a result of the strong expansion of bank credit, financial assets increased from nearly 450 per cent of GDP in 1995 to over 650 per cent in 2008, while both household and non-financial corporations' gross debt reached the highest levels among EU Member States.

In the present context we focus on the effects of financialisation in Portugal on the long-run macroeconomic development and, especially, on the financial and economic crises that hit the country in recent years. The remainder of the chapter is divided into four main sections. In Section 11.2 we discuss the main features of the development of the Portuguese economy since the early 1980s until the recent economic and financial crises, as well as the main links with the changes in the domestic financial system. Section 11.3 builds on this analysis by looking in greater

* We thank Eckhard Hein and the participants in the FESSUD Conference Understanding and Responding to the Financial Crisis, October 16–17, Warsaw, Poland, for their comments. The usual disclaimer applies.

detail at four different channels through which financialisation affects the evolution of the Portuguese economy: income distribution, investment in capital stock, private consumption, and the current account. Section 11.4 addresses the crisis, and, finally, Section 11.5 presents the main conclusions.

11.2   ECONOMIC PERFORMANCE AND FINANCIALISATION IN RECENT DECADES

Between 1980 and 2013 the Portuguese economy grew at an average rate of 2 per cent per year – the 8th highest rate among the 15 Western European countries that formed the EU until 2004.[1] In spite of this median performance, the aggregate behaviour of the Portuguese economy over this period did not coincide with the EU average: first, as is typical of small countries, its business cycle is more extreme, growing faster than the average during the upturns and falling deeper in downturns. More importantly, there is a sharp contrast in aggregate economic performance before and after the turn of the millennium.

Between 1986, the year in which Portugal joined the European Economic Community (EEC), and 2000, the Portuguese economy experienced the third fastest growth rate among the EU15 countries (behind only Ireland and Luxembourg), with real GDP increasing at an impressive average annual rate of 4.1 per cent. In contrast, between 2000 and 2013 economic growth nearly stalled, with an average rate of 0.1 per cent, the second lowest in the whole EU (above only Italy's). Contrary to what occurred in other countries on the periphery of the Euro area – such as Greece, Ireland, and Spain – the dismal performance of the Portuguese economy in the recent past is not just a post-subprime crisis phenomenon. Portugal started to fall behind the EU average GDP growth rate from 2000 onwards – while the economies of the other three former 'cohesion countries' kept growing until 2007 at average growth rates that varied between 3.4 per cent and 5 per cent.

The strong growth experienced by the Portuguese economy from the mid-1980s to 2000 was mostly driven by domestic demand: private consumption was responsible for 70 per cent of GDP growth in the period, gross fixed capital formation (GFCF) for 36 per cent, and public consumption for 21 per cent.[2] Although private consumption remained the main contributor to GDP growth over the period, GFCF played an increasing role in the Portuguese growth experience of the late twentieth century, when compared with other EU15 countries (the contribution of GFCF to GDP growth in 1986–2000 was higher only in the Spanish case).

The investment dynamics in Portugal during this period were both a cause and a result of economic growth: High growth expectations fostered new investments, which in turn contributed to stimulating further growth.

In fact, the second half of the 1980s was a favourable period for the European economies, as a result of declining oil prices and the implementation of the European Single Market programme. In the Portuguese case, economic growth was also fostered by accession to the EEC (in 1986), the massive inflow of FDI (which peaked in the early 1990s) and European structural funds,[3] as well as the overall climate of economic stabilisation and liberalisation that followed an IMF-led bailout programme in 1983–1985 (which was marked by financial repression and harsh austerity measures).[4] Moreover, real wages increased quickly between 1985 and 2000, reflecting both the strong GDP growth over that period and the improvement in the wage share of GDP in the early 1990s. No less importantly, the surge in investment experienced by Portugal would hardly have been possible without the wide availability of credit for domestic firms and households, in particular from the mid-1990s onwards. This, in turn, was a result of both supply- and demand-side developments in the financial system.

On the supply-side, the Portuguese banking sector went through an extensive process of privatisation, liberalisation, and deregulation from the mid-1980s. This led to a rapid increase in the number of banking institutions (from 27 in 1989 to 47 in 1995); a strong reduction of public bank assets (from 74 per cent of total banking sector assets in 1991 to 22 per cent in 1996); the entrance of foreign banks into the Portuguese market (increasing from 3 per cent of bank assets in 1991 to 8 per cent in 1995–1996); and an increase in competition (Antão et al. 2009). These developments in the Portuguese banking sector, combined with easier access to external financing for banks, allowed for a substantial expansion of credit to the domestic economy.

On the demand side, the growth of credit was fostered by (i) a sharp decline in nominal and real interest rates[5] (as a result of the 'nominal convergence' process, in anticipation of the European Monetary Union); and (ii) an increase in real incomes, which was diffusely perceived as permanent (as a result of the extended period of strong economic growth).

Thus, between 1995 and 2000, outstanding loans to non-financial corporations (NFCs) and households more than doubled in real terms, increasing from 50 per cent to 93 per cent of GDP (Figure 11.1). Nearly three-fifths of this increase went to households, three-quarters of which was mortgage loans. Loans to NFCs also increased rapidly in the second half of the 1990s, from 28 per cent to 44 per cent of the GDP. Construction and real estate activities were responsible for a substantial part (nearly two-fifths) of the growth in credit to NFCs, although the expansion of credit

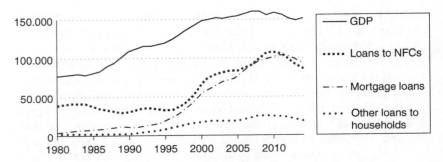

Source: Bank of Portugal and European Commission, AMECO database (available at www.bportugal.pt and http://ec.europa.eu/economy_finance/ameco/, respectively).

Figure 11.1   *GDP and bank loans to households and non-financial corporations (NFCs), 1980–2014 (in million €, at 2005 prices)*

during the period was a common feature across industries. After 2000, the pace of growth of bank credit in the Portuguese economy slowed down, and became even more focused on household mortgage credit and on credit to NFCs operating in real estate and construction industries.

By 2007, Portuguese households had the 6th highest level of debt in percentage of GDP among the EU Member States, while the Portuguese NFCs held the 4th position in the corresponding ranking.[6] Far from being a specific feature of the Portuguese economy, the rapid increase of private indebtedness from the mid-1990s until the advent of the subprime crisis was common to all the countries on the periphery of the Euro area. What is peculiar about the Portuguese indebtedness experience is the timing: While in other countries the levels of indebtedness grew slowly until the turn of the century, accelerating only after 2000, in the Portuguese case the reverse happened – private sector debt in percentage of GDP grew most rapidly in the second half of the 1990s, growing slowly thereafter (particularly in the case of non-financial firms – Figure 11.2).

While the rapid growth of credit and private indebtedness in Portugal in the second half of the 1990s is explained by developments both on the supply-side and on the demand-side of the financial markets, the slow growth of credit in the first years of the new millennium was determined by: (i) the high levels of private indebtedness, which were already evident by the turn of the century; and (ii) the aggregate performance of the Portuguese economy in the following years.

As mentioned before, the contrast between the economic performance of Portugal between 1986–2000 and 2000–2007 is overwhelming – in fact,

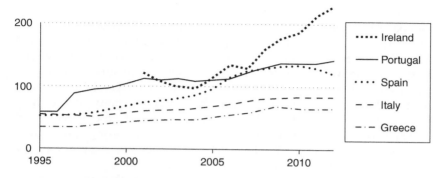

Source: Eurostat (available at http://ec.europa.eu/eurostat).

Figure 11.2   *Debt of non-financial corporations (per cent of GDP) in the periphery of the Euro area, 1995–2012*

it has no parallel among the EU15 countries.[7] A number of events account for this dramatic change of course.

Soon after the inception of the euro, in reaction to signs of overheating in the Euro area, the ECB started to tighten its monetary policy, increasing the main reference interest rate from 2.5 per cent in early 1999 to 4.75 per cent in late 2000. As a result, the Euribor 6-month rate doubled, from 2.6 per cent to 5.2 per cent. Given the high levels of debt accumulated in the previous years, the steep increase in interest rates had a significant impact on the levels of available income and, consequently, on domestic demand. In the same period, the bursting of the 'dot.com bubble' in the stock markets (starting in March 2000 and lasting through 2001) triggered the first international economic crisis of the new millennium. These two events combined had a strong negative impact on domestic demand and employment, being largely accountable for the increase in the Portuguese public deficit, which reached 4.8 per cent of GDP in 2001.[8] As a result, Portugal was the first country in the Euro area to break the EU Stability and Growth Pact (SGP). The following year the Portuguese authorities were committed to complying with the SGP rules, and followed a pro-cyclical, contractionary fiscal policy, which further contributed to the 1 per cent drop in GDP in 2003.

Concomitantly, the Portuguese economy was facing the consequences of a combination of structural weaknesses and international developments (Mamede et al. 2014). In particular, growing competition from the emerging Asian economies (largely as a result of the agreements reached by the EU at the WTO and other fora) had a substantial impact on a number of traditional industries (namely textiles, wearing apparel, footwear, wood and paper), which were responsible for a significant part of the manufacturing value added, exports and employment. Moreover, anticipating the EU's Eastern enlargement in 2004, several multinational firms (especially in the automotive and related industries) shifted their productive capacity to some of the new member states, taking advantage of lower wages, higher educational levels, and the geographical proximity to the main European markets. Additionally, after 2000 Portugal experienced a real exchange rate appreciation, largely as a result of the strong appreciation of the euro against the US dollar,[9] imposing further pressure on exporting industries that are highly reliant on cost-competitiveness.

The combination of a weak specialisation profile with deleterious trade and real exchange rate developments had a devastating impact on the traditional Portuguese productive fabric. Between 2000 and 2007 Portugal lost jobs in manufacturing at an average annual rate of 2 per cent, one of the fastest rates of deindustrialisation in the EU (Mamede 2014).[10] Similarly, the growth of manufacturing valued added in the same period was the 4th lowest in the EU (after Cyprus, UK, and Denmark), at a meagre 0.5 per cent.

When subsequent external shocks hit the international economy – namely, the successive increases in ECB interest rates in 2005–2008, the substantial appreciation of the euro against the dollar in 2007–2008, the peak in oil and commodity prices in 2008 and, finally, the Great Recession – Portugal was still going through an adjustment process characterised by low economic growth, rising unemployment rates (from 4.5 per cent in 2000 to 8.9 per cent in 2007) and, largely as a consequence, a steady rise in the public debt ratio (which surpassed the Euro area average for the first time in 2006, reaching 63.9 per cent of GDP).

11.3   LONG-RUN EFFECTS OF FINANCIALISATION THROUGH DIFFERENT CHANNELS

The long-term effects of financialisation on the economy can be transmitted through different channels. In this section we discuss the relevance of the following main channels in the Portuguese case: the distribution of income, investment in capital stock, consumption, and the current account.

Financialisation and Distribution

Financialisation processes are often associated with increasing income inequality, both in terms of functional (Stockhammer 2012) and personal income distribution (Kus 2012). Regarding the former, the adjusted wage

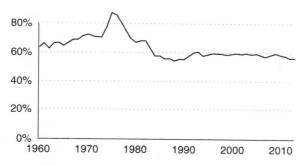

Note: Adjusted for full time equivalent employees.

Source: European Commission, AMECO database (available at http://ec.europa.eu/economy_finance/ameco/).

Figure 11.3   *Adjusted wage share (as percentage of GDP at current market prices)*

share in Portugal decreased between the mid-1970s and the early 1990s, indicating a worsening of functional income distribution (Figure 11.3). However, between 1994 and 2009 the adjusted wage share remained essentially constant, only declining after 2010 in the context of economic crises and adjustment.

If financialisation is responsible for the decline in wage share, rentiers should benefit from it. From 1980 to 2013 property income (dividends, interest and rents received less paid by households) did not show an overall positive tendency.[11] However, this type of income increased between 2003 and 2013 from 6 per cent to 8.5 per cent of the gross national income (GNI), basically due to the increase in dividends.

Inequality in personal disposable income, as measured by the Gini coefficient, increased strongly in 1989–94 (+3.1, in a scale from 0 to 100) (Rodrigues and Andrade 2013), that is, before the fast growth of finance in 1995–2009. After 1995, there was an overall decline in income inequality from 37.0 in 1995 to 34.5 in 2012, with a temporary increase in 2001–05 (+1) and another increase of 1 in the period of economic crisis (2011–12). Despite the improvement in disposable income distribution in the past two decades, in 2010 Portugal was still one of the most unequal countries in the EU15. Moreover, since 1995, the reduction in inequality was achieved by the improvement of the position of the poorest households, and not of the middle classes (with regard to the richest households). In fact, there was also a clear increase in the share of income held by the top 0.1 per cent incomes, from 1.5 per cent in 1989 to 2.5 per cent in 2005.[12] This decrease in overall inequality seems to result from the distributive policies put in place over the period: the Gini coefficient of income before taxes and social transfers in the period 2004–11 actually increased by 3.3.

In summary, we do not find a generalised increase of either personal inequality (after taxes and social transfers) or functional inequality in the period in which finance grew the most. However, three remarks need to be made. First, there may be some negative effects of financialisation on inequality because there was an increase in the Gini coefficient of disposable income between 2001 and 2005, an increase in the Gini coefficient of income *before* taxes and social transfers in the period 2004–11, an increase in the rentier income share in 2003–13, a substantial increase in the share of income held by top incomes from 1989 to 2005, and the middle class did not improve its position. Secondly, the economic crisis in Portugal, partially explained by the growth of finance, substantially increased both functional and personal income inequality. Thirdly, there were other factors that counteracted an increase in inequality at the period, namely the growth of social policies.

Financialisation and Investment in Capital Stock

The investment rate in Portugal increased to relatively high values between 1994 and 2001 from 21.6 per cent to 26.2 per cent of GDP, with two key explanatory factors being the reduction in interest rates during the period of nominal convergence in anticipation of the euro and the rapid growth of credit. Investment was also stimulated by the increase in the proportion of long-term loans in total debt from 52 per cent in 1995 to 69 per cent in 2001 (this trend continued until 2011). In contrast, after 2001 the share of *total* investment in GDP declined to 16.4 per cent in 2013 due to a combination of factors, including high levels of indebtedness of households and firms,[13] low growth prospects, the increase in interest rates, and the exhaustion of investment needs in earlier periods (Lagoa et al. 2013). Regarding the ratio of gross fixed capital formation (GFCF) of non-financial corporations (NFCs) to GDP, we observe a slightly negative trend since 1980 and especially after 2000 (Figure 11.4). The indebtedness level of NFCs may be a factor explaining the slowdown after 2000, since it increased the difficulty of getting additional funding.

There is a stream of research within the financialisation literature (Orhangazi 2008; Hein 2009, among others) that focuses on the impact of financialisation on corporate investment through two main channels: First, the rise of investment in financial assets by NFCs and, secondly, the pressure exerted over these corporations to increase their payments (interest and dividends) to financial markets.[14] In Portugal, financial receipts in

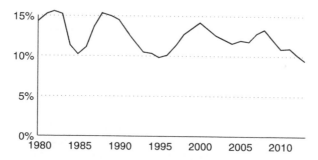

Sources: INE Contas Nacionais (up to 1994) and Eurostat (from 1995) (available at www.ine.pt and http://ec.europa.eu/eurostat, respectively).

Figure 11.4   *Gross fixed capital formation of non-financial corporations (in per cent of GDP)*

percentage of Gross Operating Surplus (GOS) increased from 11.8 per cent in 2002 to 33.7 per cent in 2008; while financial payments increased from 40.2 per cent to 88.1 per cent in the same period.[15] The main effect of financialisation may have been felt through an increase in dividends (both paid and received), which had a long-term tendency to increase since 1985.[16] Therefore, the increase of financial payments and receipts in 2002–08 may have contributed to the decline in NFCs' investment.

Econometric analysis confirms the negative effect of financial *payments* – but not of financial receipts – on NFCs' investment, mostly through the long-run relation among the variables (Barradas and Lagoa 2014). Likewise, these authors find that firms' debt has a negative effect on investment.

The effect of financialisation on investment levels of NFCs may have also resulted from the increase of household indebtedness (Mamede 2014). After household debt reached high values, it caused slow growth in aggregate demand, leading to a reduction of investment by firms oriented to the domestic market.

Arguably, financialisation leads to increasing payments by NFCs to shareholders and debtholders, thus reducing internal funds available to finance investment. In Portugal, we observe that the period of highest growth of finance was characterised by a slight decrease in the internal finance of investment: This source represented 66 per cent of NFCs' investment in 1986–94 and only 60 per cent in 1995–2008.

In conclusion, the negative effects of financialisation on investment have been felt in four areas: an increase in payments to financial investors (mainly in 2003–08), a decrease in the internal means to finance investment, an increase of the debt to equity ratio of NFCs to high values (especially after 2000), and a rise in households' indebtedness.

Financialisation and Consumption

Since the mid-1980s Portugal has witnessed a huge transformation in the behaviour of the country's households. Their savings rate dropped from more than 20 per cent to nearly 7 per cent before the economic and financial crisis beginning in late 2007. The fall was particularly pronounced during the decade that followed Portuguese accession to the EEC in 1986. Private consumption grew fast between the mid-1980s and 2000, fostered by the greater availability of credit for consumption and a reduced need of savings for precautionary reasons. This period was also marked by a change in consumption habits, evidenced, for example, by the rapid diffusion of retail trade chains, big shopping centres, and hypermarkets, all of which sold international brands at prices that were gradually becoming accessible to the expanding middle class.

The further deregulation of the financial system, and easier access to foreign funds by domestic banks from the mid-1990s onwards, led to a strong growth in credit, with mortgage credit growing faster than credit for consumption. Although bank credit to Portuguese households has been largely dominated by mortgage loans, bank credit to households for consumption and other purposes also grew considerably between 1990 and 2000, from 2.6 per cent to 14.2 per cent of GDP (Figure 11.5). In

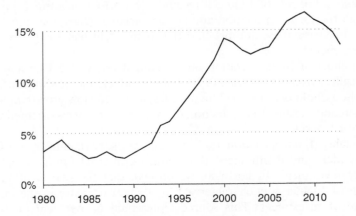

Source: Bank of Portugal (available at www.bportugal.pt).

Figure 11.5   Bank credit to households for consumption and other purposes (per cent of GDP)

order to finance their consumption (namely, of cars, home appliances, furniture, etc.), besides borrowing from banks, households also borrowed from nonbank financial institutions, especially societies for acquisition by credit and, to a much lesser extent, leasing societies.

The growth of consumption was fuelled by the liberalisation of the financial system (after a period of financial repression associated with the IMF interventions of 1977/78 and 1983/85), the significant drop in nominal and real interest rates from the early 1990s, and the strong growth of GDP and real wages until 2000.

Recall that, since the mid-1980s, the Portuguese financial system (in particular, the banking system) developed quickly. The main changes in the period include: the re-opening of the banking and insurance sector to private enterprise in 1983, the creation and development of the interbank money market from 1985, the opening of the banking sector to new entrants in 1985, the privatisation of banks allowed by the second constitutional change in 1989, the end of the credit ceilings regime (in which the central bank set the maximum amounts that each bank could lend) in 1990, and the new legislative framework 'General Regime for Credit Institutions and Financial Societies' adopted in 1992. All these factors contributed to an increase in the banking sector's ability to supply loans to meet increasing demand both from households and firms. The inflows of capital and the reduction of interest rates were also fostered by three EU related events: the free circulation of capital (with short-term capital movements being the last movements to be liberalised), the Maastricht Treaty and its convergence criteria (including the ones related to interest rates), and the Portuguese participation in the European Monetary System (which was reflected in enhanced exchange rate stability from 1993 onwards).

Financial liberalisation produced a strong wealth effect through the reduction of liquidity constraints faced by households, which translated into higher levels of consumption. Castro (2007) and Farinha (2008) both confirm this effect empirically, showing that it was higher than in the US or in other European countries. Wealth related to houses had a larger effect on consumption than financial wealth, with one possible explanation for this fact being that households use mortgage loans to finance consumption.

Thus, private consumption in Portugal grew markedly between the mid-1980s and the end of the century. After 2000, though, and even before the subprime crisis, Portugal displayed the 6th lowest level of consumption growth in the EU, reflecting the sharp slowdown in economic growth discussed in detail in Section 11.2, partly resulting from the debt accumulated by Portuguese households in the preceding period.

Financialisation and the Current Account

Portugal has historically displayed a negative current account balance, the intensity of which has changed from period to period. Between 1960 and 1973, the current account deficit remained at around 2.5 per cent of GDP, increasing to an average of nearly 9 per cent in the following decade (1974–1985),[17] due to the combination of the international crises of the 1970s and the social and political upheavals in the aftermath of the Portuguese democratic revolution of 1974.[18] The external imbalances accumulated during this period led to two IMF interventions in Portugal (1977/78 and 1983/85),[19] which favoured a rapid improvement of the goods and services balance (from −20 per cent of GDP in 1982 to −6 per cent in 1986).

The combination of gradual macroeconomic stabilisation and financial liberalisation, and the decrease in interest rates in the international markets, contributed to the improvement of the balance of net primary income from the mid-1980s onward, partly compensating for the return of the external trade deficits to levels around 10–12 per cent of GDP. As such, between 1986 and 1995 the current account deficit averaged 6 per cent of GDP, while the economy's net borrowing was around 4 per cent (given the positive contribution of capital transfers from the European structural funds to the Portuguese external balances).

After 1995 and until the subprime crisis the Portuguese current account experienced substantial deterioration, from an average of −4.7 per cent in 1995–1997 to −10.4 per cent in 2005–2007 (−2.2 per cent to −9.1 per cent, when current and capital accounts are both considered). By 2007 Portugal had the 8th highest current account deficit (as a percentage of GDP) in the EU28 and the 5th highest in the Euro area. Lately, the current account deficit peaked at 12.6 per cent in 2008 and decreased since then, turning to a modest surplus (driven by the steep improvement in the balance of goods and services) as a result of the recession and the adjustment strategy being followed since 2010.[20]

The deterioration of the current account after 1995 is common to all the countries of the Southern periphery of the Euro area, and indeed to most EU Member States.[21] The aggravation of the current account deficit in Portugal between 1995/1997 and 2005/2007 (6.9 percentage points of GDP) was, in fact, less severe than in Ireland (7.9), Spain (9.1), and Greece (11.7).

Analysing in greater detail the evolution of the main components of the current and capital accounts, before and after the turn of the century, the negative change in the Portuguese external accounts between 1996–1997 and 2006–2007 was mostly determined by the following four main factors (in order of decreasing relevance):

(i)   *the outflow of investment income*;
(ii) *the growth of imports of goods*;
(iii) *the decrease in net current and capital transfers from the EU*; and
(iv) *the decrease in remittances from emigrants* (in percentage of GDP).

The last two factors – which together account for nearly half of the weakening of the Portuguese external accounts between the mid-1990s and the eve of the subprime crisis – are essentially explained by broad institutional, demographic, and international exchange rate phenomena. That is, they cannot be directly associated with the financialisation of the Portuguese economy.

As regards the determinants of the increase in imports of goods in Portugal after 1995 (point ii above), one should distinguish between different periods. As discussed in Section 11.2, domestic demand experienced strong growth in the second half of the 1990s, fostered by the rapid expansion of credit to households (mostly in mortgage loans) and to non-financial firms (across all industries, but especially in construction and real estate). As a result, GDP grew fast, and imports rose even faster over this period, from 29 per cent of GDP in 1995 to 35 per cent in 2000. During this period, financialisation had a direct impact on the growth of imports, by fostering domestic demand. In later periods (especially after 2003), the growth of imports is explained by a combination of the aforementioned nominal exchange rate appreciation with the increase in unit labour costs (see Section 11.2): this led to an appreciation of the real effective exchange rate, leaving the traditional Portuguese industries even more exposed to competition from the emerging economies, which translated into an increasing penetration of imports in the domestic market of the corresponding industries (which are essentially based on consumer products).

Finally, the impact of the financialisation of the domestic economy on the deterioration of the Portuguese external balances after 1995 is even clearer in the case of the outflow of investment income. The growth of the latter was essentially determined by the payment of interest by residents to foreign creditors.[22] In turn, the increase in interest paid to foreigners can be explained by the strong growth of credit to households and non-financial corporations since the mid-1990s.[23]

The persistence of high external deficits in Portugal since the mid-1990s was fostered by the country's participation in the European Monetary Union. The nearly full elimination of the exchange risk premium and the easier access to intra-EU monetary markets allowed for the prolonged financing of external deficits in Portugal. Had Portugal maintained its own currency, not only would the flow of foreign capital to finance the growth of credit to domestic agents have been reduced, but the outflow of capital would also have favoured an exchange rate depreciation, which would have contributed to improving the current account.

11.4   THE ECONOMIC AND FINANCIAL CRISES AS THE CRISIS OF FINANCE-DOMINATED CAPITALISM

The first point to grasp about the nature of the successive crises that have affected the Portuguese economy since 2007 is that they did not originate either in the bursting of a domestic house price bubble or the significant exposure of the Portuguese financial system to 'toxic products'.

In Portugal, as in most European countries, there was no subprime market as in the US, despite a similar evolution of interest rates and the upward trend of house prices in some European countries (Bank of Portugal 2008). Instead, the crucial aspect of the financialisation process in Portugal was the strong increase in credit to households and firms that took place from the mid-1990s. As we have discussed in the previous sections, this has led to high levels of private debt, as well as the decrease in Portuguese banks' solvability to low levels in comparison with other European countries (Lagoa et al. 2013).

According to the Bank of Portugal (2010), Portuguese house prices have evolved in line with fundamental factors, contrary to what happened in other countries. This report quotes an IMF study stating that in 2007 deviations of house prices in relation to fundamentals were around 30 per cent in the UK, 20 per cent in Ireland, between 10 per cent and 20 per cent in France, Spain, Italy and the Netherlands; and about 7 per cent in the US. In Portugal, the deviation was close to 0 per cent.

In the same vein, Portuguese banks did not hold 'toxic financial products' in their portfolios, having avoided the losses associated with these products. The main problem faced by Portuguese banks in the immediate aftermath of the subprime crisis was the difficulty in obtaining funding in international financial markets.

Still, this funding difficulty was overcome by the Portuguese government's scheme of state guarantees for the issue of securitised debt by Portuguese banks, as well as by the huge liquidity offered by the ECB. Moreover, the ECB reduced its key interest rate from 4.25 per cent in October 2008 to 1.00 per cent in May 2009, also putting in place extraordinary full-allotment refinancing operations. After a temporary increase during 2011, the ECB started reducing again its key interest rate from 1.5 per cent in July 2011 to 0.05 per cent in September 2014.

Additionally, in a context of high risk aversion and the intensification of flight-to-quality, the increase in demand for deposits by households (Synek 2009) helped to mitigate the funding difficulties of Portuguese banks. During this period, Portuguese banks adopted aggressive strategies for attracting deposits, offering high interest rates compared with other financial instruments such as treasury bonds.

Nonetheless, the profitability of Portuguese banks fell strongly in 2008, reflecting the drop in commission fees, the increase in funding costs, and losses in investment portfolios. The international activity of banking groups mitigated these negative results, namely through the increase of the financial margin.

Yet the increase in perceived credit risk led Portuguese banks to increase interest rate spreads in credit, which implied a considerable negative impact on private consumption and GFCF. According to the Bank of Portugal (2010), Portuguese households also decreased their investment in housing due to the higher level of interest rates. This contributed to the slowdown in the growth of house prices between 2007 and 2009. Given the deterioration of consumer confidence, as well as the reduction in employment, the saving rate has reversed the downward trend observed since 2005, which also impacted negatively on private consumption.

In this context, the Portuguese economy began to decelerate in the first quarter of 2008 and slipped into a recession in the third quarter of 2008, similarly to most advanced economies.

Initially, the Portuguese economy was not especially affected by the subprime crisis, experiencing a decrease in GDP that was smaller than the Euro area's in 2009. In part this was a result of the counter-cyclical effect of both discretionary and non-discretionary fiscal policies that were in place in 2009.[24] However, this led to an increase in the public deficit that was more pronounced than the Euro area average. This took place in a country that struggled to maintain the public deficit below 3 per cent of GDP between 2001 and 2008. As a consequence, Portuguese public debt increased to levels considerably above the Euro area average in 2010 and 2011, when it was close to that average in 2009.

With a record of dismal GDP growth since 2000, high levels of indebtedness of both firms and households, a gradual increase in public debt until 2008 and a rapid one thereafter, the Portuguese economy was particularly vulnerable to the speculative attacks against sovereign bonds in the Euro area which started in late 2009. Following Greece in early 2010 and Ireland later that year, Portugal submitted a request for financial assistance to the European Financial Stability Facility (EFSF) and the International Monetary Fund (IMF) in April 2011. The Memorandum of Understanding between the Portuguese government and the troika composed of the European Commission, the European Central Bank and the IMF – which established the terms of the adjustment programme that would accompany the EFSF's loan – fixed as its main objectives the rebalancing of Portuguese public finances and the adoption of a number of measures to strengthen the competitiveness of the Portuguese economy.

In general, the adjustment programme implemented in Portugal between May 2011 and May 2014 did not represent a dramatic break with the recent past with regard to the measures relating to public finances.[25] Several policy initiatives in this field had been adopted in previous years, including the following: reducing the number of public sector workers and their real wages; reducing the number of public agencies and managers; cutting back social expenditure; downsizing public investment programmes; privatising state-owned firms; decreasing tax benefits for household expenditure on education and healthcare; imposing extra taxes on pensions and decreasing tax benefits for pensioners; increasing the value added tax rate; increasing the maximum marginal rate in personal income tax; introducing a new tax on stock market capital gains; and extending the base of social security contributions to previously excluded forms of compensation. The Portuguese adjustment programme essentially emphasised the need to proceed with the implementation of the measures already in place and, in some cases, to reinforce some of them (for example, imposing stricter limits on social benefits, greater cuts in public investment, and stricter control of the budgetary process at all levels – central and local administration, quasi-public agencies, and state-owned firms).

Such austerity measures have resulted in a steep decrease in economic activity and employment, which was much more severe than initially foreseen: While the original adjustment programme forecast a GDP year-on-year change of −1.8 per cent in 2012 and 1.2 per cent in 2013, the actual figures were −3.2 per cent and −1.4 per cent, respectively; the unemployment rate was expected to peak at 12.9 per cent in 2012, but reached 16.5 per cent in 2013 (notwithstanding the historically high levels of emigration). These outcomes had a negative impact on public finance targets: The budget deficit was expected to be cut from 9.1 per cent of GDP in 2010 to 3 per cent in 2013, but by the end of this year it was still at 5 per cent; public debt was expected to peak at 108.6 per cent of GDP in 2013, but it was by then near 130 per cent – and growing. The failure to achieve the fiscal targets led the troika and the national authorities to introduce additional austerity measures, which further hindered the economic recovery.

One area in which the programme was considered successful was the evolution of the external balances. According to the initial programme, the current account deficit was expected to decrease from 10 per cent of GDP in 2010 (a value similar to the average of the decade ending in that year) to near 0 per cent in 2015. Such an impressive result was expected to accrue from the combined effects of low wage growth and reforms to the labour market (namely, easing dismissal restrictions, restricting the scope of collective agreements, reducing the duration and amount of unemployment benefits, etc.), which, it was expected, would help restore the competitiveness of the Portuguese economy. In fact, the Portuguese current account became slightly positive in 2013. This, however, is largely explained by the steep decrease in imports, due to the drop in domestic consumption and investment, raising doubts regarding the sustainability of the recent improvement in the current account in the event of a recovery.

11.5 SUMMARY AND CONCLUSIONS

To sum up, the process of financialisation in Portugal was essentially characterised by a large increase in bank credit to the private sector. Even though at first this fostered rapid growth of GDP led by private demand, ultimately it translated into high levels of private indebtedness, which proved to be unsustainable. In this sense, the experience of the Portuguese economy in the past two decades has not been substantially different from those of Greece, Spain, and Ireland – although in the case of Portugal the period of fast growth induced by easier access to cheap credit ended earlier. Thus, we suggest that the experience of those four countries, notwithstanding some national specificities, could be subsumed under the label 'debt-led domestic demand growth' – rather than distinguishing, as Hein (2012) does for the early 2000s before the crisis, the Portuguese experience from the remaining three cases (labelling the former case 'domestic demand-led growth' and the latter cases 'debt-led consumption boom').

In this chapter we discussed more deeply the effects of financialisation on the development of the Portuguese economy through four different channels: income distribution, private consumption, real investment and the current and capital accounts. While the impact of financialisation on the external accounts is clear – as was mentioned above, it is essentially related both to the increase in interest payments and to losses in cost competitiveness – its impact through the remaining channels is less obvious.

As regards income distribution, we have shown that the levels of personal income inequality (after taxes and social transfers) and functional inequality have not changed substantially during the period in which finance grew the most (1995–2009). However, it should be noted that other factors were at work during this period that affected income distribution in Portugal, namely the growing size of social policies.

The wide availability of cheap credit had a strong impact on corporate investment in the second half of the 1990s. Investment was also favoured by the extension of average maturities of bank loans. In contrast, after 2001 the share of total investment in GDP declined in Portugal due to a combination of factors, including the high levels of indebtedness of households and firms. The available econometric analyses conclude that financialisation has had a negative impact on investment through the growth of financial payments by Portuguese firms. This suggests that corporate investment in Portugal was negatively affected by a reduction in 'internal means of finance' (borrowing the expression from Hein, 2009, 2012; and Hein and Dodig, 2013), one of the channels through which, according to the literature, financialisation may constrain real investment.

Finally, the growth of private consumption in Portugal from the late 1980s benefited not only from the expansion of credit for consumption and house purchase (which was partially used for consumption purposes), but also from the wealth effects caused by the drop in real interest rates (especially since the mid-1990s). However, as argued before, the increasing levels of household indebtedness ultimately contributed to reducing income available for private consumption, putting a further constraint on consumption growth (on top of the growth in unemployment since the turn of the century, which is itself partially related to the process of credit-led accumulation of debt).

NOTES

1. Data for Germany before 1991 refer to the Federal Republic of Germany only. Unless mentioned otherwise, the data presented in this section is drawn from the AMECO database of the European Commission.
2. This means that net exports had a negative contribution to GDP growth in this period.
3. Leading to considerable annual surpluses in the capital account – see Section 11.3.
4. The IMF intervention in Portugal in this period was due to a balance of payment crisis, which resulted from a combination of external factors (relating to the oil crises of the 1970s) and internal ones (mostly associated with the social, economic and political upheaval that followed the 1974 democratic revolution). See Lagoa et al. (2013).
5. Real long-term interest rates in Portugal fell from an average of 4.8 per cent in 1993–1996 to 1.8 per cent in 1997–2000.
6. Debt of non-financial corporations include: Securities other than shares, excluding financial derivatives; loans; and trade credits and advances.
7. The difference in average annual GDP growth rates between the two periods is 3 p.p. in the case of Portugal (4.1 per cent to 1 per cent), followed by Ireland with 2 p.p. (6.9 per cent to 5 per cent). Both the Spanish and Greek economies grew actually faster in 2000–2007 than in 1986–2000.
8. This is both a result of automatic stabilisers and discretionary policies: according to the Bank of Portugal, the change in the structural primary balance of the Portuguese government was moderately negative, both in 2000 and in 2001.
9. See Section 11.3 on Financialisation and the Current Account.
10. Nearly two-thirds of the jobs lost in Portuguese manufacturing occurred in the

country's traditional export industries, namely textiles and textile products, footwear, and wood and cork products.

11. Data obtained from INE Contas Nacionais (up to 1994; available at www.ine.pt) and Eurostat (from 1995).
12. Data is from the The World Wealth and Incomes Database (available at http://www.wid.world/).
13. Note that we are referring to *total* investment, which also includes household mortgage investment.
14. Even though in Portugal financial markets are not very relevant, we generalise this reasoning assuming that the pressure for payments is exerted also outside financial markets.
15. The data regarding Portuguese NFCs' financial payments and receipts is drawn from INE and Eurostat, financial transactions and National Accounts.
16. Note that such trend is not observed for *total* financial receipts and payments.
17. Unless stated otherwise, the data presented in this section is drawn from the AMECO database of the European Commission.
18. These factors translated into capital flight, higher imports and lower exports (see Lagoa et al. 2013).
19. The measures of the IMF interventions during this period included the following: adoption of a crawling-peg exchange rate regime (with regular and pre-announced devaluations of the currency) from 1977, strong restrictions on capital movement, credit limits aiming to control aggregate demand and the external deficit, direct control of credit growth, administrative restraints on interest rates, and the liberalisation of foreign trade.
20. See Sections 11.2 and 11.4.
21. The exceptions are Lithuania, Denmark, the Czech Republic, the Netherlands, Malta, Sweden, Austria, and Germany – a group which largely overlaps with the 'export-led mercantilist' economies in Hein's (2012) typology.
22. To a lesser extent, it was also influenced by the negative change in net direct investment income. During this period, especially after 2002, there was some increase in the inflows of investment income related to Portuguese direct investment abroad, but this was insufficient to compensate for the growth in investment income outflows.
23. Note that the relation between Portuguese households and firms and foreign creditors is mostly indirect, being mediated by domestic banks.
24. The public deficit in 2009 amounted to 14.1 billion euros, representing a deterioration of 8.9 billion compared with 2008 as a result of a 6.1 billion euro decrease in revenues and an increase in spending of 2.8 billion euros. Of these, only 824 million euros correspond to discretionary, counter-cyclical measures (Abreu et al. 2013).
25. The following discussion is based on Jorge (2014), who presents a detailed analysis of the original adjustment programme for Portugal and its subsequent revisions, and of the contrast between the initial macroeconomic estimates and the actual performance of the Portuguese economy.

REFERENCES

Abreu, A., H. Mendes, J. Rodrigues, J.G. Gusmão, N. Serra, N. Teles, P.D. Alves and R.P. Mamede (2013), *A Crise, a Troika e as Alternativas Urgentes*, Lisbon: Tinta da China.
Antão, P., M. Boucinha, L. Farinha, A. Lacerda, A.C. Leal and N. Ribeiro (2009), 'Integração financeira, estruturas financeiras e as decisões das famílias e das empresas', in Bank of Portugal, *A Economia Portuguesa no Contexto da Integração Económica, Financeira e Monetária*, Lisbon: Bank of Portugal.
Bank of Portugal (2008), *Annual Report 2008*, Lisbon: Bank of Portugal.

Bank of Portugal (2010), 'Box 1.1 housing markets in the euro area', *Annual Report 2010*, Lisbon: Bank of Portugal.

Barradas, R. and S. Lagoa (2014), 'Financialisation and the Portuguese real investment: A supportive or a disruptive relationship?', DinâmiaCet-IUL Working Paper 2014/06, October, Lisbon.

Castro, G.L. (2007), 'O efeito riqueza sobre o consumo privado na economia portuguesa', *Bank of Portugal Economic Bulletin*, Winter, 37–57.

Farinha, L. (2008), 'Wealth effects on consumption in Portugal: A microeconometric approach', in Bank of Portugal, *Financial Stability Report 2008*, Lisbon: Bank of Portugal.

Hein, E. (2009), 'A (Post-)Keynesian perspective on "financialisation"', Macroeconomic Policy Institute (IMK) at Hans Boeckler Foundation, Studies 1/2009, Düsseldorf.

Hein, E. (2012), *The Macroeconomics of Finance-dominated Capitalism – and its Crisis*, Cheltenham: Edward Elgar.

Hein, E. and N. Dodig (2013), 'Financialisation, distribution, growth and crises – long-run tendencies', FESSUD Working Paper Series 23, University of Leeds.

Jorge, R.P. (2014), *Os 10 erros da Troika em Portugal*, Lisboa: Esfera dos Livros.

Kus, B. (2012), 'Financialisation and income inequality in OECD nations: 1995–2007', *The Economic and Social Review*, 43 (4), 477–495.

Lagoa, S., E. Leão, R. Mamede and R. Barradas (2013), 'Report on the financial system in Portugal', FESSUD Studies in Financial Systems 9, University of Leeds.

Mamede, R. (2014), 'Financial (in)stability and industrial growth: the cases of Italy and Portugal', DinâmiaCet-IUL Working Paper, Mimeo.

Mamede, R., M.M. Godinho and V.C. Simões (2014), 'Assessment and challenges of industrial policies in Portugal: Is there a way out of the "stuck in the middle" trap?', in A. Teixeira, E. Silva and R. Mamede (eds), *Structural Change, Competitiveness and Industrial Policy: Painful Lessons from the European Periphery*, London: Routledge.

Orhangazi, Ö. (2008), 'Financialisation and capital accumulation in the non-financial corporate sector: A theoretical and empirical investigation on the US economy: 1973–2003', *Cambridge Journal of Economics*, 32 (6), 863–886.

Rodrigues, C.F. and I. Andrade (2013), 'Growing inequalities and their impacts in Portugal', *GINI Country report for Portugal*, GINI – Growing Inequalities' Impact Project, available at www.gini-research.org.

Stockhammer, E. (2012), 'Financialisation, income distribution and the crisis', *Investigación Económica*, 71 (279), 39–70.

Synek, C. (2009), 'Impacto da recente crise financeira internacional na riqueza das famílias em Portugal e na Área do Euro', *Boletim Mensal da Economia Portuguesa 02/2009*, GPEARI-MFAP.

12. Financialisation and the financial and economic crises: the case of Turkey*

Serdal Bahçe, Hasan Cömert, Nilgün Erdem, Elif Karaçimen, Ahmet Haşim Köse, Özgür Orhangazi, Gökçer Özgür and Galip L. Yalman

12.1 INTRODUCTION

Neoliberal economic policies have changed the structure of the Turkish economy since 1980.[1] Deregulation in labour markets and trade liberalisation have been integral parts of this process of structural adjustment. As a result of the liberalisation of cross-border capital movements and domestic financial markets, finance has gained considerable importance both at the national and international levels and the 1990s and early 2000s witnessed a series of financial crises in developing countries.[2] Although Western countries suffered from a major financial collapse in 2007, developing countries had been the main victims of a series of crises since the 1980s. Financial liberalisation seems to play a big role in these crises. In many developing countries, current account deficits and debt accumulation could be observed regularly, following financial liberalisation (Akyüz 2012). The volatility of many macroeconomic variables increased significantly. The Turkish economy demonstrates many traits of a typical developing country that has experienced such neoliberal transformation. High volatility in macroeconomic indicators and high frequency of crises have been among the characteristics of the economy since the 1980s.

Turkish current account liberalisation, which aimed to replace import-substitution industrialisation with export-oriented growth, started in 1980.

---

* This chapter is built upon Bahçe et al. (2015), 'Financialisation and the Financial Economic Crises: The Case of Turkey', *Country Report on Turkey, FESSUD Studies in Financial Systems No. 21*, Turkey Country Report. Henceforth this study will be referred to as FESSUD Turkey Country Report WP3.

By the mid-1980s import quotas were mostly removed, customs tariffs were reduced, and generous incentives were offered to exporters. Trade liberalisation was followed by the liberalisation of the capital account and the convertibility of the Turkish Lira (TL) in 1989. Foreign exchange controls on capital outflows were removed, and both current and capital accounts were completely liberalised. Capital account liberalisation was concomitant to domestic financial market liberalisation. Interest rate controls were abandoned in the 1980s and the Istanbul Stock Exchange Market was established in 1986. The weight of the public sector in financial markets gradually decreased and foreign entities were allowed to operate in Turkish financial markets. The importance of foreign investment in Turkish financial markets has increased considerably, especially since 2002.

Capital account liberalisation, accompanied by decreasing constraints on domestic financial markets, has transformed the Turkish economy considerably. However, Turkish financial markets remained shallow relative to those in developed countries. In other words, in Turkey, a classical domestic financialisation trend in the form of exponential growth in financial balance sheets, household debt and non-financial firms' financial activities was not as apparent as in the case of developed countries. As of 2010, the banking sector total assets to GDP ratio was around 90 per cent. Until 2001, government securities dominated banking sector assets. Similarly, many financial innovations such as derivatives, mortgages, and asset backed securities were only introduced after 2002. Until very recently, stock buybacks were not allowed and there has not been a significant shareholder activism forcing non-financial companies (NFCs) to change their behaviour. Besides, bank financing is still very important for NFCs and households. Households still hold their financial assets mostly in the form of deposits. Furthermore, although there has been an increase in the ratio of household debt to GDP, it stood at only about 22 per cent in 2012.[3]

Under these conditions, domestic financial markets have been very sensitive to movements of foreign financial flows. Although the symptoms of domestically driven classical financialisation are not very apparent, the Turkish economy has been greatly shaped by global financialisation trends. The Turkish economy has been suffering from chronic current account deficits and dependence on foreign capital for a long time. Stagnant and low investment has gone hand in hand with an increasing role of consumption. Furthermore, a declining labour share and increasing debt of households have been characteristics of the Turkish economy. All these developments in the Turkish economy seem to justify classifying the Turkish economy as a debt-led growth regime.

This study puts substantial emphasis on the role of financial flows in understanding macroeconomic developments in the era of neoliberalism.

To this end, we will first evaluate the growth pattern of the Turkish economy, as well as the role of financial flows. The second section investigates income distribution in Turkey focusing on the period after 2001. As debt-financed consumption has become a major issue in the Turkish economy in the last decade, these issues will be discussed in the third section. The implications of financialisation on real investment activities will be discussed in the fourth section. The fifth section attempts to document developments in the current account under the neoliberal regime. These discussions will be followed by a penultimate section on the implications of the recent crisis on the Turkish economy. We will conclude with some final remarks about how macroeconomic dynamics have changed in the Turkish economy since the 2000s.

12.2 THE GROWTH PATTERN AND FINANCIAL FLOWS DRIVEN CYCLES

In the early 1980s, liberalisation of foreign trade and the capital account was seen as the basis for economic growth in Turkey. The McKinnon-Shaw Hypothesis was the theoretical background of this policy change. McKinnon (1973) and Shaw (1973) suggested liberalisation of the financial markets and high returns on deposits particularly in developing countries, where the most valid saving method is bank deposits, would bring higher investment and growth. According to this view, financial liberalisation would restore growth and stability by raising savings and enhancing economic efficiency. Furthermore, many developing countries were lured by the export-led growth strategy with trade liberalisation, high subsidies to exports and increasing pressures on wages. Turkey was not an exception. However, neither the promises of financial liberalisation nor trade liberalisation were fulfilled in the Turkish case. An investigation of the main components of GDP can assist us to better understand the general picture.[4]

Turkey's economic growth and its demand decomposition in terms of main components of GDP is reported in Table 12.1. Since the liberalisation of the 1980s, the Turkish economy has aspired to achieve an export-driven growth model. However, even though the volume of trade has increased significantly, the contribution of net exports to growth has stayed negative. As discussed below, Turkish exports are highly dependent on imported energy, intermediate and capital goods. Therefore, an increase in exports has always been accompanied by an increase in imports, preventing net exports from being positive.

Chronic current account deficits have meant accumulation of liabilities which should be sooner or later paid back. Unless the current account

Table 12.1 Basic economic indicators

	2001	2002	2003	2004	2005	2006	2007	2008	2009	2010	2011	2012	2013
GDP growth rate (%)	-5.70	6.16	5.27	9.36	8.40	6.89	4.67	0.66	-4.83	9.16	8.77	2.13	4.12
Growth contributions to GDP (%)[1]													
Consumption	-4.50	3.21	6.79	7.66	5.56	3.27	3.80	-0.22	-1.57	4.72	5.31	-0.32	3.41
Investment	-5.54	2.03	3.13	5.61	3.14	3.11	0.59	-1.97	-4.44	5.41	4.40	-1.09	0.08
Government spending	-1.11	1.01	-0.95	0.41	0.99	0.91	0.85	0.60	0.76	0.91	0.41	1.02	1.61
Change in inventories	-1.06	2.10	-0.43	-1.92	0.06	-0.09	0.65	0.35	-2.31	2.50	-0.25	-1.49	1.60
Net exports	6.52	-2.19	-3.27	-2.40	-1.35	-0.30	-1.21	1.90	2.74	-4.38	-1.09	4.01	-2.57
Financial balances (percentage of GDP)													
Government		-14.43	-10.44	-4.38	-0.81	-0.69	-1.95	-2.71	-6.08	-3.44	-0.63	-1.42	-1.52
Current account balance	1.92	-0.26	-2.49	-3.62	-4.44	-6.01	-5.84	-5.52	-1.97	-6.20	-9.69	-6.15	-7.94
Private sector[1]		14.17	7.95	0.76	-3.63	-5.32	-3.89	-2.81	4.11	-2.76	-9.06	-4.73	-6.42
Real interest rate on government borrowing[1]	41.80	18.83	19.71	15.08	6.75	8.64	10.04	8.82	6.41	-0.11	2.26	-0.06	0.17
Export/Import ratio[1]	1.13	1.03	0.96	0.90	0.86	0.82	0.82	0.84	0.96	0.80	0.73	0.83	0.79

Adjusted wage share (percentage of GDP)	46.21	43.32	42.28	37.20	35.08	33.86	33.83	32.98	34.58	34.07	30.14	31.79	32.66
Household debt statistics[1]													
Interest payments household disposable income ratio			0.02	0.03	0.04	0.04	0.05	0.06	0.05	0.05	0.04	0.05	
Household debt, GDP ratio			0.03	0.05	0.08	0.10	0.12	0.14	0.15	0.18	0.19	0.21	
Household debt, household disposable income ratio			0.08	0.13	0.20	0.25	0.30	0.37	0.36	0.44	0.47	0.49	

Note: [1] Authors' estimations.

Sources: IMF (2014), TSI (2014), European Commission (2015) and CBRT (2006, 2008, 2010, 2011, 2013).

balance is improved, debt servicing capacity of developing countries would be vulnerable to sudden stops or reversals in financial flows. With declining demand from developed countries in a deep recession as in the case of the recent global crisis, the limitations of the export-led growth strategy become even more obvious.

Private consumption has been a major demand-generating force of the Turkish economy, with the exception of economic crises. The contribution of investment demand to the growth of Turkish GDP has been erratic and cannot be a match to that of private consumption. In the last three crises of 1994, 2001 and 2008–9, a sharp negative movement in investment expenditures is very apparent.

The contribution of government spending to economic growth has been limited. The high government debt stock and debt servicing have put an enormous burden on the government budget and forced the government to cut its expenditures significantly from time to time. The Turkish government followed tight budget policies especially in the midst of the crises of 1994 and 2001. Following the 2001 turmoil, due to the structural reform program implemented under the auspices of the IMF, contribution of government expenditures to GDP growth remained very low if not negative.[5] The government followed a relatively expansionary policy during the last crisis. However, this did not prevent the economy from experiencing one of the worst crises in its history. The contribution of consumption and investment to GDP growth turned negative in late 2008 and 2009; yet, the Turkish economy quickly recovered in 2010. Monetary and fiscal policy measures had limited impacts and the quick return of foreign capital in the form of short-term flows in 2010 was mainly responsible for this recovery.

Domestic expenditures have traditionally been higher than total income in Turkey. This has caused an accumulation of external and internal liabilities in the balance sheets of the private sector. The financial balances of the private sector have been negative for a long time (Table 12.1). In other words, the growth of demand of households and firms depended on their borrowing activities. As it will be further evaluated in the next section, the adjusted wage share declined in the 2000s (Table 12.1). As a result, consumer debt increased in this era as discussed below. Similar to households, firms benefited from decreasing interest rates and bank loans became the major source of funding for NFCs after the crisis of 2001. The profitability of NFCs declined with the 2001 crisis. Even after the recovery, it could never reach the pre-crisis levels (Bahçe et al. 2015). And similarly, fixed investment expenditures and tangible fixed assets to total assets ratio of NFCs could never return back to the pre-2001 levels.

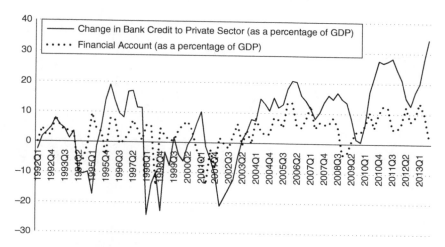

Source: Estimated from the Central Bank of the Republic of Turkey Statistics (2014).

Figure 12.1 Financial flows and domestic bank credit to private sector

The borrowing of the private sector increased considerably. Low interest rates due to capital inflows and a declining wage share strengthened this tendency. In this era, capital inflows have been a major driving force of credit expansion in the Turkish economy and as shown in Figure 12.1, there is a clear association between capital inflows and domestic credit expansion. Financial flows have dominated the course of the current account through their impacts on credit.

As a result of these developments, capital flows have dominated the growth process of the Turkish economy in the post-liberalisation period (Figure 12.2). Since the completion of external financial liberalisation in 1989, the Turkish economy has been subject to a series of financial shocks and crises, mostly associated with boom-bust cycles of the capital flows. Booms have generally been driven by an increase in capital flows; and when the flows declined, the process was reversed causing a parallel decline in domestic demand. In this sense, throughout the period, the correspondence between financial flows and growth of the economy has increased. The simple correlation between net financial flows and economic growth has been found to be 0.45, 0.66, and 0.75 for the periods of 1980–9, 1990–9, and 2000–12 respectively. The post-1990 years exhibit four downturns (1994, 1999, 2001 and 2009). In all these four crises, a sudden stop of capital inflows and/or a decline in export revenues triggered the collapse.[6]

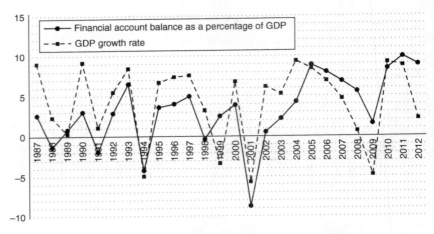

Source: Estimated from the Central Bank of the Republic of Turkey Statistics.

Figure 12.2   Financial flows and economic growth (%)

12.3   INCOME DISTRIBUTION

The macroeconomic conditions and economic policies after 2002 had profound effects upon income distribution; and at first glance, according to household data, there seems an improvement in income inequality in the early 2000s. However, the share of wages in total income has decreased in the same era. Beside this, increases in consumption especially among lower income groups could not be matched by increases in their incomes. As a result of this, lower income groups in particular have relied on borrowing (Bahçe et al. 2011).

Table 12.2 indicates that the share of the highest quintile decreased from 2002 to 2007, then rose in 2008 and 2009.[7] The losses of the highest quintile seem to be the gain for all the remaining quintiles. Without any exception, the shares of the other four quintiles increased between 2002 and 2007. Nevertheless, in 2008 (the year of global crisis) and 2009 (the year in which contagion effects of the global crisis were felt to the utmost degree in Turkey), this trend was reversed. The share of the highest quintile rose again while the shares of the others decreased.

The last two columns in Table 12.2 show the change in Gini coefficients.[8] Both Gini coefficients declined until 2007, and then increased between 2007 and 2009; after this year they both declined again. Our estimation of the Gini coefficient has always been higher than the official one except for 2006. The highest values for the coefficients were observed at the beginning

Table 12.2 *The distribution of household disposable income by quintiles (per cent)*

	Quintiles							
	1	2	3	4	5	P5/P1	Gini	Gini_TSI
2002	6.46	11.12	14.83	20.35	47.24	7.32	0.46	0.44
2003	7.13	11.68	15.36	20.63	45.19	6.34	0.43	0.42
2004	7.26	11.98	16.34	21.43	42.99	5.92	0.41	0.40
2005	7.27	12.78	16.74	22.24	40.96	5.63	0.40	0.38
2006	7.80	13.27	16.66	21.88	40.40	5.18	0.39	0.40
2007	8.03	13.16	16.86	21.85	40.10	4.99	0.38	0.39
2008	7.73	12.60	16.72	22.09	40.86	5.28	0.39	0.39
2009	7.09	12.61	16.54	21.49	42.27	5.96	0.41	0.39
2010	7.85	13.03	16.45	21.65	41.02	5.22	0.40	0.38
2011	7.66	12.75	16.53	21.88	41.18	5.38	0.40	0.38

Sources: Authors' calculations from HBSs, except for Gini_TSI. It is the official estimate of the Turkish Statistical Institute. The figures for Gini_TSI are from two different surveys. The figures for the period 2006–2011 are the results from *Income and Living Conditions Surveys, 2006–2011*. The figures for the period 2002–2005 are from *Household Budget Surveys, 2002–2005*.

of the period, as these were the years of slow recovery from one of the worst crises of Turkey. According to our calculations, the Gini coefficient dropped from 0.45 in 2002 to 0.39 in 2011. However, despite the improvement in the period, Turkey has the third worst income distribution among OECD members (following Chile and Mexico) (OECD 2013).

These Gini coefficients are estimated from household surveys; but macro level data, e.g. functional income distribution, can give different information on inequality. GDP figures estimated through an income approach are more likely to provide a complete view of the functional income distribution since this measure also incorporates retained profits.[9] The changes in the adjusted wage share are reported in Table 12.1, and as the figures indicate the wage share decreased throughout the 2000s until Turkey was hit by the financial crisis in 2009.[10]

12.4 FINANCIALISATION AND CONSUMPTION

Private consumption has become a key driver of Turkish economic growth over the last decade, and household borrowing played an important role in this process. Accordingly, the share of private consumption in GDP rose from an average of 68 per cent in the 1990s to 71 per cent in the post-2001 crisis era. Between 2002 and 2007, private consumption contributed 5.2 per cent to Turkey's average GDP growth rate of 6.8 per cent. Like many East Asian and Latin American countries, in Turkey, consumer credit stimulated consumption in the late 1990s and early 2000s (IMF 2006; Hanson 2005). According to Banking Sector Regulation and Supervision Agency (BRSA) statistics, the ratio of consumer loans and credit card expenditures to consumption of resident households increased from 3 per cent in 2002 to 31 per cent in 2013, demonstrating the increasing penetration of credit into the daily lives of people.[11]

This rising use of credit to finance consumption has been accompanied by a remarkable decline in private savings, which has reached its lowest level since 1998. According to the data from the Ministry of Development, the private saving ratio as a share of GDP declined from 25.7 per cent in 1998 to 12 per cent in 2012 (Karacimen 2014). The data breakdown of private savings by corporate and household sectors is not available. Nevertheless, according to the estimations of Van Rijckeghem and Üçer (2009), household savings as a percentage of household disposable income fell from 17 per cent in 2004 to 8 per cent in 2008. More recent data from the Central Bank shows that from 2008 to 2012, household savings fell further to 7.3 per cent in 2012 (CBRT 2013). As a result, consumption grew faster than income, and households, especially from low income groups, resorted to borrowing for further consumption (Bahçe et al. 2015). However, increases in borrowing activities were not limited to consumption, as housing loans also increased in this era (Karacimen 2014).

Although household debt levels increased, they are still low in comparison with that of developed countries. As argued throughout this chapter, financial markets are relatively shallow in Turkey, a phenomenon that is also valid for the consumer credit market. Household debt, as a percentage of GDP, increased from 3 per cent in 2002 to 21 per cent in 2012 (Table 12.1). Strikingly, household debt reached 49 per cent of disposable personal income in 2012, implying a seven-fold increase since the end of 2003.[12] Along with the rising debt, the burden of debt servicing increased as well. The share of interest payments in the disposable income of households increased from 2.2 per cent in 2003 to 5 per cent in 2012 (Table 12.1), indicating increasing transfers of household income to the financial sector. Higher interest rates on consumer debt relative to other debt instruments, especially on credit cards, were important determinants of the rise in Turkey's consumer debt service burden. In response to rising public discontent against high interest rates on credit cards, there were significant interest rate cuts after 2006. Although the interest rates fell, the rising debt levels led to a rise in the debt service burden in the upcoming years.

Throughout this period, banks have increasingly turned towards providing consumer credit as an alternative way of making profit. The share of consumer loans in total banking sector loans increased remarkably, rising from 13 per cent in 2003 to 34 per cent in 2012 (Karacimen 2014). One of the key questions that needs to be addressed related to the rising usage of consumer credit is whether this increased access is accompanied by a rise in asset holdings of households. However, the rise in financial wealth is rather weak. Indeed, in Turkey the rise in household financial assets is well below the rise in household liabilities as evident in the sharp increase in the household leverage ratio, as seen in Table 12.3 below.

The table shows that households hold their financial assets mostly in deposits. It is striking to see that while the importance of deposits has declined in many countries in the age of financialisation, the opposite has been the case in Turkey. The total share of domestic and foreign currency deposits increased from 64.3 per cent in 2003 to 70.8 per cent in 2012. Another important observation is that, together with the introduction of the private pension system in 2003, there has been a steady, albeit small, increase in the share of private pension funds in household portfolios. On the other hand, there has been a decline in the share of government

Table 12.3   *Composition of household financial assets in Turkey (per cent)*

	2003	2004	2005	2006	2007	2008	2009	2010	2011	2012
TL deposits	29.1	33.3	41.2	40.6	45.5	51.2	49.9	52.7	51.9	50.7
FX deposits	35.2	32.2	27.2	26.8	25.0	24.2	23.3	20.1	20.6	20.1
Currency in circulation	6.4	6.5	8.3	8.8	8.4	8.3	8.4	9.3	9.1	9.0
Government securities and Eurobond	22.4	20.5	14.8	10.1	6.3	5.3	3.3	2.0	1.9	1.0
Mutual funds	n.a	n.a	n.a	6.3	7.2	5.6	6.2	5.9	4.7	4.3
Stocks	5.1	6.5	7.1	5.6	5.6	2.9	5.9	6.8	5.5	6.3
Private pension funds	0.0	0.2	0.5	1.0	1.5	1.7	2.1	2.5	2.6	3.4
Repos	1.78	0.8	0.7	0.7	0.6	0.6	0.5	0.3	0.3	0.6
Precious metal deposits	n.a	n.a	n.a	n.a	0.0	0.1	0.3	0.5	2.5	2.9
Total assets (billion TL)	157.6	190.5	219.5	279.7	313.6	368.3	420.4	481.7	543.2	605.1
Household liabilities / assets (per cent)	8.5	14.8	22.2	26.3	33.2	35.0	35.1	39.7	46.3	49.4

Sources: CBRT (2006, 2008, 2010, 2011, 2013).

securities and Eurobonds, due to their declining yields. Overall, it can be seen that the remarkable increase in financial liabilities is not matched by a corresponding increase in the asset holdings of households in Turkey. Furthermore, there is no major shift in household portfolios towards riskier asset types, suggesting that the financialisation of household balance sheets has mainly taken place through a rise in liabilities. As a result, the household leverage ratio increased from 8.5 per cent in 2003 to 49.4 per cent in 2012, as can be seen from Table 12.3.

In sum, the analysis of the household dynamics in Turkey indicates that financialisation of household balance sheets is not comparable with that of developed countries. The most outstanding observation is the rapid rise in household debt levels over the last decade, albeit from a low basis. However, it is unquestionable that the rising debt levels put a considerable burden on households through a rise in their debt stock and debt service burden. As the rise in financial assets does not show a similar increase, the burden of increased debt levels does not seem to be compensated by a rise in gains from asset acquisition.

12.5   FINANCIALISATION AND INVESTMENT IN CAPITAL STOCK[13]

In the financialisation literature, most of the studies focused on advanced economies, looking at the changing relationship between NFCs and financial markets in the last couple of decades. These changes are twofold: On the one hand, nonfinancial corporations began increasing their acquisition of financial assets and deriving an increasing share of their income from financial sources. On the other hand, the management of nonfinancial corporations came under increased pressure from financial markets to maximise shareholder value, which led to increased payments to financial markets in the forms of interest payments, dividend payments and stock buybacks (Crotty 2003; Stockhammer 2004; Orhangazi 2008). These studies argue that the changes in the relationship between financial markets and NFCs had a negative impact on the levels of investment.

A number of recent studies examined similar issues for the case of Turkey. Demir (2007) in a cross-country study including Turkey suggested that financial liberalisation led to a channelling of nonfinancial sector savings to speculative short-term investments instead of long-term investment projects and this has changed the pattern of nonfinancial corporate sectors' capital accumulation. In a study on the investment and saving behaviour of nonfinancial corporations, Özmen et al. (2012) argued that in Turkey the financial sector remains limited in mobilising funds for firms that are dependent on external financing for investment. However, they have not analyzed to what extent corporations use their internal savings for investment in fixed capital as opposed to financial investments. Gezici (2007) examined the effects of financial liberalisation on the investment decisions of manufacturing firms in Turkey. She contended that:

> (the) negative impact of uncertainty on investment is worsened under financial liberalisation, while there is no evidence of declining importance of liquidity. Overall, results suggests that financial reform policies did not lead to expected benefits for the investment of real sector firms while producing increased uncertainty that impedes investment further.

Akkemik and Özen (2014) observed that nonfinancial corporations in Turkey have shifted significant amounts of working capital from productive activities to the acquisition of high-yield interest bearing assets in an effort to gain short-term interest revenues and argued that they have done so as a response to highly uncertain macroeconomic conditions.

In terms of financialisation, it should be mentioned that stock market capitalism is relatively undeveloped in Turkey, since shareholder activism is very limited, corporations are still controlled by large groups, stock buybacks were not allowed (until very recently), and most corporations are organised as holding companies which also include affiliated banks (Demirag and Serter 2003).

The Company Accounts of Turkey (CBRT 2014) covers the aggregate data on NFCs for the period 1997–2012 and this data set is used in order to evaluate the impacts of financialisation in Turkey.[14] Gross fixed capital formation as a percentage of GDP, in this era, has oscillated around 20 per cent except during recessions and the following years. The profitability of NFCs experienced a decline in the 2001 crisis, it recovered in the following years but could not reach pre-crisis levels, and the profit before tax to equity ratio oscillated around 11 per cent. On the liability side, the leverage ratio, defined as total loans as a percentage of total assets, declined significantly following the 2001 crisis; and bank loans have constituted more than 40 per cent of total loans to the NFCs at the end of the period, showing that bank finance is an important channel for NFCs. In terms of financial activities, financial incomes as a percentage of operating profits significantly declined starting in 2000; it had reached a remarkable rate of 74 per cent by 1999, yet levelled around 25 per cent after the decline. During the 1990s, government bonds used to be the main sources of financial income for NFCs as the yields on these bonds were very high. However, as interest rates of these assets declined this type of financial revenue source dried up.

In conclusion, we make a couple of complementary observations about NFCs in Turkey. First, a hallmark of financialisation in advanced economies has been the increase in payments to the financial markets, especially in the form of dividends and stock buybacks. For the Turkish NFCs, dividend data is limited in our database. However, due to the institutional differences, stock buybacks were not possible until very recently. Shareholder pressure was also not visible as shareholder activism has been limited. This is a major institutional difference. Second, bank financing is still a very important channel. Third, there is an increase in financial asset holdings, although financial incomes are declining in the post-2001 era. This is partly due to declining interest rates especially on government bonds. In the pre-2001 era, Turkish NFCs were earning high short-term interest revenues through investments in government bonds. Overall, the framework based on classical financialisation literature derived from the experiences of advanced countries would not easily account for the stagnant nature of investment in Turkey, though high volatility in financial flows might contribute to this trend by increasing uncertainty in the economy.

12.6   CURRENT ACCOUNT BALANCE OF TURKISH ECONOMY

The Turkish economy has been suffering from chronic current account deficits for decades, and these deficits have grown in size in the 2000s and 2010s. The recession of 2009 led to a contraction in the current account deficit, however, unlike previous recessions, the current account still remained in deficit. The current account deficit as a percentage of GDP reached a record level of 9.7 per cent in 2011 and 7.9 per cent by the end of 2013 (Table 12.1). Chronic and large current account deficits render the economy vulnerable to slowdowns in capital inflows, which could create problems in terms of financial stability and economic growth.

Various explanations have been put forward to explain the chronic and large current account deficit of the Turkish economy. Two dynamics behind those deficits can be identified (Bahçe et al. 2015). The first one is the structure of Turkey's trade with the rest of the world and the composition of exports and imports. Turkey imports large amounts of energy items, intermediary and capital goods, while it exports, to a large extent, relatively low-value added products. The second one is the impact of capital inflows. Capital inflows have direct and indirect effects on the current account deficit. The direct effect is through the exchange rate. Periods of large capital inflows coincide with the appreciation of the domestic currency, which leads to increasing imports while holding back export growth. If the opposite was true, that is if a current account deficit was the cause of capital account inflows, then rising deficits should lead to a depreciation of the local currency and/or rising interest rates. Yet, the Turkish economy experienced both currency appreciation and declining interest rates in this era of widening current account deficits. The indirect effect of capital inflows on the current account deficit works through the domestic dynamics of the economy. Large capital inflows lead to an expansion of domestic credit, increased asset prices, and decreased interest rates. As a result, domestic economic activity increases and, given the high import content of domestic production, this leads to an increase in imports of both consumption goods and investment goods (energy, intermediary goods, and capital goods) imports.[15]

For the first dynamic, the details of the current account balance provide very insightful information. First of all, even though the volume of foreign trade has increased since 2001, the export-import ratio declined to its lowest level (79 per cent) by 2013 (Table 12.1, and TSI 2014). Secondly, contrary to common fallacy, intermediate and capital goods, not consumption goods, have the largest share in Turkish imports. Intermediate goods and capital goods have constituted 70 per cent and 20 per cent of all imports, respectively, on average since 1989 (TSI 2014). In a different classification of total imports, energy items such as oil and natural gas accounted for 25 per cent of all imports on average in the 2000s and 2010s (TSI 2014). Thirdly, as regards the export side of the economy, Turkey has managed to update its product variety so as to adapt itself to changes in the product composition of developing economies. However, the rank of the Turkish economy in the global production value-chain has not changed since the 1950s; Turkey could not improve its rank in international markets, yet it could keep its position (Taymaz et al. 2011). Even though Turkey managed to transform its production base, the export sector specialised in mid-level technology products with relatively low market growth potential (Taymaz et al. 2011).

The structure and composition of exports and imports can explain why the Turkish economy has experienced chronic current account deficits for a long time, but to explain the growing deficit in the 2000s and 2010s we need a further elaboration of the second dynamic; i.e. the role of capital flows. The dynamics of capital inflows to Turkey are related to changes in the global economy. According to Boratav (2010, p. 24), as US current account deficits started to grow in the late 1990s, many developing economies benefited from rising current account surpluses. However, a small group of developing countries took a different path and benefited from rapid growth through foreign capital inflows in the 2000s; these economies were Eastern European economies, Turkey, South Africa and some of the Latin American economies. In this respect, financial liberalisation changed the causality between current account deficits and capital flows (Boratav

2010, p. 25). Before liberalisation, economic growth was responsible for the rise in imports and current account deficits, and thus the need for foreign capital inflows through foreign debt. However, in the era of financial liberalisation, capital flows have become *autonomous* from the current account as these flows are determined by the international financial system. It can be argued that these flows are determined by global liquidity and search for yield not by the size of Turkish current account deficit.

Capital flows lead to economic growth mainly through three channels in the Turkish economy:[16] First, capital inflows lead to credit expansion, which increases demand, consumption and imports (and hence contribute to the current account deficit). Second, capital inflows lead to appreciation of assets, especially the stock market index. Third, periods of surges in capital inflows are associated with appreciating currency and thus by making imported capital goods cheaper contributes to increased investment. As a result domestic economic activity increases. Moreover, lower interest rates also gave a further stimulus to overall economy. Thus, a surge in foreign capital boosts domestic demand and economic growth (of excess capacity), and these developments give way to a rise in imports and current account deficits (Boratav 2010, p. 25).

As foreign debt constituted most of the capital inflows to the Turkish economy (Bahçe et al. 2015), a chain-reaction emerges out of these developments: greater capital inflows will be needed for further economic growth in the following years (BSB 2008, pp. 131–132). Thus, the fate of the Turkish economy, similar to other fragile economies, is directly linked to global interest rates and credit conditions. A stress in these areas can send shockwaves to the Turkish economy as experienced in 2009 and again briefly in the summer of 2013. The main fragility here is that the Turkish economy not only needs uninterrupted capital inflows but also greater amounts compared with previous years for economic growth (BSB 2008, p. 132).

12.7   THE RECENT CRISIS AND THE TURKISH ECONOMY

Along with massive financial flows related to the mainly positive global outlook, the Turkish economy experienced its Great Moderation from 2002–8 with high growth and low inflation, although the problem of high unemployment could not be addressed. However, the global financial crisis ended this honeymoon, and the Turkish economy fell into a significant recession.

Although the crisis began in advanced economies, it quickly spread all over the world and caused negative GDP growth and significant increases in the unemployment rate in Turkey and in many other developing countries. Turkish GDP growth began to decline in the third quarter in 2008 and the fall continued until the third quarter of 2009. The Turkish economy experienced 0.7 per cent annual real GDP growth in 2008. In 2009, GDP shrank by −4.8 per cent. Indeed, the Turkish economic performance was one of the worst in the world in this period. Excluding small economies from the sample, Turkish economic performance was better than just a few ex-Eastern bloc countries and raw material exporters. The negative growth performance of the economy deteriorated the already weakened employment conditions further. As a result, the unemployment rate rose to record levels of 15.0 per cent in April 2009. The capacity utilisation rate in the manufacturing sector declined from 80 per cent to about 60 per cent in 2009. Overall, economic growth significantly deteriorated and the economy experienced one of its worst recessions since the Second World War.

The initial impact of the crisis took place through declines in consumption and investment spending due to the worsening expectations of investors and consumers. The contraction of consumption was larger compared to the 2001 crisis (Cömert and Çolak 2014). The negative growth of investments lasted for seven consecutive quarters. This investment shock was as large as the shock during the 2001 crisis. Similar to consumption and investment, exports also declined during the global crisis as demand from the EU largely stopped. While exports had increased during the 1994 and 2001 crises due to large depreciations of the Turkish Lira, export earnings in 2009 declined by 20 per cent (Cömert and Çolak 2014). The contribution of the fall in exports to the negative GDP growth of 2009 was around 25 per cent and the fall in exports to Europe explains directly about 20 per cent of the recession in 2009. Similar to many other developing countries, Turkey did not experience a financial system collapse during the global crisis. And, relative to the 1994 and 2001 crises, the financial system of Turkey recovered from the global crisis very quickly. While 18 banks went bankrupt during the crisis of 2001, no single bank collapsed during the global crisis. Moreover, the profitability of the banking sector did not even decline and their capital to asset ratios further increased during the global crisis (Uygur 2010).

According to the literature, developing countries owe the resilience of their financial systems to large accumulated reserves, flexible exchange rate regimes, financial stability policies, and banking reforms (Ammer et al. 2011; Llaudes et al. 2010; Alvarez and Gregorio 2013). Although these factors might have mitigating roles, we believe that the Turkish financial system was not substantially tested in the global crisis. Since

Turkish financial markets were not exposed to toxic assets of the advanced countries, there was no direct deterioration of balance sheets. Even though financial flows declined in 2008 and 2009, in comparison to earlier crises, there was no reversal of capital flows and they returned quickly to pre-crisis levels after 2009 (Cömert and Çolak 2015).

The authorities adopted a wide range of policy measures in order to mitigate the impact of the financial crisis, despite criticisms that they were too late to respond.[17] These measures might be grouped into three categories: monetary responses, fiscal policy measures, and financial sector measures.

The Turkish monetary responses to the crisis preceded the fiscal actions starting in the first half of 2008. The primary objectives of monetary policy during this period were to stabilise inflation and to meet the FX demand (to ease the pressure on the exchange rates) and TL liquidity needs of the private sector. In the initial phase of the crisis, the Central Bank of the Republic of Turkey (CBRT) did not adapt an expansionary stance until November 2008. In this period, the measures taken by the Central Bank were mostly concerned with inflation and financial stability without much emphasis on growth and unemployment issues. When Lehman collapsed in the third quarter of 2007, it was apparent that a plunge in aggregate demand and recession was looming for advanced countries. Hence, these countries significantly cut their policy rates. In contrast, the CBRT took a tightening stance in this period and did not cut its rates. Indeed, it even increased the policy rates further in the second quarter of 2008. Nevertheless, when the inflation pressure abated in the last quarter of 2008, monetary policy was relaxed significantly with a cutting of policy rates by 10.5 basis points in 11 months from November 2008. Moreover, considering the threat of short-term volatile cross border flows, the Turkish monetary authorities started implementing a nonconventional monetary policy in 2009. In addition to the conventional inflation targeting regime, the CBRT targeted financial stability as another objective and utilised nonconventional policy instruments with particular emphasis on credit expansion and exchange rate volatility (Kara 2011). Several macro prudential measures have been taken as well.

Compared with advanced countries and many other emerging market countries, the Turkish government was slow and reluctant in its fiscal response to the crisis. For example, while the advanced countries decided to implement huge stimulus packages in the second quarter of 2008, the first significant fiscal measures by the Turkish government were only taken in the first quarter of 2009, when the crisis had already affected the Turkish economy.[18]

Besides fiscal and monetary authorities, BRSA adapted measures specifically geared towards financial sector stability and the health of bank balance sheets. In order to tighten liquidity conditions some balance sheet adjustments were made. In particular, the amount of provisions set aside for loans was reduced and the calculation of liquidity adequacy ratio was adjusted downward. Furthermore, in order to strengthen the capital structure of the banking sector, profit distributions to shareholders were limited and only allowed under the control of BRSA. Also, to decrease the amount of risky assets, the risk weights on credit card usage were raised. Finally, in coordination with the Central Bank, a wide range of debt relief regulations were put into practice.

12.8 CONCLUSION

Capital account and domestic financial liberalisation of earlier decades increased the importance of financial markets, yet the Turkish financial markets still remain shallow relative to those in developed countries. Financialisation in the form of non-financial firms' activities in financial markets did not take place, and domestic financial markets are still dominated by the banking sector. However, the financialisation process is not non-existent, and it is dominated by international financial flows; and economic growth has been very erratic under the influence of such flows.

During the 2000s and 2010s, private consumption has been the main contributor to economic growth. Although investment has partially contributed to the growth of the economy, investment expenditures have been much more volatile than consumption, as expected, aggravating the size of the growth cycles. Since 2005 the government budget showed a primary surplus (Hazine 2015) and the financial balance of the government sector remained less than 3 per cent of GDP with the exception of 2009. And together with chronic current account deficits, this development meant rising liabilities, usually in the form of debt accumulation, for the private sector. Benign conditions in the international capital markets reinforced this trend again with the exception of 2009. In the light of these developments, a declining labour share and increasing debt of households justify labelling the structure of the Turkish economy as a debt-led growth regime based on the classification of Hein (2013) and Dodig et al. (2016).

These developments also had implications on the income distribution in Turkey after 2001. Even though an initial analysis shows a decline in income inequality between 2002 and 2011, an analysis of the functional income distribution indicates a reduction of the wage share throughout the period. Consumption spending rose while the wage share declined and income inequality worsened; these developments might also have reinforced households' indebtedness.

The global economic crisis hit Turkey in late 2008 and 2009, yet the economy returned to pre-crisis patterns as capital flows resumed after 2009. Unlike in many developed economies, the banking sector was not seriously affected as banks did not have US or European toxic assets in their balance sheets. Beside this, there was no reversal of capital flows and they returned quickly to pre-crisis levels. The crisis hit Turkey through deteriorations in expectations, trade and financial activities.

Declining wage share, household indebtedness, the importance of consumption for economic growth and chronic current account deficits have been major points of weakness for the Turkish economy throughout this era. And the availability of foreign capital only exacerbated these problems as policy-makers and their voter constituents did not have incentives for any major economic changes. As Akyüz (2012, p. 89) has noted, financial flows to developing countries 'has been creating or adding to macroeconomic imbalances and financial fragility in several recipient countries in large part because they have been shy in applying brakes on them'. Our analysis suggests that Turkey is a case in point. The biggest concern is the large current account deficit and the short-term and volatile nature of capital inflows; and if these flows are ever reversed in the future, the Turkish economy has no cover or limited countercyclical policy tools against such events.

NOTES

1. Bedirhanoğlu et al. (2013). Comparative Perspective on Financial System in the EU: Country Report on Turkey, FESSUD Studies in Financial Systems No. 11, http://fessud.eu/deliverables/, provides an overview of the economic and social developments in general, and the financial system in particular since 1980. Henceforth this study will be referred to as FESSUD Turkey Country Report WP2.
2. The Turkish and the Mexican Tequila crises of 1994, the East Asian crisis of 1997, the Brazilian and Russian crises of 1998, the Turkish crisis of 2001 and Argentinian crisis of 2001–2002 can be counted among the major crises in developing countries.
3. Although a growing problem of household indebtedness is evident from the rising ratio of household obligations to household disposable income, which increased from 7.5 per cent in 2003 to 51.7 per cent in 2011, the indebtedness is still low relative to that of advanced countries.
4. One should be careful in investigating the contributions of different demand components to GDP growth. Since each of these components can be considered as endogenous variables, the determination of direct and indirect contributions of each demand component to GDP is much more complicated.
5. For details see FESSUD Turkey Country Report WP2.
6. For details see FESSUD Turkey Country Report WP2.
7. The data set is obtained from the Household Budget Surveys (HBSs), which have been annually conducted by the Turkish Statistics Institute (TSI) since 2002. Household Survey Data is only available after 2002.
8. There are two different Gini coefficients here. One is from our own calculations;

the second one is the official Gini estimate by the TSI. We included these two measures as there is an important difference between these two. The official one assumes homeowners have an extra income called *imputed rent*. This is the amount of rent they would have paid if they did not own a house or apartment. And thus TSI adds the amount of *imputed rent* to the homeowners' income and then estimates the income distribution. In our own Gini estimations we omitted this *imputed rent*.

9. The former covers only the household income and does not include undistributed profits of firms. On the other hand, the denominator in the wage share incorporates undistributed profits. When this last item is included, the course of the wage share radically changes. This change casts doubt upon the analytical validity of the size distribution analysis.

10. The wage share is defined as the ratio of total compensation of employees – adjusted with the wage component of self-employment income – to GDP. TSI stopped providing GDP at income approach series in 2006. In order to fill the gap we used the data provided by the Annual Macro-Economic Database (AMECO) of the European Commission.

11. https://www.bddk.org.tr/websitesi/English.aspx.

12. It is important to insert a caveat here. Private disposable income data is estimated either through macro aggregates or Household Budget Surveys released by the TSI. It is well known that there is a discrepancy between the two data sets. This mainly derives from an implicit tendency of households to under-declare their incomes. Disposable income data in Table 12.1 comes from the Household Budget Surveys. Therefore household debt to disposable income ratios in the figure might be higher than actual ones. Nevertheless, the ratios are still important in showing the remarkable increase over a short period of time.

13. For an extensive version of the debate on financialisation in Turkey, see FESSUD Turkey Country Report WP3.

14. For details see FESSUD Turkey Country Report WP3.

15. For details see FESSUD Turkey Country Report WP3.

16. For details see FESSUD Turkey Country Report WP3.

17. A relatively detailed analysis of the policy responses can be found in Bahçe et al. (2015).

18. Several reports by the OECD and the IMF reveal that Turkey was among the slowest respondents in terms of fiscal stimulus compared with other countries. Besides the slow response, costs comparisons reveal that the costs of adopted fiscal measures as a ratio of GDP were among the lowest among countries. An OECD report (2009) identifies Turkey and Greece as the only two OECD economies having no fiscal stimulus package until March 2009. An IMF report (2009) on G20 economies' fiscal measures in crisis demonstrates that while the average cost of fiscal measures already amounted to 0.5 per cent of G20 GDP, Turkey did not announce any measure in 2008. And the costs of discretionary fiscal measures enacted in 2009 in Turkey were among the lowest in G20 economies and far below the G20 emerging markets average.

REFERENCES

Akkemik, K. A. and Ş. Özen (2014), 'Macroeconomic and institutional determinants of financialisation of non-financial firms: case study of Turkey', *Socio-Economic Review*, **12** (1), 71–89.

Akyüz, Y. (2012), *The Financial Crisis and the Global South: A Development Perspective*, London, UK: Pluto Press.

Alvarez, R. and J. D. Gregorio (2013), 'Why did Latin America and developing countries perform better in the global financial crisis than in the Asian Crisis',

Paper presented at Fourteenth Jacques Polak Annual Research Conference, Washington.

Ammer, J., F. Cai and C. Scotti (2011), 'Has international financial co-movement changed? Emerging markets in the 2007–2009 financial crisis', in J. A. Batten and P. G. Szilagyi (eds), *The Impact of the Global Financial Crisis on Emerging Financial Markets* (Contemporary Studies in Economic and Financial Analysis), Bingley: Emerald Group Publishing Limited.

Bahçe, S., F. Y. Günaydın and A. H. Köse (2011), 'Türkiye'de toplumsal sınıf haritaları: sınıf oluşumları ve sınıf hareketliliği üzerine karşılaştırmalı bir çalışma', in S. Şahinkaya and N. İ. Ertuğrul (eds), *Bilsay Kuruç'a Armağan*, Ankara, Turkey: Mülkiyeliler Birliği Yayınları.

Bahçe, S., H. Cömert, N. Erdem, E. Karaçimen, A. H. Köse, Ö. Orhangazi, G. Özgür, and G. Yalman (2015), 'Financialisation and the financial economic crises: the case of Turkey', Country Report on Turkey, FESSUD Studies in Financial Systems, No. 21, University of Leeds.

Bedirhanoğlu, P., H. Cömert, I. Eren, I. Erol, D. Demiroz, N. Erdem, A. Gungen, T. Marois, A. Topal, O. Türel, G. Yalman, E. Yeldan, and E. Voyvoda (2013), Comparative perspective on financial system in the EU: Country report on Turkey, FESSUD Studies in Financial Systems, No. 11, University of Leeds.

Boratav, K. (2010), 'Türkiye'nin dış açığı, gümrük birliği ve döviz kurları', in T. Subaşat and H. Yetkiner (eds), *Küresel Kriz Çerçevesinde Türkiye'nin Cari Açık Sorunsalı*, Ankara, Turkey: Efil Yayınevi.

BSB (Bağımsız Sosyal Bilimciler) (2008), *2008 Kavşağında Türkiye*, Ankara, Turkey: Yordam Kitap.

CBRT (2006), *Financial Stability Report*, December, Ankara, Turkey: Central Bank of the Republic of Turkey.

CBRT (2008), *Financial Stability Report*, May, Ankara, Turkey: Central Bank of the Republic of Turkey.

CBRT (2010), *Financial Stability Report*, December, Ankara, Turkey: Central Bank of the Republic of Turkey.

CBRT (2011), *Financial Stability Report*, November, Ankara, Turkey: Central Bank of the Republic of Turkey.

CBRT (2013), *Financial Stability Report*, November, Ankara, Turkey: Central Bank of the Republic of Turkey.

CBRT (2014), 'Company Accounts', *Real Sector Statistics*, available at: http://www.tcmb.gov.tr/wps/wcm/connect/tcmb+en/tcmb+en/Main+Menu/STATISTICS/Real+Sector+Statistics/Company+Accounts/.

Cömert, H. and M. S. Çolak (2014), 'The impacts of the global crisis on the Turkish economy and policy responses', ERC Working Paper, No. 14/17, Ankara, Turkey: Economic Research Center.

Cömert, H. and M. S. Çolak (2015), 'Can financial stability be maintained in developing countries after the global crisis: The role of external financial shocks?', PERI Working Paper, No. 379, Amherst, MA: Political Economy Research Institute.

Crotty, J. (2003), 'The neoliberal paradox: The impact of destructive product market competition and impatient finance on nonfinancial corporations in the neoliberal era', *Review of Radical Political Economics*, **35** (3), 271–279.

Demir, F. (2007), 'The rise of rentier capitalism and the financialisation of real sectors in developing countries', *Review of Radical Political Economics*, **39** (3), 351–359.

Demirag, İ. and M. Serter (2003), 'Ownership patterns and control in Turkish listed companies', *Corporate Governance*, **11** (1), 40–51.
Dodig, N., E. Hein and D. Detzer (2016), 'Financialisation and the financial and economic crises: theoretical framework and empirical analysis for 15 countries', in E. Hein, D. Detzer and N. Dodig (eds), *Financialisation and the Financial and Economic Crises: Country Studies*, Cheltenham: Edward Elgar.
European Commission (2015), *AMECO Database*, available at: http://ec.europa.eu/economy_finance/db_indicators/ameco/index_en.htm.
Gezici, A. (2007), 'Investment under financial liberalization: channels of liquidity and uncertainty', *Ph.D. Thesis*, Amherst, MA, USA: University of Massachusetts-Amherst.
Hanson, J. A. (2005), 'Post-crisis challenges and risks in East Asia and Latin America', in G. Caprio, J. A. Hanson and R. E. Litan (eds), *Financial Crises: Lessons from the Past, Preparation for the Future*, Washington, DC, USA: The Brookings Institution.
Hazine (2015), *Kamu borç yönetimi raporu*, Ankara: T.C. Hazine Müsteşarlığı.
Hein, E. (2013), 'The crisis of finance-dominated capitalism in the euro area, deficiencies in the economic policy architecture, and deflationary stagnation policies', *Journal of Post Keynesian Economics*, **36** (2), 325–354.
IMF (2006), *Global financial report April 2006*, Washington, DC, USA: International Monetary Fund.
IMF (2009), *The State of Public Finances Cross-country Fiscal Monitor: November 2009*, Washington, DC, USA: International Monetary Fund.
IMF (2014), *International Monetary Fund World Economic Outlook database*, April 2014, available at: https://www.imf.org/external/pubs/ft/weo/2014/01/weodata/index.aspx.
Kara, H. (2011), *Monetary policy in Turkey after the global crisis*, CBRT Working Paper, No. 12/17, Ankara, Turkey: Central Bank of the Republic of Turkey.
Karacimen, E. (2014), 'Financialisation in Turkey: The case of consumer credit', *Journal of Balkan and Near Eastern Studies*, **16** (2), 161–180.
Llaudes, R., F. Salman and M. Chivakul (2010), 'The impact of the great recession on emerging markets', IMF Working Paper, 10/237, Washington, DC, USA: International Monetary Fund.
McKinnon, R.I. (1973), *Money and Capital in Economic Development*, Washington DC, USA: The Brookings Institution.
OECD (2009), *Fiscal Packages Across OECD Countries: Overview and Country Details*, Paris: OECD.
OECD (2013), 'Crisis squeezes income and puts pressure on inequality and poverty: new results from the OECD income database', available at: http://www.oecd.org/els/soc/OECD2013-Inequality-and-Poverty-8p.pdf.
Orhangazi, Ö. (2008), 'Financialisation and capital accumulation in the non-financial corporate sector: A theoretical and empirical investigation on the U.S. economy, 1973–2003', *Cambridge Journal of Economics*, **32** (6), 863–886.
Özmen, E., S. Şahinöz and C. Yalçın (2012), 'Profitability, saving and investment of non-financial firms in Turkey', CRBT Working Paper, No. 12/14, Ankara, Turkey: Central Bank of the Republic of Turkey.
Shaw, E. S. (1973), *Financial Deepening in Economic Development*, New York, NY, USA: Oxford University Press.

Stockhammer, E. (2004), 'Financialisation and the slowdown of accumulation', *Cambridge Journal of Economics*, **28** (5), 719–741.
Taymaz, E., E. Voyvoda and K. Yılmaz (2011), 'Uluslararası üretim zincirlerinde dönüşüm ve Türkiye'nin konumu', *TÜSİAD- T/2011, 12: 522*, Istanbul, Turkey: TÜSİAD.
Turkish Statistical Institution (TSI) (2014), 'Imports by chapters', available at: http://www.turkstat.gov.tr/PreIstatistikTablo.do?istab_id=623.
Uygur, E. (2010), 'The global crisis and the Turkish economy', Türkiye Ekonomi Kurumu, Working Papers, No. 2010/3, available at: htp://www.tek.org.tr/dos yalar/TURKEYUYGUR-FF.pdf.
Van Rijckeghem, C. and M. Üçer (2009), 'The evolution and determinants of the Turkish private saving rate: What lessons for policy?', *ERF Research Report Series*, No. 09-01, Istanbul, Turkey: Koc University-TÜSİAD Economic Research Forum.

13. The impact of the financial and economic crises on European Union member states

Carlos A. Carrasco, Jesús Ferreiro, Catalina Gálvez, Carmen Gomez and Ana González

13.1 INTRODUCTION

Although the Great Recession is a global phenomenon, with roots outside the European Union (EU), its impact has been deeper and longer lasting in the EU than elsewhere. Indeed, according to the World Economic Outlook Database (April 2015) of the IMF, the long-term economic growth forecasts (up to the year 2020) for the EU are much lower than those of the other regions of the planet. Thus, in 2014 the real GDP of the EU and the Euro area were only 4.6 per cent and 2.1 per cent higher respectively than in 2006. The IMF forecasts that in 2020 the real GDP of the EU and the Euro area will be 17 and 12 per cent higher respectively than in 2006. In contrast, the IMF forecasts the real GDP of the United Kingdom, the United States of America and Asian emerging and developing economies will be, respectively, 22, 28 and 169 per cent higher in 2020 than in 2006.

However, the impact of the Great Recession has not been the same in all the European countries. The objective of this chapter is to analyse the different effects of the economic and financial crisis among the European Union member states, focusing on the behaviour of a number of real and financial variables since the year 2003 to evaluate the impact of the crisis. Thus, we will analyse the performance of seventeen economic variables grouped into seven categories:

1. Economic activity:
   - rate of growth of real GDP
   - rate of growth of GDP per capita

- rate of growth of potential GDP
- output gap
2. Labour market:
    - employment growth
    - unemployment rate
    - rate of growth of real wages
    - rate of growth of real unit labour costs
3. Income distribution:
    - adjusted wage share
    - Gini coefficient
4. Inflation:
    - rate of inflation (CPI)
5. Balance of payments:
    - balance on current account
6. Public finances:
    - public budget balance
    - public debt
7. Financial balance sheets of total economy and sectors:
    - financial assets
    - financial liabilities
    - net financial assets

While the effects of the above mentioned variables were different between Euro area and non-Euro area countries of the EU, the effects also varied within the Euro area itself. To analyse these differences, we will study the impact of the Great Recession on European countries analysing the outcomes of the aforementioned seventeen variables for three groups of European Union member states:

- The first group includes the countries that joined the euro at the time of its creation in 1999: Belgium, Germany, Ireland, Spain, France, Italy, Luxembourg, the Netherlands, Austria, Portugal, and Finland (EMU-11).
- The second group is formed by those countries that joined the euro after 1999: Estonia, Greece, Cyprus, Malta, Slovenia and Slovakia (EMU-6).
- The third group includes the EU economies that do not belong to the Euro area: Bulgaria, Czech Republic, Denmark, Lithuania, Latvia, Hungary, Poland, Romania, Sweden and the United Kingdom (EU-10).

Since we have used data until 2013, we have excluded Croatia from the EU countries because it joined the EU in this year. Likewise, as Latvia and

Lithuania adopted the euro in 2014 and 2015 respectively they are included in the non-Euro area group for this study.

For the three groups, the individual-national values of the analysed variables have been weighted according to the respective shares of total GDP of the group. The reason is that our objective is to analyse the economic performance of the whole groups. This procedure suffers from two problems. First, the economic performance of each group is dominated by the behaviour of larger countries.[1] Second, the results obtained in each group may hide significant individual differences between and within groups.

The existence of significantly different impacts of the Great Recession on the European economies questions the sustainability of the current institutional setting of the European Union and the Euro area (Benczes and Szent-Ivanyi 2015). Many studies argue that the increasing heterogeneity in economic performance in the EU as a whole and the Euro area countries in particular is the direct consequence of the incorporation of economies with differing structures to those in the pre-existing member states (Arestis and Sawyer 2012; Bitzenis et al. 2015; Carrasco and Peinado 2015; Gibson et al. 2014; Mendonça 2014; Perraton 2011; Onaran 2011). This higher heterogeneity increases the possibility of asymmetric shocks, and, simultaneously, reduces the effectiveness of single and common rules for macroeconomic policies (Dodig and Herr 2015).

The different impacts of the Great Recession on the 'old' and 'new' euro economies emphasises the problems of consistency in the enlargement process of the European Monetary Union, as far as this enlargement implies greater (macro)economic heterogeneity and increased coordination problems with (possibly) more frequent asymmetric shocks.

13.2   THE IMPACT OF THE GREAT RECESSION IN THE EUROPEAN UNION

Effects on the Economic Activity

Table 13.1 collects the data of the four variables related to the evolution of economic activity in the European Union during the period 2003–2013, namely, the rate of growth of real GDP, the rate of growth of the GDP per capita, the rate of growth of potential GDP, and the output gap.

If we focus on the rate of growth of real GDP, we can see that the EMU-6 recorded the highest rate of economic growth before the crisis whilst the EMU-11 performed worst. However, this pattern significantly changed with the onset of the crisis, and since 2009 the EMU-6 has been the group

Table 13.1 Evolution of economic activity

	Rate of growth of real GDP (%)			Rate of growth of real GDP per capita (%)			Rate of growth of potential GDP (%)			Output gap (% potential GDP)		
	EMU-11	EMU-6	EU-10	EMU-11	EMU-6	EU-10	EMU-11	EMU-6	EU-10	EMU-11	EMU-6	EU-10
2003	0.61	5.26	3.55	-0.09	5.14	3.45	1.83	4.38	3.07	-0.27	0.45	0.04
2004	2.14	4.47	3.71	1.57	4.22	3.41	1.82	4.00	2.92	0.06	1.30	0.38
2005	1.67	3.40	3.41	1.05	2.89	2.96	1.74	3.25	2.77	-0.02	0.51	0.75
2006	3.17	5.99	3.69	2.59	5.66	3.43	1.74	3.18	2.61	1.34	3.45	2.05
2007	2.93	5.09	3.72	2.27	4.78	3.16	1.74	2.83	2.46	2.53	5.79	2.82
2008	0.35	1.16	0.25	-0.08	0.81	-0.13	1.36	2.04	2.04	1.63	4.58	1.27
2009	-4.41	-4.16	-4.71	-4.81	-4.38	-5.20	0.59	0.40	1.07	-3.47	-1.17	-3.88
2010	2.15	-2.01	2.33	2.01	-2.01	1.70	0.66	-0.42	1.19	-1.95	-3.17	-2.77
2011	1.80	-3.35	1.77	1.41	-3.33	1.15	0.74	-0.88	1.24	-0.80	-6.69	-1.94
2012	-0.50	-4.00	0.44	-0.89	-3.93	-0.50	0.41	-1.26	1.09	-1.78	-8.87	-2.51
2013	-0.37	-2.34	1.55	-0.49	-0.05	1.28	0.51	-1.33	1.25	-2.68	-9.33	-2.22

Source: Our calculations based on Eurostat.

worst affected by the crisis. Indeed, the EMU-6 recorded negative growth from 2009 onwards, with the result that the GDP in these countries in 2013 was 15 per cent lower than in 2008. In the case of the EMU-11, although these countries recorded positive economic growth in 2010, growth became negative again in 2012 and 2013, meaning GDP in 2013 was 1.5 per cent lower than in 2008 for this group. Conversely, the EU countries that do not belong to the Euro area recorded positive economic growth since 2010, and, thus, their GDP in 2013 was 1.2 per cent higher than in 2008.

Therefore, the negative effects of the Great Recession have generally been more pronounced in the Euro area countries. The annual average rate of growth of GDP in the EU-10 has fallen from 3.6 per cent in the period 2003–2007 to 0.3 per cent in 2008–2013, whilst in the EMU-11 and the EMU-6 GDP growth decreased from 2.1 per cent to −0.2 per cent, and from 4.8 per cent to −2.4 per cent, respectively for the same periods.

The impact of the crisis is even larger when we look at the evolution of GDP per capita. The differences among the three groups of countries remain similar to those detected in the analysis of GDP growth. However, the novelty is that between 2009 and 2013, the three groups have recorded a decline in the GDP per capita: −0.3 per cent for the EU-10, −0.6 per cent for the EMU-11, and −2.7 per cent for the EMU-6.[2] As a consequence, the GDP per capita in the EU-10 in 2013 was 1.3 per cent lower than in 2008, compared with 2.9 per cent lower in the EMU-11 and 13 per cent lower in the EMU-6.

The collapse in economic growth also led to a sharp decline in the rates of growth of potential GDP, mainly in the case of the EMU-6. In these countries, the average rate of growth of potential GDP before the crisis (in the years 2003–2007) was 3.5 per cent, and the estimation for 2013 is −1.3 per cent. For the EU-10 and the EMU-11 the fall in the potential growth is less marked: from 2.8 per cent in 2003–2007 to 1.3 per cent in 2008–2013 for the EU-10, and from 1.8 per cent in 2003–2007 to 0.7 per cent in 2008–2013 for the EMU-11.

As far as we identify the estimations of the rate of growth of potential GDP as a correct proxy of the medium and long-term rates of economic growth, we can evaluate the impact of the Great Recession on the European economies in the near future. For both the EMU-11 and the EU-10, the economic and financial crisis has led to a significant fall in potential growth: in both groups the rate of growth of potential GDP in 2013 is 1.2 percentage points lower than in 2007, although the potential growth remains positive. However, the decline of potential growth is much more accentuated in the EMU-6, which records negative rates of growth of potential GDP since 2010, and, as a consequence, in 2013 the rate of growth of its potential GDP is 4.2 percentage points lower than in 2007.

Finally, Table 13.1 shows the evolution of the output gap, a variable that could be interpreted as a proxy of the sign and the size of the cyclical fluctuations, and, therefore, a proxy of the size of the impact of the Great Recession. Table 13.1 shows that before the eruption of the financial crisis in 2008, the European economies were in an expansionary phase (that is, a positive output gap), where the EMU-6 recorded the strongest expansion (in 2007 and 2008, the output gap was estimated at 5.8 and 4.6 per cent, respectively). Since 2009, the three groups have entered a recession (negative output gap). In the case of the EMU-6, its output gap is continually rising, reaching an output gap of −9.3 per cent of potential GDP (the output gap for Greece in 2013 would be −13.8 per cent). In the case of the EMU-11 its output gap declined between 2009 and 2011, but since 2012 it has risen again, although the size of the negative output gap is below that recorded in 2009. In the EU-10, the output gap worsened in 2012, but in 2013 recorded a small recovery, and like in the EMU-11, the size of the negative output gap is below that recorded in 2009.

In sum, the impact of the Great Recession in terms of the fall in the economic growth and the size of the recession has been more intense in the Euro area than in the non-Euro area countries, and has been even deeper in the member states which joined the euro after 1999.

Effects on Labour Markets

The slowdown in economic growth resulting from the crisis has had various impacts on European labour markets. There has been an obvious effect on the evolution of employment in EU economies. The data in Table 13.2 shows that before the Great Recession the highest growth in employment took place in the EMU-6 (an annual average growth in employment of 1.9 per cent between 2003 and 2007), a result directly related to the high economic growth in these countries. However, the differences with the other two groups are not as pronounced as the difference in GDP growth. Furthermore, the countries included in the EMU-11 group were creating employment at a higher rate than the EU-10 countries (1.6 per cent and 1 per cent, respectively).

This similar performance registered before the crisis has diverged since 2009. The Great Recession has led to a deep process of employment destruction, mainly in Euro area countries. Since 2010, the EU-10 countries created employment at an annual rate of close to 1 per cent, with the result that in 2013 employment in the EU-10 was 0.5 per cent higher than in 2008. Differently, in the EMU-11 and the EMU-6 employment in 2013 was, respectively, 1.7 per cent and 16.5 per cent lower than that recorded in 2008.

Table 13.2 Labour market outcomes

	Rate of growth of total employment (%)			Unemployment rate (%)			Rate of growth of real compensation per employee (%)			Rate of growth of real unit labour costs (%)		
	EMU-11	EMU-6	EU-10	EMU-11	EMU-6	EU-10	EMU-11	EMU-6	EU-10	EMU-11	EMU-6	EU-10
2003	1.08	1.94	0.37	10.49	9.01	8.75	0.66	3.11	3.44	−0.01	−1.52	−0.32
2004	0.83	1.30	0.77	10.20	9.58	8.89	0.38	1.73	2.28	−1.06	−0.84	−0.87
2005	1.73	1.43	1.12	9.21	9.02	8.53	0.18	5.38	2.02	−0.59	1.65	−0.46
2006	2.00	3.44	1.35	8.03	8.16	8.19	0.29	0.67	2.97	−0.97	−2.60	−0.31
2007	2.13	1.47	1.15	6.67	7.42	7.40	0.31	2.59	2.96	−0.95	−0.67	0.06
2008	1.07	1.34	1.13	6.17	6.92	7.36	0.81	−0.15	−0.32	1.88	0.84	0.79
2009	−1.53	−1.66	−1.57	8.75	8.80	10.12	2.59	1.97	−0.02	3.21	4.31	2.84
2010	−0.33	−2.76	−0.40	10.72	11.17	11.05	0.62	−2.91	0.04	−1.40	−1.25	−1.83
2011	0.76	−4.67	0.57	10.39	14.25	11.26	−0.15	−3.29	−1.61	−0.37	−2.24	−1.45
2012	−0.17	−5.33	0.91	10.83	18.11	12.19	−0.08	−2.06	−0.14	0.57	−2.98	1.02
2013	−0.40	−3.24	1.00	11.01	19.97	12.55	0.60	−3.04	0.55	−0.21	−3.49	−0.27

Source: Our calculations based on Eurostat (Labour Force Survey) and AMECO (Gross Domestic Product (Income Approach), Labour Costs).

The evolution of the active population means the evolution of the unemployment rate differs to the employment rate. As data in Table 13.2 shows, until 2006 the EMU-11 economies recorded the highest unemployment rates, but if we analyse the five-year period 2003–2007 we can see that the average annual unemployment rate was very similar in the three groups of countries: 8.3 per cent in the EU-10, 8.6 per cent in the EMU-6 and 8.9 per cent in the EMU-11.

Since 2008, unemployment rates increased in all three groups, although the highest increase was recorded in the EMU-6, where the unemployment rate rose from 7 per cent in 2008 to 20 per cent in 2013. It is remarkable that although the crisis was deeper in the EMU-11 than in the EU-10, the unemployment rate is lower in the EMU-11 than in the non-Euro area countries: in the EMU-11 between 2008 and 2013 the unemployment rate rose from 6.2 per cent to 11 per cent, whilst in the EU-10, the unemployment rate increased from 7.4 per cent to 12.6 per cent.

The Great Recession has also had a different impact on the evolution of real wages in the European Union. In the case of the EMU-11, with the exception of 2009 when real wages rose 2.6 per cent, the growth of real wages has remained very stable, and after the crisis, with the exceptions of 2011 and 2012, real wages have maintained their rising trend, though at very low rates of growth. Thus, between 2010 and 2013 real wages in the EMU-11 have grown at an annual rate of 0.3 per cent, 0.1 percentage points below the average growth recorded in 2003–2007. As a result, in the EMU-11 real wages in 2013 were 6.4 per cent higher than in 2002 and 3.6 per cent higher than in 2008.

Conversely, the impact of the Great Recession on wages has been more intense in the EU-10 and even more so in the EMU-6. In the EU-10, real wages have fallen, except in 2009 and 2013. As a result of this wage moderation, although real wages in 2013 were 12.7 per cent higher than in 2002, they were 1.2 per cent lower than in 2008. But it is in the EMU-6 where wage adjustment has been most severe. Between 2003 and 2007, real wages were growing at an average annual rate of 2.7 per cent (a similar rate to the EU-10). Real wages suffered a small fall in 2008, but they rose by 2 per cent in 2009 (something that also happened in the other Euro area countries). From 2010 onwards, real wages in the EMU-6 collapsed and fell at an annual rate of 2.8 per cent. The result of this adjustment is that although real wages in 2013 were 3.6 per cent higher than in 2002, they were 9.1 per cent lower than those recorded in 2008.

Finally, Table 13.2 shows the growth of real unit labour costs (ULCs). The outbreak of the crisis in 2008 caused greater divergence in the real ULC growth rates of the three groups. Thus, in 2007 real ULCs in the

EMU-11 were 3.5 per cent lower than in 2002, 4 per cent lower in the EMU-6 and 1.9 per cent lower in the EU-10. However, in 2013 real ULCs in the EMU-6 were 5 per cent lower than in 2007, whilst they were 1 per cent higher in the EU-10 and 3.7 per cent higher in the EMU-11.

Effects on Income Distribution

The evolution of employment and real wages has directly affected the share of wage incomes in GDP. Data from Table 13.3 shows significant differences between the three groups of countries. First, we can see that the share of wages is much lower in the EMU-6 than in the other two groups, whose wage shares are at a similar level. Second, we can observe that the impact of the crisis on the wage share has been different.

At the beginning of the crisis, following the usual pattern of the wage share to increase in recessions, the wage share increased in the three groups in the years 2008 and 2009: 2.8 percentage points of GDP in the EMU-11, 2.9 percentage points of GDP in the EMU-6, and 1.3 percentage points of GDP in the EU-10. Since 2009, due to the declining real wages and the fall in employment, the wage share has fallen, although it slightly increased in 2012 and 2013, but only in the EMU-11 and the EU-10. Thus,

Table 13.3   Income distribution

	Adjusted wage share (percentage of GDP at current market prices)			Gini coefficient of equivalised disposable income		
	EMU-11	EMU-6	EU-10	EMU-11	EMU-6	EU-10
2003	56.1	51.0	56.7	na	na	na
2004	55.5	50.4	56.1	na	na	na
2005	55.3	52.6	55.8	28.9	31.1	32.1
2006	54.7	50.8	55.8	28.7	32.0	30.9
2007	54.2	50.4	56.0	29.6	31.4	30.8
2008	55.2	50.9	56.2	30.1	30.5	31.6
2009	57.1	53.3	57.4	29.9	30.5	30.8
2010	56.3	52.9	56.4	30.0	30.6	30.9
2011	56.0	52.3	55.2	30.2	30.7	31.1
2012	56.4	51.1	55.5	30.0	31.1	30.1
2013	56.4	49.5	55.4	30.2	31.1	29.5

Note: na – not available

Source: Our calculations based on Eurostat (Income and Living Conditions) and AMECO (Gross Domestic Product (Income Approach), Labour Costs).

between 2009 and 2013, the wage share declined by 0.6 percentage points of GDP in the EMU-11, 3.8 percentage points of GDP in the EMU-6, and 1.9 percentage points of GDP in the EU-10. This evolution implies that although in the EMU-6 and the EU-10 the wage share in 2013 is lower than that recorded in 2007, the wage share in the EMU-11 is 2.2 percentage points higher than in 2007.

Besides affecting the functional income distribution, the economic and financial crisis has also affected personal income distribution, as the three last columns of Table 13.3 show. In the case of the EMU-11, rising inequality is detected since 2006, that is, before the onset of the Great Recession. Since 2009, the Gini coefficient remains relatively constant with minor changes, thus implying that the crisis by itself has had no impact on income inequality in the EMU-11.

Contrary to the EMU-11, the countries of the EMU-6 recorded a declining trend of income inequality before the crisis. Since 2009, income inequality started to rise. This change implies that, besides leading to a fall in the GDP for this group of countries, the Great Recession has made the income distribution less egalitarian, and, thus, since 2012, the EMU-6 group presents the least egalitarian income distribution in the European Union.

Conversely, since 2010 the Gini coefficient in the EU-10 noticeably declined, and, therefore, income distribution is more egalitarian after the crisis than before it. Indeed in 2013 the non-Euro area countries are those with the lowest inequality in income distribution, well below that recorded in the Euro area.

Table 13.4   Inflation rate (based on National CPI) (%)

	EMU-11	EMU-6	EU-10
2003	2.0	4.3	1.8
2004	2.0	3.5	2.0
2005	2.0	3.3	2.1
2006	2.0	3.3	2.3
2007	2.1	3.1	2.7
2008	3.1	4.6	4.1
2009	0.2	1.2	2.1
2010	1.4	3.6	3.0
2011	2.6	3.3	4.1
2012	2.3	2.2	2.8
2013	1.3	0.1	1.9

Source: Our calculations based on AMECO (Consumption, Consumer Price Index).

Inflation

Before the crisis, during the period 2003–2007, the inflation rates in the European Union were significantly different. In the EMU-11, inflation rates remained at 2.0 per cent, but in the EMU-6, although inflation had a declining tendency, it remained well above the 2 per cent target and in 2007 the inflation rate was 3.1 per cent. In the case of the non-Euro area countries, inflation had a rising tendency, moving from 1.8 per cent in 2003 to 2.7 per cent in 2007. Therefore, the lowest inflation rates were recorded in the EMU-11.

At the beginning of the crisis, after a significant increase in inflation in 2008 in all groups, but particularly in the EMU-6, inflation rates decreased to unparalleled low levels in 2009, falling to 0.2 per cent and 1.2 per cent in the EMU-11 and EMU-6, respectively. These low rates were well below the target set by the European Central Bank. Closer to this target was the inflation registered in the non-Euro area countries (2.1 per cent).

Since 2010, inflation rates started to rise, mainly in the EU-10, but in 2012 inflation in the European Union tended to decline again, leading in 2013 to really low inflation rates: 0.1 per cent in the EMU-6, 1.3 per cent in the EMU-11, and 1.9 per cent in the EU-10. The low inflation rates were due to, among other reasons, weak demand, the fall in energy prices and wage moderation.

When we look at the whole period 2003–2007, the highest inflation rates were recorded for the EMU-6, with average inflation amounting to 3.5 per cent. The annual average inflation rate in the EU-10 was 2.2 per cent, while the EMU-11 recorded the lowest annual average inflation rate of 2.0 per cent. For the crisis years (2008–2013), average inflation rates declined in the Euro area (to 1.8 per cent in the EMU-11 and 2.5 per cent in the EMU-6), while inflation increased in the non-Euro area countries to 3.0 per cent.

This data implies a marked divergence in the inflation outcomes in the Euro area. Since 1999 the average inflation rate in the Euro area has been above the target set by the European Central Bank: thus, for the seventeen Euro economies analysed in this chapter, the weighted average inflation rate in the period 2003–2013 has been 1.95 per cent, slightly below the target rate of 2 per cent, although this is due to the exceptionally low inflation rates recorded in 2009 and 2013. However, average inflation rate in the EMU-11 has been 1.91 per cent, whilst the inflation rate in the EMU-6 has been 2.95 per cent, implying the existence of an inflationary bias in the new members of the Euro area.

Balance on Current Transactions

Like previous variables, the behaviour of the balance on current transactions registers significant differences between the groups of countries. While the EMU-11 maintained a surplus in its balance on current transactions for the observed period (with the only exception being 2008), both the EMU-6 and the EU-10 have continually registered deficits. These deficits reached extraordinary levels in the EMU-6, peaking at 13.1 per cent of GDP in 2008. However, the deep recession these countries have suffered since 2009 has contributed to the adjustment of the balance on current transactions reducing it in 2013 to below 1 per cent of GDP, lower than that of the EU-10.

In the case of the EU-10, it seems that the Great Recession has not affected its external deficit: thus, the average deficit in the period 2003–2007 amounted to 1.5 per cent of GDP, and in the period 2008–2013, the deficit of the balance on current transactions was only slightly higher at 1.7 per cent of GDP. Between the periods 2003–2007 and 2008–2013, the surplus of the balance on current transactions in the EMU-11 increased from 0.9 per cent to 1.2 per cent of GDP. Indeed, this surplus has seen a rising tendency, and in 2013 it peaked at 2.6 per cent of GDP, implying a mercantilist (export-led) growth strategy in these countries during the crisis.

As a consequence of the crisis and the subsequent deep recession, the EMU-6 has registered the greatest variation of its balance on current

Table 13.5   Balance on current transactions with the rest of the world (% GDP)

	EMU-11	EMU-6	EU-10
2003	0.63	−8.76	−0.84
2004	1.36	−8.16	−1.49
2005	0.63	−8.52	−0.78
2006	0.76	−10.85	−1.66
2007	0.93	−12.69	−2.49
2008	−0.03	−13.10	−2.98
2009	0.78	−9.64	−1.55
2010	0.83	−8.85	−1.36
2011	0.89	−7.19	−0.85
2012	2.12	−2.53	−1.82
2013	2.60	−0.95	−1.57

Source: Our calculations based on AMECO (Balances with the Rest of the World, National Accounts).

transactions. In the period 2003–2007, the average annual deficit in the balance on current transactions was 9.8 per cent of GDP, while in the crisis period 2008–2013 this deficit decreased to 7 per cent of GDP on average. During the latter period, the deficit decreased from 13.1 per cent of GDP in 2008 to 1 per cent of GDP in 2013.

Public Finances

The situation of public finances in the European Union has been characterised by the existence of fiscal deficits, with the EMU-6 being the group that registers the highest fiscal deficits (see Table 13.6). Although between 2003 and 2005, the situation of public finances was very similar in the EMU-11 and the EU-10, since 2006 public deficits have been lower in the EMU-11 than in non-Euro area countries.

The evolution of the public budget balances is the same in the three groups: they improve until 2007, worsen until 2009, and from 2010 onwards public budget deficits improve again in the three groups. However, while the improvement in the public finances is continuous since 2010 in the EMU-11 and the EU-10, the public deficits in the EMU-6 increased again in 2013 by 3 percentage points amounting to 9.9 per cent of GDP.

Table 13.6   Public finances

	Net lending (+) or net borrowing (−) of general government (% GDP)			General government consolidated gross debt: Excessive deficit procedure (% GDP)		
	EMU-11	EMU-6	EU-10	EMU-11	EMU-6	EU-10
2003	−3.1	−4.9	−3.4	67.7	75.8	39.6
2004	−2.8	−5.7	−2.8	68.0	76.2	40.9
2005	−2.5	−4.3	−2.3	68.8	82.6	41.3
2006	−1.3	−4.7	−1.9	67.1	79.2	40.9
2007	−0.6	−4.5	−1.5	64.8	77.5	40.5
2008	−1.9	−7.0	−3.4	68.4	80.3	46.1
2009	−6.1	−12.4	−8.8	77.8	95.5	57.0
2010	−6.1	−9.1	−7.7	83.2	107.3	64.1
2011	−4.0	−7.7	−5.5	85.4	122.0	67.8
2012	−3.6	−6.9	−4.8	90.3	114.2	70.4
2013	−2.8	−9.9	−4.3	92.3	127.3	71.6

Source: Our calculations based on AMECO (General Government, Excessive Deficit Procedure, and Gross Public Debt, Based on ESA 2010 and Former Definitions Linked Series).

Despite the fact that the variation in the public budget balance was very similar in the three groups, the intensity of this change differs markedly. Between the years 2003 and 2007, all groups recorded an improvement in their public finances, however, the size of the fiscal adjustment in the EMU-6 (+0.39 per cent of GDP) was much lower than in the other two groups (+2.53 per cent of GDP in the EMU-11 and +1.89 per cent of GDP in the EU-10). But during the period of implementation of expansionary fiscal policies (in 2008 and 2009), it is the EMU-6 who registered the greatest deterioration in their public finances: −7.94 per cent of GDP compared with −5.5 per cent and −7.28 per cent of GDP in the EMU-11 and the EU-10, respectively. Since 2010, all the groups implemented fiscal consolidation strategies, but, as happened before the crisis, the size of the fiscal adjustment was smaller in the EMU-6 economies: +3.25 per cent of GDP in the EMU-11, +4.43 per cent of GDP in the EU-10, and +2.51 per cent of GDP in the EMU-6.

The economic crisis, accompanied by the deterioration of public finances, has increased the size of public debt in all the European economies, exceeding the threshold of 60 per cent of GDP set for the Euro area countries. Again, the figures corresponding to the EMU-6 stand out, being above 127 per cent of GDP in 2013. But it is also important to emphasise that the size of public debt is higher in the Euro area than in non-euro countries, despite the fiscal rules operating in the Euro area.

Again, among the three country groupings the EMU-6 is the group that continually recorded the highest public debt level and that also registered the greatest increase in public borrowing: 49.7 percentage points of GDP between 2008 and 2013. In the EU-10 and the EMU-11, the rises are similar to each other and lower than those of EMU-6 registering 31 per cent and 27.5 per cent of GDP, respectively.

Financial Balance Sheets

In this sub-section, we will focus our analysis on the impact of the crisis on financial variables, namely, on the evolution of the size of financial assets and liabilities, both for the whole economy and the main institutional sectors. The analysis will be made using the data provided by Eurostat corresponding to the financial balance sheets. Given that at the time of writing, the data for 2013 was not available for all European countries, the last year analysed will be 2012.

Table 13.7 shows the data of financial liabilities and assets (measured as a percentage of GDP) of EU countries for the years 2003 to 2012. Some conclusions can be obtained from this data. First, the size of financial assets and liabilities, a proxy of the size of finance in the economies, is

Table 13.7   Financial assets and liabilities: total economy (% of GDP)

	Financial assets			Financial liabilities			Net financial assets		
	EMU-11	EMU-6	EU-10	EMU-11	EMU-6	EU-10	EMU-11	EMU-6	EU-10
2003	773.7	393.3	853.9	781.9	443.2	870.7	−8.2	−49.9	−16.9
2004	800.4	417.5	963.2	808.6	473.6	984.7	−8.3	−56.1	−21.5
2005	865.4	463.5	1,074.7	870.5	524.3	1,093.6	−5.0	−60.7	−18.9
2006	909.8	473.4	1,123.3	920.8	547.9	1,147.0	−11.0	−74.6	−23.7
2007	938.5	505.3	1,190.0	950.9	589.7	1,213.7	−12.4	−84.4	−23.7
2008	962.8	481.7	1,478.0	973.1	560.2	1,490.4	−10.3	−78.5	−12.3
2009	1,035.5	528.8	1,366.9	1,046.0	619.2	1,391.0	−10.5	−90.4	−24.0
2010	1,045.6	544.4	1,402.9	1,054.9	631.1	1,421.1	−9.2	−86.6	−18.3
2011	1,047.2	541.9	1,439.6	1,053.4	615.6	1,453.9	−6.2	−73.6	−14.2
2012	1,081.3	572.9	1,397.7	1,087.6	671.6	1,420.8	−6.4	−98.8	−23.0

Source: Our calculations based on Eurostat (Annual Sector Accounts ESA 2010, Financial Flows and Stocks).

significantly higher outside the Euro area than in the Euro area, and it is in the EMU-6 where the smallest financial markets are recorded. Second, until 2012, financial assets and liabilities had a rising tendency, with the exception of the EU-10, where in 2012 a small decline in the size of financial assets and liabilities was registered.

The third conclusion is that in the three groups the size of financial liabilities is smaller than that of the assets, implying the existence of net external borrowing of the European economy from the rest of the world. Although the three groups have maintained a negative net financial balance throughout the whole period, the volume of these negative net financial positions has remained quite stable in the EMU-11 and the EU-10, with an average size of −9 per cent of GDP and −20 per cent of GDP respectively. On the contrary, the net financial liabilities of the EMU-6 have had a rising tendency that continued after the outbreak of the crisis, and, thus, net financial liabilities in the EMU-6 reached 99 per cent of GDP in 2012.

Next, we will study the impact of the crisis on the financial balance sheets of the institutional sectors in the three groups of EU countries.

Table 13.8 shows the data of financial assets and liabilities of the general government. It can be seen that the Great Recession has led to a marked increase of financial liabilities, as a result of the public budget deficits generated during the crisis and the borrowing necessary to finance the public support to the financial institutions in crisis.

Before and after the crisis, the lowest public debt has been registered in the non-Euro area, well below that existing in the EMU-11 and in the EMU-6. Despite the fall in the financial liabilities recorded in the

Table 13.8 *Financial assets and liabilities: general government and households and non-profit institutions serving households (% of GDP)*

	GENERAL GOVERNMENT									HOUSEHOLDS								
	Financial assets			Financial liabilities			Net financial assets			Financial assets			Financial liabilities			Net financial assets		
	EMU-11	EMU-6	EU-10	EMU-11	EMU-6	EU-10	EMU-11	EMU-6	EU-10	EMU-11	EMU-6	EU-10	EMU-11	EMU-6	EU-10	EMU-11	EMU-6	EU-10
2003	30.2	41.6	33.0	81.2	101.0	50.4	−50.7	−59.4	−17.4	192.4	116.8	207.7	60.0	30.6	75.2	132.3	86.2	133.7
2004	30.6	43.9	33.2	82.3	103.6	51.2	−51.2	−59.8	−18.0	197.3	124.2	211.0	61.9	35.0	79.7	135.5	89.2	132.6
2005	32.4	46.2	34.1	83.4	103.7	52.0	−50.5	−57.5	−17.9	206.1	135.9	229.4	64.9	41.9	81.3	141.3	94.1	149.5
2006	32.4	45.4	34.0	79.9	106.9	50.5	−47.0	−61.4	−16.5	208.4	139.9	236.3	66.9	46.1	86.4	141.5	93.8	151.3
2007	33.3	47.0	33.9	76.7	103.1	49.6	−42.7	−56.1	−15.7	204.5	138.7	232.8	67.6	50.6	88.8	137.0	88.1	145.1
2008	34.8	40.7	37.0	82.4	103.0	57.2	−46.9	−62.4	−20.2	190.9	114.8	204.4	68.1	53.6	89.5	122.8	61.3	116.1
2009	38.4	46.0	40.8	92.9	117.6	68.7	−53.6	−71.6	−27.9	207.1	126.1	234.0	72.6	56.6	92.9	134.4	69.4	142.4
2010	41.3	46.3	40.4	98.2	111.0	75.2	−56.2	−64.7	−34.8	208.2	123.6	237.4	72.7	62.7	89.7	135.6	60.9	148.9
2011	41.0	44.8	41.4	100.0	95.6	85.5	−58.6	−50.9	−44.2	202.3	121.3	229.8	71.7	64.5	87.5	130.6	56.8	143.4
2012	45.0	62.8	43.9	110.7	131.1	88.5	−64.9	−68.3	−44.6	210.3	126.6	238.1	71.5	63.6	86.9	138.8	63.0	152.5

Source: Our calculations based on Eurostat (Annual Sector Accounts ESA 2010, Financial Flows and Stocks).

EMU-6 in 2011 (−22 per cent of GDP with respect to those registered in 2009) as a result of the haircut applied to private holders of Greek public debt, liabilities in 2012 had increased again reaching unparalleled levels. Between 2007 and 2012 the increase recorded in the public financial liabilities is quite similar in magnitude in the three groups: 22 per cent of GDP in the EMU-6, 34 per cent of GDP in the EMU-11 and 38.9 per cent of GDP in the EU-10. While at first glance these figures may seem surprising, they can be explained by the restructuring of the Greek sovereign debt.

Like financial liabilities, the financial assets of general governments in Europe have also increased during the crisis, mainly in the EMU-6, as a direct consequence of the public support to troubled financial institutions. Thanks to the increases in financial assets the increases in the net financial liabilities of the general government have not been as strong as in the case of the gross financial liabilities. Again, the smallest increase in net financial liabilities was recorded in the EMU-6 (+12.2 per cent of GDP), followed by the EMU-11 (+22.2 per cent of GDP) and the EU-10 (+28.9 per cent of GDP). Nonetheless, in 2012 the net financial liabilities of the general governments in the EU-10 seemed to stabilise, while in the Euro area they continued to deteriorate.

In Table 13.8 we also show the evolution of the financial assets and liabilities of European households. The largest financial balance sheets are registered outside the Euro area, and the smallest size of the financial assets and liabilities are found in the EMU-6. It is relevant to note that the larger differences in the size of the financial balance sheets are found in the size of the financial assets: thus, the gap between the financial assets in the EU-10 and the EMU-6 amount to 100 per cent of GDP, while the gap in the case of the financial liabilities is below 40 per cent of GDP. Therefore, the difference in the size of the net financial assets is mainly explained by the differences registered in the size of financial assets.

The impact of the Great Recession on the European households' financial assets and liabilities has been different among the groups. In 2008 the size of financial assets fell dramatically in all three groups, but started recovering from 2009 onwards. However, while in 2012 the ratio of household financial assets to GDP was about 5 percentage points larger than in 2007 in the EMU-11 and EU-10 groups, it was still 12 percentage points below the 2007 level in the EMU-6 group. Regarding the households' financial liabilities to GDP ratio, it was 1.9 percentage points lower in the EU-10 in 2012 in comparison to 2007, but it increased in the Euro area (+3.9 percentage points in the EMU-11 and +13 percentage points in the EMU-6), despite the fact the ratio began to fall in 2011 in the EMU-11 and in 2012 in the EMU-6.

As a result of this evolution, in 2012 the households' net financial wealth in the EU-10 is larger than that recorded before the crisis, and in the EMU-11 households' net financial wealth is close to the peak recorded in 2006, merely 3.8 per cent of GDP smaller. However, in the EMU-6 the net financial wealth has dramatically declined, and, is 31 per cent of GDP below its peak recorded in 2005.

Table 13.9 shows the data of financial assets and liabilities of financial and non-financial corporations. Regarding the latter, the financial balance sheets of the non-financial corporations in the EMU-6 countries are the smallest (100 per cent of GDP smaller than in the other groups). Financial liabilities of the non-financial corporations are slightly higher in the EMU-11 than in the EU-10 countries, while the size of financial assets is higher in the EMU-11 than in the EU-10 non-financial corporations (about 40 per cent of GDP higher).

Although at the beginning of the crisis there was a strong decline in the gross indebtedness of non-financial corporations, the financial liabilities of these corporations started to rise again from 2009, with the result that in the three groups the size of the financial liabilities is very similar to that recorded in 2006. In the case of the financial assets, they have maintained their tendency of low but sustained growth in the EMU-11, so that despite the fall in 2008 and 2011, the financial assets to GDP ratio was at the highest level in 2012. In the EU-10, despite the fall registered in 2011, the size of the financial assets of the non-financial corporations is larger than before the crisis. Conversely, in the EMU-6 financial assets of these corporations have not recovered from the declines during the crisis so that the ratio is below the pre-crisis level.

The conclusions are different when we look at the net financial assets of non-financial corporations. The highest and the smallest net indebtedness of non-financial corporations for most years are registered in the EU-10 and the EMU-6, respectively. Generally, net indebtedness is larger outside the Euro area than in it.

The onset of the crisis in 2008 implied a strong decline of the net indebtedness of non-financial corporations, mainly in the EU-10, where net financial liabilities fell by 33 per cent of GDP. This improvement in the financial balance sheets of non-financial corporations lasted until 2012 when net indebtedness rose again, mainly in the EMU-6, where it increased by 13 per cent of GDP, exceeding the net financial liabilities of the non-financial corporations in the EMU-11. In any case, the net indebtedness of non-financial corporations in 2012 is smaller than in 2007, with a decrease that amounts to 11.3 per cent of GDP in the EMU-11 and the EU-10, and 2.6 per cent of GDP in the EMU-6.

In the case of financial corporations, the largest aggregate financial

Table 13.9 *Financial assets and liabilities: non-financial and financial corporations (% of GDP)*

	NON-FINANCIAL CORPORATIONS									FINANCIAL CORPORATIONS								
	Financial assets			Financial liabilities			Net financial assets			Financial assets			Financial liabilities			Net financial assets		
	EMU-11	EMU-6	EU-10	EMU-11	EMU-6	EU-10	EMU-11	EMU-6	EU-10	EMU-11	EMU-6	EU-10	EMU-11	EMU-6	EU-10	EMU-11	EMU-6	EU-10
2003	151.2	68.3	121.0	235.8	139.6	230.4	−83.3	−71.4	−108.0	400.2	167.1	492.2	404.9	173.3	516.0	−4.7	−6.2	−23.9
2004	153.7	70.5	122.5	242.8	147.7	236.7	−87.8	−77.3	−112.8	419.0	179.0	596.5	421.8	187.2	618.5	−2.7	−8.3	−22.0
2005	166.6	78.5	137.3	259.1	166.4	266.8	−90.9	−87.8	−128.3	460.5	202.8	674.0	463.1	212.3	694.6	−2.6	−9.5	−20.7
2006	180.4	79.5	144.5	282.2	172.8	281.3	−100.0	−93.3	−135.4	488.6	208.7	708.5	491.8	222.3	730.1	−3.2	−13.7	−21.7
2007	185.1	86.9	142.7	292.1	183.3	278.6	−104.9	−96.3	−135.6	515.5	232.7	780.6	514.6	252.8	797.0	0.9	−20.1	−16.4
2008	170.1	73.5	146.0	261.9	149.7	249.5	−91.0	−76.2	−102.9	567.1	252.7	1,090.7	560.7	253.9	1,094.9	6.4	−1.2	−4.2
2009	185.6	75.8	148.5	283.7	160.2	277.7	−97.1	−84.4	−128.0	604.4	281.1	943.7	596.7	284.8	952.9	7.7	−3.7	−9.2
2010	186.8	73.5	152.0	286.9	155.4	280.8	−98.8	−81.8	−127.6	609.3	301.0	973.2	597.0	302.0	976.6	12.2	−1.0	−3.5
2011	182.7	72.4	145.3	274.5	153.1	265.7	−91.2	−80.6	−119.1	621.3	303.4	1,023.0	607.3	302.3	1,016.3	14.0	1.0	6.7
2012	189.4	74.1	147.1	283.6	167.8	273.2	−93.6	−93.7	−124.2	636.6	309.3	968.5	621.9	309.2	974.0	14.7	0.1	−5.5

Source: Our calculations based on Eurostat (Annual Sector Accounts ESA 2010, Financial Flows and Stocks).

317

balance sheets are in the EU-10 and the smallest in the EMU-6. But the most striking fact is the size of this difference, because the size of the financial balance sheets is much larger outside the Euro area, and, moreover, the size in the EMU-11 is much larger than in the EMU-6. Thus, in 2012 the size of financial assets of financial corporations in EU-10 was 1.5 times larger than in EMU-11 and 3.1 times larger than in EMU-6.

Since the outbreak of the crisis in 2008 the size of the financial sector in the EU has increased. In 2008, in all groups, but mainly in the EU-10 (as a result of the increase in the size of the financial balance sheets of British financial institutions), there was a noticeable increase in the size of the financial sector. Since 2009 the increase in the size of the financial sector has slowed down, actually decreasing in size slightly in the EU-10 in 2009. Overall, however, the size of the financial sectors in the three groups is larger in 2012 than before the crisis.

But the most striking fact is that the crisis has reversed the net borrowing position of financial corporations, mainly in the Euro area. In 2007, in the EMU-11 and in 2011 in the EMU-6, financial corporations became net lenders. In the EMU-11 and in the EU-10, the net financial liabilities of these institutions fell dramatically reaching a position close to equilibrium.

13.3   CONCLUSIONS

The analysis in the previous section has shown the marked differences in the impact of the crisis on the European economies. The group of countries that form the EMU-6, that is, the countries that joined the Euro area after its creation in 1999, have been the most affected by the crisis, much more than the other Euro area countries and the non-euro EU economies. However, this conclusion must be taken very cautiously.

First, because the analysis, as explained, is biased by the outcomes of the largest economies, thus hiding the impacts of the crisis on individual countries, for example, Ireland, Portugal or Spain in the EMU-11, Cyprus or Greece in the EMU-6, or Latvia and Lithuania in the EU-10. A deeper analysis of the consequences of the crisis on European economies, outside the scope of this chapter, should, therefore, be based on individual countries and not on groups of countries (new versus old euro economies, euro versus non-euro economies, the so-called PIIGS countries – Portugal, Ireland, Italy, Greece, Spain – peripheral versus core countries, etc.).

Second, the outcomes are conditioned by the inclusion of Latvia and

Lithuania in the group of the non-euro EU countries. Actually, these countries joined the Euro area in 2014 and 2015, respectively. If we included Latvia and Lithuania among the new euro member states in the Euro area, forming the EMU-8, the performance of the (reduced) non-euro EU countries (EU-8) would improve substantially in parallel to the deterioration of the new euro countries (EMU-8).

This outcome not only highlights the poor economic performance of the Euro area during the crisis, but also that the new euro countries have been the most damaged in the Great Recession. This larger heterogeneity of the Euro area implies a larger incidence of asymmetric shocks, because although the national business cycles may be highly synchronised, the impact of a common shock may be amplified by national factors, questioning the effectiveness of single economic policies, like monetary policy, in highly heterogeneous regions.

NOTES

1. In 2013, in the EMU-11 the GDP of the three largest economies, Germany, France and Italy, amounted to 30 per cent, 22 per cent and 17 per cent, respectively, of the GDP of that group. In the case of EMU-6, Greece, Slovakia and Slovenia amounted to 58 per cent, 19 per cent and 11 per cent, respectively, of the GDP of that group. Lastly, in the EU-10, the United Kingdom, Poland, and Sweden amounted to 61 per cent, 10 per cent and 10 per cent, respectively, of the GDP of the group.
2. Between 2003 and 2007, the real GDP per capita in the EU-10 grew at an annual rate of 3.3 per cent, 1.5 per cent for the EMU-11, and 4.5 per cent for EMU-6.

REFERENCES

Arestis, P. and M. Sawyer (eds) (2012), *The Euro Crisis*, Basingstoke: Palgrave Macmillan.

Benczes, I. and B. Szent-Ivanyi (2015), 'The European economy in 2014: fragile recovery and convergence', *Journal of European Market Studies*, **53** (S1), 162–180.

Bitzenis, A., N. Karagiannisand and J. Marangos (eds) (2015), *Europe in Crisis. Problems, Challenges and Alternative Perspectives*, Basingstoke: Palgrave Macmillan.

Carrasco, C. A. and P. Peinado (2015), 'On the origin of European imbalances in the context of European integration', *Panoeconomicus*, **62** (2), 177–191.

Dodig, N. and H. Herr (2015), 'Current account imbalances in the EMU: an assessment of official policy responses', *Panoeconomicus*, **62** (2), 193–216.

Gibson, H. D., T. Palivosand and G. S. Tavlos (2014), 'The crisis in the Euro area: an analytical overview', *Journal of Macroeconomics*, **39**, Part B, 233–239.

Mendonça, A. (2014), 'The European crisis and global economy dynamics:

continental enlargement versus Atlantic opening', *Panoeconomicus*, **5**, Special Issue, 543–569.

Onaran, Ö. (2011), 'The crisis in Western and Eastern EU: does the policy reaction address its origin', in P. Arestis, R. Sobreiro and J. L. Oreiro (eds), *An Assessment of the Global Impact of the Financial Crisis*, Basingstoke: Palgrave Macmillan.

Perraton, J. (2011), 'Crisis in the Euro zone', in P. Arestis, R. Sobreiro and J. L. Oreiro (eds), *An Assessment of the Global Impact of the Financial Crisis*, Basingstoke: Palgrave Macmillan.

Index